THE RIVER COTTAGE
FAMILY COOKBOOK

THE RIVER COTTAGE FAMILY COOKBOOK

Hugh Fearnley-Whittingstall & Fizz Carr

Photography by Simon Wheeler

TEN SPEED PRESS
Berkeley | Toronto

1⊕

Ten Speed Press
PO Box 7123
Berkeley, California 94707
www.tenspeed.com

Distributed in Canada by Ten Speed Press Canada.

First published in Great Britain in 2005 by Hodder and
Stoughton, a division of Hodder Headline

Cover design by Betsy Stromberg
Text design by Georgia Vaux
Typeset in Fournier, Archive Tilt, and Archive Antiqua

Photography by Simon Wheeler
(email: simonwheeler@onetel.com)

ISBN-13: 978-1-58008-925-8
ISBN-10: 1-58008-925-9

Library of Congress Cataloging-in-Publication Data

Fearnley-Whittingstall, Hugh.
  The River Cottage family cookbook / Hugh Fearnley-
Whittingstall & Fizz Carr ; photography by Simon Wheeler.
     p. cm.
  Summary: "U.S. edition of the best-selling British cooking
primer for children and families, featuring a broad range of
recipes that can be made by children age ten and older" –
Provided by publisher.
  Includes index.
  ISBN 978-1-58008-925-8
  1. Cookery – Juvenile literature. 2. Cookery, English –
Juvenile literature. I. Carr, Fizz. II. Title.
  TX652.5.F42 2008
  641.5942 – dc22
                          2007039028

Printed in Korea

2 3 4 5 6 7 8 9 10 — 12 11 10 09 08

We'd love to know how you're getting along with *The River
Cottage Family Cookbook*, and we'd love to have your own
best cooking tips and favorite variations. Please tell us on our
website, www.rivercottage.net.

*For Charlotte, Georgie, Joey, Mattie,
and Ted, my wonderful girls. And for
Steve, with much love.* F. C.

*For my family — Oscar, Freddie, Chloe,
and Marie — with love.* H. F.-W.

Hugh Fearnley-Whittingstall

Hugh is widely known as a writer, broadcaster, and campaigner for his uncompromising commitment to real food. His various British television series for Channel 4, most recently *Beyond River Cottage*, have earned him a huge popular following. His first book in the River Cottage series, *The River Cottage Cookbook*, scooped the top British food writing awards, including the Glenfiddich Trophy and the André Simon Food Book of the Year. His next book, *The River Cottage Year*, was a passionate polemic for shopping, cooking, and eating in tune with the seasons. *The River Cottage Meat Book* aimed to help cooks understand meat better and invited readers to join the campaign to improve quality and welfare in the production of British meat. In recognition of this, he again won both the André Simon prize and the Glenfiddich Trophy.

Hugh is patron of the National Farmers' Retail and Markets Association (FARMA). Last year he set up River Cottage HQ, converting some old dairy buildings into a venue for courses and events expounding the River Cottage food philosophy, and celebrating the very best local, seasonal food.

Hugh lives in Dorset with his wife, Marie, and their three children, Oscar, Freddie, and Chloe.

Fizz Carr

Fizz was born and brought up in Sussex. After graduating from Exeter University, she was runner-up in the annual *Vogue* talent contest for young writers; she then worked in London for several years in magazine publishing.

After starting a family with the birth of twins in 1992, she moved back to the South Downs to farm with her husband, Stephen. Fizz is a passionate advocate of animal welfare and regularly holds farm visits for schools. Through her contact with children, she has become painfully aware of how little so many young people know about the food they eat, how it is produced, and where it comes from. An active member of her local branch of the European Movement, she would like to see a more ambitious legislative program to improve the welfare standards of animals on E.U. farms.

Fizz has five daughters – Charlotte, Georgie, Joey, Mattie, and Ted – all of whom are enthusiastic about food and cooking.

CONTENTS

What Is a Family Cookbook?   8

FLOUR   14

MILK   54

EGGS   86

FRUIT   118

VEGETABLES   166

FISH & SHELLFISH   220

MEAT   258

THE CUPBOARD   302

SUGAR & HONEY   336

CHOCOLATE   380

Glossary   404

Index   408

Acknowledgments   416

WHAT IS A FAMILY COOKBOOK?

This is a book that everyone in the family can pick up and use. If you're around ten to twelve years old, we reckon you'll be able to cook from it with maybe just a little adult help. Twelve-plus and you might be able to tackle most of the recipes on your own. And if you're an adult with younger children, we hope you'll enjoy cooking from it too, with your kids alongside, fully engaged in the mixing, sifting, stirring, and rolling. In fact, now that we've finished the book, we think it will be useful as a kitchen "primer" for cooks of any age.

The River Cottage Family Cookbook was effectively cooked up by five families – our own, plus those of our designer, Georgia Vaux; our photographer, Simon Wheeler and our editor, Richard Atkinson. All the food that you see on the following pages was made by our children and their friends (with a bit of help from us). Simon walked around the kitchen taking pictures as they cooked. The fish on page 227 really was gutted by Mack, aged nine. The drop scones on page 116 are just as eight-year-old Josephine made them – with a bit of help from her little sister, Georgia, aged five.

The older children cooked many dishes entirely on their own – although one of us was never far away. The younger children "helped" us, doing what they could (and what they felt like doing). As we cooked, phones rang, babies crawled about, and family life carried on regardless. We did it like this because we imagine you'll be cooking the same way . . .

Starting young

If you are a parent, perhaps you're wondering at what age your children can begin to take an interest in cooking. The answer is, we believe, long before they could even attempt to read the simplest word in this book. The baby who sits in a highchair watching you washing and steaming some carrots, or peeling a banana, then whizzing his or her food in a blender, is learning that the true story of lunch begins with raw ingredients, rather than with the opening of a jar.

The toddler who walks past a field of sheep and asks what they are doing there should not be fobbed off with stories of woolly jumpers. Far better to pick up some lamb chops on the way home and show your child how you cook them. And the child who has a chance to grow some food, even if it's just mustard and cress on a wet flannel on the windowsill, has learned a vital lesson about where food comes from.

Not just how, but why

For experienced cooks in a rush, a recipe that is merely a set of instructions may be useful. But children (and adults) who are still learning about food want and deserve more – the tools and rules for a lifetime's cooking.

And so in our book, the "whys" of cooking are at least as important as the "hows." Why

do you rub butter into flour when you make pastry, and why do you have to put so much effort into kneading bread dough? Once you know the answer, you'll make better pastry and better bread, because you'll understand the reasons behind what you're doing.

You may think that some of our recipes look rather long. Does it mean that they're really hard? On the contrary, we've written them longer to make them easier! It's true that we could tell you how to make garlic mayonnaise in 37 words. We could say: "Mix crushed garlic, salt, egg yolks, pepper, mustard. Add half the oil a drop at a time. Add tablespoonful of lemon juice. Add rest of oil in steady stream, beating constantly. Add rest of lemon juice. Refrigerate."

That would be a short, easy recipe for making mayonnaise. But it would only be easy if you've made it before. If you're going to make really good mayonnaise for the first time, you should know why you add the oil a drop at a time, and why you can add it more quickly once you've stirred in some lemon juice. We try to answer the kind of questions that might come into your head as you're cooking. And that's why our recipe for mayonnaise is about twelve times as long!

The "whys" of cooking are a mixture of art, science, history, and geography (the most interesting and fun bits, we think, of all these subjects). We have tried to reflect this by including short sections (in blue ink, with their own headings) giving stories about our food culture that we think are both important and enjoyable. We also suggest a number of "projects" (usually one or two per chapter) that go beyond day-to-day cooking and take you on a bit of a food adventure.

Kitchen-sink dramas

While you're cooking, we hope you'll particularly enjoy those moments when, if you stop to think about it, something quite amazing is happening. For example, mixing flour and water doesn't sound like the most ambitious recipe. But when you come down to breakfast the next morning to find that the gluey paste that you set aside the night before is now bubbling away of its own accord, you're entitled to get excited. Suddenly you're Dr. Frankenstein, and that bowl of fizzing gloop is your Monster. You have created life! Or, how is it that you can shake a jar of cream for minutes on end and then suddenly it turns, in the space of a second, into a lump of butter sloshing around in a milky liquid? Where did that come from? And is it really possible that a slippery, jellylike egg white will whisk into a mass of white bubbles so thick that you can hold a bowl of them upside down above your head?

You'll soon discover that cooking and eating engage all the senses — not just taste. Every time you tackle a recipe you'll be using your eyes and fingertips, almost without knowing it, to keep you on track. Your nose and ears are important as well. Few smells are as good as a chopped onion frying gently in a little butter — and the sound is pretty mouthwatering, too. Should you happen to forget those onions, so they start to burn, it's your nose that will alert you to the problem — and tell you that it's probably time to start all over again.

Of course, there will be plenty of times when things just don't turn out as you planned, but don't be discouraged. Comfort yourself with the thought that you often learn more about cooking when you get things wrong than when you get them right. And you probably won't make the same mistake again. In fact, *again* is a very important word in cooking. Cooking becomes easier, more fun, and more interesting the more you do it. We hope this becomes an "everyday" book in your kitchen — or at least an "every week" book.

The best ingredients

One message that we hope is loud and clear throughout the book is that the best food is always prepared with the best possible ingredients. The way to appreciate this is by knowing those ingredients in their whole, raw form. So we show you how to cook a whole chicken before we give you a recipe that uses only breast meat or thighs. And we'd love to persuade you to grow your own tomatoes so you can taste just how wonderful they are straight from the plant, when they're allowed to ripen fully on the vine — so much tastier than the dull, watery ones that are sold by so many stores. You'll find plenty in the pages ahead about where our food comes from, how it's processed, and why that matters so much.

In fact, the whole structure of the book is based on key ingredients – the building blocks of good cooking. You'll find chapters headed Flour, Eggs, Meat, and Fruit, for example. This means that we can talk about particular ingredients and the different things they can do in one place, rather than scattering information about them all over the book. If you want to get to the recipes quickly – if you suddenly have the urge to make a cake for tea, for example – then turn to the index at the back of the book and look up *cakes*.

Safety first

If you learn good habits early on, then cooking need never be a dangerous activity. But it does involve sharp knives, boiling liquids, scorching ovens, and hot pans. All these things should be used carefully, and treated with respect. Some of the recipes in this book are suitable for younger children to try because any hot work with the oven comes right at the end of the recipe, and can be the adult's job. Other recipes are a bit more challenging and need a little careful thought beforehand, as well as an adult on hand at all times. We wouldn't advise anyone cooking for the first time to start off by making fudge, for instance. But we put the recipe in, along with some other delightful sugar-boiling recipes like Turkish delight and bramble jelly, flagged up with our "warning – boiling sugar!" message. We've taken the trouble to explain them very carefully, so you can learn to treat the boiling syrup with the utmost caution.

Only a parent can decide how much freedom and responsibility to give his or her children in the kitchen. But generally speaking, we feel that preteens should never be left to cook entirely on their own. Pans can flame, water can boil over, knives can slip – all in the space of a few seconds. An adult and a first-aid kit should always be on hand . . . just in case. And remember the golden rule about first aid for all minor burns – immersion in cool water (a running tap or a large bowl of cold water) for minutes rather than seconds.

Future cooks

We hope that if you use this book often, you'll soon be experimenting, changing ingredients, and thinking about food and flavor, rather than just blindly following recipes. We hope it will lead you to approach other cookbooks with confidence and understanding.

When you've learned enough about your ingredients that you often say to yourself, "This is a good recipe, but wouldn't it be even nicer if I . . . ," then you've graduated from this book, and the whole world of cooking is yours to explore. (Though we do hope you'll come back and visit us from time to time, like an old friend.)

FLOUR

See those crumpled bags of flour in your
kitchen cupboard? They may not look
much but without them you'd have
no bread to spread with butter and jam,
no spaghetti to twirl around your fork,
no crunchy pizza with its tangy, cheesy,
tomatoey topping. Not to mention
no cakes, no biscuits, no croissants,
no pies, no pancakes, no scones . . .
no wonder this is the first chapter.

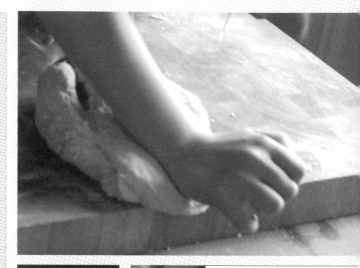

easy flat breads, page 38

sourdough bread, page 25

pasta, page 30

a loaf of bread, page 41

pizza, page 48

raisin bread, page 43

FLOUR

Flour. Let's face it, it's not the most exciting thing in the kitchen cupboard. Yet flour is the key ingredient of many of our favorite foods – bread, pasta, pizza, not to mention almost all cakes and biscuits. Glance through any cookbook and you'll find flour in every section – even in soups, sauces, and meat dishes – yet it's never even mentioned in the index. It's the unsung hero of the kitchen.

Flour is so important because of what it does. Rub butter into it and it will bake to a crisp pastry on top of a pie. Mix it with butter and milk and it becomes a velvety sauce. Knead it with eggs and you get silky strips of pasta. Add milk to the same mix and you have a pancake batter. Combine it with water and yeast, let it rise, bake it in the oven, and you have wonderful, crusty bread.

What is flour?

Flour isn't just one food, it's a description of a family of foods – and of a process that has happened to all of them. It means a fine powder that has been ground from a grain, a bean, a nut, or a seed (you can even get potato flour and chestnut flour). But the everyday flour that you might use for making jam tarts or a loaf of bread has almost always been ground from wheat – the tall, grassy stalks that ripen to a golden yellow in the summer fields. Each stalk of wheat has an "ear" made up of a tight cluster of grains, and each grain is a seed that can grow new stalks of wheat.

You may have seen huge combine harvesters cutting through fields of wheat or other cereals in late July, August, and September. These machines cut off the ear and most of the stalk of the plant, shake out the seed from the ear, store the seed in a great tank, and then chuck the straw and any dust and seed casings out of the back of the machine – they look like great mechanical beasts having their lunch.

If you crush grains of wheat and grind them finely, you get whole-wheat flour, which is a mixture of the bran (the outer skin of the grain), the germ (the tiny embryo – the part that would sprout if you covered the grain with soil), and the endosperm (the starchy white center, which is the food for the seed). A few mills still grind wheat the traditional way between two great revolving stones, producing whole-wheat flour that contains all the bran and the germ – these can be sifted out to make white flour. But in most modern mills, the wheat is sheared open to separate the bran from the endosperm, then sifted and rolled many times to refine the flour. White flour is more versatile for general cooking. But whole-wheat flour has more of the goodness left in, and is great for making bread.

What does flour do?

Flour thickens liquids. So if you cook flour and butter together and add hot milk, you make a white sauce for, say, layering with pasta and meat to make lasagne. A sauce like this can be flavored – with cheese, or herbs and spices.

Flour makes a crisp coating. Sometimes meat or fish is tossed in flour to give it a light coating before it is fried. As the flour fries in oil or butter, it turns golden brown and crisp (black and very crisp if you overdo it). This gives a little crunch to fried foods that most of us find really appealing.

Flour stops things from sticking. If you're rolling out pastry for a pie or tart, you'll need a little extra flour to sprinkle on the work surface and the rolling pin or your pastry will stick. And you'll need to grease and dust your cake pans with flour, or your perfectly risen, golden brown cake may refuse to come out.

But most of all, flour is used to make doughs, batters, and other mixtures that are baked in the oven to give us all kinds of breads, cakes, tarts, and biscuits. You wouldn't use the same flour to make all these different sorts of foods. There are various flours, all with their own properties. And the biggest influence on how a flour behaves is a substance called gluten. Gluten is a protein that's activated when flour is mixed with liquid. In some mixtures, such as bread dough, you need lots of it because it makes the dough strong and stretchy. But in other doughs – for example, the kind you'd use for biscuits or pies, where you want a tender, buttery, melt-in-the-mouth mixture – you need only a little gluten. As different flours contain different amounts of gluten, it's important to use the right one for the job.

Different flours

Even a small corner shop will have several different types of flour. It's easy to get confused. Here's a quick rundown of the flours you might come across and what you could use them for:

All-purpose flour is made from a mixture of soft and hard wheats. It's the standard flour used in the U.S. for most baking, including pastries and yeast breads. In Britain, the flour used to make pastry, egg pasta, and sauces – but not yeast breads – is called plain flour; the American equivalent is called pastry flour.

Self-rising flour is pastry flour with several additives – the same ones you find in baking powder – that help scones and cakes "rise" to become light and spongy when you cook them. The main one is baking soda, which fizzes, like sherbet, in the liquid of a cake batter to make tiny bubbles of carbon dioxide. These expand when the mix is baked, and are trapped when the batter sets to a solid as it cooks.

Some recipes in this book call for self-rising flour, but if you don't have any in the cupboard, you can still make some. Just add a heaping teaspoon of baking soda and a good pinch of cream of tartar to every 2/3 cup of all-purpose or pastry flour, mix thoroughly, and then sift it.

Bread flour is ground from hard wheat with a high gluten content. It comes mainly from North America and is the most popular flour for bread, as the gluten produces an elastic dough, which expands to form the larger, distinctively textured bubbles we like in our bread.

Whole-wheat flour is made from the whole grain, with nothing taken away. As it has quite a distinct flavor and texture, it doesn't tend to be used for general cooking (unless this is exactly what you want), and is mainly used for making bread, where it produces a brown loaf. You can "lighten" whole-wheat flour by mixing it with all-purpose – a great mix for soda bread (see page 46).

FLOUR AND CIVILIZATION

Without cereal crops to grind into flour, we'd still be living in small groups in our animal skins, following the herds of mammoths and bison, gathering wild fruits, and taking fish from rivers and seas.

But around 10,000 years ago, our ancestors realized that if they put seeds into the ground and waited around to harvest the plants that grew from them, they could live in permanent settlements, growing cereal crops and grinding them to make cereals and bread. It was no longer necessary to be constantly on the move, searching for food. They could stay in one place.

This is how civilization was born. Safe and well fed, the population grew tremendously. Settlements became villages, which in turn grew into towns and cities. Peace and prosperity for these villages was largely dependent on the cereal crops that provided their inhabitants with grain all year round. The price of civilization was dependence on agriculture. Then, as now, a failed crop and a shortage of food led to hunger, tension, raids on other settlements – and at worst, it led to famine and war.

BREAD

Take flour, water, yeast, and a little salt. Mix them into a smooth, squishable dough. Watch it slowly rise and swell. Bake until golden brown and crusty. You have just made one of the most important foods in the world.

In fact, wherever you go on the planet you will find bread in all sorts of shapes and sizes – long, thin French baguettes; flat Indian naan and chapati; oval pita pockets from Greece, Turkey, and North Africa. Bread is quite simply the most basic food of almost every culture on earth. It is the food of life.

However, in Britain, many people's first idea of bread is rows and rows of plastic-wrapped loaves on the supermarket shelf. If that's how it is for you, then perhaps it's time you had a go at making your own.

Why make bread?

Bread is easy to buy and fairly cheap. So why make your own?

Well, not only does the end result taste fantastic, but there's something very satisfying about every stage of making it: stirring the water into the flour and feeling the dough change beneath your hands from a rough, soggy mass to a smooth, stretchy dough; watching the dough swell in the bowl; pressing the dough down in the bowl; crafting it between your hands into the shape you choose; and finally watching the miraculous transformation of this ball of dough into a crusty loaf.

Best of all, you can eat it while it's still warm from the oven. Watching a generous blob of butter melt onto the first slice of your own homemade bread or the inside of a hot, crusty roll is a guaranteed thrill. With a bit of luck, it will taste fresher, crustier, and more delicious than the bread you normally buy.

Once you get the hang of it, bread making is a chance to experiment, to invent your own customized loaf by adding things that appeal to you: sweet things, such as raisins, dried apricots, or honey; or savory things, like cheese, garlic, or olives; or crunchy things, like nuts and seeds.

The importance of yeast

You can make a very basic kind of bread with just flour and water, but it will hardly rise at all. Most of the bread we eat is plump and risen and full of tiny bubbles of air. To get bread to rise up in this way, and then keep its shape without collapsing, means adding something else to the flour and water. Yeast.

Yeast is a remarkable organism – a fungus related to mushrooms, but virtually invisible. It has a magical effect on dough, transforming the taste and texture of the bread. It can be dried into a powder and stored in airtight packets or tins for many months, or it can be kept fresh in the fridge for about a fortnight – alive, but cold and dormant in a compressed block, a bit like a lump of light brown cheese.

If you add warm water to active yeast, it is "activated," frothing up like a cross between a soup and a bubble bath. When you add this

yeasty froth to flour and mix it to a dough, the yeast starts to feed on the flour, growing and multiplying. As it does so, it gives off the gas, carbon dioxide, which forces itself through the dough, making it rise and puff up. This is how bread gets its bubbles of air. Dry yeast works in roughly the same way, only instant dry yeast (the one that we use in the recipes on pages 41 and 43) is always sprinkled straight onto the flour and salt rather than being mixed with water first.

Bashing the dough down won't kill the yeast – it'll just start rising again. In fact, it won't die until it either runs out of food or is killed by a high temperature. And this is what happens when a loaf of bread is baked in a hot oven. The soft, elastic dough becomes firmer and drier – so dry on the outside that it forms a hard crust. The yeast is killed by the heat, but the bubbles it has made are trapped in the bread, leaving a light, crumby texture.

Choosing flour for bread

We've already described various types of flour on pages 17 and 18, not all of which are suitable for making bread. You need flour made from wheat that is high in gluten – the thing that will make your dough nice and stretchy, and trap those air bubbles in the bread. For yeast breads, choose all-purpose flour or bread flour.

Many bread-making flours have a recipe or two for bread on the back of the packet.

ALL YOU NEED TO KNOW ABOUT KNEADING

In theory, you could just mix up your flour, water, and yeast into a dough and pop it into the oven. But it wouldn't rise properly, and you'd end up with a heavy, dense loaf like a lump of stone. And some homemade bread does end up like this! To get a nice, elastic dough that will rise well and make a good, light crumb, you need to stretch the gluten by working the dough with your hands. This is called kneading.

Pin down part of the dough with one hand and use the base or heel of your other hand to stretch the dough away from you on the work surface. Then fold the dough back on itself, give it a quarter turn, and repeat again and again. It *is* quite hard work, as you end up using the whole of your upper body to lean into the dough. If you're cooking with someone else, then you could do it in turns.

After a good few minutes (maybe 10) of kneading, you'll notice that the dough becomes smoother and bouncier and feels as if it's fighting you back. Prod it with your finger, and the dent you make will start to smooth out again. At this point, you can shape the dough into a ball and let it rise (or "proof") in its bowl, covered with plastic wrap or a damp tea towel (kitchen towel).

These often work well, but it's good to have your own recipe up your sleeve. We have a nice easy recipe for a white loaf on page 41.

Remember the salt!

You can make a beautiful loaf, but if you've forgotten the salt no one will want to eat it. Too much salt is almost as bad and will stop the yeast working properly. If you're making up your own recipes, then around 2 teaspoons salt for 3¼ cups flour is about right.

Different shapes?

You have your dough, it has risen, what now? Do you fancy making a "proper" loaf in a loaf pan, a batch of soft, floury little rolls, or a big, round, crusty loaf? You really don't need any special equipment. A deep, round cake pan will do if you don't have a bread tin; or just shape the dough into a round and put it on a baking sheet. The size of the pan isn't crucial – just make sure there's plenty of room for the dough to expand during its second rising. A large roasting pan or baking sheet will hold 12 good rolls.

If you're feeling artistic, you can make three long ropes of dough, braid them together, and put them on a baking sheet. There really is no end to the possibilities.

Whatever pan or sheet you use, remember to grease it before you put the dough in it or your loaf will stick. A scrap of lard (rendered pig fat) is the best thing to use, but vegetable oil will work fine. Pour in a drop or two and rub it around the base and sides of the pan with a piece of paper towel.

Varying your recipe

Once you've got the hang of the basic bread recipe on page 41, you can have a lot of fun trying out different recipes – and, best of all, inventing your own. Try the following ideas:

Seed bread Add a handful of pumpkin seeds, sunflower seeds, sesame seeds, and poppy seeds (any or all of them).

Cheese and onion bread Add a large handful of grated cheese and a gently fried chopped onion, plus a few twists of black pepper.

Tomato bread Add a tablespoon of tomato purée and some chopped sun-dried tomatoes. When making the bread dough, you could use oil from the sun-dried tomatoes instead of plain olive oil.

Blending flours

Seeds from other cereal plants, such as barley, rye, rice, and maize, can all be ground to flour and added to all-purpose or bread flour to make bread. Part of the fun of bread making is that you can do your own flour blending. You are the cook and therefore in charge, so you can bake whatever bread you feel like eating.

Mix whole-wheat with white flour, or add some rye flour to the whole-wheat. A tablespoon or two of barley flour mixed in with wheat flour makes delicious bread (although it doesn't make good light bread on its own, as there's not much gluten in barley flour).

Some yeasty bread recipes

A Loaf of Fresh White Bread, page 41
Raisin Bread, page 43

WHITE OR BROWN? If you take some whole-wheat flour and sift a spoonful of it into a bowl, you'll see that little brown, shiny flakes are left in the sieve – this is bran, the outer covering of the wheat seed. This bran, together with most of the germ of the wheat seed, is generally sifted out in order to make white flour. Whole-wheat flour is flour made from the entire seed – nothing is sifted out.

Today, we're all encouraged to eat whole-wheat bread rather than white because it's higher in fiber and vitamins, so it's better for us. But until the mid-nineteenth century, people ate brown bread only if they couldn't afford to eat anything else. Traditionally, the best bread (the most expensive and therefore eaten by the wealthy) was thought to be the bread made from flour that had all this coarse bran sifted out. Rye flour or oatmeal often replaced most of the wheat flour in a poor man's loaf because oats and rye were cheaper and easier to grow in a cold or wet climate.

Nowadays, people tend to buy the sort of bread they like best. When it comes to making bread at home, there's nothing to stop you from mixing whole-wheat flour with white to get the best of both worlds. The white flour will help the loaf to rise well (breads made from just whole-wheat flour only rise a little, so they can be heavy to eat) and the brown flour will add flavor as well as healthy fiber.

WILD YEASTS AND SOURDOUGH

Stand in the middle of an empty space, hold out your hands, and look around you. You might not have realized it, but you are surrounded by all sorts of different tiny wild yeasts. You can't feel, see, or smell them. They're with you the whole time, though, drifting around in the air like those tiny dust particles that you suddenly notice floating in a bright shaft of light from a sunny window.

Capture the right sort of yeasts and make them work for you and you have a whole life-form at your disposal: a life-form that will help you turn a flour and water paste into a mouthwatering crusty loaf. But if you want to use wild yeasts in cooking, you'll have to look after them. In fact, you'll need to turn yourself into a sort of yeast farmer — breeding, feeding, and watering your invisible livestock. This is not a fast-food project. With a bit of patience and a little luck, you'll end up with a spongy, bubbling bowl of sourdough, ready to raise flour and salt into bread.

Be warned — these wild yeasts can be a tricky bunch. You can start two identical batches of sourdough and one will start to bubble and froth while the other might go black and smell nasty. Frustrating, but that's just part of the magic and mystery of the whole thing. It may be that you'll have more success if you've been baking bread with commercial yeast recently, so that your kitchen is still full of yeasts floating around in the atmosphere.

The basic idea of sourdough is to attract the right wild yeasts that float about in the air to come and settle on a sloppy mixture of flour and water and then breed. As they breed and multiply, they give off carbon dioxide, producing gassy bubbles that can be used to raise a loaf of bread.

You can use this mixture as a starter, feeding it and building it up with more flour and water for a few days. Finally, you add salt and enough flour to turn it into the usual bread dough, which you proof and bake as normal.

In many parts of the world, sourdough bread making is still common practice. It's even said that some sourdough starters are decades old, passed from one member of the family to the next like a rather ancient pet.

Bread made from wild yeasts is very different from bread made with yeast that you buy in a shop. It has a much stronger flavor and doesn't usually rise nearly as much. You may think it is even nicer, or you may not like it quite as much. But you won't know until you've tried!

Project:

MAKING SOURDOUGH BREAD

This method of making sourdough uses wild yeasts to create a loaf of bread. If your dough starts to bubble and froth on its own, then you'll know that you've truly managed to breed these invisible yeasts. However, if no bubbling happens despite your best efforts, we give a slightly "cheaty" alternative just to help you along your way.

We also give you directions on how to make a semi-sourdough loaf at the same time, so that even if you find your pure sourdough loaf just a bit too challenging you've got something both interesting and completely scrumptious to eat for tea.

Day one Measure 3 heaping tablespoons of organic all-purpose or bread flour into a large bowl (it's best to use organic flour because nonorganic flour could contain tiny traces of chemicals that might prevent the wild yeasts from breeding). Add a tablespoon of organic whole-wheat flour. Tip in the juice of half an orange and enough lukewarm still mineral water or rainwater (tap water contains chemicals that might kill your yeasts) to make a thick but just stirrable dough – about $1/4$ cup.

Stir this mixture and then beat it with a wooden spoon or a balloon whisk for a couple of minutes to drive air into it. You'll notice that the dough gets almost stretchy as you beat it; this is the gluten developing in the flour.

Cover the bowl with some plastic wrap. Write a label to warn everybody not to throw your precious mixture away, then set it aside

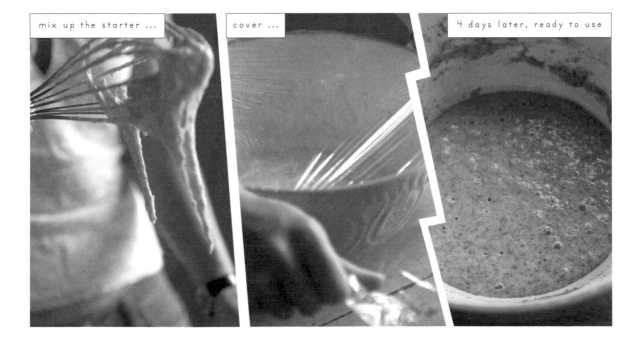

mix up the starter ...

cover ...

4 days later, ready to use

in a warm place – near (but not on) a radiator, perhaps, and away from drafts.

Day two Check for frothy bubbles – signs that your mixture is "breeding" and therefore producing carbon dioxide gas. Beat in another $1/4$ cup white and whole-wheat flour just as before, plus $1/4$ cup water. Cover once more with plastic wrap and let bubble overnight. If your mixture is looking very unbubbly – flat and unpleasant smelling rather than nicely sour – it's probably not worth continuing with this batch of dough. Try the alternative below instead.

Day three Hopefully, your dough will be looking quite active – bubbling furiously and rising up the bowl. It's time to build it up a little more. Beat in another $1/4$ cup flour and $1/4$ cup water. Cover and leave overnight as before.

Day four Add 6 tablespoons of organic flour – 5 of white and 1 of whole-wheat. Stir well and allow the dough to rise again but just for 2 to 3 hours this time, until it looks puffy. Take out 2 tablespoons of dough and put it in a small bowl to one side.

Add $1/2$ cup water and about 2 cups organic white flour, plus 2 teaspoons salt and enough warm water to make a smooth dough. Mix, knead, proof, shape, and bake the dough just as if you were making the bread recipe on page 41, but allow for the fact that this dough will take much longer to rise and won't rise nearly as much.

Meanwhile, if you're in an experimental mood, try the semi-sourdough version to bake alongside. Make up the basic white loaf recipe on page 41, halving the amount of yeast but adding to the mix the 2 spoonfuls of wild yeast batter that you set aside. You'll need a bit less water than you would in your normal bread dough. Proceed as with the basic white loaf recipe, but allow extra rising time. This will make a semi-sourdough loaf that you can try alongside your pure sourdough version. You should find that it has a slightly less challenging taste but still has a nice sour kick.

Cheaty alternative

Add just a bit of compressed yeast or a pinch of active dry yeast (not the instant variety) to the flour and water on day one. This will help to attract the right sort of wild yeasts.

Sourdough pancakes

If you want to spend hours rather than days on your sourdough project, then why not use some of the bubbling mixture from the end of day two to make a batch of sourdough pancakes? Mix $1/2$ cup sourdough batter into 1 cup white flour, along with an egg and around 1 cup milk. Whisk well and then cook in the usual way (see page 114). This gives you a slightly thicker pancake with a lightly yeasty taste, which is delicious with maple syrup as well as lemon and sugar.

SODA BREAD

Three o'clock? Want some homemade bread for tea? Think you've left it too late? Relax! Forget the yeast and pick up the baking soda instead. You shall make bread – perhaps not quite like bread you've ever tasted before, but maybe all the better for that.

Soda bread is fast bread – no kneading, no proofing, no fiddling about. This is its great strength. It became popular in the nineteenth century when chemical leaveners became readily available, particularly in rural areas where fresh yeast could be difficult to get hold of.

Soda bread is made to rise with baking soda rather than yeast. It works better with all-purpose or pastry flour than with bread flour because the whole rising thing happens so fast that there's no time to knead the flour and stretch that gluten. The end result is rugged and crusty on the outside, soft and moist on the inside. Soda bread is really a very large, loaflike scone.

How does it work?

Put a teaspoon of baking soda into a glass of warm water mixed with a teaspoon of lemon juice and you'll see it immediately start to fizz with frothy bubbles. This is because the acid in the lemon reacts with the alkaline soda. It's another way of producing that carbon dioxide gas – and it's even faster than using yeast. In fact, it works so fast that you need to use not-quite-so-acidic yogurt or buttermilk in a soda bread dough, otherwise the reaction is all over before the dough has even reached the oven.

Some bread recipes with soda

Soda Bread, page 46
Sultana Scones, page 47

PASTA

After bread, probably the commonest way for us to eat flour is when it has been made into pasta. Thirty years ago, pasta was still a bit exotic in the U.K. Canned spaghetti and spaghetti served with the popular Italian meat sauce bolognese were about the only familiar types. Now, we eat huge amounts of the stuff, in all kinds of shapes, with a variety of different sauces and ingredients thrown in. But we still don't eat anything like as much pasta as they do in Italy — most Italians eat pasta nearly every day.

Different types of pasta

There are two main sorts of pasta: flour-and-water pasta and egg pasta. Much of the pasta that we buy in Britain, including our adopted national favorite, spaghetti, is simply flour — made from a hard wheat called durum — mixed with water. This sort of flour-and-water pasta is always bought from shops rather than made at home because of the industrial equipment needed to process the dough.

Egg pasta is made from a simple dough of flour and eggs, kneaded until smooth and then rolled very thinly. It's made from softer flour than flour-and-water pasta and is the sort of pasta that you can make at home, since it needs no special equipment. You can buy special Italian pasta flour called 00 flour, but all-purpose or white pastry flour will make perfectly good pasta too.

Pasta made at home tastes quite different from bought pasta. It has much more flavor and a smooth, soft texture that absorbs sauces better than industrial flour-and-water pasta.

WHICH PASTA SHAPE?

You could cook a sauce and it would taste nice with a bowl of spaghetti, but that same sauce might taste twice as nice with a different shape of pasta. Certain pastas go particularly well with certain sauces. Pasta shapes aren't designed to look different simply for the fun of it; their shapes give them special eating qualities, too.

Long, thin spaghetti, for example, is traditionally eaten with smooth, oily sauces that cling to the pasta when you twirl it on your fork, not with meaty sauces. The wide ribbons called tagliatelle, which wrap around a sauce rather than fall off it, and big, fat tubes of pasta such as penne or rigatoni are perfect for meaty sauces.

Smaller pasta shapes, such as shell-like conchiglie or corkscrew fusilli, have hollows and spirals to help catch and hold even quite smooth or thin sauces. Bigger pasta shapes, such as lasagne, tubes of cannelloni, and giant shells, are meant to go in the oven, to be filled or layered with sauce, rather than boiled separately and then coated in it. Tiny pasta shapes are designed for adding to soups such as minestrone.

It's great fun, pretty quick (quicker than bread making!), and not at all difficult once you get the hang of it. A pasta machine that will roll out the dough for you as you turn the handle makes the job even easier – and they're not expensive. Rolling the dough out by hand with a rolling pin takes longer and is harder work, but will make very good pasta.

Cooking dried pasta

Always cook pasta in a large pan containing plenty of fast-boiling water. Just before you add the pasta to the pan, drop in a good tablespoonful or two of salt. Add the pasta all at once and stir it gently until every strand or piece is submerged beneath the surface. Keep the water at a rolling boil the whole time and stir the pasta occasionally to stop bits sticking to each other as they cook.

Most commercial dried pasta takes 8 to 12 minutes to cook. Look at the back of the package for guidance, but fish out a piece of pasta with a fork a couple of minutes early, blow on it to cool it, then taste it to see whether it's right for you. Some people like a little "bite" to it – this is called *al dente*. If it feels too hard, let it boil on and test again a minute or two later.

Take care when draining the pasta from its boiling cooking water. Empty the pasta and water into a large sieve or colander set in the sink, let the water drain away, and then gently stir the pasta into your chosen sauce straight away before it has a chance to stick together. Or, if you're planning to serve the pasta plain, you can toss it with a little butter or olive oil.

Some recipes with pasta

Spaghetti Carbonara, page 51
Macaroni and Cheese with Bacon, page 71
Pasta with Four Herbs, page 207
Spaghetti Bolognese, page 287

Project:

MAKING PASTA DOUGH

As you can see, you need about $2/3$ cup white pastry flour or all-purpose flour for each large egg and, using that basic ratio, you can make as much or as little pasta dough as you like. You can make an extra-rich pasta with two egg yolks instead of each whole egg. The amount below will make enough for about 4 people.

You will need:
White pastry flour or all-purpose flour, about $2^1/_2$ cups, plus a few shakes for working and kneading
Free-range eggs, 4 large

Sieve, mixing bowl, fork, tea towels, rolling pin or pasta machine, sharp knife

1. Sift the flour into the mixing bowl. Make a hole in the center of the flour and break the eggs into it. Whisk the eggs with the fork and then start knocking a little of the flour from the sides into the egg well, stirring it with your fingers until you have a rough, eggy-floury mixture. You may not need all of the flour.

2. Turn the mixture out onto a work surface sprinkled with flour, rub your hands clean, and then start to knead the dough. If it feels sticky, sprinkle in some extra flour. Keep kneading until the dough feels smooth and silky and not sticky at all. Five minutes should do it. Then a couple more for luck.

3. Wrap the ball of dough loosely in a damp tea towel and let it rest for 15 minutes. Lay a tea towel on a work surface or table nearby.

4. If you don't have a pasta machine, flour the work surface and the rolling pin and start to roll out the pasta, stretching it with the rolling pin until it's very thin – so thin that if you were to slip a piece of newspaper under it you'd be able to see the print (even if you couldn't quite read the article).

5. If you're using a pasta machine to roll out your dough, then assemble the machine and turn the rollers to the widest setting. Break off about a sixth of the dough (keep the rest wrapped in the damp towel so it doesn't dry out) and feed this carefully through the rollers. Fold it in half, turn it, and repeat.

6. Do this 2 or 3 times until the dough feels silky and pops as you feed it through the rollers. Then turn the machine to the next setting so that the rollers close up a little and pass the unfolded strip of dough through. If the dough starts to stick to the rollers, smooth a little flour over the pasta strip.

7. Keep closing the rollers and passing the dough through until you get a long sheet of very thin pasta (do the newspaper test to see if it's thin enough). Cut it in half at any stage if it gets too long to handle. Lay the sheet of pasta out flat on the tea towel while you roll out the other pieces, starting back on level one.

mix the dough

roll the pasta

cutting tagliatelle

pinching farfalle shapes

Making pasta shapes

Let the pasta dry out on the tea towel for just a couple of minutes before you cut it into shapes.

Tagliatelle (ribbons) If you're using a pasta machine, pass a strip of pasta through the wider ribbon cutter of the machine. If you've rolled the pasta by hand, then fold it over in loose flat rolls and cut it straight across into $1/4$-inch-wide strips. Unravel the strips and spread them out on the tea towel.

Farfalle (butterflies/bow-ties) Cut the pasta into little rectangles roughly the size of 2 postage stamps set side by side. Place the tip of your first finger in the middle of the rectangle and draw up the pasta top and bottom with your thumb and second finger, pinching the dough together so that it forms a bow-tie shape. Let rest on the tea towel.

Lasagne Cut the pasta into big rectangles (at least the width of your hand) and drop them a couple at a time into a large pan of boiling water for 1 minute. Fish them out with a slotted spoon and drop them into a bowl of cold water to stop them cooking. Then lay them out on a tea towel while you precook the rest.

Drying pasta

If you want to keep your homemade pasta for a day or two, you'll need to let it dry out pretty thoroughly or it will stick together horribly. With sheet pasta or tagliatelle, this is easily done by hanging it over a clean stick or a broom handle suspended between two chairs, or over the back of a wooden chair or a coathanger. A pasta "tree" is designed to make it even easier to hang out your pasta to dry. If you have made short pasta shapes, just spread them out on a tea towel. When your fresh pasta has dried, you can store it in plastic containers in the fridge for 3 to 4 days. A light dusting of semolina or rice flour will help to keep it dry.

Cooking your homemade pasta

Homemade pasta cooks much faster than dried pasta. If you've just finished making it, it will take only a minute or two (taste a piece after 1 minute to see if it's done). If you've left it to dry for a few hours or overnight, it will take 3 to 4 minutes. As with dried pasta, cook it in a large pan of boiling water to which you have added a generous 1 or 2 tablespoonfuls of salt. When it's done, drain it carefully through a large colander set in a sink and use straight away.

How to eat your homemade pasta

You don't have to make a sauce to serve with your homemade pasta. It is delicious enough to eat with just a slosh of olive oil or melted butter and a little bit of grated cheese. The Italians love Parmesan but any good grating cheese will do.

If you do want to get saucy, try the carbonara on page 51, the herb sauce on page 207, or the bolognese on page 287.

PIZZA

Can it really be right that pizza was invented only around 200 years ago? Something as simple as a flat platter of bread dough, sprinkled with a few tasty ingredients, and quickly baked in the oven? You'd have thought the ancient Romans, with their sophisticated cooking know-how, might have perfected something a little less exotic than roast dormouse and poached sea urchin – if only for comfort eating at home.

But of course there was one crucial ingredient missing. The pizza as we know it today is nothing without the tomato. And tomatoes weren't a popular ingredient in European cookery until the early nineteenth century. It's said that a baker from Naples in southern Italy made the very first pizza, which he topped simply with tomato, garlic, and herbs. Note that there were no slices of stretchy mozzarella cheese – the famous Margherita pizza came later.

Making pizza

Pizza dough is bread dough. So if you are making a loaf of bread and suddenly get hungry, you could always tear off a lump of your risen dough and make a pizza with it. (Perhaps that Neapolitan baker just got very hungry one day. So many great recipes started originally with a "what if I?")

Once you have made the dough and it has risen, you have all the fun of shaping it. There are two ways of doing this. You can roll the dough out by bringing it to the edge of the work surface so that part of it hangs slightly over the edge, trap the hanging-down bit with your (aproned) body, and then use the rolling pin to roll and stretch the dough away from you. Give the dough a quarter turn and repeat until you have a thin, circular shape.

Alternatively, you can leave the rolling pin in its drawer, pull the dough into a roughly round shape, and then use your fingers and knuckles to stretch and ease the dough into a larger circle. Pick the dough up at one edge and jiggle it in mid-air and you'll be using the weight of the dough to help stretch it out. Put it down again, then pick up another part of the edge, and do the same thing, and the dough should stretch reasonably evenly. And if it doesn't? A teardrop shape will taste just as good. Stretched by hand rather than rolled flat, it will probably be a little thicker at the edges than in the middle – which is just as it should be.

See page 48 for a pizza recipe.

PASTRY

If bread is little more than flour and water, then pastry is little more than flour and some sort of fat (usually butter, vegetable shortening, or lard). And just as you can make hundreds of different sorts of loaves by varying a basic bread dough recipe, so a slight change in technique or quantity can make all sorts of different pastries. You can make one that's just right for covering a mound of soft, sweet apple slices, or one that's strong enough to raise and support a pork pie crammed with meat and herbs, or one that's light and puffy enough to be stuffed with whipped cream and coated with a slick of chocolate for an éclair.

The first thing you do when you start to make pastry – even before you've found a package of flour – is to get out the measuring cups. When it comes to pastry, measurements matter. Too much flour and your pastry will crumble; too much butter and it'll be difficult to roll out; too much liquid and it will be as tough as old boots.

Pastry making involves some different techniques from bread making. You even use a different part of your hands to make this sort of dough. When you make bread, it's the heel of your hands – where the palm meets the wrist – that does the work. With pastry, it's your fingertips.

Why? As with bread – it's all down to gluten. When you make bread, you're doing everything possible to release and develop the gluten in the flour so that it will trap the yeasty air bubbles. But with most types of pastry you're doing everything possible *not* to develop it. Too much gluten will make your pastry tough and chewy, not light and melt-in-the-mouth. So you have to handle most pastry doughs with a lot of care, kneading and stretching them as little as possible.

As a general rule, you need to keep your pastry very cool at every stage. Chilled butter, chilled flour, even a chilled kitchen, all help to inhibit the development of the dastardly gluten. Most pastry recipes tell you at some point to let the dough rest for 30 minutes or so in a cool place, usually the fridge. This is so it can relax and shrink back after being handled or rolled. Some sorts of pastry – for instance, hot water crust (used for pork pies) and choux (used for éclairs), which both use hot melted fat – do break most of the rules. But the kind of pastry that you want for an everyday tart or pie is generally a variation of shortcrust pastry. In pastry terms, *short* means easily crumbled. Basic shortcrust pastry is a blend of about two parts flour to one part fat and uses water as a binder to glue the pastry together. The recipe on page 52 makes a rich, sweet shortcrust pastry and uses egg yolks to bind the butter, flour, and sugar together.

Rubbing in

After you've measured your flour into the bowl and added the fat cut into small cubes, many pastry recipes tell you to rub in the fat. With the palms of your hands facing down, scoop up some of the flour and butter with

rubbing in

bringing it together

flouring the pin

rolling out

rolling up the pastry

lining the pan

pricking the bottom

your fingers and start to break down the lumps of butter by gently grinding them into the flour. The pads of your thumbs will rub against the tips of your fingers just as if you were sprinkling seeds onto the ground.

Keep going and you'll very quickly find that the butter lumps get smaller and smaller. Most books say that you should keep going until the mixture looks like bread crumbs, but it's more of a coarse, sandy sort of look and feel, like ground almonds or cream-colored coffee granules. Shake the bowl every now and again, and any remaining butter lumps will rise to the surface.

Go to wash your buttery hands under the cold tap and you'll find that the water lies in droplets on your skin. The butter is acting as a barrier between your skin and the water. This is exactly why you have just rubbed the butter into the flour – you've given the flour an oily coating that will protect it against the liquid that you'll have to add later in the recipe to get the pastry to bind together into a solid mass. Yet again, it's all down to gluten, which starts

to develop when flour is mixed with liquid. So the more buttery the flour, the less liquid gets to the flour and the less gluten is developed. A little liquid does get through, and you need this or your pastry would be very crumbly and wouldn't be strong enough to do its job, i.e., supporting a filling in a pie or tart. This is why pastries with lots of butter in them taste delicious but can be difficult to roll out – there's so little gluten, or "glue," to bind the dough together.

It's worth bearing in mind that a sweet pastry mix, rubbed to the coarse meal or crumb stage, with no water or egg to release the gluten or bind the mix together, is, in fact, a British crumble! It has no load-bearing potential, but still makes a great topping.

Some recipes with pastry

Lemon Tart, page 52
Summer Fruit Tart, page 148
French-Style Apple Tart, page 150
Spicy Lamb Pie, page 289

BAKING BLIND If you're making a pastry shell for a filling that doesn't need to be cooked, or needs only light cooking, then you're going to have to cook it empty. This is known as baking "blind." The problem is, if you simply put a newly rolled-out pastry case in the oven to cook on its own, it will brown very quickly, lose its shape, puff up like a balloon, and not cook very well. So the solution is to line the pastry shell with foil or parchment paper and fill it with beans – either ceramic pie weights, which you can buy specially for the job, or ordinary dried beans. The pastry shell is then cooked for about 15 minutes, the beans and the foil are taken away, and the pastry is put back in the oven for another 5 to 10 minutes, until it's lightly colored.

EASY FLAT BREADS

The simplest breads of all are made with nothing more than flour, salt, and water, sometimes with a little oil or fat added. They hardly rise at all, and are more like bready pancakes. But freshly made, they are delicious.

Tortillas, eaten in Mexico, are made from a special corn flour or wheat flour. Mixed with a little water to make a dough, they are rolled or pressed very thin and cooked quickly on a hot pan or griddle. Indian chapatis are cooked in a similar way and then held over a naked flame for a few seconds so that they rise up suddenly like balloons before gently deflating again.

Flat breads like these are often used to wrap food or to scoop it up – so you don't have to use a knife and fork.

To make 8:
All-purpose or white pastry flour, 1²/₃ cups,
    plus extra for dusting the work surface
Salt, 1 level teaspoon
Olive or sunflower oil, 1 tablespoon
Warm water, about ²/₃ cup

Sieve, mixing bowl, teaspoon, tablespoon, measuring cup, rolling pin, heavy frying pan, tea towel, plate, metal spatula, oven rack (for puffing the flat breads)

1. Sift the flour into the mixing bowl along with the salt.

2. Spoon the oil into a measuring cup filled with the warm water (notice how it floats on the surface of the water like a slick). Pour the liquid over the flour in a thin stream, stirring well all the time with the fingers of your other hand. Bring the flour and water into a soft mass of slightly sticky dough. Rub off any dough that sticks to your hands.

3. Sprinkle a little flour onto the work surface and take the dough out of the bowl. Start to knead it by pushing the heel of your hand (where the palm meets the wrist) into the dough

to stretch it. Fold it over, give it a quarter turn, and then stretch it again. If the dough feels too sticky, sprinkle in a little more flour. Keep on kneading for about 5 minutes, until the dough feels smooth and plump.

4. Cover the ball of dough with an upturned mixing bowl and let it rest for at least 15 minutes. This allows it to relax and makes it much easier to roll out. If you're using your flat breads as wraps for a filling, you could make the filling while you're resting the dough.

5. When you're ready to cook the flat breads, roll the dough into a sausage shape and divide it into 8 pieces. Roll each piece into a ball. Flour

the work surface and the rolling pin and then roll out a ball of dough into a very thin round roughly the size of a small plate.

6. Put the frying pan on the stove top and turn it on to high heat. Get the pan good and hot and then turn the heat down to medium-low. Have ready a tea towel on a plate next to the stove where you can put your cooked flat breads and wrap them to keep warm and soft.

7. Pass the rolled-out flat bread from one hand to the other to shake off any excess flour, which would toughen the bread. Carefully lay the flat bread in the hot pan. Let it sit for between 30 seconds and 1 minute, until you see little white spots forming on the surface, then flip it over with a spatula; it should be patched with brown underneath. Cook the other side for another half a minute. Wrap the cooked flat bread in the tea towel while you roll out and cook the others, one at a time.

8. To make your flat breads extra special, they can be puffed up over a hot flame as they come out of the frying pan. Stand a metal oven rack over a gas or electric burner on medium heat, slip the cooked flat bread from the pan to the rack, and watch it bubble with air as it meets the intense heat. This will take only a few seconds. Quickly flip it over with a spatula to scorch the other side, and then scoop it off the heat. The bubble in the bread means it can be split and filled — a bit like a pita bread, only slightly more delicate.

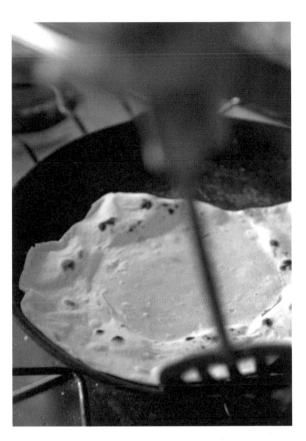

How to eat your flat breads

Eat them as soon as you can hold them, spread with a little butter, and they'll taste wonderful just as they are. Or you can roll them up like a carpet around a tablespoon of spicy filling.

Once you've got into the filling thing, the possibilities are endless. So why not have a flat bread party? Everyone takes turns rolling out and baking their own bread. Put out bowls of fillings – Spicy Bean Stew with Sausages on page 330, perhaps, with some tasty guacamole (page 215), chopped lettuce, and sour cream – and then everyone can create their own tacos at the table.

kneading, at least 10 minutes

proofing the dough (till doubled in size)

the shaped loaf

done!

A LOAF OF FRESH WHITE BREAD

Bread isn't difficult to make, but you do need to leave time for the dough to rise twice. So if you fancy a special loaf of bread for tea, start making the dough in the morning.

If you don't have instant yeast, you can use ordinary active dry yeast and follow the instructions on the packet. It's important that the yeast is well within its use-by date, as it loses its powers after a time, especially if the packet has been opened. If you use active dry yeast, you'll need to mix it with the water and sugar or honey first, letting it stand for about 5 minutes, or until foamy, before adding the oil and stirring it into the flour and salt.

To make 1 loaf:
All-purpose or bread flour, about 4 cups,
  plus extra for dusting the work surface
Salt, 2 teaspoons
Instant yeast, 1 packet or 2^1/$_4$ teaspoons
Olive oil, 2 tablespoons
Sugar or honey, 2 teaspoons

Warm (110°F) water, about 1^1/$_4$ cups
Butter or olive oil for greasing the pan

Large mixing bowl, wooden spoon, tablespoon, teaspoon, large glass measuring cup, plastic wrap or tea towel, loaf pan or baking sheet, wire rack

1. Put the flour into a mixing bowl, add the salt and the granules of yeast, and stir with the wooden spoon so they are all combined.

2. Spoon the olive oil and sugar or honey into the measuring cup and fill with warm water to just over the 1^1/$_4$-cup mark. Stir well.

3. Pour the oily water onto the flour in the bowl, a little at a time. Either with the wooden spoon or with your hands, work the water into the flour and gradually bring it all together into a mass of soft, slightly sticky dough. If the dough feels very sticky, add a little more flour. If it feels as if it won't come together, then work in some more warm water – a soft dough is much easier to knead.

4. Flour the work surface and turn the dough out onto it. It'll look rough and saggy at this stage, so it has to be kneaded until it's smooth and bouncy. Keep kneading (see page 21) for as long as you can – at least 10 minutes, if possible.

5. When you feel that your arms are ready to drop off, shape the dough into a neat ball, put it back in the bowl, and cover the bowl with some plastic wrap or a damp tea towel to proof. This is when the yeast starts to work and the dough begins to rise. Ideally, the dough needs to sit somewhere fairly warm, away from drafty open doors and windows. Too hot a place, though, and the yeast will die, so keep it away from direct heat such as a radiator. If you don't have a suitable warm place, then normal room

temperature will do. In fact, dough doesn't actually need warmth at all to rise – it's just that the rising takes much longer if it sits somewhere cold. You could make your dough in the evening and leave it to rise overnight in the fridge if this suits you better. Many people say a slow rise gives a better flavor.

6. Grease the base and sides of the pan or baking sheet with a scrap of butter or a few drops of olive oil.

7. After about $1^1/_2$ to 2 hours, your dough should have risen to a great big puffy, ballooned mass, at least twice its original size. Push your hand into the dough to flatten it (this is a truly wonderful feeling). Now pull it out of the bowl and knead it gently for half a minute on the work surface.

8. Form the dough into a fat sausage, roughly the size of the pan. Tuck the sides of the sausage underneath the base, so that it begins to look more like a plumped-up pillow. This helps the dough rise upward rather than just outward. Place it in the middle of the pan or baking sheet and sprinkle the top with a little flour. Cover with a clean, dry tea towel. Let it rise again for about 30 minutes – it will rise much more quickly this time, but don't let it quite double in size, as you want the yeast still to have some energy left before the loaf goes in the oven. Set the oven temperature to 475°F (or, if it doesn't go this hot, to the maximum heat – it must be at least 400°F).

9. Oven gloves on. Place the pan gently in the oven and set the timer to go off in 10 minutes. Then turn the oven down to 400°F for another 10 minutes. Oven gloves on. Take the pan out of the oven. Lift the loaf out of the pan and gently turn it upside down. Put it back in the pan and return it to the oven for 5 to 10 minutes to brown the base. Tap the base of the loaf – if it sounds hollow, then the bread is done; otherwise, leave it a little longer.

10. Turn off the oven, take the pan out, and unmold or place the loaf on a wire rack on the work surface to cool.

How to eat your bread

If you can bear to, leave your bread for an hour or so before you eat it, to let the crust harden. Then cut off a thick slice. Spread it thickly with butter and . . . eat it up. Save the jam or honey for your second, or third, slice.

While you're waiting for the dough to rise, you could make some lemon curd (see page 143) to spread on your bread. You could even make some jam-jar butter (page 64) for an entirely homemade feast.

Variations

You can play around with all kinds of tastes and textures in your bread by adding seeds, spices, herbs, and other ingredients. Turn to page 22 for some ideas.

RAISIN BREAD

This is really just a large, shiny currant bun. The syrupy glaze that you brush on the loaf after it comes out of the oven makes it look quite extraordinary – it's as if someone has suddenly turned a spotlight on it.

To make 1 loaf:
All-purpose or bread flour, about 4 cups,
  plus extra for dusting the work surface
Salt, 2 teaspoons
Instant yeast, 1 packet or 2¹/₄ teaspoons
Raisins, ³/₄ cup
Milk, ¹/₂ cup
Warm water, ¹/₂ cup
A large free-range egg
Orange marmalade, 2 good tablespoons
Butter or canola oil for greasing the pan

For the glaze:
Sugar, 1 tablespoon
Water, 2 tablespoons

Large mixing bowl, teaspoon, large glass measuring cup, fork, tablespoon, wooden spoon, plastic wrap or tea towel, large loaf pan about 5 by 9 by 3 inches (or a round cake pan), small saucepan, wire rack, pastry brush

1. Put the flour in the mixing bowl with the salt, yeast, and raisins.

2. Measure the milk and water into the glass measuring cup. Break in the egg and whisk everything together with the fork. Pour the eggy liquid into the bowl of flour. Spoon in the marmalade.

3. Mix the flour and liquids together, either with your hands or with the wooden spoon. When it becomes difficult to stir the dough, turn it out onto a floured work surface. Knead the dough (see page 21), adding more flour a handful at a time if it is really sticky. The dough will become smoother and smoother.

4. When you feel that your arms are ready to drop off, poke a fingertip into the dough – if the dent you make bounces back and leaves just a little mark, then you've kneaded enough. Shape the dough into a neat ball, put it in the bowl, and cover the bowl with plastic wrap or a damp tea towel.

5. Let the bowl of dough rise in a warm (but not hot) place, away from open doors and windows, for 1¹/₂ to 2 hours, until doubled in size.

6. Grease the bread or cake pan with a scrap of butter or a drop of canola oil.

7. When your dough has risen to a great big puffy, ballooned mass, twice its original size, flatten it with your fist. Now, pull it out of the bowl and knead it gently for a few seconds on the work surface.

8. Flatten the dough out a little into a round disk, then roll it up roughly like a carpet so that you get a puffy sausage shape. Place the dough sausage in the loaf pan – it should come about halfway up the sides. (If you're using a round cake pan, then shape the dough into a ball and tuck the sides of the dough underneath to make the ball pillow up, then put it in the pan.) Cover with plastic wrap or the tea towel again and let rise for 20 to 25 minutes. Meanwhile, preheat the oven to 425°F and place a rack in the center.

9. Oven gloves on. Place the pan gently in the oven and bake the bread for about 12 minutes. Then turn the oven down to 375°F for another 10 minutes. Oven gloves on. Take the pan out of the oven. Turn the bread out of the pan and tap the bottom to see if it sounds hollow. If not, put the loaf directly on the hot oven rack for 10 minutes to color the sides and bottom.

10. Meanwhile, make the glaze. Put the sugar into a small saucepan with the water. Place on the stove, turn the heat to medium, and stir with the wooden spoon until the sugar has dissolved to make a syrup. Let it simmer for a minute, then turn off the heat.

11. Turn off the oven, take the bread out and let cool on a wire rack. Now brush the top and sides of the bread with the warm syrup. It will shine beautifully.

How to eat your raisin bread

This loaf is probably at its best when slightly warm. Spread thick slices of it with butter and eat, licking your sugary fingers. If you've got any bread left the next day, eat it toasted and dripping with butter.

Variations

If you fancy a spicier loaf, you can add a teaspoon of ground cinnamon, nutmeg, or allspice (or a mixture of the three) to the flour in the bowl. And you can shape the mixture into little buns rather than one big loaf if you prefer. Bake the buns on a large greased baking sheet for about 15 minutes at a slightly lower temperature, 400°F.

SODA BREAD

The liquid in this loaf can be buttermilk or natural yogurt. In the past, most country households had buttermilk to spare, left over from the butter-making process (see page 64). But the important thing is that you give the soda something acid to react against. So yogurt, full of lactic acid, works very well too.

To make 1 loaf:
A little olive oil or butter for greasing
All-purpose or white pastry flour, 1²/₃ cups
Salt, 1 level teaspoon
Baking soda, 1 level teaspoon
Soft brown sugar, 2 teaspoons

Buttermilk or plain yogurt, scant 1 cup

Baking sheet, mixing bowl, sieve, teaspoon, large glass measuring cup, wooden spoon, sharp knife

1. Preheat the oven to 450°F. Grease the baking sheet with a little oil or butter.

2. Sift the flour, salt, and soda into the mixing bowl and add the sugar.

3. Stir in the buttermilk or yogurt, at first with the wooden spoon, then bringing it all together into a doughy mass with your hands. It should feel soft and firm, not sticky. Add a little more flour if the mixture is too wet.

4. Knead the dough lightly in the bowl for about half a minute, until smooth, then shape it into a ball, as deep as you can make it. Place it on the greased baking sheet. Slash a deep cross in the top of the loaf with the sharp knife. This will allow the bread to open out as the soda starts to work and expand the dough.

5. Oven gloves on. Bake in the hot oven for about 12 minutes, then turn the oven down to 400°F and bake for another 15 to 20 minutes, until the bread sounds hollow when you tap it.

How to eat your soda bread

Give the bread 15 minutes to cool, cut it into thick slices and eat with salty butter and fruit jam. Savory foods such as cheese or crisp fried bacon taste especially good with it, too.

Soda bread tastes much better when it's eaten warm. Breads without yeast in them don't tend to keep well, but even slightly stale they make great toast.

Variations

For a wheatier loaf, you can substitute whole-wheat flour for some of the white flour.

A lovely Irish-style soda bread is made with half whole-wheat and half all-purpose flour, or all whole-wheat pastry flour, and a tablespoon of rolled oats to give a crumbly texture and a mildly oaty taste.

SULTANA SCONES

Scones are just a daintier way of making soda bread. Baking powder is a ready-mixed combination of baking soda and an acid chemical. It quickly loses its chemical powers, so you'll need to buy a new can every few months.

To make about 16:
Self-rising flour, 3 cups, plus extra for dusting the work surface
Salt, ½ teaspoon
Baking powder, 2 teaspoons
Butter, 6 tablespoons
Superfine sugar, ½ cup
Sultanas (Golden raisins), ½ cup

Milk (or a mixture of milk and plain yogurt or buttermilk), about 1¼ cups

Mixing bowl, sieve, teaspoon, wooden spoon, large glass measuring cup, rolling pin, 2-inch biscuit cutter, baking sheet

1. Preheat the oven to 450°F.

2. Sift the flour into the mixing bowl along with the salt and baking powder.

3. Cut the butter into little cubes and add them to the flour. Rub the butter into the flour with your fingertips (see page 34) until the butter has basically disappeared into the flour and the flour looks like coarse meal.

4. Add the sugar and the raisins and give everything a good stir.

5. Using a wooden spoon, stir in the milk until you have a slightly sticky, rough mass of dough; you might not need quite all the milk.

6. Turn the dough out onto a lightly floured work surface. With the rolling pin, press the dough gently into a round about ³/₄ inch thick.

Dip the biscuit cutter in flour and use it to cut out as many scones as possible. Gather up the trimmings, press them together, and cut out more scones, until you've used up all the dough.

7. Lightly sprinkle the baking sheet with flour. Place the scones on the baking sheet. Oven gloves on. Bake the scones for 10 to 12 minutes, until they are golden brown.

How to eat your scones

Let your scones cool for just a few minutes, so that they're still warm as you split them. Scones taste fantastic with a teaspoon of jam or lemon curd and a generous dollop of whipped or clotted cream. There's a lot of argument as to whether you should put the cream or the jam on first. What do you think?

PIZZA

When you're making pizzas with family and friends, it's nice to have a wide choice of toppings so that everyone gets to make a pizza they're excited about. But when it comes to your turn, you needn't feel that you have to overload your pizza with a huge array of toppings – it's far better to keep it simple. Most of your work has gone into creating a delicious pizza base, so you really want to taste that as much as anything else. Just choose two or three things to scatter on it, along with herbs, salt, and pepper.

To make 4 pizzas:
A Loaf of Fresh White Bread dough,
page 41
Olive oil
Salt and black pepper

For the tomato sauce:
Garlic, 1 clove
Plum tomatoes, 14^1/$_2$-ounce can
Olive oil, 1 tablespoon
Sugar, 1 teaspoon

Toppings:
You can invent your own toppings, but some
tried and trusted favorites include:
Chopped or shredded mozzarella cheese
(or try a semihard goat's cheese for
a change)
Olives

Chopped garlic
Dried oregano
Slices of ham or cooked bacon
Sliced mushrooms
Slices of pepperoni or Spanish chorizo
sausage
Basil leaves, torn in half (add when the
pizza comes out of the oven)
Arugula leaves (add when the pizza
comes out of the oven)
Shrimp
Anchovies
Capers

. . . maybe not all at once, though

Cutting board, knife, medium saucepan,
tablespoon, wooden spoon or potato masher,
teaspoon, large baking sheet, rolling pin

1. Make the dough and knead it until it feels very smooth and stretchy – in fact, until you feel that you just can't knead it any longer. Put the dough back in the bowl, cover it with some plastic wrap or a damp tea towel, and leave it in a warm place for 1^1/$_2$ to 2 hours, when it should swell to about double its size.

2. Meanwhile, make the tomato sauce. Peel the garlic clove, place it on the board, and crush it with the flat of the knife blade until it turns into a coarse paste. Add the tomatoes into the pan with the olive oil and garlic. Break them up with a wooden spoon or a potato masher. Add the teaspoon of sugar. Turn the heat to medium and let the tomatoes bubble furiously,

stirring every now and again to make sure that they don't stick to the bottom of the pan. Let them bubble for about 5 to 10 minutes, until most of the juice has evaporated and you have a thick, pulpy sauce. Then turn off the heat and let the sauce cool.

3. When the dough has risen, press it down with the palm of your hand (always a very satisfying moment) and take it out of the bowl. Divide it into 4 pieces.

4. Turn the oven to its hottest setting (the ideal pizza cooking temperature is 500° to 550°F). Put the baking sheet in it to get hot.

5. Sprinkle some flour onto the work surface. Take one of the dough pieces and shape it roughly into a circle. Then continue to shape it as described on page 33 – either with your hands or with a rolling pin. Shape the other pieces in the same way.

6. Oven gloves on. Get the hot baking sheet out of the oven. Carefully lay 1 (or 2, if you can fit them both on) of the circles on the hot sheet. Spread a quarter of the tomato sauce over the pizza, leaving a bit of bare dough around the edge.

7. Scatter on your chosen ingredients. You might start perhaps with chopped mozzarella, then a few strips of ham, and a good sprinkling of oregano. Trickle a very little olive oil on top. Finish with a little salt and a grind of pepper. Put your oven gloves back on and the pan back in the oven. Bake the pizza(s) for 8 to 10 minutes, until the base looks cooked and the cheese is bubbling and spotted with brown. Cook the remaining pizzas in the same way.

8. Eat as soon as you can.

SPAGHETTI CARBONARA

This is an easy recipe to rustle up at any time, provided you can lay your hands on a few slices of bacon, a couple of eggs, a blob of cream, and some grating cheese.

To serve 4:

Make a batch of pasta as on page 30 and cut it into tagliatelle (or use store-bought pasta)
Garlic, ½ clove (optional)
Good bacon, 6 slices
Cheddar, Parmesan, or other grating cheese, 2 ounces, plus extra to serve
Free-range eggs, 2

Heavy cream, 2 tablespoons
Salt and black pepper

Large saucepan, cutting board, sharp knife, kitchen scissors, frying pan, grater, small bowl, tablespoon, fork, colander, wooden spoon

1. To cook the pasta, fill the large pan three-quarters full with water and place over high heat to come to a boil.

2. Meanwhile, peel the garlic (if you're using it) and chop it as finely as you can. With the scissors, snip the bacon into thick strips.

3. Put the frying pan over medium heat, add the bacon, and fry until it is brown and just turning crisp on both sides. Turn the heat down and add the chopped garlic, if using.

4. Grate the Cheddar, Parmesan, or other cheese into the small bowl. Break in the eggs and add the cream, then, using the fork, mix them into the cheese. Season the mixture with a few twists of black pepper.

5. Add 1 tablespoon salt to the pan of water. When it comes back to a boil, put the pasta in. If the pasta is freshly made, it will take just a minute or two to cook. Otherwise, look at the back of the package for guidance. When the pasta is done, drain it in the colander over the sink, then return it to the still-hot pan.

6. Toss the crisp bacon in with the pasta and pour the cheesy, creamy, eggy mixture in as well. Leave for a moment, then mix thoroughly with the pasta, using the wooden spoon. The heat of the pasta will gently scramble the eggs and melt the cheese, making a wonderful gooey concoction that sticks to the pasta. You can put the pan back on a gentle heat to help this happen, if necessary. Serve straight away, in warm bowls. Pass around some more grated cheese.

LEMON TART

This intensely lemony tart is made by baking the pastry shell blind and filling it with a creamy lemon curd mixture. The tart can then be placed under a hot broiler for just a minute or so until the filling starts to bubble and fleck with brown. Chefs used to do this with a metal tool called a salamander, which was heated until it was red hot and held over the food to brown it. Modern chefs use a blowtorch instead, but the broiler is a lot safer.

To serve 6 to 8:
For the sweet pastry:
All-purpose or white pastry flour, 1¼ cups, plus extra for dusting the work surface
Confectioner's sugar, 2 tablespoons, plus extra for dusting the top of the tart
A pinch of salt
Butter, ½ cup (1 stick)
Free-range egg yolks, 2 (see page 88 for details of how to separate eggs)

For the lemon curd filling:
Unsalted butter, 6 tablespoons

Superfine sugar, ¾ cup
Free-range eggs, 2 whole, plus 1 yolk
Lemons, 3

Plus:
Heavy cream, 6 tablespoons

Sieve, mixing bowl, knife, plastic wrap, large baking sheet, rolling pin, 9½- to 10-inch tart pan, fork, aluminium foil or parchment paper, dried beans, tablespoon, wire rack

1. First make the pastry. Sift the flour and sugar into the bowl. Cut the butter into little cubes and add them to the flour with the salt. With your fingertips, rub the butter into the flour and sugar (see page 34) until the mixture looks like bread crumbs.

2. Add the egg yolks to the mixture, stirring them in with a knife. Then use your hands to make the dough into a ball (you may need a very little cold water if your egg yolks are small). Knead it very lightly until it's smooth. Flatten the ball of dough out slightly, wrap it in plastic wrap or a plastic bag, and put it in the fridge for 1 to 2 hours.

3. Meanwhile, make the lemon curd, following the recipe on page 143, and let cool.

4. Place the baking sheet in the oven to heat up. Preheat the oven to 375°F.

5. Sprinkle a little flour on the work surface and rub some over the rolling pin. Unwrap the by-now chilled pastry and put it in the middle of the floured area. Carefully start to roll out the pastry, always rolling the pin away from you and giving the circle of pastry a quarter turn every other roll so that it makes an even shape. Dust the rolling pin and the work surface with a little more flour if the pastry starts to stick, but try not

to use too much extra flour. Stop rolling when the pastry is about an inch larger than your pan (remember it's got to cover the sides, too). Pick up the pastry by rolling it carefully up on the rolling pin and then drape it over the pan.

6. Line the pan as best you can, pressing the pastry into the base and up the sides. Patch and mend if you get gaps or tears – the pastry will glue together as the tart cooks (it's actually a very good sign if your pastry breaks up a little as you line the pan). Trim off any overhanging pastry by running your rolling pin over the top of the pan, then put the pan in the freezer for just 10 minutes. (This will help to firm up the pastry after all that handling.)

7. Lightly prick the base of the pastry shell all over with the prongs of a fork. Tear off a piece of foil or parchment paper and use it to line the bottom and sides of the pastry. Pour in the beans and spread them out evenly.

8. Oven gloves on. Put the tart on the now very hot baking sheet in the oven and bake for 15 minutes, or until the foil or paper lifts off easily. Oven gloves on again. Lift the foil or paper and beans carefully off the pastry shell and put it back in the oven for 3 to 4 minutes or so, until the pastry is a light brown. Turn off the oven, take the pan out, and let cool for a few minutes.

9. Stir the cream into the lemon curd and fill the pastry shell with the mixture. Sift a little confectioner's sugar over the filling.

10. If you like, you can glaze the top. Preheat the broiler. Cover the rim of the pastry shell with some strips of foil to protect it from the heat. Oven gloves on. Place the tart under the hot broiler for just a minute, until the sugar starts to fleck brown on top of the lemon filling, but watch carefully that the sides of the pastry shell don't burn. Turn off the broiler and let the tart cool on a wire rack for 5 to 10 minutes, until it is just warm.

How to eat your tart

This kind of tart, like many eggy dishes, tastes better and more lemony when it's eaten warm rather than hot. Eat it with plenty of cream, and if there's any left over you can eat it cold for tea.

MILK

All mammals produce milk to feed their young. But one grass-eating, cud-chewing, stringy-tailed mammal — the cow — produces a versatile milk that makes an astonishing contribution to the human diet. It gives us butter for our toast, cream for our strawberries, yogurt for all sorts of sweet and savory delights, and, as if that's not enough, well over a thousand different cheeses worldwide.

cheesecake, page 77

cream cheese, page 7

omemade butter, page 64

milkshake, page 85

MILK

Take a bottle or carton of milk from the fridge and pour some into a glass. The chances are you do this every day. But think about it for a moment. Isn't this an extraordinary liquid, filling up the clear, empty space in the glass with its intense, pure whiteness? How amazing, don't you think, that it comes straight from inside the body of an animal? That it has been made, by a cow, as the perfect food for its baby – a calf? And that it's also a pretty brilliant food for us humans, too?

If milk seems so familiar and everyday that you find it hard to get excited about it, try another thought. Imagine not having milk. No milk for your cereal, tea, or coffee, or for hot chocolate or a milkshake. Worse than that, perhaps, no butter on your toast – and none for making cakes and biscuits, either. No cheese in your sandwich, no cream on your strawberries, and no ice cream at all.

Milk and the many products we make from it are among the foods we depend on most, day in, day out. And they are some of our favorites. How could we do without them?

Dairy cows

It's no wonder that for thousands of years, all around the world, the cow has been a symbol of wealth. Their gift to us is their amazing ability to convert their favorite food, grass, not only into the bones, muscles, and body parts that keep them alive and well but also into milk – and plenty of it.

Like all mammals (including humans), cows produce milk as a first food for their babies, who suck it directly from their mothers' teats (the pointy bits on their large, milk-filled udders). The milks of different mammals are never quite the same. Human milk is different from cows' milk, which is different from the milk of dogs or donkeys. Each is specially made by the mother to help the babies of that species grow quickly and stay healthy.

Cows' milk is not a suitable food for tiny human babies. But as they grow, children are more tolerant of different foods. For many thousands of years, cows' milk and all the products that are made from it have been vital foods for children and adults the world over.

Almost all the milk sold in the U.K. is cows' milk – taken from female cattle that start producing milk once they have given birth to a calf. Our generally wet and mild climate grows plenty of grass for a large part of the year, so we have a long history of keeping cattle for milk. Sheep and goats are also raised for milking in this country, and you can buy their milk in specialty food stores and some large supermarkets. But most sheep's and goats' milk is used for making cheese.

Not all the cows that you see on farms are kept for milking – some are kept to produce calves for raising into beef (we both raise beef cattle on our farms). You can usually tell a dairy cow from a beef cow simply by looking at her – a bony back end and a large udder, like pink bagpipes swinging between her legs,

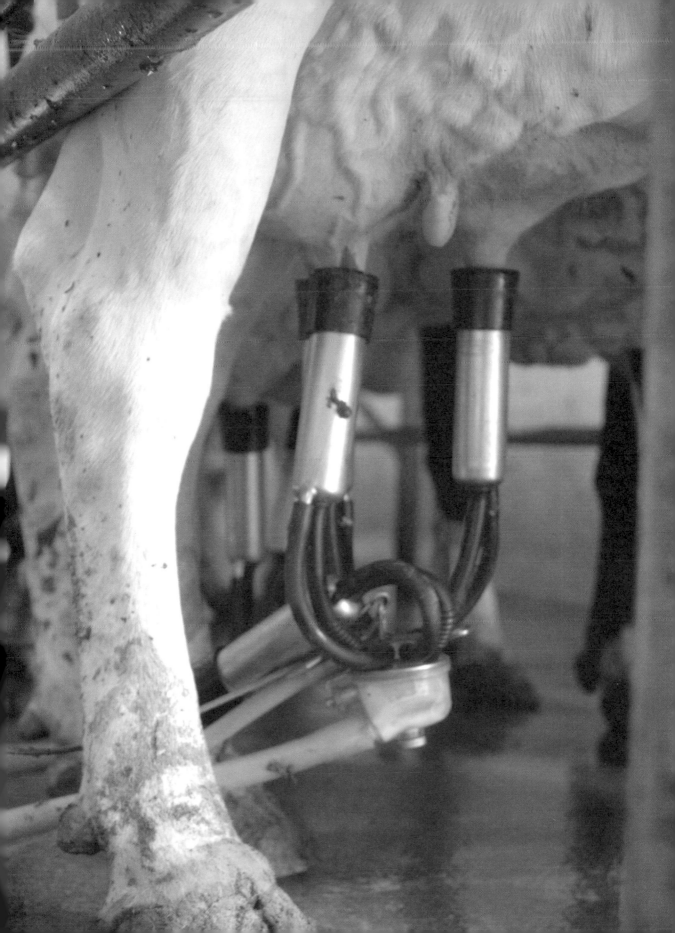

are sure signs of a cow kept for milk rather than meat. Today, most milk-producing cows in the U.K. are Holstein Friesians – the familiar big black and white breed.

It wasn't always like this. It's only in the last 300 years that cattle have been bred specially for eating or just for milking. Before then, cows of whatever breed were milked, and male cattle, called steers or oxen, worked on the farm, pulling plows or harrows. Both cows and steers were eaten only at the end of their productive working life.

But as Britain changed from being mainly a rural nation, where most people lived and worked on the land, to an urban nation, where most people lived and worked in towns and cities, the demand for milk went up and up. Farmers wanted to produce more milk than they could use themselves, so they could sell the extra to city dwellers. Dairy farming, as it is called, became a specialist part of the farming business, and cows like the Friesian were bred selectively to produce as much milk as possible.

THE PROBLEM OF DAIRY CALVES

Dairy cows need to have a calf every year so that they can keep producing milk. Sometimes, dairy farmers need to replace the older cows in the herd with younger dairy cows, and some of the female calves will be kept for this purpose.

But of course not all, in fact no more than about half, of the calves born are female. Male dairy calves have a less certain future. They won't produce milk, and they obviously won't produce calves themselves. Their fate often depends on the price of beef at around the time they are born. If the price is high, farmers may raise these male calves for beef in the hope that they will be profitable to rear; some pure-bred dairy calves are also reared for veal (see page 267). If the price is low, then farmers will not risk keeping these calves. Many of them will be killed very shortly after they are born. A partial solution to the dairy calf problem is to use beef bulls to make the dairy cows pregnant. The resulting calves, both male and female, keep the mother cow producing milk and are also meaty enough to be raised for good beef. The female calves born from a beef bull are not good enough at producing milk to replace the old cows in the dairy herd. But they can, along with the male calves, be reared for beef.

This connection between beef and dairy farming is one of the reasons strict vegetarians, often called vegans, avoid milk and other dairy products as well as meat. They are opposed to killing animals for meat, and they realize that dairy farming plays a vital part in the meat business.

Today, a good Friesian dairy cow can produce a staggering 10,000 quarts of milk a year. That's roughly 18,000 bottles of milk. A beef cow, such as an Aberdeen Angus, would produce just a fraction of that – little more than enough to feed her calf.

Different kinds of milk

In the old days, many farms had their own dairies, where the dairy maid would separate the milk from the cream, turn the cream into butter, and make cheese from the milk. Few farms nowadays process and sell their own milk, so it's collected from the farm by tankers that take it to a commercial dairy. Today's dairies are huge buildings, factories really, where milk is processed. These days they are full of high-tech machinery, which separates the milk at enormous speed.

If you leave a bucket of whole milk – milk straight from the cow – to sit around for a few hours, you'll find that the cream in the milk, being lighter than the milk itself, rises to the top and forms a separate thick layer. If you were to ladle off this cream with a spoon, you'd be left with skimmed milk.

Modern dairies have machines that spin the milk by centrifugal force, which means that the cream stays in one area while the heavier milk is driven into a different part of the machine. Varying amounts of cream can be taken out of the milk. So skimmed, or nonfat, milk is milk where virtually all the cream has been taken out, while 1 or 2 percent milk has had only some of the cream taken away.

Whole milk, cream, 1 or 2 percent milk, and nonfat milk can all be used and processed in different ways, and their different properties contribute to the vast array of foods that we refer to, collectively, as "dairy products."

Cooking with milk

Nearly every chapter in this book contains a recipe where milk plays a vital part. Hot chocolate, fish pie, pancakes, fudge, rice pudding – all impossible without milk. But you'll also find milk in quite unexpected places. In this book, for instance, it turns up in spaghetti bolognese, where it mellows and enriches the meaty, tomatoey sauce. Elsewhere you might find it used for braising pork, say, where the pork stews very gently and the milky liquid surrounding it simmers down into a sauce. One of the reasons milk is used in recipes like these is because of its sweetness. You might not have thought of milk as sweet, but simmer it in a pan for a long time to evaporate away the water it contains into steam and you are left with a kind of fudge.

One important thing to remember when heating milk on the stove: it boils over amazingly quickly, rising up the pan to froth over the top and make a horrendous mess. So, easy does it.

Béchamel sauce

One of the most useful things you'll ever learn to cook is a basic milky sauce called béchamel. It's the sauce that you sandwich between sheets of pasta and meat for lasagne.

If you cook a fish pie, it's béchamel that you mix with fish and herbs and top with plenty of mashed potatoes.

You make it by cooking together equal quantities of butter and flour in a saucepan, then adding enough warm milk to give a smooth, creamy sauce. It needs to be flavored – at the very least with salt and pepper. Usually, spices such as nutmeg, mace, or cayenne are added for a little kick. If you were making a fish pie (see page 248), you'd cook the fish in milk and then use this milk to make the béchamel. Or you can steep vegetables and herbs, such as onions, carrots, celery, and parsley, in hot milk and use this to make a simple but well-flavored sauce. Béchamel is the basis of a classic cheese sauce.

Some milky recipes

Macaroni and Cheese with Bacon, page 71
Frozen Strawberry (and Other) Milkshake(s),
   page 85
Pancakes, page 114
Creamy Fish Pie, page 248
Rice Pudding, page 322
Real Hot Chocolate, page 388

· ·

CREAM

We take milk for granted – getting out a bottle to slosh on our cornflakes or add to a cup of tea without a second thought. Cream, though, is a different matter. We think of it as a luxury. We pour it over strawberries, whose juices turn it streaky-pink; or whip it and pile it between exploding meringue halves; or, best of all perhaps, sweeten it, flavor it, and freeze it into velvety ice cream. Cream is the luxurious, special-occasion, upper-crust end of the milk bottle.

Quite literally. Look at a glass bottle of whole milk and you'll see an inch or so at the top that's thicker and more yellowy than the rest (even more so in the summer months, when the cows are gorging themselves on the best grass). That's the cream. Of course, you don't have to separate cream from your own milk. You can buy it in pots, ready to use.

Different creams

The most popular creams you see on shop shelves are called half-and-half and heavy whipping cream. Each contains different amounts of butterfat and is suited to its own particular uses in the kitchen. You'll also find sour cream, crème fraîche, and clotted cream.

Half-and-half is half heavy cream and half whole milk. It's similar to light cream. It's good for pouring on puddings and for making custard – perhaps to turn into ice cream (see pages 113 and 374). Because it has a low butterfat content, it's lighter in taste than other creams – just a bit greedy rather than very greedy. It's delicious trickled onto hot porridge in winter.

Heavy cream, also called heavy whipping cream, is thicker than half-and-half. You can use it in sauces, dollop it onto puddings, or whip it up with a whisk until it's thick and mousselike. It's the best cream to use when making butter (see page 64). Make sure not to buy ultra-pasteurized heavy cream; it lasts longer, but it doesn't taste as good or whip as easily.

Clotted cream, also called Devonshire cream, is a special cream to look out for if you are in the southwest of England. Very thick and yellowy, with a sparkling, buttery crust, this is the king of creams, made from the richest milk from cows that have eaten the lushest grass. It's perfect for spreading lavishly over a fresh scone along with a big spoonful of good strawberry jam. It's so thick you'll need to push it off the spoon with your finger.

Crème fraîche and *sour cream* have both been cultured with bacteria so that they become thicker and sharper flavored than normal heavy cream. They're useful when you want a less sweet alternative to cream – to eat with spicy Mexican food, perhaps, or in a cheesecake recipe to tone down the richness.

Cooking with cream

Heavy cream is so rich and delicious, we've come to use it as a kind of sauce – poured on an apple pie or topping an ice cream sundae, for example. But cream is very important in cooking, too, hidden inside dishes rather than showily displayed on top. Gently cooked egg yolks, sugar, and cream make wonderful custard, either for eating warm with puddings, or cooled and frozen to make a rich ice cream. Cheesecakes are baked mixtures of cream, cream cheese, eggs, and sugar. Chocolate truffles are made by melting lots of chopped-up chocolate into hot cream.

Cream isn't just for sweet things. Savory tarts, such as French quiches, are egg custards baked in pastry with ingredients like bacon, ham, cheese, or mushrooms. Often, cream is poured into soups at the end of the cooking time to make them richer, or used to thicken or finish simple sauces. For example, if you're frying a steak, then after you've cooked the meat and put it aside, pour a little cream in the pan to mix with the juices and crusty bits. Heat it gently, stirring and scraping all the time until it bubbles, add a little salt and pepper to taste, and your creamy sauce is ready.

Some recipes with cream

Homemade Cream Cheese, page 72
Creamy Brussels Sprouts Gratin, page 75
Real English Custard, page 113
Strawberry Fool, page 141
Custard Ice Cream, page 374
Chocolate Éclairs, page 397

BUTTER

You probably eat butter every day – in a cake or pastry, in a sauce, or simply spread on a piece of bread or toast. Butter is just cream that has been beaten or sloshed around until all the fat in the cream sticks together and forms a lump of butter. This is drained away from the rest of the liquid (called buttermilk; more on page 65), then washed and pressed into blocks. Sometimes salt is added to butter, which makes it keep better. Salted butter tastes wonderful on freshly baked bread, but unsalted is better for cooking sweet things.

Cooking with butter

There aren't many better cooking smells than that of a chopped onion gently sizzling in foaming-hot butter, but butter is used a great deal less in cooking than it was a generation ago. Oils, particularly olive oil, now play a much bigger part in cooking, mostly because food from Mediterranean countries such as Italy and Spain has become so popular.

But butter still has a very important role. Unlike many cooking oils, it flavors the food it is cooked with. Cakes, biscuits, and pastries made with butter have a much richer, fuller taste than those made with margarine (which is made from vegetable oil). So, if you're going to put some effort into making a cake one afternoon, do justice to it and use butter, even if it is a little more expensive than margarine.

There is one big problem when cooking with butter – it burns very easily. When you are melting butter for a recipe, watch it carefully because it can quickly turn brown and then black. Brown butter has a delicious, toasty taste, but black butter tastes bitter and, with a few unusual exceptions (fish is sometimes cooked in black butter), this is not what you want. Adding a little cooking oil such as sunflower or olive oil to the butter will help prevent it from burning. Indian cooking, which involves a lot of frying, gets around this problem by turning butter into an oil. The butter is melted in a pan and cooked very slowly until all the milky solid parts of the butter fall to the bottom and turn brown. It is then strained through a cloth and the resulting clear, golden liquid, called ghee, can be heated to a much higher temperature without burning. So can clarified butter, which is made the same way, but without browning the milk solids.

Project:

MAKING BUTTER AT HOME

Butter is very easy to make yourself. Until the nineteenth century, nearly all butter was made at home, in churns with paddles or plungers. Anything that stirs or agitates cream in a steady, regular way will eventually turn it to butter. People have even made butter sitting in a rocking chair with the cream in a jar on their lap. Feel how the cream thickens as you shake it, and wait for the sudden, satisfying slosh as it turns into butter.

You will need:
Heavy cream

That's the only ingredient! (It's better if the cream has been sitting in the fridge for a couple of days; really fresh cream takes longer to turn into butter.)

Mason jar (as big as you can comfortably hold; it needs a tight-fitting screw-top lid), mug, wooden board, wooden spoon

1. Take the cream out of the fridge and let it warm to room temperature for about half an hour (so it doesn't feel cold on your finger when you dip it in).

2. Pour enough cream into the Mason jar to come a third of the way up the sides. You need to leave plenty of air space so that the cream can really move around.

3. Screw on the lid tightly. Now shake the jar up and down and all around so that the cream bounces against the lid. It's important not to stop shaking until the butter starts to form.

4. First you'll feel the cream slop around in the jar, then you'll notice that it stops slopping and goes silent. At this stage you just have whipped cream. Keep shaking – pretend

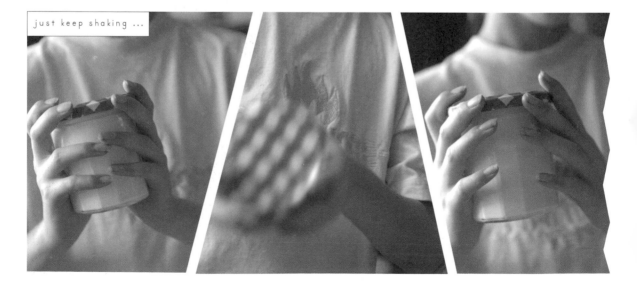

just keep shaking ...

you're playing the maracas! It may take 10 minutes or it may take half an hour.

5. All of a sudden the sound and the sensation will change. You'll have a big lump sloshing around in a thin, watery liquid. The lump is your butter and the liquid is buttermilk – carefully open the lid and take a look inside.

6. Now you have to wash your butter under the cold tap: drain the buttermilk off into a mug and fill the jam jar with cold water. Swirl the lump of butter around in the water and pour the water carefully away. Do this again and again until the water is clear.

7. Put the butter lump on the board and press down on it with the back of the wooden spoon (or use your hands) to force out any buttermilk still inside. This is important, because any buttermilk left inside it will make it go sour.

8. You can now wrap and refrigerate your homemade butter – or eat it straight away.

How to eat your butter

Eat your butter dripping over hot toast, on bread still warm from the oven (see page 41), or on toasted crumpets – basically anything hot that makes the butter melt.

If you're not going to eat your butter straight away (which, let's face it, is pretty unlikely), you can mold it into a shape (any shape you like), wrap it in waxed paper, and keep it in the fridge.

Make some scones (page 47) and some lemon curd (page 143). Homemade scones, eaten warm with homemade butter and homemade lemon curd – it'll be the best afternoon tea you've ever had.

For a savory treat, mix your homemade butter with crushed garlic and chopped herbs and make garlic bread or garlic toast.

it's definitely butter!

mold your butter

CHEESE

Leave a bottle or carton of milk in a warm kitchen overnight by mistake and you probably won't want to pour it on your cereal in the morning. Milk goes sour very quickly if it's not kept cool. Nowadays, we have refrigerators to keep food cold. But imagine that you are living in an age when there is no electricity – no fridge, no freezer, no reliable way of keeping things cold. Your cow, full of good summer grass, is producing far more milk than you can possibly drink. Unless you can find some way of making the milk keep, you will have to throw it away or give it to your pig. What do you do with it? You make cheese.

How cheese is made

Cheese is simply milk or cream that has been turned to a solid by adding a substance that will make it curdle. You can make a very basic sort of cheese by adding a little lemon juice to warm milk until it forms lumps and then draining the lumps in a cloth. This leaves you with curds (the lumpy bits) and whey (the liquid). Just what Little Miss Muffet was eating in the nursery rhyme. Curds are the basic ingredient of most cheeses.

Most cheese is curdled with rennet rather than lemon juice. Rennet is a substance extracted from the stomachs of young calves. Stirred into warm milk, it makes the milk form a firm curd. This is then cut into pieces and salted. The pieces are piled into a mold and pressed so that all the liquid runs out and the lumps of curd firm together into a cheese. (Some cheeses are curdled with vegetarian rennet, which is usually made from a fermented kind of fungus.)

Virtually all the milk we buy nowadays is pasteurized – heated to 162°F for at least 15 seconds and then rapidly cooled. This process kills all the harmful bacteria that can cause diseases such as tuberculosis and brucellosis, which used to kill people by the thousands. You might have whole milk, nonfat milk, or low-fat milk in your fridge at home. But unless you have bought them directly from a farm that is specially licensed to sell unpasteurized milk, it's sure to have been pasteurized. The problem is, this pasteurization process is very effective at killing all the bacteria that start growing in the milk, including the bacteria that make the lactic acid that form the milk curds. So when cheese is made from pasteurized milk, special bacteria have to be added to it at the beginning of the process.

While certain groups of people – pregnant women, very young children, and the elderly – are advised not to drink unpasteurized milk, it's safe for these groups to eat unpasteurized hard cheese because bacteria called listeria that can cause food poisoning can't tolerate the long maturing process that hard cheeses undergo. However, people in these groups should avoid soft, mold-ripened cheeses such as Camembert, and blue cheeses such as Stilton, whether they're made from unpasteurized or pasteurized milk.

Different kinds of cheese

Thousands of different cheeses are made all over the world – from the countless sheep's, goats', and cows' milk cheeses of France and the rest of Europe to the yaks' milk cheeses of India and Tibet. A lifetime wouldn't be long enough to taste them all. But there are some world-famous cheeses that almost everyone has heard of, and most of them are named after the places that originally started to produce them – think of Brie, Camembert, Cheddar, Stilton, and Edam.

The fascinating thing about these cheeses is that nearly all of them are produced in roughly the same way, yet they all look and taste completely different. This is because even the smallest change in the way a cheese is made can have a big effect on its taste and texture.

These differences start even before the animal is milked. What a cow or goat eats in the field or barn will make a cheese taste quite different – whether it's munching on spring or late-summer grass, or whether it's relying on hay (dried grass) for most of its feed.

How the curd is cut up alters the texture. If a hard cheese such as Cheddar is to be made, then the curd is cut up into tiny pieces so that more whey will drain out. Some cheeses are pressed very hard under weights to force out yet more whey. Softer cheeses remain soft because the curd isn't cut so finely and less of the whey drains off.

Some cheeses are kept for months or even years before they are eaten so that the flavor can develop. Others are eaten within hours.

Cheeses like Stilton have blue veins running through them. These are made by inserting large needles in the cheese, so that the blue *Penicillium* mold starts to grow in the holes. Daniel Defoe, eighteenth-century author of *Robinson Crusoe*, talks of visiting an inn where Stilton was made and being given a spoon to eat his cheese – not so much for the cheese itself but so that he could scoop up and eat the cheesy maggots that tumbled out of it. Not our idea of a treat, but he seemed to like it.

Cooking with cheese

Different cheeses play quite different roles in cooking. Strong cheeses, such as mature English Cheddar or Italian Parmesan, add a lot of flavor to food, so they're good for making a dish like cauliflower cheese or for adding to savory scones to give a good overall cheesy flavor. Soft, mild cream cheeses, such as ricotta or mascarpone, are often used for making creamy desserts, like cheesecake or Italian coffee and chocolate tiramisù. Some cheeses are valued as much for their texture as their flavor. Think of melting mozzarella on top of a pizza, stretching into long threads as you tug it with your teeth.

Some cheesy recipes

Spaghetti Carbonara, page 51
Macaroni and Cheese with Bacon, page 71
Homemade Cream Cheese, page 72
Cheesecake, page 77
Cheese Straws, page 79

THE DAIRY MAID'S STORY

Before big dairies took over the production of many of our dairy foods in the 1880s, the quality of your milk might be a pretty hit-and-miss affair. If you lived in a town in the eighteenth century, your milk might well be mixed with water to make it go further or, even worse, mixed with snail slime to make it froth and look fresh. There was no way of moving it quickly from place to place, and it was difficult to keep it cold. It wasn't being pasteurized, and bacteria from cattle with diseases such as tuberculosis were passed on to people who drank the milk.

In the countryside, good milk was easier to find – every farm had some sort of dairy herd. Wealthy country families built specially designed dairies with stone floors, tiled walls, and slate counters – all materials that could be easily cleaned and would stay cool.

In the dairy, cleanliness was all important. The dairy maid spent a large part of her day swilling pans and utensils out with hot water before she made her butter and cheese. It seems odd that centuries before people understood how important it was to boil medical instruments for operations, dairies were being scrubbed out and scrupulously cleaned to get rid of things that might spoil the milk. Dairy maids themselves had to be clean – in a time when hot water was an expensive luxury and proper baths were rare for all but the wealthy. Just as a great surge of the population was pouring into the towns to live in filthy slum conditions, the dairy maid became a symbol of health and purity.

In fact, the extraordinarily good health of the average dairy maid came to have a huge impact on medical history. One particularly nasty disease that affected a great number of the population was a virus called smallpox. At the end of the eighteenth century, a doctor called Edward Jenner realized that dairy maids never seemed to contract this disease, which left most people who survived it with dreadful scars. Instead, they caught a much less dangerous version of the virus, known as cowpox, from the cows that they milked.

Jenner injected the cowpox virus into a small boy. After the child had recovered, he injected him with smallpox virus. The boy didn't contract smallpox. Antibodies against the cowpox had built up in the child and protected him from smallpox. A huge program of vaccination followed across the country, and within 100 years, smallpox had virtually disappeared.

YOGURT

Only 50 years ago, few people in the U.K. had ever heard of yogurt, let alone tasted it. Today, it's as much a part of our weekly shopping as butter or cream. You're sure to have tried it sweetened and flavored with fruit. But you've missed a treat if you've never made your own yogurt, where you add the fresh fruit yourself, with a bit of sugar, and stir it all up. It's better than anything you can get at the supermarket. Or try it with runny honey and toasted nuts or cornflakes. Delectable. Make a smoothie, with yogurt, ice, and fresh fruit in the blender. It's a whole new breakfast.

Certain types of bacteria turn milk into cheese. The transformation of milk into yogurt is a similar process but with different bacteria doing the work. These bacteria multiply in the warm milk and turn the natural milk sugars into something called lactic acid. The milk thickens and turns to yogurt.

Yogurt is very easy to make at home, although you don't really make it so much as grow it. The bacteria needed to ferment the milk can be found in tubs of "live," or natural, plain yogurt that you buy in a natural foods store, delicatessen, or supermarket. Just two tablespoons of this will turn two cups of milk into creamy yogurt, perfect for your favorite smoothie. "Live" yogurt sounds a bit alarming, but all it means is that the bacteria in the yogurt are still active and capable of growing.

The bacteria in live yogurt are generally considered "friendly," which means they are the same as, or at least work well with, the ones that occur naturally in your stomach. This is what gives live, natural yogurt its status as a health food.

Some recipes with yogurt

Soda Bread, page 46
Sultana Scones, page 47
Homemade Yogurt, page 82
Cucumber Raita, page 83
Peach, Pear, and Raspberry Smoothie, page 161
Chicken Curry, page 298

MACARONI AND CHEESE WITH BACON

Macaroni and cheese is one of those creamy, cheesy, comforting foods that are just right to eat on winter evenings, when everybody's feeling a bit cold inside. A couple of slices of well-cooked bacon makes just the right crisp contrast to the oozy sauce.

To serve 4:
Macaroni, 2 cups
Smoked bacon slices, 8

For the cheese sauce:
Milk, 3 cups
Unsalted butter, 3 tablespoons, plus extra
  for greasing the dish
All-purpose flour, 3 tablespoons
A bay leaf

Sharp Cheddar cheese, 6 ounces
Parmesan cheese, 2 ounces
Cayenne pepper, ¼ teaspoon
Salt and black pepper

*Large saucepan, medium saucepan,
large pitcher, wooden spoon, balloon whisk,
grater, teaspoon, ovenproof dish about
8 inches square, colander, frying pan*

1. Preheat the oven to 400°F.

2. Fill the large pan three-quarters full with water and put it on high heat to boil.

3. Meanwhile, make the sauce. Using hot milk to make a béchamel greatly reduces the risk of a lumpy sauce, so start by pouring the milk into the medium saucepan and place it over medium heat until the milk is hot but not quite boiling. Pour the hot milk into the pitcher and keep it standing by.

4. Now put the butter in the medium saucepan and melt it over low heat. As soon as it's melted, add the flour. Turn up the heat a little. Stir the flour and butter with the wooden spoon to make a thick paste called a roux. It's very important to cook this roux a little or you'll end up with a floury-tasting sauce, so keep stirring it for a minute or two while it sizzles gently.

5. Pour in about a quarter of the hot milk and stir it carefully into the roux. Swap the wooden spoon for the whisk and you'll find it much easier to blend in the milk. Gradually add the rest of the milk and keep whisking gently until it's all thoroughly mixed in. Add the bay leaf. Bring the sauce to a boil and then turn the heat down low. Let the sauce gently simmer and blip bubbles for about 5 minutes. Stir every minute or so just to keep it from sticking to the bottom of the pan. Meanwhile, shred the Cheddar and grate the Parmesan, keeping them separate. Grease the ovenproof dish with plenty of butter.

6. Season the sauce very well with the cayenne pepper, a good grinding of black pepper, and a

generous sprinkling of salt. Add the shredded Cheddar cheese to the sauce and stir well.

7. When the water in the large pot starts to boil, add 2 tablespoons of salt and the macaroni and cook the pasta for 2 minutes less than the time it says on the package. Drain in the colander over the sink.

8. Add the pasta to the cheese sauce and stir them together until thoroughly combined. Pour the cheesy macaroni into the ovenproof dish. Spread evenly and sprinkle it with the grated Parmesan.

9. Oven gloves on. Place the dish in the preheated oven and bake for about 20 minutes, until the cheese on top has turned golden brown and the sauce is bubbling. Meanwhile, grill or fry the bacon until brown and crisp, turning it once halfway through cooking.

How to eat your macaroni and cheese

Serve it up straight away, making sure that everybody gets a couple of crisp bacon slices on top of their helping of creamy macaroni. Generous hunks of crusty bread would be very nice, too.

. . . .

HOMEMADE CREAM CHEESE

It's bacteria that turn milk into cheese, but virtually all the bacteria in milk or cream are killed when it is pasteurized, so you need to put some bacteria back in at the start of any cheesemaking process. This bacteria is known as a "starter."

You can make a very easy soft cream cheese using cultured buttermilk as a starter. This is quite different from the buttermilk you get when you make butter in a jam jar, as on page 64. Cultured buttermilk is milk that has been skimmed of its cream and then blended with lactic bacteria. You can buy it in many natural foods shops and in some large supermarkets in the dairy aisle, usually near the cream and sour cream section. It tastes like thin yogurt, and you can use it in the same way – for making bread and scones (see pages 46 to 47) and for whizzing up with fruit into smoothies.

Use heavy cream that has had a couple of days to sit in the fridge rather than one straight from the store shelf.

You will need:
Heavy cream, 2 cups
Cultured buttermilk, 3 tablespoons

Saucepan, 2 heatproof bowls, tablespoon, candy thermometer, plastic wrap, sieve, large clean handkerchief or square of cheesecloth, string

spooning in the curds and whey

hanging the bag

unwrapping the cheese

adding chopped herbs

1. It's very important that all your cheese-making equipment be sterilized with boiling water before you start, so put the kettle on to boil. Stand the saucepan and one of the bowls in the sink and put the tablespoon and the thermometer in the bowl. Pour boiling water from the kettle into the bowl and saucepan and over the utensils. Turn the cold tap on to cool the water down, then take everything out of the sink and shake it dry.

2. Pour the cream into the saucepan and set the pan over low heat, stirring all the time with the clean tablespoon. Stand the thermometer in the pan. When the temperature gets to 75°F — which won't take very long at all — take the pan off the heat and pour the cream into the bowl. Check that the temperature hasn't risen above 75°F. If it has, stir the cream until the temperature drops back.

3. Stir the buttermilk into the cream. Stretch some plastic wrap over the top of the bowl and leave it in a warm place, such as on or near a radiator, for about 8 hours or overnight.

4. The cream should now have set into a fairly firm curd with a watery whey. Scald the sieve, the handkerchief or cheesecloth, and the second bowl with boiling water in the sink as before. Then line the sieve with the handkerchief or cheesecloth and set the sieve over the bowl.

5. Spoon the curd into the lined sieve. The whey will start to trickle through the cloth and into the bowl. Gather up the 4 corners of the cloth and twist them gently together. Tie a piece of string around them, tie the other end to a hook or a suitable cupboard door handle, and suspend the bag of cheese over its bowl so that the whey keeps on dripping into it (you can use the whey for making bread or scones).

6. The cheese solidifies as more and more whey drips out of the bag. When it seems fairly firm (probably after about 2 hours), take down the bag and scrape the cheese into a bowl. Keep it in the fridge until you want to use it.

Tip
Instead of buttermilk, you can use the same amount of cultured crème fraîche to make a slightly fresher-tasting cream cheese.

How to eat your cream cheese
The beauty of this cream cheese is that you can turn it into something sweet or savory. You could stir it up with a little salt and some black pepper and eat it on bread or crackers, maybe adding some finely chopped herbs such as parsley and chives.

If you fancy something sweeter, mix the cheese with a couple of teaspoons of your favorite jam.

CREAMY BRUSSELS SPROUTS GRATIN

Some people think they don't like Brussels sprouts. This recipe should change their minds. Make sure you choose small, young sprouts with tightly packed leaves rather than large, flabby ones.

To serve 4:
Brussels sprouts, 12 ounces
A little butter
White country bread, 1 to 2 slices
Heavy cream, about 1/2 cup
Sea salt and black pepper

Medium saucepan, sharp knife, cutting board, colander, shallow baking dish about 22 x 8 inches square, food processor or blender

1. Preheat the oven to 375°F.

2. Half fill the saucepan with water and bring it to a boil.

3. Meanwhile, trim the tough end off each sprout and peel off the outer layer of leaves.

4. Add the sprouts carefully to the boiling water and simmer them for 5 to 6 minutes, until they're just tender but not at all soggy. Drain the sprouts in the colander and let them cool for about 10 minutes.

5. Butter the baking dish. Trim the crusts off the bread with the knife and whiz the bread to small crumbs in the food processor or blender.

6. When the sprouts are cool enough to handle, chop them coarsely into quarters (or halves if they're very small) and add them to the greased baking dish. Grind in some sea salt and lots of black pepper. Pour the cream over the top, then sprinkle on the bread crumbs and dot with small pieces of butter.

7. Oven gloves on. Place the dish in the oven and bake for 20 to 25 minutes, until the top of the mixture is browned and the cream is bubbling.

How to eat your sprouts

A creamy vegetable dish like this is a lovely wintry treat to tuck into after you've been outside in the cold. Serve it with roast chicken or sausages. If you can't find good sprouts, you can use 4 washed and trimmed leeks (see page 204) instead. Cut the leeks into slices 3/4 inch thick and simmer for 5 minutes. Then drain them and carry on with the recipe as above.

CHEESECAKE

A cheesecake is just a sweetened, very creamy version of a baked egg custard (see page 94). It's always eaten well chilled, after the cheese has set into a delicious, almost fudgy mass. Like many baked custards, this is cooked in a pan of hot water (sometimes called a bain marie) so that it bakes slowly and evenly. Take extra care getting it out of the oven.

Most cheesecake recipes make enormous cakes. This is much smaller than usual, but it will still serve 6 people easily.

To serve 6 to 8:
Butter, 5 tablespoons, plus extra for
   greasing the pan
Graham crackers, 14 (3 ounces)
Unsalted cream cheese, 12 ounces
   (homemade, as on page 72, if you like)
Superfine sugar, 2/3 cup
Lemon, 1
Free-range eggs, 2
Free-range egg yolks, 2 (see page 88 for
   details of how to separate eggs)

Vanilla extract, 1 teaspoon
Heavy cream, 6 tablespoons

*8-inch round cake pan about 2 inches deep
(either a springform pan or one with a
removable bottom), aluminium foil, small
saucepan, plastic bag, rolling pin, wooden
spoon, mixing bowl, grater or zester, plastic
spatula, roasting pan large enough to hold
the cake pan, wire rack*

1.   Preheat the oven to 325°F. Butter the base and sides of the cake pan. Tear off a large piece of aluminium foil, fold it in half, and use it to wrap around the base and side of the pan (this will protect it from the boiling water that it is going to sit in). Put the kettle on.

2.   Make the crust for the cheesecake: Melt the butter very slowly in the small pan over low heat. Before it starts to sizzle, take the pan off the heat. Put the graham crackers in the plastic bag, squeeze out the air from the bag, and crush them with a rolling pin until there are no lumps.

3.   Stir the crumbs into the melted butter with the wooden spoon and mix well. Put the buttery

crumbs into the bottom of the cake pan, pressing them to the edge in an even layer. Let cool, then put the pan in the fridge to set.

4.   Put the cream cheese and sugar into the mixing bowl. Beat them together with the (washed) wooden spoon until they are smooth and creamy.

5.   Grate the zest from the lemon, making sure you leave behind the bitter white pith. Break one of the eggs into the bowl and beat this into the mixture just until everything is well combined. Repeat with the other egg. Beat in the yolks one at a time, along with the vanilla extract and the lemon zest.

6. Gently stir in the cream. Pour the mixture into the chilled pan, scraping it out of the bowl with the plastic spatula.

7. Place the cake pan in the roasting pan. Pour just an inch or so of hot water from the kettle into the roasting pan – not too much, or it will be too dangerous to carry.

8. Oven gloves on. Very carefully, place the pan in the preheated oven and bake for about 40 minutes – but check after 30 minutes to make sure your cheesecake isn't getting too brown on top. The cheesecake is ready when it is firm around the outside but still wobbles a little in the center; it will finish setting as it cools.

9. Turn off the oven. Oven gloves on. Carefully take the roasting pan out of the oven. Lift out the cake pan and place it on the rack until the cheesecake has cooled. Then put it in the fridge for at least 2 hours. The sides will shrink away from the pan a little.

10. Either unclip the sides of the pan or, if you used a pan with a removable bottom, stand the pan on top of a small bowl or mug and the ring will slide down, leaving the cake balanced on the bowl or mug.

How to eat your cheesecake

This cake is delicious eaten just as it is, or you could have it with some soft fruit such as raspberries or blackberries, either piled on top or served on the side. You could even push the fruit through a sieve to make a sauce if you feel like making a really fancy dessert. Sweeten the sauce with a little sifted confectioners' sugar if you think it needs it.

CHEESE STRAWS

Quick and easy to make, cheese straws are just a very buttery, cheesy pastry. It's important that the cheese you use is really strong and well flavored.

To make about 24:
Butter, for greasing
Aged Cheddar cheese, or a mixture of
  Cheddar and Parmesan, 5 ounces
All-purpose or white pastry flour, $^2/_3$ cup,
  plus extra for dusting the work surface
Cayenne pepper
Black pepper

Butter, 6 tablespoons
Free-range egg yolk, 1 (see page 88 for
  details of how to separate eggs)

*Large baking sheet, parchment paper,
grater, mixing bowl, sieve, butter knife,
rolling pin, sharp knife, wire rack*

1. Preheat the oven to 425°F. Lightly grease the baking sheet and cover it with a piece of parchment paper.

2. Finely grate the two cheeses into the mixing bowl. Sift in the flour and add a sprinkling of cayenne pepper (remember it can be very spicy). Grind in some black pepper.

3. Cut the butter into little cubes and rub them into the mixture with your fingertips (see page 34) as if you were making pastry (which you are). When the butter has almost disappeared into the flour and you're left with a crumbly mixture, stir in the egg yolk with the butter knife.

4. Gather the pastry into a ball of dough (it should come together very easily). Dust the work surface with plenty of flour. Carefully roll out the cheese dough into a rough square. It should be about 2 inches thick. Neaten the edges with the side of your hand.

5. With the sharp knife, cut the square into strips, then each strip into fingers. Gently lift them onto the lined baking sheet, leaving a little space between each one.

6. Oven gloves on. Place the baking sheet in the oven and bake for about 8 minutes, but check after 5 or 6 as oven temperatures vary tremendously. The cheese straws should be a very pale golden brown. They're extremely fragile when they come out of the oven, so let them sit for 5 minutes before you try to move them. Then carefully lift up the parchment paper and transfer everything to the wire rack to cool just a little more.

How to eat your cheese straws

Cheese straws are at their best while they're still warm from the oven, either just as they are or dipped into a bowl of sour cream.

SHORTBREAD

When a recipe has as few ingredients as this, each one plays a vital role. The all-purpose or pastry flour provides body, the rice flour lightness, and the sugar sweetness. But it's the butter that really works hard here, giving the shortbread its fantastic flavor and melting texture.

To make 8 to 16 pieces:
All-purpose or white pastry flour, 3/4 cup
Rice flour, 3 tablespoons
A pinch of salt
Unsalted butter, 7 tablespoons, firm but not
  fridge cold
Superfine sugar, 1/4 cup, plus 1 teaspoon
  for sprinkling

Sieve, mixing bowl, butter knife, 8-inch round cake pan, wire rack

1. Preheat the oven to 325°F.

2. Sift the flours and salt into the bowl. Cut the butter into little cubes and add them to the flour. Add the sugar.

3. Using your fingertips, rub the butter into the flour, just as if you were making pastry (see page 34).

4. When the butter has been absorbed, you'll be left with a sandy sort of mixture. Start to clump it together with your hands until you get a smooth, cakelike mass. No liquid is needed; it's just the butteriness of the mixture that holds everything together.

5. Put the mixture into the center of the cake pan (there's no need to grease or line it). Using your knuckles or the back of a spoon, gently press out the shortbread to fit the pan in an even layer.

6. Oven gloves on. Put the pan in the oven and bake for 15 to 20 minutes, until the shortbread is just beginning to take on the faintest trace of color.

7. Oven gloves on again. Remove the pan from the oven, place it on the wire rack, and leave the shortbread untouched in the pan for about 10 minutes to harden up.

8. Sprinkle the cake with the teaspoon of sugar. With a sharp knife, cut the cake in half, then half again, then cut these quarters into half again to make eighths, and cut one last time to make sixteenths. Allow the shortbread to cool completely, so it becomes firm and brittle.

How to eat your shortbread
This is very good with creamy puddings such as the fools on pages 141 and 142. It's also lovely with a cup of tea or a glass of milk.

HOMEMADE YOGURT

Homemade yogurt tends to be thinner than the yogurt you buy in shops, but you can add a little nonfat milk powder to the recipe to thicken it. Use only freshly bought plain yogurt with a long sell-by date to breed your own yogurt, and make sure it says "live cultures" on the carton (see page 70).

You will need:
Whole milk, 2 cups
Nonfat dried milk powder, 2 heaping tablespoonfuls (optional, if you want thicker yogurt)
Live plain yogurt, 2 to 3 tablespoons

Balloon whisk, tablespoon, candy thermometer, large mixing bowl with lid (or use plastic wrap), medium-sized saucepan, towel

1. When you make yogurt, it's important that everything you use is very clean, so you don't start growing the wrong kind of bacteria. Put the kettle on. Place the whisk, the tablespoon, and the thermometer in the mixing bowl and put them in the sink. Pour boiling water into the bowl and leave for a few seconds. Turn the cold tap on to cool the water down, then take everything out of the sink and shake it dry.

2. Pour the milk into the saucepan and whisk in the dried milk powder, if using. Place the pan on the stove over medium heat. Clip the thermometer to the pan and watch it like a hawk. Stir the milk gently.

3. When the temperature reaches 114°F (which won't take long), take the saucepan off the stove and pour the milk into the mixing bowl. Check that the temperature hasn't gone beyond 114°F. If it has, stir the milk until the temperature drops back. Whisk in the yogurt so that it blends in with the milk.

4. Now cover the bowl with the lid or some plastic wrap. Wrap the bowl in the towel and put it somewhere warm – in a turned-off oven that has a pilot light, maybe, or above a radiator.

5. Check the yogurt after 6 to 8 hours (you can leave it overnight). If it's still runny, give it another hour or two wrapped up in the warm place. If it has thickened and looks set, then put the bowl straight into the fridge.

How to eat your yogurt

If you like plain yogurt, you'll find it delicious to eat as it is, straight from the fridge, perhaps with a little sugar sprinkled on top. Sliced banana with yogurt and runny honey makes a great snack or breakfast. But if you fancy a quick dessert, mash up some strawberries or raspberries with a little superfine sugar and stir them in to make your own fruit yogurt. In winter you could whisk in some of your favorite jam – the nicer the jam, the nicer the jammy yogurt.

CUCUMBER RAITA

Of course, yogurt doesn't just make good snacks and desserts. If you're eating something spicy, such as a curry, then a cool yogurt sauce tames that fiery tiger in your mouth much better than a glass of water. The classic soothing yogurt sauce from India is called raita. Here's a cucumber version. It serves 4 people, eating it with curry or kebabs.

You will need:
Cucumber, 1/2
Salt
Mint leaves, 4 to 5
Plain yogurt, 5 heaping tablespoons

Black pepper
Ground cumin, a good pinch

Vegetable peeler, grater, sieve, cutting board, sharp knife, bowl, wooden spoon

1. Peel the skin from the cucumber and shred the flesh into the sieve. Sprinkle the mushy cucumber with a little salt and let it drip over the sink for 5 minutes to get rid of some water.

2. Meanwhile, chop the mint leaves very finely. Put the yogurt into the bowl.

3. Squeeze out the liquid from the cucumber and add it to the bowl with the mint. Grind in some black pepper and add the cumin. Stir well with the wooden spoon, then put the raita in the fridge until you're ready to eat it.

How to eat your raita

This is especially good with the chicken curry on page 298, or served with lamb kebabs for dipping (see page 292). But it also works as a zesty, refreshing dip for chunks of raw vegetables, or crispy bits of toasted pita bread.

FROZEN STRAWBERRY (AND OTHER) MILKSHAKE(S)

Here's the easiest way possible to whip up a lovely, slushy, creamy, ice-cold milkshake.

To serve 2 to 4:
Strawberries, 2 cups
Superfine sugar, 1 tablespoon
Whole milk, about 1¹/₄ cups, cold from
   the fridge

*Small sharp knife, blender, tall glasses,
thick straws*

1. Remove the leafy bits from the strawberries. Put the strawberries in the freezer until they're either completely frozen, or very nearly frozen (about 2 to 3 hours should do it).

2. Put the frozen strawberries in the blender, add the sugar, and pour in the cold milk; it should come almost to the top of the straw-berries (but not more than two-thirds of the way up the blender, or it might squirt out of the top when you switch it on).

3. Whiz! (Until thick, slushy, completely blended, and gloriously pink.)

4. Pour into tall glasses and drink through thick straws. Or pour into thick glasses and drink through tall straws.

Variations

You can use various frozen fruits to make these delicious ice-cold milkshakes. Bananas are always good – especially if you add a tablespoon of oatmeal to the blender. Cut the banana into thick slices before freezing it. Other "fleshy" fruits, such as peaches, nectarines, and cherries (in all cases, with the pits removed) work extremely well too. And you can make up combinations – banana and blueberry is a good one!

If you suddenly feel like a milkshake and you don't have time to wait for fruit to freeze, then add a few ice cubes to the blender along with the fresh, unfrozen fruit. The effect won't be quite as fruity, but it should be pretty delicious all the same.

EGGS

An egg is the perfect environment for a growing chick. But when there's no chick at home, it's a brilliant, multipurpose cooking ingredient for us. Hidden inside the shell are the round, sunny yolk and the gloopy, see-through white. Between them, they have inspired cooks for hundreds of years, giving us custards and cakes, mousses, and meringues. And, of course, boiled eggs with toast fingers.

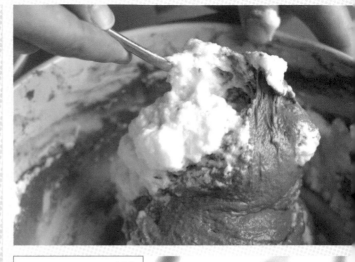

meringues, page 108

French omelette, page 10

boiled egg, page 101

Victoria sponge cake, page 111

pancakes, page 114

eggy bread, page 103

real English custard, page 113

scrambled eggs, page 101

EGGS

If you've got an egg, you've got a meal. Boil it in water, scramble it with butter, flip it in hot oil as it sizzles in the pan, or crack it into boiling water and poach it – an egg is a different breakfast or supper for every day of the week.

But there's a *lot* more to eggs than that. They are one of the most amazing ingredients there is. This is because eggs, with their slippery whites and unctuous yolks, can do the most extraordinary things. Cakes, meringues, custard, mousses, soufflés, and sauces – all would be impossible without eggs.

What is an egg?

An egg laid by a hen is an entire food pantry designed for a tiny developing chick to feast on until it hatches out. But unless you keep your own chickens, and have a rooster too, the eggs you are using, bought from the shops, will almost certainly be unfertilized – there'll be no chick at home. So this great pantry is all yours, to use in a thousand and one different recipes.

Of course, if you do keep your own hens, the eggs they give you will be the best you ever get. And if you have a rooster, too, you can hatch out baby chickens, keep the hens for laying, and fatten up the roosters for roasting! (To find out about keeping poultry, see our website, www.rivercottage.net.)

In many recipes, eggs are used whole: the shell is cracked open and the round, yellow yolk and clear, jellylike white are poured into a bowl. Whisk them together and the yolk breaks. Keep whisking and the white and yolk will mix together into a pale yellow, creamy gloop. Mixed-up whole eggs are used in many recipes – for example, four eggs, beaten with equal quantities of sugar, butter, and self-rising flour, make a simple pound cake.

Often, though, cooks will "separate" an egg – taking the yolk away from the white. This is because, on their own, the yolk and the white do very different things in recipes. Meringues, for instance, are made from whites beaten stiff with sugar. English custard is made from yolks beaten with sugar and stirred into hot milk or cream, then heated gently until they thicken.

Eggs can carry a risk of salmonella poisoning. Because of this, raw or very lightly cooked eggs should not be eaten by babies and toddlers, pregnant women, or elderly people.

Cracking an egg

Unless you're boiling an egg in its shell for breakfast or tea, you'll need to break that shell before you start cooking. If you want to use the whole egg (both yolk and white together), tap the middle of the egg gently but firmly against the side of a bowl or mug until a crack appears. Now, with the egg in both hands and the bowl underneath, put your thumbs into the crack and pull the shell apart so that the egg drops into the bowl.

Separating an egg

So many recipes ask for either the yolk or the white, or use them at different stages, that all

good cooks soon learn how to separate eggs. Find two bowls or mugs. As before, crack the middle of the egg with one smart blow on the side of the bowl. But now proceed with a little more caution. With one of the bowls underneath, tilt the egg to one side and pull the halves of the shell apart, making sure the yolk drops back into one half of the shell (ideally the bigger half). Now pass the yolk backward and forward between the two shells, each time letting a little of the white drop down into the bowl. Finally, drop the yolk into the other bowl.

If you're going to be whisking the egg whites, it's important that not a scrap of yolk gets mixed up with them or they won't whisk properly (the yolk contains a lot of fat, which will stop the white foaming up – just like soap in a bubble bath). If a little yolk does get in the white, fish it out with half of the empty shell, or a teaspoon. If you have a total disaster and the yolk breaks everywhere into the white, start again with another egg. And have scrambled eggs for supper.

Egg whites

If you feel the egg white with your fingers, you'll find that it has a strange, slightly slimy texture, like jelly that's just started to set. It seems odd that we call this transparent gloopy substance the "white" of the egg. Odd, that is, until you cook it, and it almost instantly turns completely white.

You can see it turn white more slowly if you whisk it in a bowl. As the bubbles begin

to form, it slowly becomes opaque, and if you keep whisking it soon becomes a mass of brilliant white froth. Many recipes call for egg whites to be beaten until they form stiff peaks. Carry on whisking until, when you lift the whisk out of the foam, the foam stands up on its own, like a little snowy mountain. In fact, if you've whisked for long enough, you should be able to turn the whole bowl upside down without any egg white sliding out. Do you dare to hold it above your head?

What's actually happening when you whisk up egg whites to make them foam is that you are trapping lots of tiny bubbles of air. Cooks have discovered that this is one of the best ways of getting air into their recipes.

THE GENTLE ART OF FOLDING

This is a way of blending a new ingredient into a mixture. Sometimes, you're adding a delicate ingredient to a thick mixture (like whisked-up egg whites to a cake mix), and sometimes you're adding a heavy ingredient to a delicate mixture (superfine sugar to whisked egg whites for meringues, say). Unlike beating, which uses all of your arm, with folding it's the spoon and your wrist that do all the work, turning the mixture over and over like a scooping sort of paddle (see the picture opposite). For folding, you use a metal spoon rather than a wooden one, because it has a thin edge and doesn't work the mixture so much. After each scoop of the spoon, give the bowl a quarter turn with your other hand – this helps to make the blending more even.

Meringues, for instance, are made of thousands of tiny sugar-and-egg-white bubbles, dried out gently in a low oven.

In many recipes, the snowy beaten egg white is gently combined with a mixture of other ingredients – usually at the very last minute before the dish is baked in the oven. Some cakes are made in this way, as well as the extraordinary soufflé, which doubles or triples in size as it cooks.

Beaten egg whites need to be treated gently and with respect. As they are usually added to other, much heavier ingredients at the end of a recipe, you need to fold them in carefully, using an up-and-over movement with a large metal spoon. If you were simply to mix or beat them into other ingredients with a wooden spoon or whisk, you'd squash out all that lovely air that you worked so hard to get in. (See "The Gentle Art of Folding," above.)

Beaten egg whites have to be used quite quickly, otherwise they slowly deflate back to a slimy puddle, so always whisk them up at the last minute before folding them in.

Some recipes with egg whites

Meringues, page 108
Peppermint Creams, page 363
Marshmallows, page 368

Egg yolks

Whether you are dipping a toast finger or serving your eggs sunny-side up, that bright yellow yolk surrounded by its snowy white is a remarkable sight. Some yolks are darker than others. If you keep hens in your garden or buy eggs from hens that roam outdoors, you'll notice that the yolks aren't so much yellow as a sunset orange. The grass and plants that the hens eat affect the natural pigments in the yolk and make it darker. (This doesn't necessarily mean that an egg with an orangey yolk has come from a free-range hen, though. Sometimes hens that are kept inside are fed supplements to turn their egg yolks orange.)

Separated from its white, the yolk plays a different role in cooking. If you beat an egg yolk with milk or cream, or into a sauce, and heat it gently while stirring, then it will thicken the mix. This is how custard and many other sauces are made. Bake a mixture of egg yolks and cream and it will set firm. This is how sweet and savory tarts, such as custard pies and quiches, are made. Slowly mix or stir a sweet-flavored custard while it freezes and you end up with ice cream, made the old-fashioned way.

The yolk can perform these tricks because the proteins in it start to cling together when they reach a certain temperature, thickening the liquids that they're cooked with. It's a subtle process, though – overdo the heat and instead of gentle thickening, you'll have solid lumps – scrambled eggs, in fact.

However, egg yolks don't have to be hot to thicken and bind other ingredients together. You can mix lemon juice or vinegar with olive oil to make a dressing for a salad, but they won't stay mixed for long. Within a few minutes they separate back into layers, the lemon juice or vinegar sitting on top of the oil. But whisk the lemon juice or vinegar with an egg yolk first and you will find that you can mix in the olive oil, little by little, to make a thick, creamy mayonnaise – perfect with some cold chicken in a crusty sandwich or to dip French fries into.

Some recipes with egg yolks

Real English Custard, page 113
Crudités with Garlic Mayonnaise, page 212
Strawberry Parfait, page 371
Custard Ice Cream, page 374
Real Hot Chocolate, page 388

Is it fresh?

Nearly everyone at some stage in their life cracks open an egg and immediately wishes that they hadn't. The smell of a rotten egg is about as bad as a smell gets. But luckily you can tell whether an egg is fresh or rotten – or even somewhere in between – without cracking it open.

Gently place the egg in a bowl of cold water. If it's really fresh, it should sink and lie flat on its side. If it stands on a point at the bottom of the bowl, then it's more than just a couple of days old but it should be okay. If it bobs about on top of the water, then don't even think about cracking it open.

The reason a bad egg floats is that as an egg gets older, the white shrinks and the egg starts to fill up with air. The more air, the older and "badder" the egg and the more it wants to float.

Before you crack open another egg, though, you might want to know a little more about the hen that laid it.

The chicken and the egg

When we talk about hens and chickens, it's important to sort out the difference between the kind of chickens that are farmed for their eggs (layers), which are always female, and the chickens that are farmed for their meat (broilers). If you were keeping a few chickens in your back garden, you could choose a breed that would provide you with some eggs but still be plump enough to make good eating. If you're buying eggs from a shop, though, they'll certainly be from a chicken that has been bred solely to lay eggs. These hens use the food that they eat to produce lots of eggs (usually one almost every day) rather than putting on weight and getting meaty.

What sort of eggs should I use?

Wherever you buy your eggs, be it the supermarket, produce market, farmers' market, or corner store, you will find some important information about them written on the box. For example, it will tell you how big they are   ranging from small to extra large – and perhaps the breed of hen that laid them. Most importantly, though, it will give you some idea of the sort of life the hens that laid them are leading.

While egg producers have to tell the truth about what they are selling, the box labels can still be very misleading. "Farm Fresh Eggs" in big letters on the label means that the contents of the box are fresh, laid on a farm, and are certainly eggs. But you'll have to peer at the small print to read that they're actually "eggs from caged hens."

A hen from a caged system – also known as battery, or factory, farming – will spend most of its life in a cage with three other birds, each bird having roughly the size of a sheet of typing paper to move about in. This is not enough room for the birds to move around freely and therefore restricts much of their natural behavior. Oddly enough, the boxes that contain these sorts of eggs often have pictures of sunrises and crowing roosters printed on the front. But the hens that laid them will never have seen either.

Cage free, or barn, eggs come from hens that live uncaged in large sheds, though these sheds aren't quite as picturesque and charming as the labels on the box sometimes might have you think. These birds can fly to perches off the ground and share nesting boxes where they can lay their eggs. Again, these hens do not go outside or see natural daylight, and many are kept in extremely crowded conditions.

Free-range eggs come from hens that have access to grassy fields. This means that the hens that get outside can wander freely, scratching and pecking the ground, and dust-bathe in soil. Some free-range flocks, however, are a bit more free range than others. While some hens may live in relatively small groups with easy daytime access to pasture, others may live in a flock of thousands, in a single large barn with just a few small doors to get in and out, so many of them never make it outside. Farmers' markets and farm shops usually sell free-range eggs, and

here you can ask about what sort of life the hens are leading.

Organic eggs come from hens that have had a free-range lifestyle and a diet that's free from artificial pesticides and fertilizers. The routine use of antibiotics is banned.

So check the label on the box very carefully and try not to be influenced by pretty pictures of egg cups, healthy-looking people, or rolling countryside. Look at the words. And if it doesn't say "free range" or "organic," then you can be sure it isn't.

Eggs from other birds

Nearly all the eggs we eat come from chickens (hens), but you can also buy eggs from other birds to cook with. Duck eggs are slightly larger than hens' eggs and are usually white or pale blue in color. They can be used just like hens' eggs. You might find goose eggs for sale at some farm shops, and now that ostriches are farmed in the U.K. it's even possible to buy ostrich eggs. A creamy white color, ostrich eggs measure around 6 inches long and are incredibly heavy – 21 times the weight of a hen's egg and the largest egg of any living bird. You can even stand on them.

Some more eggy recipes

Boiled Egg, page 101
Scrambled Eggs on Toast, page 101
Poached Egg, page 102
Eggy Bread, page 103
French Omelette, page 104
Spanish Omelette (Tortilla), page 106
Victoria Sponge Cake, page 111

. . . .

CUSTARD

There are two main kinds of English custard. There is the kind that you buy in Britain powdered in tins, which is flavored cornstarch to which coloring has been added so that it turns bright yellow when the powder is mixed with milk. This is what you might reasonably call "fake" custard.

Then there's real English custard, made from eggs, milk, and/or cream and sugar. It's not showy – positively boring in color, in fact – but it tastes absolutely delicious.

When you make tin or packet custard, you're simply mixing hot milk with flavored and colored cornstarch, which thickens it to a creamy sauce. But when you make real English custard, you use egg yolks to do the thickening rather than cornstarch. The egg yolk and milk mixture is heated very gently so that the temperature rises slowly. When it reaches a certain temperature, the proteins in the egg yolks start to link together and the mixture thickens and makes a sauce. The custard has to be stirred all the time so that parts of the mixture don't heat up more quickly than

others. If the temperature gets too high, the eggs go completely solid and you end up with sweet and lumpy scrambled eggs.

In Britain, the word *custard* usually refers to this sweet, hot sauce — the kind that's poured over a steamed pudding or an apple pie — which is known in the U.S. as English custard, or crème anglaise. Left to cool, it can be poured over cake and fruit to make trifle, or mixed with thick cream and flavoring to make ice cream (see page 374). In the U.S., *custard* usually means baked custard, made from the same ingredients.

However, custards don't have to be sweet. Savory tarts, such as quiches, are basically custards made of eggs, milk, and cream, baked in a pastry shell with added ingredients such as bacon, onions, mushrooms, and cheese.

For both sweet and savory custards, the richness is determined by whether you use milk or cream, and whole eggs or only yolks. Thin custard sauces can be made with creamy milk and whole eggs. You can make them richer and thicker by using half cream, half milk, and egg yolks only. The thickest, richest custards are made with pure heavy cream and egg yolks. They'll set fairly firm when cold — and that's how crème brûlée is made.

Some custard recipes

Real English Custard, page 113
Custard Ice Cream, page 374

. . . .

PANCAKES

When eggs are mixed with flour, you are usually well on the way to making some kind of cake. But the simplest cake of all, without doubt, is the pancake, which in the U.K. is really a crêpe.

Why don't we eat pancakes every day? They're cheap, they're quick, and they're easy to make. You don't even need a special shopping trip to get the ingredients. Flour, eggs, milk, and a pinch of salt — all things you've almost certainly got sitting in your kitchen right now — whisked up together into a thin batter and fried. Have you ever met anyone who has said no to a pancake?

Especially one dripping with lemon juice and gritty with sugar?

Outside the U.K., pancakes are an everyday food. Crêpes in France are eaten all year round, in the street, in the market, at home — anywhere, in fact. Stuffed with delicious fillings and sauces, both sweet and savory, they're available at street stalls and at expensive restaurants, served in a paper cone with lemon and sugar or flamed at your table by the head waiter.

Throughout North America, pancakes are eaten for breakfast, a great pile of them smothered in maple syrup. In Russia, blini are eaten with sour cream and fish or meat. In India, the batter for dosas is made with rice

ANCIENT PANCAKES People have been making pancakes for thousands of years, long before the celebrations of Shrove Tuesday, or Pancake Day in Britain, which often involves a pancake race (see page 99). A Roman writer called Apicius recorded this recipe almost 2,000 years ago: *"Whisk up four eggs, some milk, and some oil so that it makes a smooth mixture. Pour a small amount of oil into a frying pan, heat it until it bubbles and add the prepared mixture. When one side has been cooked, turn it over, spread some honey on it, sprinkle with pepper and serve."*

As the Romans didn't have sugar, they sweetened their dishes with honey. Pepper sounds a rather strange thing to sprinkle on a pancake topped with honey but try it – it tastes nicer than you might think.

flour and yogurt rather than eggs and wheat flour, but they're just pancakes all the same.

Yet in the U.K. it's as if pancakes don't exist for 364 days of the year. Then, on so-called Pancake Day, everyone goes mad for them!

It's true, of course, that pancakes have traditionally been eaten on Shrove Tuesday for many generations. The following day is Ash Wednesday, the beginning of the Lenten fast, when fat and eggs were not to be eaten. So Shrove Tuesday naturally became a day when everybody gorged themselves on as much fat and eggs as they had. Pancakes were an easy, obvious, and appetizing way of eating up all those just-about-to-be-forbidden ingredients. But that doesn't mean that pancakes weren't eaten during the rest of the year – only not in Lent. It's a great shame that they are now saved for just one day, especially as they're so quick, simple, and delicious. So break with "tradition" and cook them whenever you like. All our kids love pancakes and have them for breakfast, tea, or supper, or all three, *at least* once a week!

Different sorts of batter cakes

Pancakes don't have to be just the lemon and sugar type of wide, flat pancakes that we're used to seeing on Shrove Tuesday. There are all sorts of different batter "cakes." Some, like pancakes, are fried in a frying pan or on a griddle – originally a stone that was heated in the fire. American-style pancakes, and British drop scones, are made with baking powder. Fritters are chunks of food dipped in batter and fried in hot oil. Toad-in-the-hole is a giant batter pudding of sausages, baked in the oven, surrounded by a great pillow of puffy batter. Yorkshire pudding is another baked batter cake that's as essential to a roast beef dinner as the roast beef.

Some pancake recipes

Pancakes, page 114
Drop Scones, page 117

and the winner is

Project:

HOSTING A PANCAKE RACE

Shrove Tuesday will always seem like the best day of the year for a fully fledged pancake party. But now that you're eating pancakes all year round, what's to stop you from holding a pancake race whenever you feel like it?

You will need:

Ingredients for pancake batter (milk, all-purpose or white pastry flour, eggs, and salt), sunflower oil for frying, frying pan for each team, posts or obstacles to run around, tape for finishing line, plates, lemons, superfine sugar, spoons, jams, etc.

Optional. **Strings of pennants, aprons, or paper chef's hats**

Preparations

Mark out the area where you're going to race — it could be your garden, a nearby park or field, or, with the school's permission, a school playground. As well as a start/finish line, you'll need a couple of obstacles for people to run around or markers to show them where they need to toss their pancake. You can hang up strings of pennants or banners. This instantly gets people in the mood for racing. You can even put a string of pennants across the race track — you go under and the pancake has to go over!

You'll only need one pancake per team to race with (tip: make extra thick "racing pancakes" — they'll be easier to toss and less likely to fall apart), but you're bound to work up an appetite, so make up a big batch of pancakes (see page 114) and keep them warm, ready to feast on as soon as the race is over.

Decide on the penalty for dropping the pancake — perhaps the racers just have to keep tossing the pancake until they get it right, or maybe they will have to be penalized in some other way, like performing a trick.

Think about who is going to start the race and who'll make sure that everybody runs the race according to the rules. Finally, how about a prize for the winning team? Or maybe they just get to be the ones to tuck in first.

The race

Divide the number of pancake racers into teams — the teams can be as big as you like. Give the first person to run a frying pan containing a pancake, and either an apron or a chef's hat to wear. When the whistle blows, the first member of each team runs down the course, around the first post, tosses the pancake (successfully), runs to the end of the course, circles another post, tosses the pancake again, and then runs back for home. They then pass the apron or hat and frying pan to the next member of the team.

Finally, and most importantly, at the end of the race, get your (hot) plate of pancakes out of the oven and devour them immediately, with a choice of everyone's favorite toppings on hand.

SOFT-BOILED EGG

As eggs vary in size, it's difficult to be precise about boiling times. If you like a firmly set white with a slightly runny yolk, then $4^1/_2$ minutes' boiling is about right for a large egg starting at room temperature. The traditional 3-minute egg will be very runny indeed!

To serve 1:

1 really fresh free-range egg, at room temperature

Small saucepan, tablespoon, egg cup

1. Fill the saucepan three-quarters full with water and set it on the stove to boil.

2. When the water starts to boil, place the egg in the curved "bowl" of the spoon and gently lower it into the water, using the side of the saucepan to ease the egg in. Immediately turn the timer to $4^1/_2$ minutes. Keep the water bubbling gently the whole time.

3. When the timer goes off, scoop the egg out of the boiling water with the spoon, taking as little water as possible, and put it in the egg cup.

How to eat your soft-boiled egg

Slice off the top of the egg with a knife (or bash it, then scoop it with a spoon), sprinkle with a little salt and pepper if you like, and eat with a teaspoon and toast fingers for dipping.

. . . .

SCRAMBLED EGGS ON TOAST

Make the toast first and keep it warm on a plate while you scramble the eggs.

To serve 2:

Free-range eggs, 3 to 4
Salt and black pepper
Butter
Buttered toast

Small bowl, fork, small nonstick saucepan, wooden spoon

1. Break the eggs into the bowl. Add a pinch of salt and a twist of pepper. Whisk with the fork.

2. Place the saucepan over low heat, and melt a tablespoon of butter. When it starts to bubble, pour in the eggy mixture and start stirring.

3. As the mixture gets hotter and hotter, the egg will start to thicken into soft lumps. Keep stirring for another 10 seconds or so, then turn off the heat. The egg mixture will keep on thickening in the heat of the pan. Spoon onto buttered toast and eat straight away.

POACHED EGG

If you're poaching lots of eggs, it's best to do them one at a time rather than trying to do them all at once. The fact is, it's impossible to poach two eggs in the same pan using this method – though you could, if you're getting very good at it, do two pans at a time.

To serve 1:
1 really fresh free-range egg
Salt and black pepper

Medium saucepan with tight-fitting lid, cup, wooden spoon, slotted spoon, plate

1. Fill the saucepan three-quarters full with water and bring it to a boil on the stove.

2. Break the egg into the cup and stand it within easy reach of the stove (if you want to eat your poached egg on toast, start toasting the bread now).

3. When the water is bubbling quite fiercely (what cookbooks sometimes call a "rolling boil"), pick up the wooden spoon and start to stir the water around in one direction. Do this gently at first until a whirlpool effect starts, then more firmly for 20 to 30 seconds. Stop stirring, and quickly slip the egg into the center of the whirlpool. Cover the pan straight away with its lid, turn off the stove, and set the timer to go off in 2 minutes.

4. When the timer goes off, scoop up the egg from the bottom of the pan with the slotted spoon, give it a couple of gentle shakes to get rid of any water, and transfer it to a warmed plate (or put it on the hot buttered toast). Season with a little salt and pepper.

How to eat your poached egg

On toast is the classic way to serve it, but a poached egg is very good slipped into a creamy soup like White Winter Soup (page 195), or served on top of Green Peas with Roasted Red Peppers and Chorizo (page 208).

EGGY BREAD

Perfect camping food, perfect breakfast food, perfect snack food any time, eggy bread is a great addition to a full breakfast or simply a lovely thing to eat on its own.

To serve 2:
White or light brown bread, 2 slices
Free-range eggs, 2
Salt and black pepper
Sunflower or olive oil, 1 tablespoon

Knife, cutting board, shallow dish, fork, frying pan, tablespoon, metal spatula, plate

1. Cut the crusts off the bread. You can either use whole slices or cut them into fat fingers.

2. Break the eggs into the shallow dish. Add a pinch of salt and a twist of pepper and beat well with the fork until the yolks and whites have frothed up together.

3. Lay the bread slices in the eggy mixture, turning them over and letting them sit in the bowl for a couple of minutes so that the egg really soaks in.

4. Put the frying pan on the stove over medium heat and pour in the sunflower or olive oil.

5. As soon as the oil is hot, carefully place the eggy bread slices in the pan. The egg will bubble up and sizzle nicely in the hot oil. After about a minute, the slices should have turned golden brown underneath, so flip them over with the metal spatula and cook the other side. When they're done, lift them out of the pan and put them on a warm plate.

How to eat your eggy bread

Try it sprinkled with a little grated cheese. Or turn it into French toast: leave out the pepper, but mix a teaspoon of sugar into the beaten egg. Serve with raspberry jam, maple syrup, or sliced fresh strawberries.

FRENCH OMELETTE

Made properly, an omelette has to be one of the most delicious dishes ever created. It's important to have everything ready – eggs beaten and seasoned in the bowl, pan nice and hot, filling prepared and to one side – before you put the butter in the pan.

To serve 1:
Free-range eggs, 2
Butter
Salt and black pepper

Small bowl, fork, small frying pan or omelette pan, butter knife

1. Break the eggs into the bowl, add some salt and pepper, and whisk briefly with the fork to combine the yolks and the whites.

2. Set the pan over medium heat. After about a minute, add a tablespoon of butter – not too much, just enough to swirl around the base of the pan.

3. As the butter starts to foam in the pan, whisk the eggs again with the fork. As the bubbles of butter die down, pour the eggs into the frying pan.

4. Let the mixture sit for a few seconds, until a white line begins to form around the edge. Using the tip of the knife, push the egg from the outer edge to the middle so that it wrinkles up into soft folds. Tilt the pan so that the liquid egg runs back into the bare space. Keep pushing the edges to the middle until there's no more liquid egg to run back in.

5. At this point, if you're adding a filling to the omelette (see "How to Eat," below), spoon it onto one half of it.

6. Slide the omelette onto a plate, flipping one half of the omelette over the other as you do so.

How to eat your French omelette

Eat straight away. Omelettes just hate being kept waiting!

If you want to add a filling to your omelette, here are a few suggestions: some of your favorite cheese, grated; sliced mushrooms, cooked gently in butter for 5 minutes; chopped ham or fried bacon; little cubes of fried potato; an onion, finely sliced and gently fried.

Some ingredients, like chopped green onions or finely chopped herbs, can simply be stirred into the whisked, seasoned eggs, rather than added to the omelette while it is cooking.

ush the egg to the middle

flip one half over the other

SPANISH OMELETTE (TORTILLA)

This tortilla is a classic Spanish omelette – quite different from Mexican tortillas. Made with sliced potatoes, the Spanish version is thick and filling, and can be eaten in slices, hot, warm, or cold.

To serve 2 to 4:
Potatoes, 5 to 6 small waxy ones, such as
   Red Rose or Yukon Gold
Olive oil
Free-range eggs, 6
Salt and black pepper

Cutting board, sharp knife, medium frying pan, metal spatula, mixing bowl, fork, small knife, big plate

1. Scrub the potatoes if they look dirty and dry them on some paper towels. Cut each potato in half lengthwise, put the flat side down on the cutting board, and cut each half into thin slices.

2. Put the frying pan over medium heat. Pour enough olive oil into the pan to cover the base. Before the oil gets really hot, carefully slide all the potatoes into the pan and let them start to fry. Turn the heat down a little if they start to

brown too quickly – they need to fry gently. Turn the potato slices with the spatula from time to time so that they cook evenly.

3. While the potatoes are cooking, break the eggs into the mixing bowl. Grind in some pepper and add about ½ teaspoon of salt. Beat the eggs with the fork until the yolks and the whites are combined.

4. The potatoes are ready when they look quite crisp but not yet brown and when a slice feels soft if you stick the small knife into it. Take the pan off the heat and, using the spatula (which will lift out the potatoes but not the oil), transfer all the potatoes to the bowl of beaten egg. Give it a stir. Put the oily pan back on the heat (again, low to medium) to warm up again. Preheat the broiler.

5. Pour the egg and potato mixture into the pan. It will bubble up a little at the sides. Let the omelette cook gently for 6 to 8 minutes or until it is turning golden brown underneath (check by sliding the tip of the spatula down the side of the omelette and levering it up so that you can see). It should only be slightly liquidy on top.

6. The easiest (and safest) way to cook the top of the tortilla is to put it under the hot broiler for just a minute or two. Watch it like a hawk. The tortilla should look set and dotted with golden brown. When it looks ready, turn off the broiler and slide the tortilla onto a big plate.

7. To turn a tortilla the bold (and Spanish) way, you'll need a large, flat plate that's a bit bigger than the frying pan. And you'll need to take considerable care. Oven gloves on. Remove the pan from the heat and place the plate over the pan. Use both gloved hands to hold the plate firmly over the pan. Lift the pan and plate together and flip them upside down. Place the plate on the table and lift off the frying pan, putting it back down on the stove. You can now slide the tortilla back into the pan, runny-side down. Cook it for another 3 to 5 minutes, until that side too is nicely browned.

How to eat your Spanish omelette

Unlike a French omelette, which needs to be eaten almost as it slides out of the pan, a tortilla is best eaten warm rather than hot. You can even wrap it up in foil and take it on a picnic.

You can add other things as well as potatoes when you make a tortilla – for example, thin slices of chorizo sausage, chopped red bell pepper, sliced onions (gently fried until golden, then added with the potatoes), or shreds of leftover cooked chicken. Best not to add too many different things to one omelette, though – just stick to two or three.

MERINGUES

These are classic individual meringues, baked slowly and very gently until they dry out and become crisp and brittle. But there is another kind of meringue, too. If you bake meringue quickly in a hot oven, you get a crisp, browned outside and a soft, whipped texture inside – desserts such as lemon meringue pie have meringue tops like this.

To make about 15 to 20 small meringues:
Free-range egg whites, 2 (see page 88 for details of how to separate eggs)
Superfine sugar, 1/2 cup

Very clean mixing bowl, rotary or electric mixer or balloon whisk, metal spoon, baking sheet, baking parchment, 2 teaspoons

1. Preheat the oven to 225°F.

2. Put the egg whites in the bowl and start to whisk. At first you'll get great big frothy bubbles but, as you carry on whisking, the egg whites will stiffen and the bubbles get smaller.

3. When the egg whites have formed soft peaks, add half the sugar. Whisk again so that all the sugar is blended into the egg white. The mixture will get thicker and thicker still, and shiny, like shaving foam. When it's so thick that you can turn the bowl upside down without anything sliding out (do this cautiously at first), then you can stop.

4. Fold in the rest of the sugar very gently, using the metal spoon.

5. Line the baking sheet with parchment paper. Using one of the teaspoons, scoop up a dollop of meringue and use the other teaspoon to help it off the spoon onto the lined baking sheet. Dot the meringues all over the baking paper. Swirl each one with the top of the spoon.

6. Place the baking sheet in the oven and leave for 1½ to 2 hours, until the meringues can be lifted off the paper easily and are beginning to look slightly cracked. The mixture won't spread or rise at all in the oven – it just sets firm. Every tiny swirl of meringue should be exactly as it was when you put the tray in the oven. Remove from the oven and let cool completely.

How to eat your meringues

Traditionally, meringues are sandwiched together with thick, softly whipped cream, and this is very hard to beat. A giant meringue base, smothered with whipped cream and fresh fruit, is called a Pavlova, and a "bashed-up" version of this, where broken meringue is mixed with cream and fruit (usually mashed strawberries) into a kind of fool, is called Eton Mess. Both are delicious.

whisk till you get soft peaks

sk in half the sugar

fold in the rest of the sugar

on onto parchment

... and into a very low oven

VICTORIA SPONGE CAKE

Victoria sponges are always made with equal quantities of butter, sugar, flour, and eggs. In the States, they are known as pound cakes. If you look down the ingredients list below, you can see that there are no measurements given in this recipe. Instead, weigh the eggs together in their shells on the scales and whatever the total weight, use the same weight of butter, of sugar, and of flour. So if your four eggs weigh 9 ounces, then use 9 ounces of butter, 9 ounces of sugar, and 9 ounces of flour.

Our recipe tells you how to make a Victoria sponge the old-fashioned way – mixing all the ingredients by hand. But you can make a nearly-as-good version with an electric mixer.

To make an 8-inch cake:
Free-range eggs, 4
Unsalted butter, softened but not melted
Superfine sugar
Self-rising flour (see page 18)
A pinch of salt
Pure vanilla extract, 1 teaspoon
A little milk, if needed
Good jam (raspberry or your favorite),
  about ¼ cup

Superfine or confectioners' sugar for
  dusting the top of the cake

Two 8-inch cake pans, parchment paper, pencil, scissors, large mixing bowl, wooden spoon, medium bowl, sieve, teaspoon, metal spoon, knife, wire rack

1. Preheat the oven to 350°F and position a rack in the center of the oven. Grease the cake pans carefully with a scrap of butter on a piece of paper towel. Place a cake pan on the parchment paper and draw around the bottom. Cut out the circle and use this to line the bottom of the pan. Repeat for the other pan, then put both pans to one side.

2. Put all the eggs (still in their shells) on the kitchen scales and make a note of their total weight. Put the eggs to one side.

3. Weigh the same amount of butter and put it in the mixing bowl. Using the back of the wooden spoon, beat – or cream – it until very soft. Weigh the sugar and add it to the butter a third at a time, beating with the wooden spoon to blend the butter and sugar together. After a little while, you'll notice that the mixture becomes quite fluffy. And if it doesn't, you should keep going until it does!

4. Weigh the flour, add the pinch of salt to it, and set aside.

5. Break one of the eggs into the butter mixture and beat it quite hard until it is completely blended in. Add the other eggs in the same way, one at a time. Sift in a tablespoon of the flour

with the last egg; this will help stop the mixture curdling as you beat the egg in. Stir in the vanilla extract.

6. Set the sieve over the mixing bowl and add all the flour to the sieve. Shake it all gently into the bowl.

7. With the metal spoon, start to fold the flour into the cake mixture (see page 91), using an up-and-over turn of the spoon like a paddle.

8. When the flour has been folded in, test the consistency of the mixture – whether it's stiff or sloppy. Scoop up a tablespoon of mix and turn it upside down over the bowl. If it drops down reasonably easily, then the mix is just right. If it sits stubbornly in the spoon, fold in a tablespoon or two of milk just to lighten the mixture a little.

9. Spoon the mixture equally between the 2 prepared cake pans and gently smooth the tops with a knife. Oven gloves on. Put the cakes in the preheated oven and bake for 25 to 30 minutes.

10. The cakes are ready when you can stick a knife or a skewer into the center and it comes out clean. As you take each cake out of the oven, hold it level about a ruler's length above the work surface and drop the cake, in its pan, straight down. Look carefully at the surface of the cake and you'll see that some of the tiny little bubbles on the surface have broken open.

This allows the steam inside the cake to come out and stops the cake from sinking in the middle.

11. Let the cakes cool for a few minutes, then run a knife around the edge to loosen them from the pans and turn them out onto the wire rack. Let cool completely.

12. Turn one of the cakes upside down so that its flat surface is uppermost and place it on a serving plate. Spread the jam over the upturned cake and sit the other cake on top, right way up. Sprinkle a little superfine sugar over the top of the cake, or if you'd rather you can sift a little confectioners' sugar over it instead.

Variations

Before you sandwich the cakes together, you could whisk some heavy cream (about 1 cup) until it just stands up in soft mountains when you lift the whisk. Spread the cream on top of the jam and put the other half of the cake on top.

Try flavoring your cake by adding the grated zest of a lemon instead of the vanilla extract, and "softening" the cake mixture with lemon juice instead of milk. You could fill the cake with lemon curd (see page 143) and cream.

REAL ENGLISH CUSTARD (OR CRÈME ANGLAISE)

The golden rule when making English custard is to cook it very slowly, stirring all the time with a wooden spoon, and test it carefully, according to the instructions in step 4.

To serve 6 as an accompaniment:
Whole milk, 1 cup
Half-and-half cream, 1 cup
Vanilla bean or vanilla extract
Free-range egg yolks, 6 (see page 88
  for details of how to separate eggs)
Superfine sugar, 3 tablespoons

Heavy medium saucepan, sharp knife, large pitcher or bowl, tablespoon, balloon whisk, wooden spoon, sieve

1. Pour the milk and cream into the saucepan and set it over medium heat. If you're using a vanilla bean, slit it lengthwise with the sharp knife and add it to the milk mixture. Stir from time to time until the milk starts to steam. Switch off the heat.

2. Whisk the egg yolks and sugar together in the pitcher or bowl for about a minute, until they're thick and pale. Pour the hot milk into the eggy mixture and whisk again gently for just a few seconds. Pour everything back into the saucepan and set it over low heat. Stir all the time with the wooden spoon.

3. From time to time, lift the spoon out of the mixture and inspect the back. If the mixture simply runs straight off the spoon and leaves it quite clean, then you need to continue stirring. As the mixture gets hotter and hotter, it's vital that you keep stirring. And however tempting it is to raise the heat, keep it low.

4. When the mixture coating the back of the spoon starts to look creamier, run your finger down the length of the spoon (see the picture on page 95). If the line you make stays clear and distinct, then the custard is ready (this happens at about 175°F, if you have a candy thermometer). Take the custard off the heat immediately and stir it for another minute or two to encourage it to cool down. Stir in a teaspoonful of vanilla extract if you're using it instead of the vanilla bean. Strain the custard through the sieve into a clean pitcher or bowl. If you're going to serve it cold, sprinkle a little superfine sugar on top to prevent a skin from forming.

How to eat your English custard

Pour custard over puddings such as crumbles and fruit pies. Or why not slice some bananas into a bowl of it for a quick dessert? In the summer, cold custard with fresh fruit and a dollop of yogurt is delicious.

PANCAKES

If you plan to make pancakes on a regular basis, then it's worth setting aside a dedicated pancake pan – one that's light enough to pick up easily, not too large and, very importantly, that you never wash. Just wipe out the pan when it's cold with a wad of paper towels, and in time it will build up a good, naturally nonstick layer. The same pan will make good French omelettes, too (see page 104).

To make about 15:
All-purpose or white pastry flour, 1½ cups
A pinch of salt
Free-range eggs, 2
Milk, about 2 cups, and then a little more
Sunflower oil for frying

Sieve, mixing bowl, large glass measuring cup, balloon whisk, nonstick frying pan, tablespoon, cup, ladle, metal spatula, dinner plate

1. Sift the flour and salt into the mixing bowl. Make a crater in the middle of the flour and break the eggs into the crater.

2. Pour in half the milk and start to mix the eggs and milk with the balloon whisk, whisking in the flour from the edges a little at a time. Add the rest of the milk and keep on whisking until there are no more lumps of flour. Pour the batter into the measuring cup. You may need to whisk in a little extra milk to get the right consistency – not quite as thick as half-and-half.

3. Put the frying pan on the stove over not quite full heat. Add about a tablespoon of sunflower oil, swirl it around the pan, and then pour the excess into the cup so that just a film of oil stays in the pan.

4. When the oil is hot but just before it smokes, pour a little of the batter into the pan. How much to pour really depends on the size of your pan, but you need to leave plenty of room for the pancake to spread out (use a ladle if it helps you to judge the right amount of liquid each time). Immediately tilt and rotate the pan so that the batter runs across the base and doesn't sit in a big lump in the middle.

5. As the pancake sets, loosen the edge of it with the spatula. Shake the pan gently so that you know the pancake hasn't stuck (a bit of work with the knife if it has; the first one often does). Flip the pancake over with the spatula and cook the other side for a few seconds – the second side is much quicker to cook. (Notice the intricate patterns left behind by the hot oil; each one different, like a fingerprint.)

6. Slide the pancake out of the pan and onto a warmed plate. Cook the rest of the pancakes, remembering to pour a little oil into the pan before each one, swirling it around the pan and draining it away into the cup as before.

How to toss a pancake

Once you've got the hang of making pancakes and turning them over with a spatula, then sooner or later you're going to want to toss them. Don't do it with the first of a batch. Wait until the pan is used to cooking the pancakes before you try to toss one.

You still need a spatula, to loosen the pancake from the pan. Lift the pan away from the heat and shake it gently so you know that the pancake isn't stuck to the bottom. Step back from the stove and flip the pan quickly upward so that the pancake goes up into the air, turns, and comes down again. It's impossible to describe how to do this, but obviously practice makes perfect (and any pets will be grateful for your mistakes).

How to eat your pancakes

A squeeze of lemon and a sprinkling of sugar is the classic British way to eat a pancake, but there are plenty of scrumptious alternatives. Jam (with a little cream if you're feeling really greedy) is good, and so is honey. They're also very good stacked up with layers of stewed sweetened apples between them.

Pancakes don't have to be sweet. A quick and delicious savory way of eating them is *ficelles Picardie*. To make these, you roll up a thin slice of ham in each pancake, lay them in a buttered shallow baking dish, pour over some cheesy béchamel sauce (see page 71), then sprinkle them with more grated cheese and bake in an oven preheated to 400°F for about 20 minutes.

... this is why they're called drop scones

DROP SCONES

These are the same as American pancakes. In Britain, they're eaten at teatime and for elevenses (a snack *before* lunch).

To make 30 to 40:
Butter, 2 tablespoons
All-purpose or white pastry flour, $1^1/_2$ cups
A pinch of salt
Baking powder, 1 teaspoon
Superfine sugar, 2 tablespoons
Free-range eggs, 2
Milk, about 1 cup

A little sunflower oil for frying

Small pan, sieve, medium bowl, teaspoon, large glass measuring cup, balloon whisk, large, heavy frying pan (or a cast-iron griddle), paper towels, tablespoon, metal spatula, warm plate, tea towel

1. Gently melt the butter in the small pan over low heat, then remove from the heat.

2. Sift the flour into the bowl with the salt and baking powder and add the sugar.

3. Break in the eggs and add about half the milk. Whisk, gently at first, and then as you start to get a thick paste, add the rest of the milk and the melted butter. Beat until you get a creamy batter. It should be thick but pourable.

4. Put your frying pan on the stove. Pour a few drops of sunflower oil into the pan and rub the base of the pan with a paper towel until it's lightly greased. Turn the heat on to medium.

5. Give the pan a minute to heat up, then pour a tablespoon of batter into it so that you get a disk about 2 inches across; you should be able to fit about 4 or 5 in the pan. After about a minute, little bubbles will start to appear on the surface of the drop scones. As soon as they cover the scones, flip them over with the spatula (the first batch may stick, as all first pancakes like to do).

6. Cook the other side for half a minute or so, then transfer the drop scones to a warm plate and cover them with a tea towel so they stay soft, or put them in a low oven to stay warm. Cook the other drop scones in the same way, adjusting the heat level if they start browning too quickly and regreasing the pan with oil and a thick wad of paper towels as necessary.

How to eat your drop scones

When all the batter has been used up, spread each drop scone with a little butter and sprinkle a little sugar on top. You could also serve them buttered and spread with jam, lemon curd, or honey. This hardly needs to be said, but eat quickly, while they are still hot. You can sprinkle some raisins onto the drop scones as they cook, if you like.

FRUIT

Fruit has an unfair advantage over nearly every other food. It wants to be eaten and is crying out for your attention: oranges so bright you could only ever call them by their color; apples dangling on the tree like giant jewels; peaches bursting with tempting juice; strawberries, raspberries, cherries – red for temptation. There's no need to resist. You're really not meant to.

baked apples, page 144

lemonade, page 159

fruit tart, page 148

apple tart, page 150

fruit jellies, page 154

bramble jelly, page 156

FRUIT

Throughout history, we've been food adventurers. We call ourselves omnivores because of the amazing variety of foods that we eat – the word means "eaters of all." We pick and eat flowers, tap the sap from trees, and winkle meat out of the tiniest shells. Almost every creature and plant that doesn't actually poison us has, at some moment or other, become a part of the human diet.

But although we can adapt and thrive on so many different foods, there's one group of foods that are so tasty we simply can't get enough of them. We love them raw – pulled from the plant and eaten on the spot. We love them cooked – in pies and crumbles or just baked with sugar. They are good for us, too. It is the group of foods we call fruits.

Stand in front of a produce market's display and half-close your eyes. What demands your attention? Is it the earthy potatoes, the green spinach, or the frilly lettuce? Chances are that you're more likely to pick out the stacks of sunny oranges and lemons, the baskets of jewel-like strawberries, raspberries, or cherries, the glossy greens, yellows, and reds of the apples. Perhaps a watermelon has been cut in half, to expose its tempting red flesh.

Fruits don't need fancy wrappings to advertise their appeal to human taste buds. For most of us, just to look at them is to want them. Produce markets and supermarkets simply pile them up in crates or set them out in neat rows, in the certain knowledge that we'll take them as they are. If they are in a box or a bag, it's sure to be transparent, so we can see the naked beauty of the fruits inside.

What is a fruit?

There's a very good reason why we have the natural desire to eat fruit. A fruit is the part of a plant that carries its seeds – the seeds that will enable that plant to reproduce itself. These fruit-bearing plants have evolved a clever strategy in their desire to do this – advertising. By making their fruits as attractive and desirable as possible to a variety of hungry creatures – birds, bats, bears, squirrels, monkeys, and humans – plants increase the chances of reproducing themselves.

What we call the "fruit" is generally a skin surrounding a fleshy substance, which is the bit we love to eat. Inside this is a seed or seeds – sometimes one, sometimes a few, sometimes hundreds of them. In the case of most fruits, this is pretty obvious: cut open the fruit and you'll see the seeds. Eat the fruit whole and you'll probably end up spitting out the seeds. But swallow the seeds and they'll come out unharmed when you go to the loo. And this is all part of their evolutionary strategy.

Like us, all animals that eat fruit distribute the seeds in some way. Whether they swallow the seed and then excrete it in their dung, spit it out, or even drop the fruit and its seed while carrying it from one place to another, they are helping the parent plant to reproduce. In every case the seed is taken away from the plant to a separate place, where it has a chance

to germinate, grow, and create another plant, which can later produce more fruits, and more seeds, of its own. In some cases, the dung of the animal that ate the fruit even acts as a natural fertilizer for the growing seedling.

Sheer variety

There are thousands of varieties of plants that produce fruits as a strategy for reproduction and survival. And the size, shape, color, texture, sweetness, smell, and taste are different for every kind of fruit. Each plant tries hard to make its fruit look and taste as exciting and enticing as possible, so that some animal will take the fruits away and eat them, spreading the seeds far and wide. Some fruits "target" just one species to perform this task – a particular type of bird or monkey, for example. Others are popular with a wide range of creatures – perhaps dozens of different birds and mammals. And it's these plants that are generally the most successful in reproducing.

Seeds come in all shapes and sizes, too. Apples and pears have a cluster of seeds at their core, while peaches and plums have single large central pits. Gooseberries and strawberries have tiny seeds you hardly even notice when you eat them. Strawberries have them on the outside of the flesh, gooseberries on the inside. A pomegranate has a leathery skin that seems unpromising. You certainly wouldn't want to eat it. But crack it open and its edible treasure is revealed – a cluster of seeds, each surrounded by a juice-trapping membrane. They look like tiny polished rubies (see the picture on page 121), but you can crush them with your tongue to set the juice free, then swallow them, seeds and all.

These fruits and their seeds could hardly be more different from each other. But they've all secured their future on the planet by persuading animals to eat them. And not just occasionally, but every year, again and again and again.

So remember – the reason you can't resist a luscious ripe plum or a bright gem of a raspberry peeping out from underneath its leafy foliage is because you're not meant to resist. You've been targeted. They are daring you, begging you, to eat them. Unfortunately, their charms have a similar effect on many other creatures – especially birds. If you want to eat them, you'll have to get to them first.

Wild fruits and early humans

A hundred thousand years ago, before we learned to grow our own food by planting crops, wild fruits were a vital part of our diet. We may have had to compete with other species for our share of the best fruits, but we used our large brains to remember where the best trees were and what time of year they would produce their fruit. As a result, we were generously rewarded. Just as it is in the interests of fruit-producing plants to make their fruits tasty and good to look at, so it is in their interests to make them highly nutritious. If plants give energy and health to the animals that eat them, those animals will continue to be around to feast on future harvests and spread the seeds. So fruits are bursting with natural sugars that give energy, plus vitamins, minerals, and enzymes that keep our bodies working at the peak of performance.

The first cultivated fruits

About ten thousand years ago, humans started cultivating cereal plants such as wheat and barley. It was this early form of agriculture that meant we could start living in permanent settlements rather than following herds of wild beasts as hunter-gatherers. Yet we almost certainly began cultivating fruit-bearing plants long before this time. This is because the early humans' love of fruit often led to a form of cultivation anyway. By gathering and eating a particular fruit from a particular plant on a regular basis, then discarding or excreting the seeds in and around a temporary camp, our ancestors were giving that plant the best possible chance to reproduce. Accidental orchards would be formed. And such happy accidents inevitably led to the deliberate planting and nurturing of fruit plants.

As agriculture developed, the planting of cereal crops in a new settlement was always the top priority – they could produce a harvest of edible grain within just a few months. But as the settlements became more permanent, a greater variety of plants could be cultivated. Most fruit plants are slow-growing trees and shrubs that can take years to establish. However, once they are producing fruit, they can be harvested year after year.

The result is that the earliest civilizations prized fruits as among the very finest foods. In prehistoric times, apples, pears, and quinces, native to Eurasia, were some of the earliest fruits to be domesticated. Grapes, from which wine could be made, were first grown in North Africa and Asia, then spread throughout the ancient world by the Greeks. Apricots came from China, peaches from Persia, and both had arrived in the Mediterranean by Roman times. In fact, we're still domesticating our fruits today – making them bigger, more resistant to disease, and more prolific. Sadly, we're not always making them tastier.

When is a fruit not a fruit?

You wouldn't think twice before cutting up apples, pears, peaches, and oranges for a bowl of fruit salad. But how about avocados, tomatoes, cucumbers, zucchini, pumpkins, peppers, and chiles? They, too, have a thick layer of moist, edible flesh surrounding a stone or a cluster of seeds. Scientifically speaking, they are definitely fruits. Yet they end up in our vegetable baskets, not in our fruit bowls. What's going on?

On the whole, we expect fruits to taste good raw (at least we do when they are ripe — more on this later). We expect them to smell tempting and to taste sweet and juicy. When fruits don't match these expectations, we use them differently. Perhaps we find them more appealing with a pinch of salt than with a sprinkling of sugar. We may prefer to eat them boiled, with a piece of meat, than in a pie with custard. And so we call them vegetables.

Melons, squashes, and pumpkins, for example, all belong to the same "family" of fruits, but we use them completely differently. Melons taste sweet, drip with juice, and have a powerful floral scent, so we treat them as fruit. Their close cousins, squashes and pumpkins, look very similar but because they are drier, less sweet, and have a mealy texture, we think of them as vegetables.

It's not merely a question of sweetness, though, and sometimes it's difficult to put a finger on just why we treat some fruits as vegetables. Roast a red pepper in the oven and its flesh tastes as sweet and aromatic as any fruit. Eat a perfectly ripe tomato from the vine and it is juicy, sweet, and quite delicious. Every inch a fruit, you might have thought. Perhaps it's just that, as a vegetable, the tomato has a unique status that it would probably never achieve as a fruit. Its special talents are to bring color, sweetness, and its tomatoey tang to all kinds of savory foods, such as stews, soups, sauces, salads, and sandwiches. And in doing this job, it's probably given us at least as much pleasure as any of our favorite fruits. So let's keep calling it a vegetable. (But let's not forget one vital, fruity thing about the tomato that explains the vast difference between the best, sweetest, most scented tomatoes and the worst, sourest, dullest ones. To be at its best, to fulfill its fantastic potential to delight our taste buds, a tomato must be allowed to become ripe. All too often, it isn't.)

Some recipes with fruits pretending to be vegetables

Cucumber Raita, page 83
Sweet Chile and Red Currant Jam, page 163
Green Peas with Roasted Red Peppers
    and Chorizo, page 208
Guacamole, page 215
Quick Tomato Salad, page 216

Ripeness

The word *ripe* simply means "ready to eat," "at its best," or "pretty much perfect." It describes that window of opportunity when the combination of sweetness, flavor, aroma, juiciness, and texture in a fruit is "just right."

Think of the difference between a hard, green, sour peach and a rosy-blushed, sweet peach that drips with juice when you sink your teeth into it. That's the difference between unripe and ripe, nasty and nice, horrid and delicious. It could be the same peach — just left to hang on the tree in the sunshine a week or two longer.

Unlike vegetables, which taste best when they're picked young and tender, fruits need to be ripe to be enjoyed at their best. We don't talk about vegetables being ripe and ready to eat because most vegetables taste good as soon as they start to form. You could dig up a baby carrot the size of your little finger, pop it in your mouth, and it would taste sweet. Take a bite out of a "baby" apple, though — tiny, green and hard — and you'll be spitting it out again in a hurry. As we discussed earlier, fruit really wants to be eaten. But only when the time is right.

Some fruits keep on improving — ripening, that is — after they've been picked; something that no vegetable does. An apple will go on maturing and ripening for some days, maybe even weeks, after it has been picked, getting sweeter and tastier, before it starts to wrinkle and taste woolly (when we say it is overripe). Bananas, too, will keep on ripening after

picking, and this is one of the reasons they can be successfully exported all over the world. They can be picked and transported green and hard, when they are very resistant to bruising, then allowed to ripen when they reach their destination.

Sadly, not all fruits are as cooperative as this. Some fruits will ripen only while they're still attached to the plant (strawberries, grapes, and melons, for instance). Once fully ripe, they need to get from the plant to you as quickly as they can, before they become overripe and start to go moldy. This is a big problem for those who are in the business of growing, transporting, and selling these fruits.

Have you ever wondered why the strawberries you buy so often taste disappointing? They look beautiful, but they have only a faint strawberry flavor and they just aren't that sweet. This is because they are picked just before they are ripe. Fruit growers have to allow time for their fruit to get from the farm where they're grown to the shop where they're sold. If the fruit is grown locally and can be on the shop shelves within just a few hours of harvesting, then it can be picked as ripe as possible. But a strawberry picked in Spain while truly ripe is going to be past its best by the time it's travelled on at least two trucks and an airplane over a distance of a thousand miles to reach a produce market in the U.K. So it has to be picked a little too early in order to travel well.

If you want to enjoy the very best fruits, when they are at their best (i.e., ripe), then it

helps to know a little about which fruits are in season and when. It also helps to know which shops are likely to sell the best fruit — fruit that has been grown to taste good rather than fruit that has been grown to make money.

On the whole, the best, tastiest fruit is the stuff that has been grown to supply local markets, not to be packed up and transported halfway around the world. For Brits, that means fruit that has been grown in the U.K. to supply shops in the U.K. Better still, look for fruit that has been grown near you to be sold near you. Because the less distance it has to travel, the riper it can be picked.

Organic fruit

Some people prefer to buy organic fruit because almost no chemicals such as herbicides and pesticides are sprayed onto the crop. Instead, pests (such as aphids) are controlled by encouraging, and sometimes introducing, their natural predators (such as ladybugs). Woven ground cover is used to help keep down weeds, while the fertilizers that are used to help the fruit grow have to be organic, too — i.e., animal dung. Because so much of the work such as weeding has to be done by hand and the cost of labor is very high, organic fruit is more expensive than nonorganically grown fruit.

Seasonal fruit

It's worth getting to know the full range of your local fruit and when it's in season. All the fruits grown in the U.K., whether they appear on trees, bushes, or little plants, ripen in the summer and autumn months between May and November. The season starts with the early gooseberries, which are usually ready by the end of May and pretty much finished two months later. By the beginning of June, the first English strawberries will be ready too.

Next come black currants and red currants, which will usually be ready by early July. A week or two later the earliest varieties of raspberries should be coming on, too. Look out also for tayberries and loganberries — large, juicy relatives of the raspberry. They are not as well known, but they are delicious.

These summer berries have many varieties, which ripen at different times and so are available in one form or another right through until early September. At this point, the currants run out — but the raspberries keep going. There are autumn varieties that ripen as late as October and even November. Blackberries start ripening on the bushes at the end of August and are usually around until late September, early October.

As for the tree fruits, cherries are the first to show, with a short season that begins in July and is over by mid-August. However, imported cherries from warmer parts of Europe extend the season by a few weeks in each direction. Damson and greengage plums have a short season too, but between them various varieties can be had from late July to mid-September.

Apples span the longest stretch. In August, we look for an early type such as Discovery, with its bright red skin that stains the flesh inside with pink. Some of the later varieties, such as Orleans Reinette, are still on the trees three months later in mid-November. But what really extends the season is the amazing ability of many varieties of apples, and pears too, to store well if kept cool and dry.

So, from the first gooseberries in May to the last apples in March, some kind of British fruit is available to be eaten fresh, either raw or cooked, for around ten months of the year.

And even this "hunger gap" can be plugged – by a strange but familiar plant called rhubarb. Sometimes grown indoors by candlelight in order to keep its beautiful color, its thin, pink stalks first appear in shops in January and February. Of course, it's not really a fruit. It's a vegetable. But it does such a good job in the fruit department that it would be mean to criticize it for that.

Where to buy fruit

Where can you find some truly ripe fruit? There can be no better way to enjoy fruit than to grow some yourself and then pick it when it's absolutely perfect – warmed by the sun and bursting with sweet juice. Most fruit

FRUIT AND FOOD MILES

There is another benefit from finding fruit (and all other foods) grown as locally as possible. Fruits that are sold and eaten near where they've been produced don't require airplanes, ships, and trucks to transport them long distances, burning up diesel and petrol. So they cause less pollution and less wasted energy.

Environmentalists who are concerned about these issues calculate the energy used and the pollution caused in transporting food around the world by measuring food miles. They suggest we all contribute to reducing food miles by choosing more foods that are grown locally.

Of course, there are many fruits that we can't grow in cold climates. They include two of our all-time favorites – bananas and oranges – and other delicious fruits, such as mangoes and kiwifruits, which have become popular only recently. We can enjoy these "exotic" fruits with a clean conscience – not least because the business of growing and selling them is vital to the economy of the countries that produce them. There may, however, be good reasons for choosing some imported fruits over others. Fair Trade products guarantee that more of the money that you pay for them goes to the people who grow them, not just to the big companies that buy and sell them. You can identify products that have been traded fairly by the Fair Trade Certified label printed on the packaging.

bushes take a year or two to get going, but they're well worth the wait. Plant a gooseberry bush in your garden and you can pick delicious early-summer fruit year after year to turn into pies and crumbles. Or grow two or three red currant bushes to tempt you with their exquisite scarlet berries. You don't even need a garden to grow certain fruits. Some strawberry plants can be grown in window boxes and hanging baskets; you can sow seeds for Alpine, or wild, strawberries in late winter and harvest the tiny little berries in late summer.

The next best place to get your seasonal fruit is right on the farm where it grows. What would you rather take home? A couple of crackly plastic baskets of underripe, undersweet berries from the supermarket? Or an old ice-cream tub filled to the brim with your personally chosen crop, all glossy, ripe, and juicy? This is what a U-pick farm is all about. You'll find the perfect strawberries to eat with sugar and cream, to crush and blend into sorbet or ice cream, or to slice and sandwich with whipped cream in the middle of a fat sponge cake. And while you're at the farm, check out the other fruit that might be growing alongside – gooseberries, raspberries, red, black, or even white currants.

Apart from a U-pick farm, the best place to find properly ripe local fruit is at farm stands and farmers' markets, where they sell the best local, seasonal fruit throughout the year. Next comes a good produce market that buys its fruit from local farms and suppliers. And just about the worst place is the supermarket.

Having said that, convenience means that many people buy most of their fruit in supermarkets. So it's worth bearing in mind that the supermarkets do stock some home-grown fruit when it's in season. It's unlikely to be truly local and will have traveled from its field to the supermarket's warehouse before it turns up in your store, so will probably still have been picked slightly underripe. But as all supermarket labels must clearly state which country their fruit comes from, you can at least, when the season is right, choose fruit grown locally.

Here, we can be confident that, for example, the U.K.-grown strawberries we find in the supermarkets in summer will be a lot tastier than the ones imported from the U.S. or Spain and elsewhere at other times of the year.

Look out for local apples, too. During the autumn and winter, buy as many different locally grown varieties as you can find, as this will encourage the supermarkets to be more adventurous in the choice of apples they grow and sell. There are hundreds of varieties, and the supermarkets stock only a few.

Some raw fruit recipes

Frozen Strawberry (and Other) Milkshake(s), page 85

Strawberry Fool, page 141

Summer Fruit Tart, page 148

Mango and Orange Smoothie, page 160

Peach, Pear, and Raspberry Smoothie, page 161

Cooking with fruit

Cooking offers all sorts of possibilities for all sorts of fruits. But the most amazing transformations, the little miracles it can perform, are for the fruits that might be seriously disappointing if we tried to eat them raw. That means fruit that's out of season, not quite ripe, or just not sweet enough on its own. It's as if the intense heat of the stove, plus a little added sugar, speeds up the ripening process of the fruit.

Some varieties of fruit are almost never eaten raw. You wouldn't want a fat Granny Smith apple in your lunchbox. But Red Delicious, an eating apple, very quickly changes into a foamy pulp when it's baked in the oven or a hot pan. And it's not suitable for the kind of tart on page 150, where it's important that the apple slices keep their shape. Granny Smiths and some eating apples, like Golden Delicious, are perfect when an apple purée is called for, perhaps as a pie filling, or as a sauce for goose or pork. They're also superb with the core taken out and brown sugar and

butter stuffed in the hole, then baked in the oven until they split into crisp skin and bubbly, appley foaming syrup. The recipe on page 144 makes a real virtue of an apple that just falls apart when the going gets hot.

Raw green gooseberries wouldn't be anybody's idea of a sweet treat. But tossed with sugar and piled into a pie pan, then topped with a mixture of butter, flour, and sugar, like unsquished pastry mix, and baked, they are one of the best-loved British desserts: "classic crumble." And it doesn't just work for gooseberries. Cooking apples, sour plums, and rhubarb – all of these defy you to eat them raw. But bake them in a crumble (or a crisp, in the U.S.) and they'll love you forever – and vice versa.

Some cooked fruit recipes

Rhubarb Fool, page 142
Baked Apples, page 144
Gooseberry Crumble, page 147
French-Style Apple Tart, page 150
Rhubarb and Ginger Smoothie, page 162

. . . .

CITRUS FRUITS

Of all the fruits that we cannot grow successfully in the British climate, the ones we depend on most, and spend the most money on, are the citrus fruits: oranges, lemons, grapefruits, and the various "mini oranges" we call tangerines, satsumas, and clementines.

This family of fruits is rather different from all the others. Slice open an orange or lemon and take a look. On the very outside are the two parts of the skin: the thin, colored layer of zest and the thick, inner white pith. The zest contains very powerfully scented oils, which can be used to flavor all sorts of foods. The pith makes up for its bitter flavor by protecting the fruit brilliantly, so that it can travel and store well. Inside the peel, the fruit is divided into segments. These are made up of thousands of tiny chambers like stretched teardrops. Press with your fingernail and each chamber pops open with an explosion of juice. Every citrus fruit provides this extraordinary portable package of juice protected in its own tough wrapper.

In fact, citrus fruits are so juicy and "drinkable" that, for almost a hundred years now, a huge industry has been devoted to the business of squeezing out the juice, concentrating it, sometimes freezing it, then mixing it with water again, to sell in cans and cartons ready for drinking. However, everyone agrees that the juice of freshly squeezed oranges and grapefruits tastes far better than juice from a carton or can.

The extraordinary lemon

Its bright yellow color and pointy-ended oval shape make the lemon unmistakable. However, it is so sharply acidic that it's almost impossible to taste raw lemon juice without getting that shocked look on your face. So lemon juice must be both sweetened and diluted before we can even think of swallowing it. We'll happily go to that trouble, though, because the resulting concoctions are so tangy and delicious.

Lemons are dazzlingly versatile in the kitchen and have managed to make themselves indispensable all year round. One day you're squeezing the juice onto crisp fried fish, another you're blending it with eggs, butter, and sugar and heating it slowly into smooth lemon curd, the next you're concocting a long, tall glass of real lemonade. Then it's with eggs again, only this time whipped with oil to make creamy, zesty mayonnaise. And perhaps the next encounter is mixed with confectioners' sugar as the irresistible topping on a lemon drizzle cake.

Sometimes you want that powerful flavor to dominate everything. At other times a squeeze of lemon can work like a magic secret ingredient, enhancing other flavors almost like a pinch of salt. Adding lemon juice to strawberry ice cream just before you freeze it makes it taste, well, more like strawberry ice cream. And a few drops in a pan of frying mushrooms won't make them taste lemony – just divine.

Lemon juice is also the most natural of preservatives. This is why it will stop an apple, pear, or banana from turning brown when you've peeled it – and why it's vital when you're making a syrup for a fruit salad.

In fact, if you've made almost any dish at all and you think it needs a little something to give it a lift, think about trying – along with a pinch of salt, a twist of pepper, or a knob of butter – a squeeze of ever-dependable lemon.

Some citrus recipes
Lemon Tart, page 52
Lemon Curd, page 143
Orange and Strawberry Jellies, page 154
Lemonade, page 159
Mango and Orange Smoothie, page 160

A SCURVY TALE

You've probably been told for as long as you can remember how good it is for you to eat oranges, grapefruits, and tangerines, and to drink their juice. We take this knowledge for granted, but it wasn't until the eighteenth century that people started to realize just how important a part these fruits could play in keeping us healthy.

For hundreds of years, a particularly nasty disease called scurvy had been a common cause of death among sailors. Sickness would set in a month or two after leaving port, and, when ships arrived back home after long voyages, only a fraction of the crew were still alive – and most of them were on the point of death.

In the middle of the seventeenth century, sailors noticed that certain fresh green plants, such as cress, kale, and sorrel, both cured and prevented scurvy. But this wasn't much use to them on long voyages, as these vegetables would keep for only a few weeks. Attempts to grow the plants on board almost always failed, and were deeply resented anyway because of all the fresh water required. The best the sailors could do was to grab as many fresh green plants as possible every time they went ashore. But in foreign parts, where many plants were unfamiliar, their potluck approach was rarely successful, and sometimes led to poisoning.

In 1747, a naval surgeon called James Lind conducted a series of experiments. He fed a range of things believed by sailors to cure scurvy to patients suffering from the disease. Vinegar, a mild solution of sulphuric acid, a pint of seawater, and a medicine made from nutmeg, garlic, and mustard seeds did no good at all. Sailors who were given a quart of cider improved a little. But those whose scurvy was most effectively cured were given, simply, two oranges and a lemon.

As soon as rations of lemon juice were given to all sailors, scurvy vanished. It returned briefly around 1850, when limes from the British West Indies were used instead. But increasing the dose was found to keep the disease at bay once again. British sailors became known as "limeys" the world over (and in some places, still are).

It wasn't until the early twentieth century that the magic ingredient in all these plants was identified. It was vitamin C, which occurs naturally in some leafy green vegetables – and in almost all citrus fruits, particularly lemons. Aside from keeping scurvy at bay, it is now known to have many health benefits. And fresh citrus juice is still the best way to take it.

REAL FRUIT JELLIES

One of the simplest ways to transform the best fresh fruit into a delicious, tempting dessert is to make a real fruit jelly (not jelly that you put on toast, but a British molded gelatin dessert). And it has to be one of the most appealing and amusing puddings there is.

Why *is* a jelly so much fun? Why does it get us into party mood and make us smile? Is it because it wobbles when we carry it? Is it the way it slides down our throats, all cold and slippery? There's no doubt that jelly is a show-off. It demands to be turned out from a fluted mold or, at the very least, poured into a tilted glass so that it sets at an impossible angle. Yet for parties, lots of people set their jelly in colored cardboard bowls. Surely that *completely* misses the point. It stops it doing any of its hilarious party tricks.

Gelatin

The secret of jelly's tricks is a substance called gelatin. Gelatin is made by boiling the bones and skin of cows and pigs in water. When the water cools, the liquid sets solid — into jelly. Victorian cooks who wanted to make strawberry jellies had to boil up pig's trotters and calf's feet to extract the gelatin before they could even think about finding the strawberries. Fortunately, making jelly is much easier nowadays.

Gelatin is sold in sheets or as packets of powder. The powder looks like any old powder, but the sheets, or leaves as they are often called, are beautiful things, like diamond-paned windows for a doll's house, and great fun to use. You can also buy vegetarian gelatin, if you prefer, which has no animal-based ingredients but is made from plant extracts.

Usually, gelatin sheets are softened in cold water before being dissolved in a warm or hot liquid, while gelatin powder is poured straight into hot water — but always follow the packet instructions to the letter. Use precisely the right amount of gelatin for the quantity of liquid you want to set.

Gelatin will set nearly every liquid you stir it into. Fruit juice is the most popular, although it is worth remembering that some fruits, including pineapples and melons, contain enzymes that stop the gelatin setting properly. You don't have to use juice, though. You could blend strawberries, milk, and cream together and set that into a lovely, summery dessert. An Italian pudding, panna cotta, is cream that has been heated with vanilla and a little sugar, then set with gelatin into a mold. You could even adapt your favorite smoothie recipe (see pages 160 to 162), dissolving the gelatin in a little hot milk or water. Jellies that you make with gelatin set much more quickly than the packet jellies available in the U.K., so you can make jelly in the morning and usually eat it at teatime.

Molding a jelly

Like modeling plaster, liquid gelatin will set into the shape of whatever you pour it into.

Victorian drawings show jellies set into spectacular temple and castle molds, striped in different colors and decorated with whipped cream and fruit.

Jellies can be as simple or as grandiose as you want to make them. You can tint the juice with food coloring to make it look more dramatic, and, if you want, you can even divide the juice in two, color one half, and then let it set, one stripe at a time, for a layered effect. You could put fresh fruit such as strawberries and raspberries into the mold before you pour in the jelly. You can buy gelatin molds in many shapes and sizes, even ones in the shapes of cats and rabbits. (Why cats and rabbits and not dogs or guinea pigs?) Or instead, you could simply pour the liquid into little glasses and prop up one side of each glass while it sets, so that when you straighten it up again to eat it, you'll find it's fixed at a ridiculous angle.

Unmolding a jelly

This is definitely the tensest part of the process – but it's also the part that turns eating jelly into an occasion, a bit like tossing a pancake on Shrove Tuesday. Just before you want to eat your jelly, fill a large bowl with hot water and dip the mold carefully into it for about 10 seconds. Take it out, place an inverted plate on top of the mold, and quickly flip the plate and mold over together. With a little shake, and a bit of luck, the jelly will slide out of the mold onto the plate. If it doesn't, try dipping the mold in the hot water again for another 10 seconds. It works by melting the very outer layer of the jelly back into a liquid.

. . . .

JAM-TYPE JELLIES

In the U.K., a jelly is a gelatin dessert. We might open a cookbook looking for a sweet treat to make and think, aha! raspberry and red currant jelly, that sounds good, and imagine it as a nice, big, wobbly jelly with streams of cream running over it. But not all jellies are meant to be eaten this way. Sometimes *jelly* means a kind of preserve, meant to be spread generously on a thick slice of bread and butter, or served with a forkful of

roast lamb or crisp pork crackling. This type of jelly is really a kind of jam without the solid fruit in it. It isn't thickened with gelatin but by boiling fruit juice and sugar together until the mixture reaches a temperature that will set the juice into a solid when it cools down. Lots of sugar is used to make the jelly set (it combines with a natural ingredient in most fruits, called pectin, which helps it set), so this sort of jelly is always very sweet (unlike wobbly, party, gelatin jellies, which are only as sweet as you want them to be). Since they contain so much sugar, which is a kind of preservative, they keep very well if you store them properly in jars with good lids – just like jam, in fact.

Some of the best and most worthwhile of these "potted" jellies can be made from wild fruits. As we've seen, all our cultivated fruits once came from wild plants, and there's still a wide variety of wild plants that bear edible fruits. In the U.K., the choice of wild fruits includes sloes, rowan berries, crab apples, bullaces, and damsons (the last two are plums). They can all be found growing in hedgerows and along the edge of woodland. The last three are usually not truly wild. They are more likely to be descended from cultivated trees that have seeded themselves in the wild.

None of the above is that easy to get hold of. But there is one wild fruit that is everywhere. Wherever you live, in the town or the country, you're never far away from a bramble bush. And the fruit of the bramble bush is the beloved blackberry.

Like crackling log fires and leaves drifting down from the sky, blackberries remind us in the U.K. of the nice things about the end of the summer, before the realities of a long British winter kick in: blackberry and apple pie, bramble jelly, stewed blackberries with rivers of custard.

But maybe we like blackberries for another reason. They're one of the few things that we still go out and gather in the way that our prehistoric ancestors must have done. They are a little history lesson on why we love fruit

so much. Maybe our ancestors didn't collect them in used ice cream tubs, but they too must have grabbed at the brambles with hooked sticks and wondered why the best berries are always just out of reach.

It's true that cultivated blackberries are sold in produce markets and supermarkets. They're large, fleshy things, which can be sweet and tasty enough. But there's something sad about seeing blackberries in a plastic or paper basket – rather like seeing a tiger in the zoo instead of roaming around in the jungle. These berries belong to their wild, untamed bushes with their straggly canes whipping about on a windy day.

By the way, blackberries tend to be the one wild fruit that nearly everyone can recognize, but if you are in any doubt about what you are picking, then check with someone who knows or leave it well alone. Pick from bushes away from busy roads, or your berries will come with a free dusting of exhaust fumes.

Some jelly recipes

Orange and Strawberry Jellies, page 154
Bramble Jelly, page 156

SMOOTHIES

A smoothie is really a sort of cold fruit soup – a blend of whole fruits rather than just their extracted juice. And just as a soup is one of the easiest and most satisfying ways to enjoy eating vegetables, so a smoothie is a really lovely way to eat fresh fruit.

But when you make a smoothie you usually bypass the stove, relying instead on the blades of the blender to do all the hard work that would have been done by the heat. Spinning metal, whizzing around thousands of times a minute, reduces whole fruit to a smooth purée in seconds.

Just as in soup making, you need good, fresh ingredients for your smoothies – sweet, just-ripe fruits, not ones past their best. A very ripe banana, its skin speckled black, may be the perfect ingredient for a loaf of banana bread, but it has no place in your blender, where it will overpower and dominate everything you blend with it.

Your "stock" is milk, yogurt, fruit juice, or even water. How much you add depends on the consistency you want – certainly you need enough liquid to make your smoothie suckable through a straw. Your seasoning may be a squeeze of lemon juice or some honey, or a hint of spice such as a dash of vanilla or ginger. A small spoonful of good jam may be just the right thing to add to a winter smoothie when fruit isn't at its sweetest.

Smoothies are always best icy cold. You can either add ice to the blender or, to keep the smoothie as fruity as possible, freeze some of the fruit in advance.

You could use some tried-and-tested combinations as the starting point of your smoothie making – raspberries with red currants, melon or pears with ginger, strawberries with orange – but feel free to invent your own. If you're feeling organized, you can shop for a smoothie in advance, but most of the time it's a question of using what you've got on hand. A few strawberries could be skimmed from those plastic baskets in the fridge (would anybody notice?), a banana from the bunch on the sideboard, a squeeze of juice from an orange or lemon.

In fact, the golden rule with smoothies is to make just a little to start with. If your first attempt isn't quite what you want, change your recipe a little and try again. Use less of something, more of another thing, sharpen with lemon juice, sweeten with jam or honey. Sample as you go, but remember to turn off the blender and remove the pitcher part whenever you stir, add, or taste. Never dip a finger into the blender (even when it's unplugged – it's just a bad habit to get into) and always replace the lid properly before you turn it on once more. When your smoothie is delicious, make some more. Then pour it into your favorite glass and find a straw.

Some smoothie recipes

Mango and Orange Smoothie, page 160
Peach, Pear, and Raspberry Smoothie, page 161
Rhubarb and Ginger Smoothie, page 162

mash the strawberries

strain off a bit of juice

whip the cream

fold in the strawberries ...

... and then the sugar

STRAWBERRY FOOL

A fool is really just a blend of crushed fruit, sugar, and cream. Food writers disagree about why it is called a fool – some think it's from the French word *fouler*, meaning "to crush," but others think it's just called fool because it's a light-hearted, silly sort of dish – just as a *trifle* means "something of little importance." This fool is really just a version of strawberries and cream – a lovely, summery dessert made with fruit that doesn't need any cooking.

To serve 6:
Strawberries, 2 cups
Heavy cream, 1 cup
$^1/_2$ lemon
Confectioners' sugar, to taste

Colander, paper towels, 2 medium bowls, potato masher, pitcher, whisk or electric mixer, metal spoon, 2 sieves

1. Rinse the strawberries in the colander, then blot them dry with paper towels. If you've picked the strawberries yourself, the fluffy hull should slide out too as you pull off the stem. With bought strawberries, you'll probably have to dig out the hulls with a knife. Place the hulled strawberries in one of the bowls.

2. Pound the strawberries with the potato masher until you have a lumpy purée. If there's a lot of liquid, set a sieve over the pitcher and pour the strawberries into it to strain off some of the juice. This stops the fool from getting too runny – and you can drink the juice!

3. Whip the cream in the other bowl with the whisk or mixer until, when you lift up the beater, the cream forms little mountain peaks.

4. Using the metal spoon, fold the mashed strawberries into the bowl of cream, using the spoon like a paddle, turning gently but firmly until the strawberries are completely blended in and there are no more lumps of white cream. Add a squeeze of lemon juice, to taste.

5. How much sugar you need to add depends on how sweet your strawberries are. Sift in a little, a heaping teaspoonful at a time, folding it in well. Keep sampling until it seems just sweet enough.

How to eat your fool

You could eat your strawberry fool straight away, but a little firming time in the fridge won't hurt it. Spoon it into little glass dishes if you have them and let them sit for a few minutes out of the fridge before you eat.

Variation: Eton Mess

Instead of using sugar to sweeten your strawberry fool, stir in some crushed meringues. You will then have a classic summer dessert known as Eton Mess.

RHUBARB FOOL

Rhubarb fool is a classic — a sunshiny pudding to enjoy on one of the first really warm days of spring. And it works pretty well to cheer you up on a not-so-warm day.

To serve 4 to 6:
Orange, 1
Rhubarb stalks (i.e., no leaves), 12 ounces
Superfine sugar, 2 or 3 tablespoons
Heavy cream, 2/3 cup
Confectioners' sugar, 2 tablespoons

Citrus juicer, cutting board, sharp knife, medium-sized saucepan, wooden spoon, 2 medium bowls, rotary beater, electric mixer or balloon whisk, tablespoon

1. Squeeze the juice from the orange. Trim the ends off the rhubarb, slice it into half-finger lengths, and place in the saucepan with the sugar and orange juice. Put the pan over low to medium heat and slowly bring the fruit to a gentle simmer.

2. Cook, stirring carefully and only occasionally with the wooden spoon, until the rhubarb pieces are completely tender but some of them still have their shape. (There comes a point when you're cooking rhubarb when the stems completely disintegrate into a mush of fine fibers. It doesn't matter if it goes this far, but we think it's nice to have a few chunky pieces among the mush.)

3. Leave the stewed rhubarb to cool, then transfer it to one of the bowls and put it in the fridge to cool completely.

4. Put the cream in the other bowl with the confectioners' sugar and whip until it forms soft peaks.

5. There are two ways to assemble the fool. Either fold the whipped cream thoroughly into the chilled rhubarb with a tablespoon until it's one lovely, sloppy, fruity, creamy mess and chill it for a while before serving. Or serve it layered in glasses — spoon into each glass a layer of rhubarb, a layer of whipped cream, another layer of rhubarb, and a final topping of whipped cream. You can then leave it to the eater to do the mixing.

How to eat your fool
Fools like this are delicious served with shortbread (see page 80). You can make a lovely "trifly" fool by adding some thick, cold custard to the layered version — and even putting some sponge cake, soaked in rhubarb juice, at the bottom of the glass.

LEMON CURD

Creamy and rich, yet sweet and tangy, this is one of the best ways ever devised of capturing lemoniness – and trapping it in a jar!

To make 1 pint jar:
Unsalted butter, 6 tablespoons
Superfine sugar, ³/₄ cup
Lemons, 3
Free-range eggs, 2 whole, plus 1 extra yolk

Pint Mason jar or bowl, butter knife, small heavy saucepan, grater, sharp knife, citrus juicer, cup, wooden spoon, sieve

1. If using a Mason jar, sterilize it as described in step 1 of the recipe for Sweet Chile and Red Currant Jam (see page 163).

2. Cut the butter into little cubes and put it in the saucepan with the sugar.

3. Grate the bright yellow zest from the lemons, using the fine-holed section of the grater. Keep turning the lemon so that you only grate the zest and not the bitter white pith.

4. Cut the lemons in half and squeeze out the juice. Pour it into the saucepan and add the zest.

5. Break the eggs into a cup and add them to the saucepan too, with the extra yolk.

6. Place the saucepan on the stove over low heat. Stir the mixture from time to time with the wooden spoon until all the butter has melted and you have a yellow, runny liquid.

7. Still with the heat on low, keep stirring all the time now. The idea is to heat everything very gently until the eggs thicken the mixture and it turns to a thick sauce. This will take about 10 minutes. Too much heat, though, and you'll get lemon-flavored scrambled eggs.

8. When the mixture is thick enough to coat the back of the spoon and to leave a good clear line if you wipe your finger across it, then the curd is ready. Turn off the heat and take the saucepan off the stove. Pour the curd through the sieve into either the clean jam jar or a bowl (for eating now). Keep the cooled curd in the fridge and eat within a week.

How to eat your lemon curd

Eat with warm scones (see page 47), or with homemade bread and butter (see pages 41 and 64). See page 52 for using it to make a delicious lemon tart. Or stir 3 or 4 tablespoons of curd into ²/₃ cup whipped cream and use it to fill a Victoria sponge (see page 111).

Variation

For a tangy lemon and lime curd, substitute a couple of limes for one of the lemons.

BAKED APPLES

One of those desserts that's so simple to make and so much more delicious than you could possibly imagine. It's essential that you use a firm apple such as a Granny Smith or Golden Delicious, rather than a sweet eating apple like a Red Delicious.

You will need:
Unsalted butter
Granny Smith or Golden Delicious apples,
  1 medium per person
Soft brown or granulated sugar

Ovenproof dish big enough to hold all the apples in a single layer (remember that they will expand a little as they bake), sharp serrated knife, apple corer, tablespoon

1. Preheat the oven to 350°F. Smear a little butter over the inside of the dish.

2. With the sharp knife, carefully cut a line completely around the waist of each apple to give it a sort of thin belt. This stops the apple from exploding as the flesh foams and expands in the heat of the oven.

3. Use the apple corer to take out the core and seeds of each apple. You do this by standing the apple on a flat surface and pushing the corer downwards around the stalk. You'll probably have to turn the apple over and do the same thing from the other end of the apple (hopefully the two holes will join up!). You'll be left with a cylindrical hole right through the middle of the apple. Cut a small slice off the bottom of the apple so that it will sit in the baking dish without rocking from side to side. Stand the apples in the dish slightly apart from each other, so they don't join up and get stuck together while they cook.

4. Pour sugar into the well of each apple right up to the top. Dot a generous knob of butter on top of the sugar. Spoon a tablespoonful of water for each apple into the base of the dish.

5. Oven gloves on. Place the dish in the preheated oven and bake for about 30 minutes. The apples should be puffy and the skin a little split. Stick a sharp knife into the flesh of each apple at the thickest part near the core. If the flesh still feels hard, let the apples cook for 5 minutes longer. Turn the oven down a little if they are getting too brown.

How to eat your baked apples

Serve everyone an apple and a good spoonful of the delicious syrupy sauce poured over the top. Some people adore the skin of a baked apple; others prefer to push it to one side. But whatever you do, eat with plenty of cream, Greek yogurt, or English custard (see page 113). They're also very good with a nice, creamy rice pudding (see page 322).

GOOSEBERRY CRUMBLE

This recipe can be adapted for other cooking fruits, such as plums, rhubarb, or Granny Smith apples. If you use plums (one of our favorites), they should be halved and pitted first, then gently stewed with sugar to taste and just a little water before you assemble the crumble. This prevents all the crumble mixture from falling through the gaps between the hard, shiny plums. You can also pour off some of the juice before ladling the stewed plums into the pie dish, to stop the fruit from becoming too runny.

To serve 6:
All-purpose or white pastry flour, 1¼ cups
Unsalted butter, ½ cup (1 stick)
Superfine sugar, ⅓ cup
Gooseberries, 4 cups
Granulated sugar, about 7 heaping
   tablespoons

Mixing bowl, small knife, tablespoon, sharp serrated knife and cutting board or nail scissors, 6-cup baking dish

1. Preheat the oven to 375°F.

2. Put the flour in the mixing bowl. Cut up the butter into little cubes and add it to the bowl. Rub the butter and flour together between your fingertips, breaking down the butter into tiny lumps until the mixture looks like fine bread crumbs (or coarse sand). Add the superfine sugar and stir it in briefly. Put the bowl of crumble in the fridge while you prepare the gooseberries.

3. Top and tail each gooseberry, snipping off the ends where the flower and the stem were. You can use either nail scissors or a sharp serrated knife and a chopping board.

4. Add the gooseberries to the baking dish and spoon the granulated sugar over the top. Then scatter the crumble mix evenly over the gooseberries. If you try to press it down, it won't be nearly as nice and crumbly.

5. Oven gloves on. Put the dish in the hot oven and bake for 30 to 35 minutes. The crumble is ready when it's colored gently golden, but stick a knife into the center to see if the gooseberries are cooked – they should be completely soft and tender. If they're not, turn the oven down to 325°F and cook for another 10 minutes. Hard, green, late-May gooseberries will take longer to cook than riper, late-June ones.

How to eat your crumble

This dessert tastes delicious with a little river of cream running over the crumble topping. Or, if you're feeling very indulgent, serve it with warm custard (see page 113). Crumbles are always good eaten cold the next day.

SUMMER FRUIT TART

This tart is made with uncooked fruit, so the pastry is baked blind (see page 36) and then spread with a simple thickened custard called *crème pâtissière*, or pastry cream. The trick of making it look impressive is to arrange the fruit in some sort of regular pattern, either in rows or in spirals, as here. Use whatever soft fruit is good. Blackberries and raspberries are in season together in late August, but you could make this tart earlier in the summer with just strawberries, or really ripe apricots.

To serve 8:
Sweet Pastry (see page 52)
Blackberries and raspberries, 2 cups each
Red currant or blackberry jelly, 3 tablespoons

For the pastry cream:
Unsalted butter, 3 tablespoons
All-purpose flour, 2 tablespoons
Superfine sugar, 1/4 cup

Free-range eggs, 2
Milk, 2/3 cup
Vanilla extract, 1 teaspoon

9-inch tart pan with a removable bottom, medium saucepan, wooden spoon, balloon whisk, small saucepan, pastry brush

1. Make the pastry, line the tart pan, and bake it blind exactly as described in steps 1 and 2 and 4 to 8 of the Lemon Tart recipe on page 52. Let cool.

2. Meanwhile, make the pastry cream. Put the butter in the medium saucepan over low heat. Let the butter melt, stirring all the time with the wooden spoon; then add the flour and sugar. Break in the eggs and beat the mixture with the wooden spoon until smooth.

3. Pour in the milk and keep stirring all the time. When the sauce gets thick (and this will happen quite suddenly), turn off the heat and beat the mixture with the wooden spoon or the whisk until smooth. Put back over low heat and cook, stirring, for 2 minutes. Stir in the vanilla extract and let cool.

4. Spoon the pastry cream into the pastry shell, spreading it level, and chill for 30 minutes.

5. Now get fancy with the berries. You could alternate circles of blackberries with circles of raspberries, to get a stripy effect. You could layer the berries in spirals like the picture at right. Keep the berries as close to each other as possible so that hardly any of the custard filling shows. Try to keep them bottom up — the stalk end of each berry should be buried in the custard.

6. Finally, warm the jelly in the small saucepan over low heat and then brush it gently over the berries with the pastry brush.

7. Put the tart in the fridge for a few minutes to set the glossy glaze. Then eat!

FRENCH-STYLE APPLE TART

If you've ever been to France and goggled at the range of cakes in the *pâtisserie* shops, then you'll have noticed the extraordinary beauty of the fruit tarts in the windows: biscuity-crisp pastry shells filled with rows of glistening fruit.

This simple apple tart is a good way to start your career as a *pâtissier*. As it's made from apples, you can cook it all year round.

To serve 6 to 8:
Sweet Pastry (see page 52)
Lemon, 1
Apples, such as Golden Delicious, 5 to 6
Superfine sugar, 2 tablespoons
Apricot jam, 2 tablespoons

9¹/₂-inch to 10-inch tart pan with a removable bottom, baking sheet, medium bowl, citrus juicer, cutting board, vegetable peeler, sharp knife, colander, paper towels, tablespoon, small saucepan, small sieve, small bowl, pastry brush

1. Make the pastry and line the tart pan in the same way described in steps 1, 2, and 4 through 6 of the Lemon Tart recipe on page 52, but this time you don't need to bake the pastry shell blind first. The pastry around the edges gets quite crisp when the tart cooks, but underneath the apples it will stay soft. That's part of the charm of this tart – and it makes it quicker and easier too. Put the pan in the fridge to let the pastry rest while you deal with the apples.

dabbing on the sieved jam

2. Preheat the oven to 350°F. Put the baking sheet in the oven to heat up.

3. Half fill the medium bowl with cold water. Squeeze the juice from the lemon and add it to the water.

4. Starting with the first apple, peel it, then place it upright on the cutting board and cut it in half from stem to flower end. Cut each half through the core again to make quarters. Cut out the core of each apple. Then cut each apple quarter as thinly as possible into even slices and put the slices straight into the bowl of lemon juice and water. (The acid in the lemon helps to halt a chemical reaction that turns an apple brown when it's cut.)

5. When you've peeled and sliced all the apples, empty the slices into the colander to drain off the water. Blot them dry with some paper towels. Get the pan out of the fridge and start to arrange the apple slices in a series of overlapping rings, beginning around the rim of the pastry and working inward, packing them in tightly. Each slice of apple should half-cover its neighbor, and each ring should overlap the one outside it. When you've covered the surface of the tart in slices, sprinkle the superfine sugar evenly over the apples.

6. Oven gloves on. Put the tin on the baking sheet in the preheated oven. Bake for 40 to 45 minutes, until the pastry is a light golden brown and the apples look cooked (test them by inserting a knife into one of them; it should be just tender). Just before the time is up, heat the apricot jam with a teaspoon of water in the small saucepan until it softens and melts. Set the sieve over the small bowl and spoon the jam into it, then press it through the sieve with the back of the spoon to get rid of the lumps.

7. Oven gloves on. Take the pan out of the oven and place it on a wire rack on the work surface. Dip the pastry brush into the sieved jam and gently dab it all over the apples. Oven gloves on again. Return the pan to the oven for 5 minutes, then remove it and let it cool on the rack.

8. Let the tart sit for at least 15 minutes before you try to cut it, to give the pastry time to set. If you want to take it out of its pan, stand the pan on a shallow bowl. Press gently down on the sides of the pan and they should drop down, leaving the tart on the metal base.

How to eat your tart

Eat this tart on its own, with a little cream, or with some good vanilla ice cream (see page 374). It's equally delicious eaten warm or cold.

BANANA BREAD

Most cakes smell pretty good while they're cooking, but banana bread smells so good that it's almost impossible not to break off a little bit as it comes out of the oven.

It's important that the bananas you use for this cake are really ripe – not just yellow but generously freckled with brown spots.

To make 1 loaf:
Dried apricots, 1/3 cup
Golden raisins, 1/3 cup
Lemon, 1
Unsalted butter, 1/3 cup, soft but not melted
Superfine sugar, 1/2 cup
Free-range eggs, 2 large

Bananas, 3 large ripe ones
All-purpose or white pastry flour, 1 1/4 cups

Loaf pan measuring about 5 x 9 x 3 inches, parchment paper, cutting board, sharp knife, grater, mixing bowl, wooden spoon, fork, plate, sieve, large metal spoon, wire rack

1. Preheat the oven to 325°F. Line the loaf pan with parchment paper.

2. Chop up the apricots so the pieces are roughly the same size as the raisins. Grate the zest of the lemon.

3. Cream the butter and sugar in the mixing bowl with the wooden spoon until they're well blended. Break in an egg and beat it into the mixture completely, then beat in the other egg. Add the dried fruit and lemon zest.

4. Mash the bananas well with the fork on a plate and add them to the bowl. Stir well.

5. Sift the flour into the bowl and carefully fold this into the mixture with the large metal spoon, making sure you don't leave any lumps of flour (see page 91 for more on the art of folding).

6. Scrape the mixture into the prepared pan and gently level the top with the back of the spoon. Oven gloves on. Put the pan in the oven and bake for about an hour – but check the cake after 50 minutes. It is ready when you can insert a knife into the middle and it comes out completely clean. Leave the cake in its pan on a wire rack to cool for about 15 minutes, then turn it out of the pan and peel off the paper.

How to eat your banana bread
It's good to eat when it's still just a little bit warm from the oven. Store the cake in an airtight container and it will make good moist eating for a couple of days.

ORANGE AND STRAWBERRY JELLIES

Once you understand how to use gelatin, you can make lots of different molded desserts. You just have to turn the fruit into juice, sweeten it with sugar, and add the right amount of gelatin to set it firm (but not so firm it's rubbery). If you're making jellies for a party, remember that they will take several hours to set. The safest thing may be to make them the day before.

This recipe uses quite a lot of strawberries, so it will be much cheaper if you go to a U-pick farm for them.

To serve 8:
Valencia oranges, 6 to 8
Lemons, 2
Ripe strawberries, about 5 cups
Confectioners' sugar, about 2/3 cup
Powdered gelatin, 2 packets (2 tablespoons)

Sharp knife, cutting board, citrus juicer, 2 large pitchers, large bowl, sieve, wooden spoon, large cotton cloth or square of cheesecloth, balloon whisk, 2 mugs, two 2-cup molds for setting your jellies

1. First, extract the juice from the fruit. In the case of the oranges, one of those electric citrus juicers is the best thing to use. Or you can use the old-fashioned kind that isn't electric and doesn't turn around. Either way, slice the oranges and one of the lemons in half and squeeze them on the juicer, getting out all the juice you can. Pour it into one of the pitchers.

2. To get the juice from the strawberries, put them in the large bowl. Squeeze the juice from the second lemon, add it to the strawberries, and crush them thoroughly with your fingers, or use a fork or a potato masher if you find it easier. Set the sieve over the other pitcher and spoon this pulp into it with the wooden spoon, then use the back of the spoon to push the strawberries through. You can then put the strawberry pulp in the cloth and squeeze out the last of the juice into the pitcher.

3. Measure the two juices separately. You should have about 2 cups of each. If you're way short of this, you might want to squeeze or crush a bit more fruit.

4. Whisk half of the sugar into the bowl of orange juice until it dissolves. Taste it, and if you think it's not sweet enough, whisk in a little more sugar. Rinse the whisk and do the same thing with the strawberry juice.

5. Using just-boiled water from the kettle, add 1/4 cup water to each mug. Add 1 packet of gelatin to each mug and stir thoroughly so the gelatin is completely dissolved.

6. Pour the dissolved gelatin mixtures into the 2 juices and mix thoroughly.

7. Pour the juices into the molds you have chosen (any extra can be poured into spare or improvised molds – even a jelly in a glass, mug, or plastic cup can be turned out onto a plate). If you'd rather, you can set the jellies half and half, so that each mold is made up of two different mixtures. To do this, half-fill each mold with half of each jelly (orange in one and strawberry in the other) and put the molds in the fridge. When they're both nearly fully set, pour the rest of the mug of orange jelly onto the set strawberry one and the rest of the mug of strawberry jelly onto the set orange one. You may find that the jelly in the mugs has started to set too, in which case stand each mug in a bowl of hot (but not boiling) water and stir the jelly around with a spoon to melt it so it's pourable once more.

8. Chill the molds thoroughly until the jelly has set firm. This will take several hours.

9. Unmold! (See page 137.) Make sure that everyone has a chance to enjoy the shape and the wobble before you carve up your jelly.

How to eat your jellies

Some people like a little cream trickled over jellies, but we prefer them just as they are, so we can feel the fresh fruit flavors dissolving on our tongues and trickling down our throats!

BRAMBLE JELLY warning – boiling sugar!

Gather a friend or two, your rubber boots, and some stout gloves, search out a basket or tub, and make an afternoon of picking blackberries. Then come back to the kitchen and make this easy, jewel-colored jelly. Try it while it's still warm, thickly spread over a big hunk of bread and butter.

Jellies and jams aren't difficult to make, but you do need to watch the pan very carefully as it boils. Let the temperature get too hot and you're left with a lot of burnt jam.

To make 1 pint jar:
Blackberries, about 4 cups
A small Golden Delicious apple
Granulated sugar

Pint Mason jar or bowl, saucer, colander, large heavy saucepan, cutting board, sharp knife, long-handled wooden spoon, sieve, bowl, a piece of cheesecloth or an old clean handkerchief, large glass measuring cup, candy thermometer, ladle

1. If you want to keep your jam for more than just a week or two, you'll need to sterilize a jam jar. Do this as described in step 1 of the recipe for Sweet Chile and Red Currant Jam (see page 163). If you're just pouring the jelly into a bowl, then put this in a low oven to warm up or it may crack when you add the hot jelly.

2. Check the blackberries for bugs. Add the berries to the colander and wash them under the cold tap before draining them and putting them into the saucepan. Cut the apple into chunks (there's no need to peel or core it) and add this to the pan, too. Pour in enough water to come just to the top of the fruit.

3. Put the saucer in the fridge to get cold. Put the saucepan on the stove over low to medium heat. Soon the juice will start to run from the blackberries, staining the apple a beautiful

pink. Let the fruit simmer gently for about 10 minutes, stirring occasionally with the wooden spoon, until it is completely pulpy and soft. Turn off the heat.

4. Place the sieve over the bowl and line it with the cheesecloth or handkerchief, then pour in the hot fruit. Let the liquid drip through the sieve on its own – if you push it through with the back of a spoon, your jelly will look cloudy rather than clear.

5. When pretty well all the juice has dripped through (a matter of minutes rather than hours, unless you're desperate to get every last drop), pour the liquid into the measuring cup and make a note of how much you've got; you will need $3/4$ cup plus 2 tablespoons granulated sugar for every 1 cup juice. Pour the juice into the saucepan and add the correct amount of sugar.

6. Turn the heat to low and stir the juice in the pan with the wooden spoon until all the sugar has dissolved. Only then can you turn the heat up to a full boil and stop stirring. Watch the mixture very carefully all the time.

7. After the mixture has been boiling for 1 minute, take the chilled saucer out of the fridge so you can test for the gelling point. Very carefully scoop up a few drops of jelly with the wooden spoon and drop them onto the cold saucer. Wait a few seconds and then carefully push the blob of jelly with your finger (it will have cooled down on the chilled saucer). If it wrinkles well, then your jelly has set and you need to turn off the heat straight away. If it doesn't, then test again after another minute. If you have a candy thermometer, the temperature you're looking for is 221°F.

8. Once you've reached the gelling point, let the jelly cool down for a few minutes in the saucepan. Push any scum on the top of the jelly to one side with the wooden spoon and ladle the clear jelly into the jam jar or bowl. It will thicken as it cools. Screw the lid onto the jar right away. Store in a cool, dry place and the jelly should keep for a year or so.

How to eat your bramble jelly

Try it first on crusty bread and butter. Why not use the rest of the jelly to make a batch of jam tarts? Or stir a teaspoon into natural yogurt or crème fraîche for an instant dessert.

LEMONADE

Could this be the most refreshing drink in the world? Intensely lemony and not too sweet – just right for the hottest day of summer.

If you can, make this lemonade in a glass jug so that you can marvel at its amazing bright yellow hue. The color, and a good part of the flavor too, comes from using the zest as well as the juice of the lemons. Bear in mind that lemons and other citrus fruits are often covered in a thin layer of wax before they're packaged, to help preserve them in storage. Either buy unwaxed lemons or scrub your lemons under the hot tap before you peel or zest them.

You will need:
Water, 3 cups
Unwaxed lemons, 4
Superfine sugar, $1/2$ cup
Ice, to serve

Vegetable peeler, large heatproof pitcher, large glass measuring cup, wooden spoon, citrus juicer

1. Fill the kettle with water and bring it to a boil.

2. Meanwhile, using the vegetable peeler, peel all the yellow zest off the lemons in wide strips. Put the shaved lemons to one side. If there is a lot of white pith still attached to the underneath part of the zest, scrape off the worst of it. Put the zest strips in the heatproof pitcher.

3. Put the sugar into the pitcher with the lemon zest. When the kettle boils, measure out 3 cups water and pour it into the pitcher with the sugar. Stir with the wooden spoon until the sugar has completely dissolved. Put the pitcher to one side for a couple of hours until the lemonade has cooled down.

4. When the lemonade is cold, fish out the strips of zest and throw them away. Cut the peeled lemons in half and squeeze the juice from them. Pour the juice into the pitcher and stir well. If you like, you can strain everything into a separate pitcher to remove any stray seeds and pulp. Store the lemonade in the fridge.

How to drink your lemonade
Half-fill some glasses with ice and pour in the lemonade. If you have mint or lemon balm growing in your garden, you could chop some and add it to the glass with the ice before you pour over the lemonade.

MANGO AND ORANGE SMOOTHIE

This is a good smoothie to make in early summer, when mangoes are widely available. They turn yellow as they ripen – keep them in a fruit bowl on the table and you'll see when they're just right.

To serve 2:
Mango, 1 smallish
Valencia oranges, 3 to 4 (depending on size and juiciness)
Lime or lemon, $1/2$ to 1, to taste
Ice cubes, 2 to 3

Cutting board, sharp knife, blender, citrus juicer, serving glasses

1. Peel the mango and slice the flesh away from the pit as best you can. There are various clever ways to cut up a mango, but the only important thing is to get all the flesh into the blender, along with any juice that has spilled out in the process.

2. Squeeze the juice from the oranges and the lime or lemon. Add this to the blender along with the ice cubes.

3. Blend for about a minute, until the mixture is smooth. Pour into the glasses and serve.

PEACH, PEAR, AND RASPBERRY SMOOTHIE

This is a late-summer/early-autumn smoothie with a beautiful sunset color. You could sweeten it with a little honey if you like, but you probably won't need to.

To serve 2:
Ripe peach, 1
Ripe pear, 1
Ice cubes, 2 to 3
Yogurt, 3 tablespoons
Raspberries, 5 or 6
Runny honey, to taste (optional)

Cutting board, small sharp knife, vegetable peeler, blender, tablespoon, serving glasses

1. Cut all the way around the pit of the peach, using the crease at the side of the fruit to start the cut. Then twist the halves in opposite directions to separate them. Hopefully, you will then be able to pick the pit out quite easily, but if not, carefully ease it out with the tip of the knife. Coarsely cut up the peach.

2. Peel the pear and then, standing it upright on the board, cut the flesh away from the core.

3. Put the ice and yogurt in the blender. Cover with the lid and blend for a few seconds, until the ice crushes down. Then (still blending) take off the little topknot in the lid of the blender and drop the peach pieces through one or two at a time.

4. Add the strips of pear. Drop the raspberries in one by one and whiz for about a minute, until the mixture is smooth.

5. Switch off the blender and lift the pitcher off the machine. Test the smoothie for sweetness; if you think it needs it, add a little runny honey and blend again. Pour the mixture into glasses and serve immediately.

How to drink your smoothies

Always serve a smoothie straight away or they start to discolor and look a bit sad quite quickly. If you want to make a smoothie look very special, dip the rim of the serving glass in a little lemon juice, then dip it into a plate of superfine sugar to make a frosted rim. Put the glass in the fridge while you make the smoothie. Then pour in the smoothie and serve with a straw.

RHUBARB AND GINGER SMOOTHIE

This one's an exception to the no-cook smoothie rule. But it has a delicious spicy gingeriness that's good for perking up a dull February day.

To serve 2:
Rhubarb, 2 to 3 stems
Oranges, 2
Superfine sugar, 3 to 4 teaspoons
Stem ginger in syrup, 1 large piece
  (or a little grated fresh ginger)
Water, 2 tablespoons

Ice cubes, 3 to 4

Cutting board, sharp knife, citrus juicer, small saucepan with lid, teaspoon, tablespoon, blender, serving glasses

1. Wash the rhubarb and trim off any leaves, then cut off the slightly dried-up ends. Chop the rhubarb into $3/4$-inch chunks.

2. Squeeze the juice from the oranges. Put the rhubarb in the small pan along with the orange juice, sugar, ginger, and water. Stir until the sugar dissolves, then cover the pan and stew the rhubarb very gently over low heat until it softens. Add a little more water if the rhubarb starts to look dry. Turn off the heat and let the rhubarb cool completely. (Dip the base of the pan in cold water if you like.)

3. Put the ice cubes in the blender and whiz for a few seconds, until coarsely crushed. Add the rhubarb mixture and whiz until smooth. Pour the smoothie into glasses and drink straight away.

SWEET CHILE AND RED CURRANT JAM

warning – boiling sugar!

Despite our reluctance to use them differently, adventurous cooks prepare delicious jams, sorbets, and ice creams from peppers and tomatoes, which make the most of their fruitiness. So if you usually just think of cooking chiles in spicy Mexican stews or Thai and Indian curries, it's worth trying this wonderfully fruity chile and red currant jam.

To make 1 pint jar:
Red currants, 10 ounces
Red serrano chiles, 1 to 2 (the number
   depends on whether you want a
   slight chile fizz on your tongue
   or a real kick)
Fresh ginger, a piece about 2 inches long
Oranges, 3
Granulated sugar, 2/3 cup

Pint Mason or jam jar with lid, saucer, medium saucepan, fork, cutting board, small sharp knife, vegetable peeler, grater, citrus juicer, wooden spoon, teaspoon, sheet of newspaper

1. Sterilize a clean Mason or jam jar. You can do this either by putting it through a dishwasher cycle and using it straight away, or by putting it in a pan of cold water, bringing this to a boil, and simmering it for 10 minutes. Then carefully pour the water down the sink; use oven gloves to pick up the Mason jar and shake it dry. Put the clean Mason jar in the oven at 250°F. This is so the jar can dry out completely and get really warm. Cold jars tend to crack if you pour hot jam into them.

2. Put a saucer in the freezer to get cold. Put the red currants into the saucepan.

3. Chop up the chile(s) by holding them down on the cutting board with the fork while you cut them up with the sharp knife. Do this at arm's length because the chile can squirt up tiny amounts of juice as you cut. Slice the chile in half lengthwise. Cut away the veins and the stalk. Chop up the chile flesh and put it, along with the seeds, in the saucepan. At all times, avoid touching the chile with your fingers if you can possibly help it, because if you touch your eyes afterward the chile will really sting them.

4. Peel the knobbly skin from the ginger so you're left with just the yellow root. Grate it carefully, discarding the last bit rather than risking your fingers on the grater.

5. Using the vegetable peeler, peel off the zest from half of one of the oranges in wide strips. Scrape away any white pith attached to the back of the zest and cut the zest into thin strips.

Add the grated ginger and the orange zest to the red currants and chile in the pan.

6. Cut the oranges in half and squeeze out their juice. Add it to the pan along with the granulated sugar.

7. Turn the heat to low and stir the juice and fruit together until the sugar has dissolved. Bring to a boil and simmer the fruit for about 25 minutes, giving it a quick stir every now and again with the wooden spoon to make sure the fruit and ginger haven't stuck to the bottom of the pan.

8. Get the saucer out of the freezer and put it next to the stove. Test to see if the jam is ready by taking a teaspoonful of it and dropping it onto the cold saucer. Wait for a few seconds, then run your finger through the puddle of jam. If the jam wrinkles, then it's reached gelling point. Turn the heat off straight away. If it doesn't wrinkle and the jam still looks very liquid, keep boiling and testing every 2 or 3 minutes. The temperature you're looking for, if you have a candy thermometer, is 221°F. The jam will look darker when it's ready, and tiny bubbles will appear in the juice as you drop it onto the saucer. Let the jam cool for a minute or two.

9. Oven gloves on. Get the hot jar out of the oven and put it on a sheet of newspaper on the work surface. Tilt the pan and spoon the jam into the jar, remembering that the jam will still be very hot. Screw the lid onto the jar straight away.

How to eat your chile jam

There are lots of ways to enjoy chile jam — both sweet and savory. Jams and jellies like these are traditionally eaten with roast meat, so try serving it with your next roast lamb lunch as a change from plain red currant jelly. You could eat it spread on bread and butter — bread and jam has never been so exciting. You could even eat a little with the cheesecake on page 77 — the faint spiciness of the chiles goes well with the sweet creaminess of the cake.

VEGETABLES

Are you fussy about vegetables? Shouldn't we all be? The secret of enjoying them is freshness – crisp, cracking carrots pulled straight from the ground, just-picked peas popped from the pod, potatoes scrabbled out of the earth. Full of life-giving energy and goodness, these are also some of the most delicious foods you could ever eat. And don't let anyone persuade you differently!

vegetable fritters, page 209

garlic potatoes, page 203

oast onion family, page 204

salad garden, page 187

grow your own tomatoes, page 172

VEGETABLES

Imagine it's a warm, sunny day in June and you are walking out into the garden. You stop next to a row of tangled plants that are clambering up a mass of twiggy sticks. Green pods hang down from each plant, some slim and empty, some fat and full. You tug one down. You press your thumb into the rounded end to make a satisfying pop, then split it open. Inside the pod is a row of little green pearls. You push them into the palm of your hand and quickly stuff them in your mouth before they can escape.

Some people tell you that vegetables are just dull and boring. Are they mad? If you've never eaten a pea this way, or pulled a dainty little carrot out of the soil, then you may not know how tasty really fresh vegetables can be.

The word *vegetable* covers a huge range of different plants. A carrot doesn't have much in common with spinach or a fava bean (we eat the swollen root of one, the leaf of another, and the seed of the third), but we wouldn't be surprised to find them all on a plate together alongside our roast chicken. However, one important thing is true of most vegetables: they contain natural sugars and nutrients that make them both pleasant to eat and very good for us.

What is freshness?

The secret of eating vegetables at their tastiest and most nutritious is to eat them when they're at their absolute best — fresh and undamaged. But what does freshness mean? You might say that the freshest vegetables are the ones that are nearest to still being alive. In fact, there are probably some vegetables in your kitchen that really are still alive – onions and potatoes, for example. This means that both potatoes and onions can be kept fresh in a cool, dark place for weeks or even months. Plant them in the ground and, with a bit of luck, they'll even grow new plants.

However, most vegetables die when they are pulled, picked, or cut, so they start to "go bad" and stop tasting so good. Their natural sugars (there are sugars even in the most unlikely vegetables, such as onions) turn to boring, tasteless starch. So, think of the search for the freshest veggies as the search for the veggies that were most recently alive.

How the vegetables have been looked after once they have been picked is also important. Usually, keeping them cool slows down their decay, while exposing them to heat or light speeds it up. By the time a vegetable reaches a store, it's hard to find out when it was picked or what has happened to it since. But your eyes, nose, and fingertips can tell you a good deal. It's largely common sense. Avoid vegetables with wrinkly skin or the slightest trace of a sad, wilted look. In the case of tomatoes, zucchini, and eggplant, a smooth skin and firmness to the touch are as important as a bright color. All root vegetables should be hard, not wrinkled and bendy. And beans in their pods, such as green beans, should be firm – so you'd expect them to break, not bend. In the case of green, leafy vegetables  such as cabbages, spinach, and lettuce, yellowing, or even browning, on the edges is a sure sign of age. All fresh vegetables should either smell pleasant or not smell at all.

So where are you going to find the freshest vegetables? The problem is that many of the vegetables on sale in stores will have had to travel huge distances (sometimes halfway around the world), spend time in a warehouse, and then sit on the shelf for several days, waiting to be picked up and put in someone's shopping cart. In supermarkets, the sheer quantity of different vegetables bundled together in one long aisle, many of them shipped in from much warmer climates, can be completely overwhelming. That means that it's all too easy to overlook the fact that the bag of lettuce you've just put in your cart has been flown in from Spain, whereas there are lovely lettuces being grown only a few miles away from the store.

The fact that many vegetables on sale are scrubbed and packed in clear plastic doesn't really help you much in your search. Grabbing a bundle of prepacked carrots may be quicker as you rush around the store, but carrots stay fresher, crisper, and sweeter if stored still muddy, in a large paper sack away from the light, than if laid out in a cellophane tray wrapped in plastic wrap.

Local is best

The freshest produce will have traveled the least distance and been the most recently harvested. So shops that source most of their vegetables locally are the best places to go.

Many old-fashioned produce markets still buy vegetables from local farms, even though they probably import quite a few, too. They usually label the local stuff quite clearly, and if they don't, you can always ask.

At farmers' markets, vegetables are sold by the growers themselves – they may even have been harvested on the morning of the market. Farm stands should also be selling vegetables they have grown themselves, or at least ones from neighboring farms. And these days many U-pick farms don't grow just strawberries and other soft fruits but have branched out into vegetables, such as carrots, cauliflowers, corn, and asparagus. They do all the hard work, so you can experience all the fun of the harvest.

And wait till you get that sweet corn home. Unwrapped from its papery cocoon, its custard-colored seeds look like rows of perfect teeth. Plunge it straight into boiling water for just ten minutes. Let a knob of butter melt over the cob, then tuck in.

Frozen vegetables

Chilling vegetables slows down their deterioration, so you might expect that freezing them would stop it altogether, and that this is a good reason for preferring frozen vegetables to ones that are not quite so fresh. It's certainly true that some frozen vegetables are better than the same kind of veggies that are unfrozen but not very fresh.

Unfortunately, freezing some vegetables can damage their fragile cell structure. This is because vegetables contain a lot of water. The water expands when it's frozen, so when the vegetables are defrosted or cooked, the texture is often spoiled.

Only a few vegetables that are cooked after freezing will be as good as the fresh version. Without doubt, the most successful (and probably the most popular) are frozen peas. If they can be frozen within an hour or two of being picked, the sugar levels will be fixed and they should taste reasonably sweet.

Fava beans, sweet corn, and spinach freeze well, too, but most other vegetables don't — it's far better to make a smooth, creamy soup out of them and freeze that instead.

Some recipes with frozen veggies

Green Peas with Roasted Red Peppers
   and Chorizo, page 208
Vegetable Fritters, page 209

Growing your own vegetables

There's no doubt that the most delicious vegetables of all are the ones you grow yourself. "From field to frozen in 45 minutes" may sound impressive on the back of a package of peas, but when you grow your own you can have "from picked to pan in 45 seconds."

You may not have the space to grow a lot of vegetables, but even just a few plants can be rewarding. Very few vegetables are hard to grow, and most can be grown in the smallest of spaces. You might devote a patch of an existing flower bed to vegetables. Or you could mark out a small bed on a patch of grass and spend an afternoon digging it up. If that's not practical, then don't give up. Large flowerpots, tubs, and other containers, placed on patios or in other sunny areas, can all be used for growing vegetables. Make sure they've got some holes in the base for drainage or you'll find your plants floating after a heavy watering. Then you just need to fill them up with a good organic potting compost, or a mixture of compost and topsoil, and they're ready for seeds. Take a trip to your nearest garden center, choose a few packets of seeds of the vegetables you most like to eat . . . and follow the instructions on the back!

Growing your own food may be a slow process, but you get time to understand what's happening. You can watch the pepper plant on your kitchen windowsill turn from green to red to yellow, like a mixed-up traffic light. And fairy stories like Jack and the Beanstalk are brought to life when you watch a runner bean germinate with so much sudden violence that the shoot brings up the soil with it and the leaf literally unfurls in front of your eyes.

Some recipes with homegrown veggies

Pick-Your-Own Minestrone, page 196
Crudités with Garlic Mayonnaise, page 212

Project:

GROWING TOMATOES

The tomato is in this chapter under false pretenses. It's a fruit, not a vegetable. You may doubt the truth, but choose a good variety, give it plenty of sunshine, water it properly, then pick it when it's ripe, and it will be so sweet it couldn't be anything but a fruit.

You can buy little potted tomato plants all ready for planting from around April. But it's cheaper and much more fun to start from seed in February. Choose a seed packet that uses a phrase like "unrivaled sweetness" rather than one that talks about "prolific" cropping. Our favorite varieties are Sungold (a lovely little orange tomato) and Gardener's Delight (a larger sweet cherry tomato that can be grown outside), or, if you like big tomatoes for slicing, Marmande or Big Boy.

Where will you grow your plants – inside or outside? If outside, then choose a variety that will flourish in a sunny, sheltered spot outdoors. Bushy varieties don't need supporting stakes and are easier to look after.

You will need:
A seed tray, potting compost, tomato seeds, a fine sprayer, labels, a large, clear plastic freezer bag and a tie, 6 or more small plastic plant pots (you could always use yogurt pots or plastic drinking cups with holes made in the bottom with a sharp knife for drainage), teaspoon, 6 large pots or 2 grow bags, 6 bamboo poles for support

Part 1: Sow seeds (mid-February to mid-March)
Fill the seed tray with damp compost and smooth it flat. Make little dents in the soil in straight rows roughly 1 inch apart so that your seedlings have room to grow. Drop a tomato seed into each dent and cover it with a little soil. Spray the soil with water to dampen it. Label the tray so that you'll remember what you planted, with the name of the tomato variety and the date you sowed it. Carefully place the tray in the plastic bag, then gather up the mouth of the bag and blow air into it as if you were blowing up a balloon. Tie up the end with one of those metal ties, so the seed tray ends up sitting in its own little polytunnel. The bag will keep in the moisture until the seedlings have germinated — when the shoots appear. Put the tray in a place where you won't forget about it. It will say on the back of the seed packet what temperature the seedlings will germinate best at — but a cool room temperature is usually about right.

The seeds may take only a few days to germinate or they may take a fortnight — it all depends on the temperature and the seed variety. As soon as you see the shoots appear, take off the bag and set the tray on a sunny windowsill. Keep the compost damp with a fine sprayer, but not wet, and watch your seedlings flourish.

Part 2: Moving the seedlings (early April to early May)
When the seedlings become sturdy enough to handle, move them (called "transplanting") into little pots, where they'll have more room to grow. Water them before you transplant them. Fill the small plastic plant pots with damp compost. Smooth off the top and make a well in each one. Holding a seedling by its two leaves and not by its stalk, dig it gently out of the seed tray with the handle of a teaspoon, making sure you bring its roots and a bit of compost with it. Place it in the pot so that the soil comes to just below the leaves, and gently firm up the soil around the seedling. Label the pot and put the pots on the windowsill so that the seedlings can grow, remembering to keep the compost damp.

Part 3: Moving the plants (late May to June)
When your seedlings have become sturdy little plants 8 to 12 inches tall, you'll need to transplant them into a grow bag or a larger pot filled with compost as before. Large grow bags will take 3 tomato plants. A large pot the size of an average bucket will take one. (If you've got more healthy plants than you want, you could give the spares away to friends.)

If you're going to be growing them outside in a sunny, sheltered place, then let the plants gradually get used to the temperature of their new position, putting them outside for a few hours each day on warm days before you transplant them. If your tomatoes are going to grow inside, make sure they're in a sunny spot with space to grow upward and outward, and that there is plenty of ventilation, or they may be vulnerable to blight.

Tall-growing tomato plants will need support or they'll fall over, so drive a bamboo pole deep into the back of the pot, and secure this cane to something solid behind the pot, as the plant will become quite heavy when it's bearing fruit.

Part 4: Looking after your plants (June to July)
Tall plants will need to have their side shoots removed so that they have one main stem rather than lots of side branches, as these would use up too much of the plant's energy growing leaves rather than producing fruit. Water containers and grow bags little and often or they'll dry out.

When little green tomatoes start to form on the plants, feed the soil once a week with liquid fertilizer. You can buy this in garden shops or make it yourself by stuffing a bucket full of chopped-up weeds, filling it with water, and leaving it in the sun for a couple of weeks. Inspect and water your plants every day and watch the little green globes swell and ripen. If you water rather erratically – too much and then none at all – you risk your tomatoes splitting and developing a condition called blossom end rot, which turns the bottom of the tomato brown.

Part 5: Harvest (July to September)
All being well, you should get your first fruit toward mid-July. Keep picking, feeding, and watering your tomato plants and they should go on and on, giving you fruit well into September and beyond. Any green tomatoes at the end of the season can be picked off the plant and ripened in a warm place such as a cupboard – it's warmth that ripens them, not sunlight. You don't even have to ripen tomatoes to cook them: green tomatoes can be used in curries or chutneys.

How to eat your tomatoes

When you spot your first ripe tomato, wipe it on your shirt and eat it right next to the plant. Notice its distinctive, almost peppery smell (any tomato you buy should smell like this if it's ready to eat). Take the second tomato into the kitchen. Cut yourself a thick slice of good bread. Cut the tomato in half and smear and squeeze its cut surface all over the bread so that the flesh and seeds come out and the bread turns pink and slightly soggy. Trickle some drops of olive oil on top and sprinkle it with a little salt. Eat the bread straight away, discarding the tomato skin.

Or you could slice a couple of tomatoes and stuff them between two thickly buttered slices of bread with a little sea salt and pepper sprinkled on top.

Some recipes with fresh tomatoes
Guacamole, page 215
Quick Tomato Salad, page 216

Seasonal vegetables

Your homegrown tomatoes will prove one very important principle – that vegetables are at their best when grown and picked in the right season. It's not always obvious that vegetables have seasons – we expect to see most of them in the stores almost every month of the year. But most vegetables do taste much better grown locally and eaten at the right time of year. You just can't beat purple sprouting broccoli in April, asparagus in May, the first new potatoes in June, zucchini and green beans in July, tomatoes in August and September, and pumpkins in October.

Some people might see a seasonal approach to buying vegetables as a bit limiting, restricting your options in the kitchen. But we believe that such "restrictions" are actually quite liberating for the cook, because buying vegetables in season not only means that you get them at their tastiest, it also helps you decide what to cook, by narrowing the confusing choice of what's available at the supermarket to the simpler choice of what's best right now. And far from being a sacrifice, eating seasonally is actually quite indulgent. You can gorge yourself on strawberries, for example, knowing that you won't be seeing much of them for another year.

In contrast, a wintry treat like cauliflower cheese in the middle of June? A summery tomato salad in January? Asparagus for Christmas? It wouldn't feel right, and they wouldn't taste as good.

VEGETABLE INVASIONS

From carrots to cabbage, sweet potatoes to peppers, lettuces to zucchini, the vegetable aisle in a supermarket goes on and on. But if the early farmers of the New Stone Age had built supermarkets, the vegetable aisle would have been fairly short. Relying on just a few wild leaves, roots, and seaweed, their vegetable diet must have been hard going, and pretty limited. Eat up your nettles, dear, or you can't have seconds of mammoth.

The Romans who invaded Britain 2,000 years ago didn't just introduce us to straight roads and central heating. They also brought with them vegetables that were widely eaten in Italy, including cabbages, leeks, fava beans, peas, onions, and garlic. However, it wasn't until many hundreds of years later that some of our favorite vegetables appeared in Europe.  The Europeans who sailed across the Atlantic to conquer the New World in the sixteenth and seventeenth centuries brought back potatoes, tomatoes, green and runner beans, pumpkins, sweet peppers, and chiles. Meanwhile, vegetables such as carrots, cauliflower, and broccoli traveled up through Europe from North Africa and the Eastern Mediterranean.

Some vegetables became immediately popular, while others took much longer to catch on – not always the ones you'd expect. Tomatoes, peppers, and chiles came to Europe in the sixteenth century. But while the pepper and chile were welcomed almost straight away, tomatoes weren't widely eaten until the mid-nineteenth century. Green beans quickly entered the British diet. Runner beans didn't, and were grown more for their pretty red flowers than for their eating qualities.

Superstition sometimes influenced whether a vegetable was accepted or not. Many people in Europe were convinced that tomatoes were poisonous, comparing them to mandrakes, which were linked to witchcraft and supposedly screamed horribly when they were dug out of the ground. Other new vegetables were accepted because they were similar to familiar plants. Sweet peppers and chiles became popular because when dried they made a cheap alternative to the expensive black peppercorns that were traded from India and Africa. Strangely, today it's almost the other way around – tomatoes are eaten every day, while many people think chiles are a bit exotic.

THE MAGNIFICENT POTATO

There is one vegetable that we consume in greater quantities, and probably with more enthusiasm, than any other. So it deserves a special mention, and a bit of a discussion.

It doesn't look like much. It's not bright orange, like the carrot, or deep green, like the pea. It'll hardly grab your attention alongside the paint-box sweet peppers and pumpkins. It is, after all, only a potato.

Oval, lumpy, and covered in mud, it doesn't seem like something to get excited about. Imagine trying to live without the potato, though. It's almost as if this food is *so* important that there's really no need to make it look special.

Scrape beneath the mud, of course, and there are differences. Some have a pinky-red skin, like the Red Rose, some are even blue or purple, like the Peruvian potatoes. Their shapes vary, too. The ones that we see most in stores are smooth and regularly sized – they are easier to peel. Other knobbly varieties may be a pain to peel, but they're delicious, and a thrill for the potato lover.

When it comes to flavor, the potato doesn't shout for attention either. It's not perfumed like the carrot or the parsnip, and it doesn't have the strong personality of the leek or cabbage. What it does have is a comforting creamy, reassuring taste. It'll always fill you up, and never let you down. But its strongest asset is its versatility. You can boil it, roast it, fry it, bake it, mash it, purée it, and slice it into almost every conceivable shape and thickness. *Larousse Gastronomique* lists at least 60 ways of cooking potatoes (and these are just French recipes).

Different kinds of potatoes

Yes, we demand a lot from the spud. And it's not reasonable to expect one sort of potato to perform so many culinary tricks.

So it's just as well that there are many different varieties, some perfect for making French fries, and others, say, just right for a potato and sausage stew. In fact, there are well over a hundred types regularly grown in the U.K. This is exciting for the cook, but a little bit confusing. How do you know which one to choose? Fortunately, there's a simple way of working it out, because, broadly speaking, all potatoes divide into two basic types, known as "floury" and "waxy." These words pretty accurately describe the texture of the potatoes once they've been cooked. Waxy, or boiling, potatoes are the kind of spuds that tend not to fall apart, even when the going gets tough. Most new potatoes are waxy, at least as long as they remain new – still young, small, and flaky skinned. It makes them suitable for boiling and then eating cold, say, mixed with mayonnaise in a potato salad.

Floury, or baking, potatoes tend to disintegrate into fluffiness when they're cooked, so they're the kind of potatoes you'd use for making mashed, fried, baked, or roast potatoes.

ready for harvest

Project:

GROWING YOUR OWN POTATOES

A potato never looks more beautiful than when you've just found it in the soil. What's more, potatoes taste best when they're at their freshest. A potato that you've just dug out of the ground in June tastes much more interesting than one that's been scrubbed clean, bagged in plastic, and left around in a store for a week or two.

Potatoes belong to a group of vegetables called tubers, which we grow because of what happens beneath the soil rather than above it. They can be grown from seeds taken from the flowers of the plants, but mostly they are grown from other potatoes called seed potatoes. The seed potato is buried in the ground; then it sprouts leaves and flowers (which are inedible) while at the same time growing an underground stem.

Potatoes need darkness, both while they are growing and after they've been dug up, or they turn green, which spoils them for eating and can even make them a bit poisonous. So, as it grows, the soil to the side of the plant has to be dug up and piled on top of it, otherwise the potatoes near the surface of the soil will catch the sunlight and rapidly turn green.

Early spring is the best time of year to plant potatoes. This is when you'll find seed potatoes for sale in garden shops, hardware stores, and through mail order and the Internet (a good place for more unusual varieties). Before you plant the potatoes, it's best if they sit for a few weeks in a not too warm or sunny place, so that the "eyes" (the black bits that you often dig out of potatoes when you peel them) can start to sprout. This is called "chitting." Stand them in an old egg box and just leave them. When the sprouts are about an inch long, the potato is ready to plant.

You will need:
A big old bucket, a trash can, a half-barrel, or another large container, with holes in the bottom to allow water to drain through (you could use 4 or 5 stacked old car tires instead)

Plus:
Some stones to put in the bottom of the container, a large bag of compost or a mixture of soil and compost (some well-rotted farmyard manure is a good idea, too), and 3 or 4 seed potatoes, depending on the size of your container (look for the ones labeled "first early," as these will grow quickly and compactly; Superior is an early white potato and Norland is an early red).

Decide where your container is going to stand for the project, bearing in mind that it'll be there for a couple of months, and that once you've added soil it'll be too heavy to move. Try to put it somewhere you pass frequently, so that you'll remember to water your plants!

Line the bottom of the container (or the space at the bottom of the car tires) with stones. Add a layer of compost about a foot deep and place your seed potatoes on top, leaving space between them. Cover with another foot of soil, or soil and compost mixed, and give the soil a good water.

Watch the plants over the next few weeks, watering them from time to time if there isn't much rain. As they grow, cover them with more compost so that only the tips of the leaves show (or keep adding tires as the soil level rises). When you've reached nearly the top of the container or the last tire, stop adding more soil. Wait for the plants to flower, keeping them well watered as the flower buds appear, because this is when the potatoes are starting to swell beneath the soil.

When the plants are fully flowering (this generally takes between 90 and 100 days), roll up your sleeves and feel about in the container to see if you can find any potatoes big enough to cook. If they still seem very tiny, give them another week or two. If they're ready to harvest, you can either grub about for the potatoes when you need them, or you can tip over the container and harvest your crop in one go. All you need to do is wash them before you cook them – they won't need peeling.

How to eat your potatoes

You've spent some weeks growing your potatoes, you've lifted them out of the soil, what now? You could simply boil or steam them (add a sprig of mint while they're cooking, if you like) until they are tender when you pierce them with a knife, then drain them in a colander and eat them with butter melting over the top.

Or, as new potatoes often appear at the same time as fava beans, boil or steam both vegetables separately until just tender (tiny fava beans will need only a couple of minutes) and fry some strips of bacon in a little butter. Drain the vegetables and mix them with the bacon and plenty of butter for a delicious hot salad.

Some potato recipes

Spanish Omelette, page 106
Best-Ever Mashed Potatoes, page 199
Potatoes with Spinach, page 200
Garlic, Rosemary, and Lemon Potatoes,
   page 203

A SHORT HISTORY OF THE SPUD

No vegetable has had a more dramatic historical journey than the humble spud. From its earliest beginnings in the Andes Mountains of South America, it crossed the Atlantic Ocean with the Spanish explorers in the sixteenth century as they returned to mainland Europe. Mistrusted for hundreds of years as food fit only for pigs and cattle, it eventually became the staple diet of millions of people across the Continent. Yet within the space of just a few decades, it was at the center of one of the most terrible famine disasters in European history, when at least a million people died of starvation and many more fled – strangely enough – to the New World.

From the New World to Europe

Potatoes probably arrived in Europe in the mid-sixteenth century, brought back by Spanish adventurers along with cacao beans (for chocolate), chiles, and peppers. But this versatile tuber didn't catch on as quickly as you might have thought – in fact, it wasn't eaten with any enthusiasm in Europe until the late eighteenth century. The reasons were partly practical: much of the plant couldn't be eaten, as the potato, like the tomato, is related to the very toxic, deadly nightshade plant. They were difficult to store, too. If you leave potatoes in the light they turn green – poisonous and useless. But snobbery also played a role in people's reluctance to eat this earthy vegetable. In much of Europe it was seen as a food for only the very poorest people.

What suddenly changed everybody's minds? The fast-growing and stomach-filling potato was recognized as a food that could save millions of people from the threat of starvation. These days, we take basic foods such as bread and potatoes for granted. But at a time when there was almost constant war in mainland Europe, the threat of famine was very real.

Marketing the potato

Governments became desperate for another basic food – something that would grow fast in cold, wet climates and keep famine, and therefore revolution, at bay. Potatoes seemed to be the answer. But how do you persuade people to grow something they are suspicious of?

There are all sorts of stories about how people throughout Europe were persuaded to grow potatoes. In Paris, wealthy landowners planted fields of

potatoes and put guards around them — but only during the day. Word spread that the *pomme de terre* was now *à la mode*. "*Sacrebleu*, we must grow the potato too!" went the gossip. When the guards disappeared each night, so did the potato plants — to gardens all over France. One governor in Greece took the same cunning approach. He ordered soldiers to guard (although not too well) a huge pile of potatoes near the harbor. In the morning, all the potatoes had gone. In Austria, carts of heavily guarded potatoes were driven through the country towns. Some countries, though, used more simple methods of persuasion. The British just paid farmers a good price to grow them. The King of Prussia threatened to cut off people's noses if they didn't.

It doesn't really matter whether all these stories are true or not. They're interesting because they highlight the reluctance of so many people to accept this extraordinary plant and the lengths that others went to to persuade them.

From miracle to disaster

It's a terrible irony, then, considering the potato was seen as a great solution to the problem of mass starvation, that the failure of the crop should have triggered one of the most terrible famines in history. By the 1840s, the potato was an important crop in many European countries, but nowhere was it more depended upon than in Ireland. When a disease called blight swept across the continent, it devastated many of the potato crops in its path. There was no cure. Potatoes rotted in the field, or decayed into black and stinking messes when they were stored. In Ireland, where most people's diet depended almost entirely on a particular variety of potato that was very susceptible to blight, a million starved to death. A million more emigrated to North America to escape the famine.

And the future?

Research shows that Brits are cooking fewer potatoes than we did 10 or 20 years ago. In part, no doubt, this is because of the recent huge growth in popularity of pasta and pizza — two starchy dishes that hardly ever get served with potatoes. Yet the potato plant grows so happily in our cold, wet climate (and gives us the kind of comforting recipes that are perfect for a chilly British winter) — unlike the wheat that supplies us with most of the flour for that pizza and pasta. So what will our government dream up to get us to change our minds?

THE ONION FAMILY

Browse through most cookbooks (including this one) and you'll find a lot of recipes that start, "Peel and chop an onion." Along with the potato, the onion is one of the few vegetables that most of us buy all year round. It's amazingly versatile, and its flavor is transformed when it meets the heat of the stovetop or the oven.

Raw onions taste sharp and spicy, sometimes giving off enough chemical fumes to make your eyes water. This is perfect if you're making a salsa, where those hot flavors are just what you want, or if you want to unsweeten a salad of, say, really ripe tomatoes with a little oniony bite.

But the flavor changes when you cook them. Stir-fry a sliced onion in hot oil for 5 minutes until it's golden brown and the hotness vanishes to make way for a sweet-but-savory taste that's perfect in stews or, say, with fried lamb's liver. There's a fine line, though, between beautiful golden onions and ones that have suddenly turned black and bitter, so you need to keep an eye on them while they're sizzling.

But the onion's transformation is most extraordinary when it's cooked slowly – roasted in the oven, say, or fried very slowly in a covered pan. Any bitterness almost completely disappears, to be replaced by an amazing sweetness.

The other members of the onion family – garlic, leeks, shallots, and green onions – aren't *quite* as versatile as the simple onion but are still incredibly useful.

Garlic has the strongest flavor of the group, so it's just as well that the bulb, or "head," comes so cleverly packaged – it's easy just to break off one segment, or clove, at a time. Chopped or sliced garlic needs to be cooked quite carefully, as it can start to turn brown and bitter after just a few minutes' gentle frying. Because of this, it's usually added after the other vegetables in a recipe have been frying for some time.

Leeks have a milder flavor than onions and are good roasted, served with creamy sauces, or added to savory tarts. Vichyssoise is a delicious soup made from leeks, potatoes, and stock and is served cold with a little cream. As they are grown deep in the soil, leeks can be muddy and always need careful washing. Make a slit down the length of the leek to the center and run it under the cold tap, making sure the water gets through all the layers to flush out any dirt (see also page 406).

Shallots are like tiny onions, and their small size and mild taste make them very useful for flavoring sauces.

Green onions are generally chopped and added to salads, soups, and stir-fries. Larger ones are delicious barbecued.

Some recipes with onions
Roast Onion Family, page 204
Quick-Fried Onion and Cabbage with
  Black Pepper, page 206
Quick Tomato Salad, page 216

SALADS AND SALAD DRESSINGS

Boil a handful of green beans, drain them, and lay them on a serving plate, and you simply have a plateful of boiled green beans. But boil those beans, drain them, and toss them in a little oil and vinegar, and suddenly you have a salad.

A salad can be just one ingredient dressed in this way or a mixture of several different ingredients. Sometimes, a salad is simply a bowl of mixed green leaves tossed with oil and vinegar, and sometimes it's more substantial – a starchy ingredient such as cracked wheat or chickpeas, mixed with herbs and chopped tomatoes and dressed in olive oil and lemon juice.

A salad dressing is really a liquid seasoning (the word *salad* comes from the Latin *sal*, meaning "salt"). The idea is not to smother your leaves or ingredients with one overwhelming flavor, but to toss them with a dressing that brings different leaves and flavors together while still letting them taste exactly of themselves. It's the same idea with fruit, too – if you've made a proper fruit salad (see page 366), then you'll know what sweet dressing can do for a simple bowl of chopped fruit.

The oil most commonly used for a dressing is extra-virgin olive oil, which is made from the first pressing of the olive. Italian, Spanish, and Greek oils are all easily available and vary a lot in flavor. In fact, different regions of the same country will produce completely different-tasting oils. A really well-flavored oil makes a huge difference to a dressing.

Usually, the smooth texture and flavor of the oil in a dressing is balanced by mixing it with a sharp, acidic liquid – often vinegar. Most of the vinegar that we use for salad dressings comes from either white or red wine (the word *vinegar*, from the French *vin aigre*, simply means "sour wine"). Cider vinegar makes excellent dressings too. Balsamic vinegar comes from sweet, unfermented grape juice and is boiled down until it forms a thick, syrupy liquid that is then aged in wooden barrels. Really good balsamic vinegar should be at least 12 years old and is used by the drop rather than by the spoonful. Lemon juice can play the same role in a dressing as vinegar.

Mayonnaise is an oil and vinegar or lemon dressing made in a slightly different way: the oil is beaten drop by drop into an egg yolk before it is mixed with the lemon or vinegar. This makes a more stable and much thicker sauce, which doesn't separate into oil and watery liquid.

Some salad recipes
Crudités with Garlic Mayonnaise, page 212
Quick Tomato Salad, page 216
A Simple Green Salad, page 218

Project:

GROWING YOUR OWN LITTLE SALAD GARDEN

Our favorite salad vegetables are some of the easiest plants to grow, and you don't need a lot of space either. A sunny windowsill is useful for getting the seedlings started; then you can plant them in the garden or in a large container.

You can start your salad garden any time from April onward. And even if you don't get around to it until the start of the summer holidays, it's still worthwhile. You'll be feasting on your salad before the beginning of the autumn term.

You will need:
A selection of salad seeds – choose half a dozen of your favorites from the following:
Leafy greens (most of these can be harvested a few leaves at a time, then left to keep on growing; look for the phrase "cut and come again" on the seed packets)
Various lettuces (Romaine and butterhead types are always good, but also look out for the "cut and come again" types)
Arugula
Land cress (like watercress, but easy to grow in soil)
Mâche (also known as lamb's lettuce)
Mizuna (a newly popular spicy leaf)
Spinach (choose "perpetual" for a regular supply of baby leaves)
Flat-leaf parsley

Other good salad vegetables, such as green onions, radishes (French Breakfast and Sparkler are good types), beets (for the leaves as well as baby roots), bulb fennel

Plus:
2 or 3 seed trays – the kind divided into individual "plugs," like miniature plant pots, is ideal
Some potting compost, a spray bottle, and a watering can
A small, fairly sunny space in the garden (2 x 1 yards is fine), dug and ready for planting – or, if it's more practical, a large container (at least 16 inches deep), such as an old bathtub, wooden planter, or just a very large, wide flowerpot

Part 1: Sowing the seeds
Fill each seed tray to within $3/8$ inch of the brim with compost. Pat it down as you go, but don't pack it *too* tightly.

Count the number of "plugs," or compartments, you have in your seed trays and divide by the number of different plants you have seeds for. For example, if you've got 24 plugs and 6 different types of seeds, you can have 4 plugs for each seed type.

Carefully, with your fingertips, place 4 or 5 seeds, of one type only, in each plug. Label them so you know what's in each plug. Scatter about $1/4$ inch of compost over the plugs and pat it down gently. Water with a fine spray, then put the seed trays on a sunny windowsill (in April or May) or a sheltered sunny corner of the garden (from June onward). Keep the

plugs well watered (every couple of days should do it). If the trays are on a windowsill, turn them around once or twice a day, or the seedlings may stretch toward the light and become too "leggy" (the stems, too long and spindly, will be weak).

Part 2: Transplanting the seedlings
The seedlings are ready to be transplanted when they look strong and healthy. They should be about 4 inches with a nice clutch of leaves (look for miniature versions of the adult leaves, not just a pair). In some cases, such as fennel and lettuces, it will help to thin out a few of the weaker seedlings, leaving just 2 strong ones in each plug.

Prepare the final growing site – either by digging up and raking a small bed in the garden or by filling your chosen container with compost and/or topsoil.

Choose a shady time of day to transplant your seedlings (don't do it under a scorching sun). Water the trays well and leave for a few minutes, then carefully release each plug of soil with the seedlings in it.

Gently separate the seedlings from each other with your fingertips. Make a small hole in the prepared soil that the roots of your seedling will fit neatly into. Lower the roots into the hole and press the soil gently back around them.

You need to leave enough space between each seedling for the plants to grow without crowding each other. At the same time, you want to grow as much salad as you can. Allow 4 inches between each plant and 8 inches between each row, and you'll be about right.

Keep your salad garden weed-free and well watered.

Part 3: Harvest
Some of your salad can be harvested whole, by pulling up the whole plant: radishes, beets, fennel, and some kinds of lettuce, for example. With others, you can pick or cut the outer leaves as they look ready, leaving the small leaves in the center of the plant to continue growing. This works for arugula, perpetual spinach, and any lettuces or leafy greens described on the seed packet as "cut and come again." Keep picking them, and don't let them form buds and go to seed, and you can go on harvesting all summer and even into the autumn.

Variation: a lazy salad garden

You don't have to grow your seedlings in plugs and then plant them – although it is a very reliable way of raising strong, healthy plants. You can sow any of the above seeds directly into the ground or into your prepared containers. The important thing is to *sow thinly* – no more than a couple of seeds every half inch.

Even then, you should thin out some of the seedlings when they are a few inches high. This means pulling them up to leave more room for a smaller number of plants to continue growing. Don't waste your thinned seedlings, though. You can eat them as a sneak preview of more substantial salads to come.

HERBS

Herb is the word we use to describe leaves from certain plants that are added to other foods to give them flavor. We might tear up a few leaves of basil to mix into a tomato salad, or add a bay leaf to a stew. We might add some herbs to a salad, but generally we don't eat them on their own – they taste too strong.

So, when it comes to herbs, a little goes a long way. Which is great, because just a few plants can supply your kitchen several times a week for much of the year. Some herbs, such as cilantro and basil, need to be sown every spring because they won't survive a cold winter. Others, such as bay, rosemary, sage, and thyme, are perennial plants, which means that once you've got them established they will just keep going year after year. With the stronger-tasting herbs, such as thyme, marjoram, and sage, one plant of each will often do, because you use only a few leaves at a time. However, you'll need to grow more plants of herbs such as parsley and cilantro, because you tend to use them by the fistful. Mint is an easy herb to grow for salads and sauces, but always plant it in a pot – it grows so thickly that it will quickly take over your garden if you put it in a flower bed.

How to use herbs

Roast duck with sage and onion (remember how Jemima Puddleduck was sent by the fox to gather herbs for her own stuffing?), chicken pieces simmered in white wine with tarragon, ham served with parsley sauce, peas with mint, salmon with dill – certain herbs go particularly well with certain foods. You might prepare a leg of lamb for roasting by piercing the skin and poking stalks of rosemary and slivers of garlic into it. You can then serve it up with mint sauce. A traditional pairing like this works particularly well because the strong flavor of the herb "spices up" the fattiness of the meat.

What's really interesting is that by changing the way you use an herb, you switch into the cooking of a different culture. In Britain, we serve roast lamb with a mint sauce and think of it as a traditional British Sunday lunch dish. But grill the lamb on skewers and serve it with a bulgur wheat salad thick with chopped mint and you could be sitting in a café on a bustling street in Damascus.

The best way to find out about herbs is to experiment with them. Rub a leaf between your fingers and smell its distinctive perfume. If you like pasta, make a tomato and butter sauce by simmering together some chopped tomatoes, a finely chopped garlic clove, and a good lump of butter for about 10 minutes, until thickened. Try tearing a handful of basil leaves into the sauce just before you stir it into the cooked and drained pasta. Next time, simmer the sauce with a sprig of oregano or a stalk of rosemary. It will taste quite different.

If you're fond of green salads (see page 218), try growing some lemony-tasting sorrel, plus some peppery land cress and arugula to mix in with the more usual leaves. Sprinkle rosemary spikes and sliced garlic on top of pizza dough (see page 48), then drizzle with olive oil to make Italian focaccia bread. Chopped herbs such as thyme or parsley mixed into soft, salty butter and then chilled are delicious served on top of steaks or grilled chicken breasts. If you added chopped garlic to this herby butter, you could use it for making herby garlic bread.

Some recipes with herbs

Garlic, Rosemary, and Lemon Potatoes, page 203

Pasta with Four Herbs, page 207

Guacamole, page 215

HERBS IN TIMES PAST

Here's the ingredients list for a recipe from 600 years ago: *"Take persel [parsley], sawge [sage], grene garlic, chibolles [spring onion], oynouns, leek, borage, myntes, porrettes [a type of leek], fennel and town cressis, rew, rosemaye, purslayne . . ."*

Only the most daring modern eater would tuck into this salad with gusto – it's so full of pungent flavors. It contains herbs that are popular still, and ones such as rue and purslane that you wouldn't expect to find in your local produce market. The herb patch was the backbone of the medieval kitchen garden, where plants were grown for both food and medicine.

Over the centuries, as more people moved from the country to work in the town, habits changed. Fewer people owned gardens. Herbs became "garnishes" and gave subtle hints of flavor. When the Victorian cookbook writer, Mrs. Beeton, wrote about herbs, she used phrases like "very sparingly" and "for decorative purposes."

This cautious approach to herbs lasted for most of the twentieth century. Until about 20 years ago, only a few herbs, such as parsley and chives, were easy to buy fresh. Most were to be found away from the vegetable aisle on the dried-herb stands – rows of little jars filled with gray-green flakes to be used by the pinch. Dried herbs are still useful occasionally (see page 315), but these days a far wider variety are sold fresh. This is because, with greater opportunities to travel abroad, we've become much more interested in the foods of other countries. Yet many of the herbs that we now associate with the cooking of foreign cultures were quite common in medieval England. Basil is an herb that we think of as being completely Italian, but it was thoroughly "British" in the seventeenth century. How many people in this country had even heard of cilantro 50 years ago? Yet it was growing happily in English kitchen gardens in the thirteenth century.

VEGETABLE STOCK

A vegetable stock is a useful base for all kinds of soups, stews, and risottos. This recipe gives you a rough idea of the vegetables you could use for making stock, but it really comes down to what you have available. Avoid vegetables that might dominate the flavor of the stock, such as parsnips and cabbage. And potatoes will just melt down into a gluey mass, so leave them out, too.

To make about 6 cups:
Carrots, 3 large
Onions, 2
Lettuce, 1 head
Celery, 4 stalks
Leeks, 3
Parsley, 3 big sprigs
Thyme, a handful of sprigs

Bay leaves, 2 or 3
Peppercorns, 5 or 6

Large glass measuring cup, 2 large pans or stockpots (one with a lid), vegetable peeler, cutting board, sharp knife, sieve, ladle

1. Pour 2^1/$_2$ quarts of water into one of the large pans and put it on the stove over high heat.

2. Peel the carrots and onions. Wash the other vegetables. Now, shred the lettuce and finely chop or shred all the other vegetables.

3. Add the vegetables to the pot of water, along with the herbs and peppercorns. Bring to a boil, then turn the heat down and simmer for about 20 minutes with the lid partly on. Don't add salt – save this seasoning for the dish you make with the stock. Turn off the heat.

4. Let the stock cool down for a few minutes so that it's not so ferociously hot, then stand the sieve over another large pan and ladle the hot stock through the sieve so that the vegetables and herbs are caught. Discard the vegetables and herbs. Put the strained stock back on the stove over high heat and boil it hard for 20 minutes to concentrate its flavor.

How to use your stock

This stock can be used to make soups, such as White Winter Soup (page 195), Lentil and Bacon Soup (page 328), and Mushroom Noodle Soup (opposite). It's also perfect for risottos.

Variation: chicken stock

Add the carcass of a roast chicken (or a bag of chicken giblets) to the ingredients in the pan. Skim off any froth that rises to the surface and simmer longer – 2 hours, if possible. Then strain the stock as above.

Both stocks freeze well, and can be concentrated before freezing by boiling hard to reduce the volume. You can then dilute the frozen stock with water when you use it.

MUSHROOM NOODLE SOUP

This is a very simple soup, fragrant with ginger, that's made in one pot.

To serve 4:
Fresh ginger, a 1-inch-long piece
Baby button mushrooms, 8 ounces
Sunflower oil, 3 tablespoons
Vegetable or chicken stock (see opposite),
  6 cups
Soy sauce, 2 tablespoons
Black pepper

Green onions, 5
Medium egg noodles, 6 ounces
Bok choy, 2 heads

*Cutting board, small sharp knife,
tablespoon, large saucepan*

1. Carefully cut the knobbly skin off the ginger with the small sharp knife. Slice the yellow flesh and chop it as finely as you can. Wipe any soil off the button mushrooms with some paper towels. Cut any larger mushrooms in half.

2. Spoon the oil into the pan and turn the stove on low. Add the chopped ginger and the button mushrooms and fry them gently for 10 minutes, stirring from time to time to make sure they don't stick and burn on the bottom of the pan.

3. Pour the stock into the pan along with the soy sauce. Grind in some black pepper. Bring the soup to a boil, turn the heat down, and simmer gently for 20 minutes.

4. Prepare the green onions by cutting off the very tip of the root and peeling off the outer layer. Chop the onions finely and add half of them to the soup, putting the rest to one side. Add the noodles to the soup and simmer for 4 minutes (or according to the instructions on the package) until they are tender.

5. Meanwhile, trim the bok choy by slicing off the tough end (where the leaves are all joined together) and the very tips of the green leaves, which may be a little battered. Cut the bok choy into slices about $3/4$ inch thick and add them to the soup. Cook for 2 minutes or until the bok choy is tender. Sprinkle the remaining green onions into the soup and serve.

How to eat your soup
Ladle the soup into bowls. Give everyone a set of chopsticks and a spoon so they can alternate between picking up the noodles and slurping up the soup.

WHITE WINTER SOUP

This creamy soup uses five of the best winter vegetables, and it's very easy to make. Don't worry about precise quantities, but use the list here as a rough guide.

To serve 6 to 8:
Onion, 1
Leeks, 3 medium
Butter, 2 tablespoons
Sunflower or canola oil, 1 tablespoon
Potatoes, 1 large or 2 medium (about 8 ounces)
Cauliflower, 1 small (about 1 pound)
Celery root, ½ head (about 12 ounces once peeled)

Vegetable or chicken stock, about 3½ cups
Salt and black pepper
Whole milk, about 1 cup
Heavy cream, ½ cup

Cutting board, sharp knife, large heavy saucepan with lid, vegetable peeler, large glass measuring cup, wooden spoon, blender, ladle

1. Peel and chop the onion. Clean the leeks (see page 406) and slice them about ³/₈ inch thick.

2. Put the butter and oil in the saucepan and turn the heat on low. Add the onion and leeks, cover, and cook the vegetables gently for a few minutes so that they soften.

3. Peel the potatoes and cut into small cubes. Cut the thick stem out of the cauliflower and discard it. Break the cauliflower into florets.

4. At the last minute, peel the celery root thickly so that you're left with just the white flesh (like a banana, celeriac turns brown very quickly once it's been cut). Chop this into cubes and add to the pan, with the cauliflower and potatoes – as well as the stock, a pinch of salt, and a twist of pepper. Stir well and bring to a boil, then reduce the heat and simmer gently until all the vegetables are tender; 15 minutes should be enough.

5. Stir in the cold milk, then turn off the heat and let the soup cool for at least 15 minutes. Purée the soup in the blender a few ladlefuls at a time. You can either reheat it now, to serve immediately, or chill it in the fridge and use within 5 days.

6. Return the blended soup to the pan, stir in the cream, and reheat gently but thoroughly. It doesn't need to boil again, but it should be piping hot. Check the seasoning and add more salt and pepper if necessary.

How to eat your soup
Serve just as it is or, if you like, with an extra little swirl of cream and some chopped chives. Some bread would be nice, too.

PICK-YOUR-OWN MINESTRONE

This is a great summer soup, which, if you can get your hands on a good selection of vegetables, is practically a meal in itself. There are two variations on the theme: one where you pick all the veggies yourself from your own garden (or a friend's); the other where you choose all the best seasonal vegetables from a good produce market or farmers' market.

The ingredients below are just a list of "desirable" vegetables for a midsummer version of the dish. If you can lay your hands on 6 or more of the vegetables listed, you're doing well. The onions and tomatoes are essential, but you could cheat with the tomatoes, if you like, by using a can of good-quality chopped tomatoes.

To serve 6:
Onions, 1 to 2
Garlic, 2 cloves
Carrots, 3 to 4 medium
Beets, 2 medium
Potatoes, 3 to 4 large
Zucchini, 3 to 4 medium
Cabbage, ¼ to ½
Spinach or chard, 2 good fistfuls
Peas, 20 pods (or cheat with about ¾ cup frozen peas)
Shelling beans (borlotti or cranberry)
Green or runner beans, 2 good handfuls
Tomatoes, 3 to 4 large

Olive oil, 3 tablespoons, plus extra for drizzling
Water, 2 cups
Salt and black pepper

To finish:
About 1 cup pasta shapes (something small, such as macaroni, is ideal)

Cutting board, sharp knife, vegetable peeler, large bowl, medium saucepan, large heavy saucepan with a lid, wooden spoon, sieve, tablespoon

1. First, wash and prepare all the vegetables. The onions should be peeled and chopped fairly fine and the garlic even finer. The hard roots, such as carrots, beets, and potatoes, should be peeled and cut into small dice. Cut the zucchini into thick disks and then cut them in half. The leafy vegetables, such as cabbage and spinach or chard, should be washed and finely shredded. Shell the peas and shelling beans, then top and tail the young beans and cut

them into short lengths. It's nice to do all this vegetable preparation as a team job – outside, if it's a fine day.

2. Only the tomatoes require any special treatment. Nick the skin of each one with a sharp knife and put them in the bowl. Pour over boiling water from the kettle, leave them for a minute or so (less if they're really ripe), then drain away the water. Leave them a minute to

... ther ...

... and dig

op ...

... and shell

ok ...

... and eat

cool down, then peel off the skins. Chop the tomatoes coarsely.

3. Fill the medium saucepan three-quarters full with water and bring it to a boil for cooking the pasta.

4. Meanwhile, put the large pan on the stove and add the olive oil. Turn the heat to low and add the garlic and onions. Put on the lid and cook them very gently for 5 to 10 minutes, until softened. Stir in the tomatoes and cook gently, stirring occasionally with the wooden spoon, until the mixture is thick and pulpy.

5. Add the cold water and a good pinch of salt, raise the heat, and bring to a boil. Now add all the other vegetables. Add a little boiling water if you need to – the vegetables should be just covered. If you're using frozen peas, bring them to a boil in a little water in a separate pan and add them, water and all, to the other veggies. Bring back to a boil and simmer for 10 to 12 minutes, stirring frequently so that all the vegetables are well mixed and cook evenly.

6. When the pasta water is boiling, add a good teaspoon of salt and then the pasta. Taste the pasta a minute or two before the cooking time on the packet is up, and, when you think it is ready, carefully drain it into the sieve.

7. The soup is ready when the carrots and beets are tender, but only just. Stir in the cooked pasta. Scoop up a little of the soup in a tablespoon, blow on it to cool it down, then taste it. Add some salt and pepper to taste. Serve immediately, with a little olive oil drizzled over each bowlful.

How to eat your minestrone
Serve with crusty bread for dipping and, if you like, a hard cheese such as Parmesan for grating over it.

BEST-EVER MASHED POTATOES

Mashed potatoes are one of the most important things to learn to make really well. There's an enormous difference between these creamy, buttery potatoes and mashed potatoes made with just a drop of cold milk and a scrap of butter.

If you want to make really smooth, creamy mashed potatoes, you'll need to use potatoes with a floury texture, which break up a little as they boil, giving you a fluffy consistency when you mash them so that they soak up the butter and hot milk. You can make mashed potatoes with waxy potatoes too, but it will be more like a smooth purée than a fluffy pile of whiteness.

To serve 4 to 6:

Large baking potatoes, 2 pounds
Whole milk, 1 cup
Butter, at least 3 tablespoons, taken out of
    the fridge so it's soft
Sea salt and black pepper

*Vegetable peeler, cutting board,
sharp knife, medium saucepan, teaspoon,
colander, large glass measuring cup,
small saucepan, potato masher or ricer,
wooden spoon*

1. Peel the potatoes and cut them into large, even-sized chunks. Place them in the medium saucepan. Add enough cold water just to cover the potatoes, then put the pan on the stove, turn the heat to high, and bring to a boil. Add a teaspoon of salt to the pan.

2. Reduce the heat and simmer the potatoes for 10 to 15 minutes. Test to see if they are tender by piercing one of them with a knife; if the knife slips in easily, they are done. If the center still feels hard, give them a few more minutes before trying again. Turn off the heat and stand the colander in the sink.

3. Drain the potatoes into the colander and let them sit for a few minutes. This helps to make sure they're not too watery. Meanwhile, heat

the milk in the small saucepan over medium heat until it just starts to steam.

4. Return the potatoes to the dry saucepan. Start to mash them and break them down. Add about three-quarters of the hot milk and all the butter, and mash again. Mix in the rest of the milk if needed. (Or you could press the potatoes through a potato ricer a few at a time and then stir in the butter and hot milk.)

5. Grind in some black pepper and add a little sea salt, stir and then taste, and keep tasting until the potatoes are as salty and peppery as you want.

How to eat your mashed potatoes

Really good mashed potatoes are almost delicious enough to eat on their own, but you'll probably want to eat them with some sausages, on top of a cottage or shepherd's pie, with a roast chicken and lots of gravy, or soaking up the juices from a big, meaty stew.

Variations

You can add other things to your mashed potatoes if you feel the urge. How about a tablespoon or two of grated Parmesan or some chopped parsley? Grinding nutmeg into the potatoes makes them taste very good, too.

. . . .

POTATOES WITH SPINACH

This is a simple version of the Indian dish, sag aloo – crisp-skinned, fluffy potatoes mixed with a little spinach and some cumin seeds.

To serve 4 to 6:
Baking potatoes, 1½ pounds
Sunflower or olive oil, 3 tablespoons
Fresh spinach, 1 pound
Cumin seeds, 1 teaspoon
Salt and black pepper
Lemon, ½

Cutting board, sharp knife, tablespoon, roasting pan, metal spatula, large saucepan with lid, sieve or potato ricer, potato masher or tablespoon, teaspoon, wooden spoon, serving bowl

1. Preheat the oven to 425°F. Wash the potatoes and dry them well on a tea towel. Don't peel them, but chop them into pieces roughly the size of large dice.

2. Measure the oil into the roasting pan and toss the potatoes so that they're well covered. Oven gloves on. Put the pan in the oven. After 15 minutes, put on your oven gloves again, take

the pan out, and carefully turn the potatoes over with the metal sptaula. Then return thcm to the oven for another 10 minutes or so, until they're golden brown and crisp.

3. Meanwhile, prepare the spinach. If the leaves are large, fold each one in half and tear out the coarse stalk. Put the leaves in the washing-up bowl, turn on the cold water, and wash the leaves 2 or 3 times. Drain away the water completely, so that only the water clinging to the leaves is left.

4. Put the spinach in the saucepan, put the lid on the pan, and the pan on the stove. Turn the heat to medium and let the spinach wilt down as the water on (and in) the leaves turns to steam. After 3 or 4 minutes, take the lid off and you'll see that the pile of spinach has gone, shrunk as if by magic to just a few tablespoons of dark green pulp.

5. Take the pan off the heat, let the spinach cool for a few minutes, and then spoon it into a sieve or potato ricer. Press as much of the watcr out as possible, so that the spinach feels reasonably dry (you can do this with a potato masher or the back of a tablespoon if you're using a sieve). Then chop the spinach coarsely with the sharp knife.

6. When the potatoes are ready, carefully take the very hot pan out of the oven and place it on the stove. Turn the heat to low. Scatter in the cumin seeds and stir these around the pan for a minute or two with the wooden spoon. Then add the chopped spinach and stir this in too, so that it picks up some of the oil in the pan and mixes with the cumin seeds and crisp potatoes. Grind in some salt and pepper and squeeze in the juice from the lemon half.

7. Turn the heat off and, with the metal spatula, transfer the spinachy potatoes to a warm bowl for serving.

How to eat your potatoes

You could eat these potatoes with chicken curry, rice, and cucumber raita (see pages 298, 324, and 83), but you don't have to keep them for an Indian-inspired feast; they'd be tasty with the Spicy Bean Stew with Sausages (page 330) too. And they even make a pretty fine supper on their own.

GARLIC, ROSEMARY, AND LEMON POTATOES

This recipe shows that the rules of potato cooking are not entirely fixed. For example, you can make roast potatoes with new as well as old potatoes. The kind of traditional roast potatoes that go with the Sunday roast – fluffy inside, crispy outside – are always made with baking potatoes. But a panful of boiling potatoes, cut into thick slices or quarters, can be roasted in the oven in olive oil with garlic, rosemary, and a few drops of lemon juice until they're brown and fragrant, chewy rather than crispy.

To serve 4 to 6:
Small boiling (waxy) potatoes, 1½ pounds
A whole head of garlic
A few sprigs of rosemary
Olive oil, 3 tablespoons
Salt and black pepper
Lemon, 1

Cutting board, sharp knife, tablespoon, roasting pan, wooden spoon, slotted spoon, serving dish

1. Preheat the oven to 425°F.

2. Wash the potatoes if they are muddy, then dry them well on a tea towel – no need to peel them. Cut into halves or quarters, depending on their size. Separate the head of garlic into cloves and tear away any of the loose papery wrapper (no need to peel the cloves). Break the rosemary sprigs up into little pieces.

3. Spoon the oil into the roasting pan. Add the potatoes, garlic cloves, and rosemary into the pan and stir them around with the wooden spoon so that they are well covered in the oil. Grind in some salt and pepper and squeeze the juice of half the lemon over the potatoes.

4. Oven gloves on. Place the pan in the center of the preheated oven. Roast for 15 minutes, then put the oven gloves on again, carefully get out the pan, and stir the potatoes around with the wooden spoon. Put the pan back in the oven and leave for another 10 to 15 minutes, then remove and stir again. Return to the oven until the potatoes are golden on the outside and soft inside (5 to 10 minutes more).

5. Using the slotted spoon, transfer the potatoes to a warm serving dish and sprinkle with a little salt just before you serve them.

How to eat your potatoes

If you like really lemony potatoes, you could sprinkle the juice of the other half of the lemon over them just as you're about to eat them. Squeeze out all the delectable softened flesh from the paper wrapper of the roasted garlic. You could eat these potatoes with all sorts of things, but they're especially good with lamb chops, kebabs, or sausages.

ROAST ONION FAMILY

Although these vegetables are members of the same family, roast them in a pan together and you'll find that they all taste a little different – some mild, some slightly stronger. But what they do have in common is that they all taste remarkably sweet. This is because the heat of the oven brings out the natural sugars in the onions. As the vegetables aren't peeled, they steam in their own skins and stay really moist and tender.

To serve 4 as a side dish:

Red onions, 4
Olive oil, 3 tablespoons
Leeks, 4
Shallots, 8
Garlic cloves, 8
Bay leaves, 4
Salt and black pepper

Cutting board, sharp serrated knife, tablespoon, roasting pan, sharp knife, paper towels, wooden spoon, slotted spoon, large serving plate

1. Preheat the oven to 425°F.

2. Pull away any loose, papery outer layers around the red onions, but leave the skin on. With the sharp serrated knife, make a cross in the top of each onion through the topknot, about $1^1/_2$ inches deep.

3. Spoon the oil into the roasting pan. Add the red onions and roll them gently around in the pan to coat them in the oil. Oven gloves on. Put the pan in the oven and leave for 10 minutes.

4. Meanwhile, prepare the other members of the onion family. With the sharp knife, cut the root part off the leeks. Cut away most of the green part of each leek — you just need the long, slim white part. Wash them under the tap. If your leeks look very muddy, you'll have to run

a knife down the length of each one to cut it open, but only cut halfway through – you don't want to actually cut it in half if you can help it. Rinse the leeks under the tap and pat them dry with paper towels as well as you can. Pull any loose papery wrapper off the shallots and the garlic, but otherwise leave them unpeeled.

5. When the red onions have been in the oven for 10 minutes, turn the temperature down to 400°F. Put on your oven gloves and carefully take the pan out of the oven. The onions should have started to sizzle and the top parts to open up like a tulip. Add the leeks, shallots, and garlic cloves to the pan and stir them around gently with the wooden spoon to pick up some of the oil. Carefully tuck a bay leaf into the opened-out part of each red onion. Grind a little salt and some black pepper over

the vegetables and return the pan to the oven for another 10 minutes.

6. Oven gloves on as before. Take the pan out, stir all the vegetables gently around, and return the pan to the oven. If at any point you think that the vegetables are getting too blackened, turn the oven down. Set the timer for yet another 10 minutes.

7. Keep checking and stirring the vegetables every 10 minutes until, when you poke a knife into a red onion, it seems reasonably soft and cooked. The red onions will probably need 35 to 40 minutes in the oven, while the other vegetables will take only 25 to 35 minutes.

8. Use the slotted spoon to transfer the roasted vegetables to a warm serving plate. Grind a little more salt and pepper over them.

How to eat your onions

These onions are very good with sausage and mashed potatoes, with a simple roast chicken, or with slices of goat cheese melted on top. Make sure when you serve them that everyone gets at least one of every member of the family – leek, onion, shallot, and garlic. Peel back the coarse, papery layers of each vegetable, and inside you'll find a nugget of oniony flesh tasting quite different from the others. Which do you like best?

QUICK-FRIED ONION AND CABBAGE WITH BLACK PEPPER

In this recipe, the onion is fried quite fast before the cabbage is added, and *lots* of black pepper is ground in. This is a really tasty way of eating cabbage – no wateriness, no stale cabbagey smells . . . just delicious.

To serve 4 to 6 as a side dish:
Onions, 2 medium
Green or savoy cabbage, ½
Sunflower oil, 3 tablespoons
Sea salt and black pepper

Cutting board, sharp knife, plate, tablespoon, heavy frying pan, wooden spoon

1. Peel the onions, cut them in half from top to bottom, and slice them thinly. Put them on a plate while you prepare the cabbage.

2. Peel off the outer couple of layers of cabbage, which may be tough and a bit scraggy. Cut the half cabbage in half again and then cut these quarters into eighths. Cut away the thick core, then slice the cabbage into fine ribbons.

3. Pour the oil into the frying pan, turn the heat to medium, and let the oil heat for half a minute or so. Add the onion slices and stir them around with the wooden spoon. The heat should be enough for a good sizzle but not so ferocious that the onions brown too quickly. Fry the onions, stirring often, until they are lightly browned and starting to wilt – 5 to 6 minutes.

4. Add the sliced cabbage and stir well. Grind in plenty of black pepper and some sea salt and fry the vegetables, stirring every few seconds. After a couple of minutes, you'll notice that the cabbage starts to wilt down. Grind in some more black pepper. Keep frying and stirring for 8 to 10 minutes, until the onions and cabbage have shrunk down in the pan and both are shiny with oil. Taste the cabbage and make sure that it is tender. Fry a little longer if it still seems a bit tough, stirring often.

How to eat your onion and cabbage
Cabbage dishes like these always seem to go very well with pork – try roast pork, sausages, baked ham, or grilled chops.

PASTA WITH FOUR HERBS

This recipe uses generous amounts of four quite strong herbs, yet none of them seems to overpower with its taste. You can make this dish in the time it takes to boil a pan of pasta. If you prefer, you could toss the sauce with a batch of fresh pasta (see page 30). Remember, though, that fresh pasta cooks much more quickly than dried; start tasting it after about a minute's cooking.

To serve 4:
Fresh rosemary, flat-leaf parsley, thyme, and basil, a handful of each
Butter, 6 tablespoons
Spaghetti or dried tagliatelle, 12 ounces
Salt and black pepper
Freshly grated Parmesan cheese, to serve

Large saucepan, cutting board, sharp knife, grater, small bowl, small saucepan, wooden spoon, colander

1. Fill the large saucepan three-quarters full with water and bring to a boil on the stove.

2. Meanwhile, deal with the herbs. Pull the rosemary needles off their coarse stems and cut the thick stems off of the parsley. Strip the little thyme leaves off the stems. Pull the basil leaves off the stems. Chop the leaves of all four herbs finely. You'll need about a heaping tablespoonful each of chopped rosemary, parsley, and basil leaves and about a heaping teaspoon of thyme.

3. Grate some Parmesan cheese into the small bowl and set it on the table.

4. Put the butter in the small saucepan, place it on the stove, and melt it very gently over low heat. It should barely sizzle. Add the herbs to the butter, stir them around in the pan with the wooden spoon for a few seconds, and turn off the heat. Let the herbs sit in the butter while you cook the pasta.

5. Add a tablespoonful of salt to the boiling pasta water, then add the pasta. Set the colander in the sink, and when the pasta is just cooked (usually about a minute less than it says on the package, but check by tasting a strand), very carefully pour it into the colander. As soon as the water has drained away, pour the pasta back into the pan. Add the buttery herbs to the pasta, grind in salt and black pepper, and stir well.

How to eat your pasta
Serve the pasta straight away in bowls and pass around the Parmesan at the table.

GREEN PEAS WITH ROASTED RED PEPPERS AND CHORIZO

This is a fun recipe that features three popular but completely different vegetables – onion, peas, and peppers – coming together in one deliciously sweet and spicy dish.

To serve 4:
Red bell peppers, 3
Onion, 1
Olive oil, ¼ cup
Spanish chorizo sausage, 3 ounces
Frozen petits pois, 12 ounces
Salt and black pepper

Small roasting pan, tongs or long-handled spoon, medium bowl, plastic wrap, chopping board, sharp knife, tablespoon, frying pan with lid, wooden spoon

1. Preheat the broiler to medium. Put the peppers in the roasting pan and place them under the hot broiler. Cook, turning frequently with tongs or a long-handled spoon, for about 5 minutes, until they have charred spots on all sides. Turn off the broiler and carefully add the peppers into the bowl using tongs. Cover the bowl with plastic wrap and set it aside to let the peppers cool down.

2. While the peppers are cooling, peel the onion and chop it.

3. Tear the blackened skin away from the peppers. Slice the flesh into narrow strips, throwing away the seeds, stems, and long white veins inside.

4. Spoon the oil into the frying pan and add the onion and peppers and a sprinkling of salt. Stir everything together with the wooden spoon, then turn on the heat to low, cover the pan with a lid, and fry the vegetables very gently for 10 minutes, stirring occasionally and keeping an eagle eye on the pan to make sure the onion doesn't burn.

5. Meanwhile, peel off the papery outside of the chorizo sausage and cut the sausage into thin slices. If the sausage is the fatter sort, you'll need to cut each slice into fourths. Add the sausage to the pan, put the lid back on, and cook gently, stirring from time to time, for about another 15 minutes, until the peppers have shrunk in the pan and the onion is very soft.

6. Add the frozen petits pois and some freshly ground black pepper. Stir well. Turn up the heat until the liquid in the pan starts to sizzle, then put the lid back on the pan, turn the heat down again, and cook gently for another 10 to 15 minutes or so, until the peas are just tender. Serve straight away.

How to eat your peas

One of the nicest ways to eat this dish is to serve it with a poached egg on top (see page 102). Or you could follow the recipe for Potatoes with Spinach on page 200, leaving out the spinach and just seasoning the potatoes with salt and plenty of black pepper. The peas and red peppers are also very good cold the next day, if you have any left over. Pass around some good crusty bread.

. . . .

VEGETABLE FRITTERS

Fritters are chunks of food that have been dipped in batter and fried until golden and crisp. These dainty little fritters are filled with chopped vegetables and herbs. We've suggested two fillings here – corn and spinach, and mushroom and parsley – but once you've got the idea of cooking them, why not invent your own fillings? Just take care with wet ingredients such as tomatoes, which can make the oil spit as you fry them.

To serve 4:
Free-range egg, 1
Cold water, ½ cup (run the tap for a few seconds so the water is really cold)
All-purpose or white pastry flour, ¼ cup
Cornstarch, ⅓ cup
Sunflower oil for frying
Salt and black pepper

For the fillings:
Frozen, fresh, or canned corn kernels, 2 tablespoons
Fresh spinach leaves, a handful
Button mushrooms, 8 to 10
Flat-leaf parsley, a handful

To serve:
Greek yogurt, 3 to 4 tablespoons
Salt and black peper
Ground cumin, for sprinkling
A lemon

Small saucepan, sieve, 3 small bowls, cutting board, sharp knife, mixing bowl, balloon whisk, large plate, paper towels, small plate, heavy frying pan, tablespoon, slotted spoon, metal spatula

1. Prepare the fillings first. If you're using fresh or frozen corn, bring a small saucepan of water to a boil, add the corn, and simmer for 3 minutes, then drain through a sieve and place in a small bowl. (It's very important to boil frozen corn first or you'll find that the corn starts popping as it fries in the hot oil!) If you're using canned corn, drain off the liquid and add the corn to a small bowl.

2. Wash the spinach and remove any tough stems that run through the center of the leaves: to do this, fold each leaf in half and tear out the stem. Dry the spinach thoroughly. Pile the leaves on top of each other on the chopping board and chop them finely. Mix with the corn in the bowl. Season with plenty of black pepper.

3. Chop the mushrooms very finely (just a bit smaller than the corn), then chop the parsley leaves quite finely, cutting away any tough stems. Put these into another bowl and mix them well together. Season with plenty of black pepper.

4. Spoon the Greek yogurt into a small bowl and stir in some salt and pepper. Sprinkle a little ground cumin on top.

5. Make the batter. Break the egg into the mixing bowl and add the water, the flour, and the cornstarch. Grind in plenty of salt and pepper. Whisk well until the mixture is smooth and creamy.

6. Line the large plate with at least 2 sheets of paper towels and put it next to the stove. Cut the lemon into quarters and put it on the small plate on the table.

7. Put the frying pan on the stove, add 3 tablespoons of sunflower oil, and turn the heat to medium. Meanwhile, add half the batter to each bowl of filling and mix together well. As soon as the oil begins to smoke, pick up about 2 teaspoons of the batter mix with the slotted spoon, letting the excess batter drain off into the bowl. Drop the mixture into the pan and flatten with the back of the spoon. Repeat to make 3 or 4 more fritters. You only need the very smallest amount of batter to vegetable — just enough to hold the fritters together.

8. Fry for 1 to 2 minutes, until the bottom of the fritters is golden brown. Flip the fritters over with the metal spatula and fry the other side until golden. Then use the spatula to transfer the fritters to the plate lined with paper towels, which will absorb any excess oil.

9. Cook the rest of the fritters in the same way. You may need to add more oil to the pan from time to time. Make sure that the oil is fairly hot before you fry the fritters or they'll be stodgy. Remember to turn off the heat after you've cooked the last one.

How to eat your vegetable fritters

These fritters make a nice quick lunch served with some fresh bread and other snacky foods, such as hummus (see page 333) and olives. They'll be fiercely hot to begin with, so let the fritters cool down for just a minute or two before you dip them into the slightly spicy yogurt sauce.

CRUDITÉS WITH GARLIC MAYONNAISE

If you've been tempted to grow some vegetables, this would be a good way to serve them. Garlic mayonnaise is also known as *aioli*. Note that it contains raw eggs (see page 88).

Mayonnaise is easy enough to make, but it does need a lot of whisking, which is tiring, so it's a good idea to make it with someone and take turns wielding the whisk. It's very important that all the ingredients be at room temperature before you start to make mayonnaise, not cold from the fridge, so that there's much less risk of the mayonnaise curdling. Once made, however, mayonnaise must always be put straight into the fridge.

You will need:
A selection of young, tender vegetables,
   such as carrots, radishes, celery,
   cherry tomatoes, and cucumber

For the mayonnaise:
Garlic, 2 cloves
A pinch of salt
Free-range egg yolks, 2 (see page 88
   for details of how to separate eggs)
A pinch of mustard powder

A sprinkling of ground white pepper
Olive oil, ¾ cup (ordinary olive oil is fine,
   not extra-virgin)
Lemon juice, 2 tablespoons

*Cutting board, knife, small mixing bowl,
balloon whisk, small glass measuring cup,
damp cloth, teaspoon, plastic wrap,
vegetable peeler, large serving plate*

1. Peel the garlic, then put it on the cutting board with the pinch of salt and crush it to a rough paste with the side of the knife blade. Scrape it into the small bowl.

2. Add the egg yolks, mustard powder, and white pepper. Whisk everything together with the balloon whisk.

3. Measure out the olive oil in the measuring cup. Stand the mixing bowl on the damp cloth to prevent it from moving around the work surface, and carefully drip just ½ teaspoon of oil into the egg mixture. Whisk it in. Add another ½ teaspoon and whisk again. Keep adding the oil, ½ teaspoon at a time, whisking it in well before you add more. You'll notice that, as you add the oil, the mixture starts to thicken. Oil and water poured into a bowl together would normally separate into layers. But when the oil is whisked into a fatty liquid, such as an egg yolk, just a drop at a time, a thick mixture called an emulsion is formed. This is because the proteins in the egg yolk break down the oil drops into tiny, more stable little droplets. (If at any stage the worst happens and your mayonnaise breaks – which is hard to describe, but you'll know when it happens – start again with a new bowl and a fresh egg yolk and whisk in your broken mixture a little at a time.)

4. When you have used about $1^1/_2$ tablespoons of the oil, you can start to drip in a little more oil at a time, still from the teaspoon.

5. After you have used $^1/_2$ cup of the oil, whisk in a tablespoon of lemon juice. This will turn the mayonnaise much paler. It also makes the emulsion more stable and less likely to break because you have rebalanced the amount of watery liquid to oil. You can now add the oil a teaspoonful at a time but still whisk it between spoonfuls. After $^2/_3$ cup, you can add the oil a couple of teaspoons at a time.

6. When all the oil has been whisked in, mix in the second tablespoon of lemon juice. Taste the mayonnaise and add more salt and pepper if you think it needs it.

7. Cover the bowl with plastic wrap and put it straight into the fridge until you're ready to serve it.

8. Prepare the crudités. Cut off most of the frondy leaves from the carrots, leaving just an inch of stalk at the top. Peel the carrots with the vegetable peeler and wash them well in cold water, nipping off any stringy bits that hang from the tip of the carrot. Top, tail, and wash the radishes in the same way. Wash and trim the celery stalks and wipe the tomatoes clean. Wash the cucumber and cut off the ends. Slice it in half lengthwise so that you end up with 2 long pieces. Using a teaspoon, scoop out the seeds in the middle all the way along the cucumber and throw them away. Cut the cucumber into long strips.

9. Put the bowl of mayonnaise in the center of the largest plate you can find, arrange the vegetable crudités around the bowl, and serve straight away.

How to eat your crudités

This dish is a lovely way to start an early-summer lunch or supper, particularly if the weather is nice enough to sit outside. Just put the dish in the middle of the table and let everyone help themselves to the crudités, using them to scoop up the tasty sauce.

Or you could boil some new potatoes and toss them in some of the garlic mayonnaise to make an extra-special potato salad.

GUACAMOLE

Guacamole is a dip from Mexico, made by mashing ripe avocados with some very distinctive flavorings. You can tell when an avocado is ripe by pressing the stalk end gently with your finger. The flesh should give a little. If it seems rock hard, ripen it for a couple of days at room temperature, or on a sunny windowsill.

Jalapeño chiles vary in strength. Some are very mild, some much hotter, so always add chile a little at a time. Handle them carefully – in particular, never touch your eyes after chopping a chile or they will sting very badly! Either pin down your chile with a fork while cutting it up or wear rubber gloves.

To serve 4 to 6:
Avocados, 2 ripe ones
Lime, 1
Tomatoes, 2 medium
Jalapeño chile, 1 (optional)

Cilantro leaves, a small handful
Salt and black pepper

Sharp knife, cutting board, tablespoon, shallow bowl, fork, citrus juicer

1. Using the sharp knife, cut each avocado in half from top to bottom, slicing around the pit in the middle. Twist the halves apart and take out the slippery pit.

2. Spoon out the flesh of the avocado into the shallow bowl. Mash it well with the fork. Cut the lime in half, squeeze out the juice from one half, and mix this into the avocado flesh straight away to stop it turning brown.

3. Slice the tomatoes in half, then scoop out and throw away the seeds. Chop the tomato flesh as small as you can. Chop the jalapeño chile, holding it down with a fork and slicing the flesh of the chile away from the cluster of hot bitter seeds in the middle. Throw the seeds away. Mix the tomatoes and a little of the chile flesh into the avocado.

4. Chop the cilantro, cutting away any tough stalks, and stir it into the mixture with some salt and pepper. Taste the guacamole and add more lime juice or chile if you want to.

How to eat your guacamole

Use corn chips to scoop up dollops of guacamole, or warm some pita bread in the oven or toaster for a few minutes and use this instead. Crunchy vegetables such as carrots, celery, and cucumber taste delicious with it, too. Or you could roll the guacamole up in a tortilla (see page 38) with some spicy meat stew and sour cream.

QUICK TOMATO SALAD

Usually, tomatoes are dressed in olive oil or a mixture of olive oil and vinegar. This recipe uses no oil at all – just the tiniest amount of balsamic vinegar to bring out their natural sweetness.

To serve 2:
Ripe tomatoes, 2 to 3 medium ones
   (or 12 to 14 cherry tomatoes)
A little red onion
Salt and black pepper
A few basil leaves
A few drops of balsamic vinegar

Shallow bowl, sharp serrated knife, cutting board, serving bowl, glass, teaspoon

1. If you keep your tomatoes in the fridge, get them out at least a couple of hours before you want to eat them (even good tomatoes don't taste of much when fridge-cold). Spread them out in a single layer in the shallow bowl and leave them on a sunny windowsill or somewhere warm, to come up to room temperature.

2. Wipe the tomatoes with a clean, damp cloth, pulling off the stems as you wipe, then cut a slice off one of them. Taste and you'll be able to see how sweet they are. Thickly slice the rest of the tomatoes with the serrated knife (or cut them into quarters if they are little cherry ones) and transfer them to the serving bowl. Add the juices that collect on the chopping board to the bowl, too.

3. Chop a little red onion as finely as you can. How much onion to add to your tomatoes depends on several things: first, how much you like raw onion! But it also depends on how sweet the fruits are – the sweeter the tomato, the more onion you can get away with. Grind in a little salt and pepper, then gently stir the tomatoes and onion together so that they're really well mixed.

4. Tear a few basil leaves into pieces with your fingers and add these to the salad.

5. Uncap the balsamic vinegar and very carefully pour out a little into a glass. Take a few drops of the vinegar in a teaspoon and, little by little, stir it into the tomato and onion mixture. Sample all the time. The vinegar doesn't taste that sour – in fact, it makes the tomatoes really sweet. You'll probably end up using only about a teaspoonful.

How to eat your salad
Tomato salads like this one taste delicious with creamy foods, such as Spaghetti Carbonara (see page 51), but you could simply eat it on its own with plenty of good crusty bread.

A SIMPLE GREEN SALAD

This salad is dressed with a simple, all-purpose oil and lemon dressing but, just as different people like different amounts of salt or pepper in their food, you may well find that everybody in your family has their own ideas about what makes a really good dressing for a green salad. Your idea of a perfect oil and vinegar dressing may be just a bit too vinegary for someone else.

The solution? Experiment during the meal. Bring the bottles to the table. Include a good olive oil and red, white, and balsamic vinegars. Cut a lemon into quarters and put it on a plate. Get the salt and pepper grinders. Fill a big bowl with salad leaves, give everyone a little side bowl, and then they can make their own dressing. Try everyone else's dressing to see what you think.

You will need:

A selection of salad greens, for example:
Romaine or leaf lettuce
   (incredibly easy to grow)
Watercress
Mâche (also known as Lamb's lettuce)
Baby spinach
Arugula (this tastes quite peppery and hot)
Radicchio

For the dressing (unless you are letting everyone dress their own salad):
Lemon juice, 1 tablespoon
Salt and black pepper
Fruity extra-virgin olive oil, 3 tablespoons

Large bowl, salad spinner (or colander and tea towel), serving bowl, tablespoon, fork, salad servers

1. Fill the large bowl with icy-cold water, add your salad greens, and gently swirl them around in the water for a few seconds. Pick over the leaves for any insects, snails, or slugs.

2. Drain the greens, putting them straight into a salad spinner, if you have one. If you don't, drain them in a colander, then pile them on a clean tea towel, firmly gather up the corners, and whirl it like a lasso above your head. You have sort of become your own salad spinner.

3. Unwrap the greens, then either add them to the serving bowl and put it on the table (if you want everyone to do their own thing), or leave them in the tea towel while you prepare a "universal" dressing.

4. To make a very simple basic dressing, put the lemon juice in the serving bowl and grind in some salt and black pepper. Whisk these together with the fork, then add the extra-virgin olive oil. The oil will just sit on top of the lemon juice, so you have to make them blend together temporarily by whisking them. As soon as the dressing turns cloudy, add the greens to the bowl and turn them in the dressing, using salad servers or (clean!) fingers.

FISH & SHELLFISH

Stand in front of a fishmonger's counter and admire the edible treasures of the sea laid out before you, from sprats so tiny you could eat a dozen of them, to steaks cut from fish so large they could almost swallow you. There are underwater aliens, too, with suckered tentacles, hairy claws, and armor-plated shells. Yet all are delectable to eat, and much easier to cook than you might imagine.

undressing a crab, page 234

grilled mackerel, page 24

6 FOR £3·00

fish in foil, page 238

salmon cakes, page 245

uid (roast), page 252

FISH & SHELLFISH

When you head for the beach, along with your bucket and spade, towel, and bodyboard, why not pack a shrimping net? As the tide sweeps out, clamber over the rocks and stop to peer into the pools. Poke them with your net and watch for any signs of movement. Here's a small stone that starts to wander — hang on; it's a crab. There's a puff of sand as a shrimp darts for cover. Be quick with the net and you have it.

Rock-pool fishing can give you a fascinating glimpse into the underwater world. It can also provide the beginnings of a delicious supper. Catch a dozen fat shrimp, and you have a very tasty snack.

Look out to sea and you are looking at, not one, but a million fish suppers. When all you can see is water, it's hard to imagine the variety of life that teems beneath the swell of the waves. But it's there all right: big fish, little fish, crabs, lobsters; shoals of mackerel that swim in close to the shore chasing a silvery school of sprats; great conger eels like sea serpents from a Greek myth — all of them edible.

In fact, almost everything that lives in the sea is trying to find something to eat while trying to avoid being eaten. Only a few fish, such as sharks, tuna, and marlin, are so big and fierce that no other sea creature can hope to catch one. And even they are not out of danger — when humans come looking for a fish supper. The sea is one of the greatest food resources of our entire planet, and we have always fought for our share.

Fishmonger's shops

Fishmonger's shops are fascinating places. They are sort of sea butchers, taking in their delivery of fish just as butchers take in sides of meat. There's a big difference, though. A butcher will sell you pork and beef, chicken and lamb, maybe some game and rabbit, but the meat — once it's cut up into joints and portions — tends to look more or less the same. A fishmonger's display can and should be much more spectacular. The wealth of the water is spread out for us to admire — and much of it is whole. Silver-bellied salmon, tiger-striped mackerel, and bright red mullet; crates of whelks, lobsters swimming in tanks, and trays of scallops in their shells, familiar even if you've never eaten a scallop — all may be fighting for your attention. Then, some of the fish is "butchered" — thick white fillets of cod and haddock, and big piles of pale pink, peeled shrimp; and some of it is already prepared and ready to eat — jars of rolled-up pickled herrings, and vacuum packs of thinly sliced orange smoked salmon.

If this wonderful world of fishy possibilities is not familiar to you, it may be that you're only used to eating fish once it's been "disguised" — shaped into long rectangles and coated in bright orange bread crumbs; or deep-fried in a jacket of batter, then wrapped in white paper at the fish-and-chip shop. It's difficult to relate these meals to the fish that

were once swimming around in the sea. Take cod and plaice, for example. In the fish shop, battered beyond recognition, they look much the same. But take off their crunchy coats, put the fillets back on the bones, restore their heads, tails, and skin, and it would be hard to find two more different-looking fish (you can see them together in the picture on page 220). The plump-bellied cod has silvery sides mottled with browny yellow, and a rather sulky head with large goggle eyes and a gaping mouth. The plaice, kite-shaped and greeny brown with bright orange spots, is so flat that you could post it through a mailbox.

How fish are caught

Most of the fish that you'll find at the fishmonger's or the supermarket have been caught at sea, either in big nets from large boats or in smaller nets from smaller boats, or on long hooked lines.

There are many different designs of net for commercial fishing. Some are aimed at catching particular species in a particular depth of water, while others are dragged along the bottom of the sea like gigantic shrimping nets, scooping up everything in their way (including things that they aren't even trying to catch, which are killed nonetheless). Other

nets "float," suspending a fine mesh of near-invisible nylon a meter or so below the surface. Many of the nets and lines used these days are huge. Nets can be miles wide and catch everything that swims into them. Longlines can be 50 miles long, and they pose a big threat to seabirds attracted by the baits fixed to the hooks on the line.

Fish have been caught in such huge numbers that in some areas the populations have been almost wiped out, and environmentalists are worried about the future of certain species. For example, overfishing has meant that stocks of cod are thought to be dangerously close to extinction in the North Sea and the North Atlantic. Conservation organizations recommend that we try to avoid buying species of fish that are under threat and substitute other fish that are thought to be around in greater numbers (see "Useful Addresses" on page 407 for further information).

For years now in Europe, politicians have been introducing rules to try to protect the long-term future of fish. Sometimes these rules are simply to do with making sure that the holes in fishing nets are big enough for smaller fish to escape unharmed. And sometimes they're to do with limiting the number of fish of a particular species that a commercial fishing boat is allowed to land. These laws aim to protect the numbers of fish in our seas, as well as the needs of people who depend on fishing for their living.

However, these E.U. fishing regulations are constantly changing, and they don't usually end up pleasing anyone. Fishermen complain they can't make a living, while conservationists insist that the regulations still don't go far enough in protecting the fish. As both sides have a fair point, it feels as if this is an argument that will go on for a long time.

Fish farming

One relatively new way of providing fish for the market should, in theory at least, help the environmental problem of overfishing.

The idea of fish farming is to provide a reliable and reasonably priced source of fish from "domesticated" stock. It's a bit like poultry farming, although obviously it all happens underwater. Large female fish kept for breeding are stripped of their eggs, which are then hatched in carefully controlled tanks. The tiny fish are grown in a series of tanks until they are big enough to be released into either "stewponds" (for freshwater fish such as trout) or large floating cages in the sea (for salmon and other sea fish). They are then grown, being fed in these controlled environments, until they reach market weight.

Far more trout and salmon are now produced on fish farms than are caught wild from the sea. As a result, farmed trout and salmon are much cheaper than their wild cousins – in fact, they're among the cheapest of all fish. Recently, two sea fish, the bass and the bream, have also been farmed in large quantities in the Mediterranean, while in the fjords of Scandinavia, flatfish such as turbot are now being farmed with some success.

Although fish farming should be a solution to the falling numbers of wild fish, the huge increase in the number of these farms has created different environmental problems. The trouble is – and it's the same for all kinds of farming – that if you confine large numbers of creatures in a small space, it greatly increases their chance of getting diseases. While farmed fish can be protected against disease by chemical inoculation, the wild fish that come near the cages can easily catch these diseases and, because they're not protected, spread the disease to other wild fish hundreds of miles away from the farm.

Throughout history, our love of eating fish has made us ever more ingenious in the methods that we use to catch them or, more recently, to farm them. But it seems that we've got some way to go if we truly want to protect our fish stocks for future generations.

The freshness of fish

If you've eaten a piece of fish and haven't liked it, it may well be because it wasn't very fresh. It took too long to get from the water to your plate. Fresh fish comes in nice firm flakes and tastes almost sweet. Not-very-fresh fish is often a bit spongy, and tastes sour.

Unlike meat, which can improve with aging in a cool, dry place, once a fish has been caught and killed it begins to go bad. In order to slow down this deterioration, it needs to be kept cool, and this is done either by packing it in ice or storing it in a fridge – or both. Looked after in this way, many fish will stay fresh and pleasant to eat for up to five days — though they will certainly taste far better on day one than on day five.

If you are going to become a good fish shopper, it's useful to know how to tell when a fish is fresh. With a whole fish, look for a nice bright eye and wet, shiny-looking scales. If you are feeling brave, ask the fishmonger to show you the gills — they should be pink, not gray and slimy. If you're buying fish that's already been filleted or cut into steaks, check that the flesh looks shiny and not dull.

If you want the freshest fish, it's a good idea to go down to the fish market before you've even decided which recipe you want to cook. Look for the freshest fish in the shop and then choose a recipe to suit the fish you buy. As fish is generally very simple to cook, this really shouldn't be a problem. Take the fish home straight away, put it in the fridge, and cook it within 24 hours.

How to prepare whole fresh fish
Unless you've caught the fish yourself, or been given it by someone who has, then most fish that you buy will have been cleaned and prepared. "Cleaning" means getting rid of the guts inside the fish so that it's ready for cooking. It's usually done by slicing the belly open and pulling them out, and although it's a bit messy it's really very easy to do.

As well as cleaning the fish, you need to remove its fins and scales — the fins because some of them are very sharp and spiny, and the scales because otherwise you'll be picking fish scales out of your teeth while you eat. Scrape the scales away with a blunt knife, working from the tail to the head of the fish. If you're scaling fish in the kitchen, spread some newspaper over the counter first because the scaly sequins fly about everywhere as you scrape. Wash the fish and then, with a sharp knife, make a slit between the anal fin (on the underneath of the fish toward the tail end) and the head. Put the knife down and pull out the innards with your fingers, removing every scrap of gutty material. Throw it away. Rinse the empty cavity well under the cold tap. Fins can be snipped off with scissors. Then wipe the fish dry with some paper towels and it is ready to cook.

A whole fish recipe
A Whole Fish Baked in Foil, page 238

Fillets of fish
Sometimes, fish are sold in fillets — the idea is to give you a nice boneless piece of fish that's quick and easy to cook. A whole fillet is taken from the side of a large fish by cutting from behind the head of the fish, close to the backbone, then down to its tail. (Imagine a fat fish swimming through a very narrow slit — the fillets would be the bits on either side of the main backbone that wouldn't make it.)

Sometimes, pieces of bigger fish are sold in "steaks" — thick pieces cut not down the length of the fish but across the body, as if a knife had come down on a fish while it was swimming along.

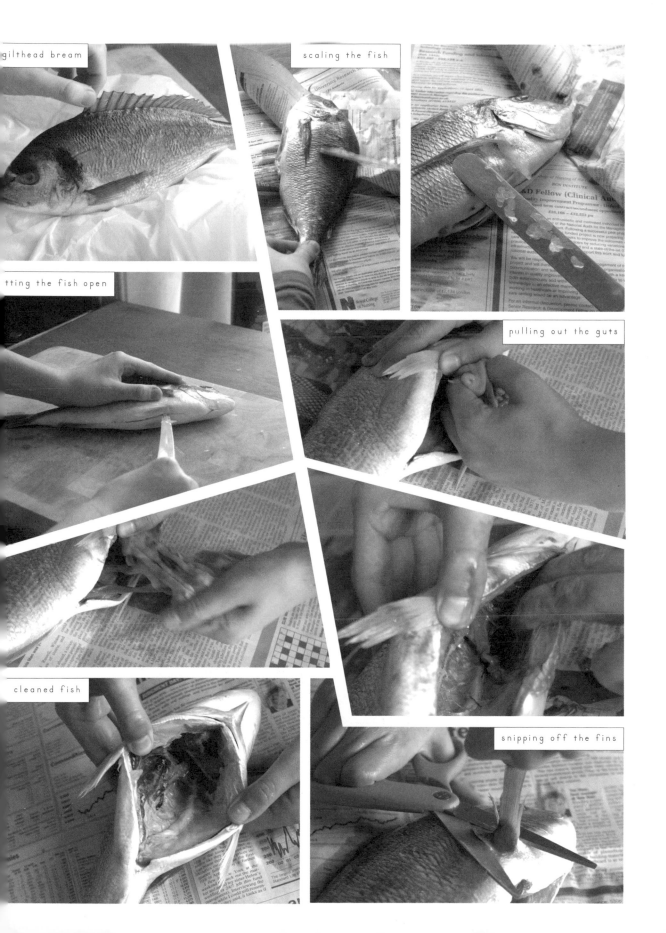

gilthead bream

scaling the fish

tting the fish open

pulling out the guts

cleaned fish

snipping off the fins

Beware of the bones

Bones in meat aren't much of a problem. They're big, easy to see, and most of them are cut out by the butcher. Those that aren't are left in because we like to gnaw around them: chicken drumsticks and spareribs, for example. But with fish, bones can be a bit of an issue – a bone of contention, you might say. They're not a problem when you're expecting to find them – when you're eating a whole fish, for instance, and delicately picking in between the little ribs to find succulent morsels of flesh. In fact, there's something rather satisfying about eating fish this way, as you end up with a cartoon fish skeleton like something out of *Tom and Jerry*.

But bones are horrible when you find them unexpectedly. It's no fun taking a great big mouthful of fluffy fish cake only to find a hard, splintery bone at the back of your throat. Don't assume that a fish fillet you've bought at a fishmonger's is boneless. If you want to make sure it is, you'd better check. And the best thing to use is not your eyes but your hands. *Feel* the raw fillets by running your clean fingers over the surface and along the edges. Any bones, however small, should just catch your fingertips. The easiest way to pull them out is with tweezers. The network of bones that makes up a fish's skeleton varies from fish to fish. Some fish – herrings, for example – are particularly bony. Others, like dogfish and monkfish, are virtually boneless.

You can also use your (clean) fingers to check for tiny bones in cooked fish – for example, if you're making fish cakes, or taking some poached salmon off the bone to serve cold. Simply flake the cooked fish between your fingers and you'll easily feel any little bones that remain.

Some boneless fish recipes

Fish Fingers, page 243
Salmon Cakes, page 245
Creamy Fish Pie, page 248

Salted and smoked fish

For hundreds of years, before refrigeration revolutionized the fish industry, there was really only one way to prepare fish for long-distance transport – by salting it. Salt draws the moisture out of foods, thereby protecting them from bacteria that would spoil the food and make it go bad. Once salted and thoroughly dried, fish can be kept not just for days and weeks but for months and even years. It then needs to be soaked in fresh water to rinse out the salt before it can be cooked and eaten.

In the late Middle Ages, British fishermen would sail across the North Atlantic to the seas around Iceland, returning home months later to sell their catches of dried salted cod and whiting. One of the reasons people went to all this trouble to get fish was that religious practice prevented them eating meat on Wednesdays, Fridays, and Saturdays.

It was also discovered long ago that "smoking" fish over a slowly smoldering fire was an effective way of preserving it – though not for as long as a thorough salting and

SOME FISHY HISTORY

Until just over 150 years ago, when there was little ice, no fridges or freezers, and terrible roads, it was almost impossible to transport fresh fish any distance before it went bad. So for most people living away from the coast, fresh fish from the sea was a luxury food. Freshwater fish from our rivers, streams, lakes, and ponds were more widely available inland – provided you could catch them. Today, you might have a pond in your garden with a few goldfish swimming idly by, but centuries ago people built ponds for a more practical reason – dinner. Wealthy landowners and monasteries kept their own "stewponds," stocked with freshwater fish such as roach, tench, and carp (all fish that British anglers catch nowadays for sport and return to the water because they're not thought to make good eating).

Surprisingly, perhaps, one type of seafood more readily available to the less wealthy was oysters. Before the pollution of the Industrial Revolution, they were plentiful, cheap, and sold by the gallon – they could be kept alive, and therefore fresh, for many days, provided they were kept wet and out of the sun.

Salmon was also once plentiful, and therefore regarded as a poor man's fish. Before the Industrial Revolution, the printing apprentices of London actually went on strike until their employers promised to give them salmon "no more than twice a week"! But overfishing and industrialization took their toll on British rivers. By the early nineteenth century, the River Thames was so polluted that salmon had completely disappeared from its waters.

Although farming has now made salmon cheap again, a truly wild fish is still a rare treat. Most people think that wild salmon, swimming freely across the breadth of the Atlantic, eating a natural diet, has a better flavor than farmed salmon, reared in a cage on a diet of fish pellets.

Fresh sea fish only became really popular and cheap to buy about 150 years ago, when transport dramatically improved. The new steamships were fast and reliable, and trawlers could venture out into the North Atlantic for the first time to bring back big catches of fresh fish in just a few hours. The building of the railways meant that traveling times across the country fell from days to hours. Ice could be shipped in from Scandinavia to keep fish fresh. For the first time ever, you could get on a train in London, go to a seaside resort, eat your fish and chips on the pier, and be back home by bedtime.

drying. However, if fish are salted very lightly and then smoked at a relatively cool temperature for a long period of time, they keep well for at least a few weeks, staying moist and tender. The fish can then be eaten without any soaking, and might not even need cooking. Countless experiments have been made in different cultures over a long period of time for us to end up with delicacies such as smoked salmon, smoked haddock, and kippers.

In parts of the world where people don't have fridges, fish is still salted and smoked in vast quantities. And we still choose to eat salted and smoked fish from time to time, not because we need to preserve food like this anymore but because we love the flavor and texture of fish treated in this way.

Some smoked fish recipes

Creamy Fish Pie, page 248
Kedgeree, page 250

Hook 'em and cook 'em

If you've never fished before, then you've never experienced the thrill of that tug on the line as a fish takes a bite. As your fish breaks the surface of the water, your first thought will be, "What is it?" Maybe your second thought should be, "How shall I cook it?"

Books on fishing tell you lots about how to fish, where to fish, and when to fish. What they rarely tell you is how to cook the fish to enjoy it at its best.

If you're near the coast, a good way to start fishing is to take a trip on one of the mackerel fishing boats that chug out from many seaside towns. The boats provide rods and tackle and take you out for a couple of hours to where the mackerel swim in their thousands. You're practically guaranteed to catch something that you'll be able to take home for supper.

In settled weather in the summer months around the south coast of England, mackerel often follow the high tide in close to the beach as they pursue their favorite food – shoals of silvery sprats. You can fish for them from the beach by attaching a line of cheap, feathered hooks to your rod, casting out, reeling the line back in, and making the hooks dance through the water. The same thing can be done from a harbor wall or pier. You might even be able to scoop out a netful of sprats, too.

By far the best way of guaranteeing a fish in your bucket at the end of the afternoon is to go with someone who has fished before – someone who can show you how to use a rod as well as tell you the best places to fish. It's also safer. Remember to be wary of tides coming in and sudden big waves that can hit the beach out of nowhere. You should never underestimate the power of the sea.

And whatever you fish for, make sure that the beach or water that you're raiding for food is far from any pollution hotspots. Keep away from beaches near sewage outfalls and water treatment works.

A catch-your-own fish recipe

Grilled Mackerel, page 240

SHELLFISH

Crabs that can only walk sideways, lobsters marching nose to tail the length of the Atlantic seafloor, oysters that grow their own pearls, squid that squirt clouds of black ink, snails that live on whales, and mussels that cling to every rock and rope – shellfish are the eccentrics of the sea. Some pincered, some whiskered, some smooth, some spiny, many completely encased in their defensive shells – here are some of the most fascinating life-forms on the planet.

Our earliest ancestors, no doubt learning from birds, bears, and otters, picked all kinds of shellfish off the beach and smashed them open with a stone. And by the first century A.D. the Romans, who loved British oysters, were shipping them back to Italy by the cartload – oyster shells from the Essex coast have been excavated from various ancient ruins in Rome itself.

Most of the shellfish we eat can be divided into two kinds. The most primitive are the mollusks, which include the various sea snails, such as periwinkles, whelks, and the giant tropical conch, as well as all the bivalves, such as cockles, clams, scallops, oysters, and mussels, whose two-sided shells are held tight together by a fleshy muscle (the bit we love to eat). Less obviously from the same family, but mollusks nonetheless, are squid, cuttlefish, and octopus. They have evolved so that what was once a shell on the outside is now a bony

cartilage and a beaky mouth on the inside of their soft bodies.

Then there are the crustaceans, which have lots of legs, jointed segments, and often a pair of claws to tackle their prey and brandish at their enemies – these are the crabs, shrimp, and lobsters.

The shells of all the shellfish are suits of armor, designed to protect them from predators. And, like any other creature who wants to eat them, we must learn the skill of getting inside the shell to reach the tender, edible parts. In most cases, cooking will do the job very well. Once boiled, whelks and clams, periwinkles and mussels, can easily be removed from their shells. The large crustaceans, such as lobsters and crabs, require a bit more work: hammers and nutcrackers are used to break open the armor plating, probing small forks to pull out the juicy flesh.

But if we want to eat shellfish raw (which can be delicious), we can expect a bit of a battle on our hands. Opening oysters takes some skill and practice, and by the time you've got the hang of it you will probably have caused yourself at least one minor injury.

Some shellfish recipes

Roast Squid, page 252
Mussels à la Marinière, page 255

Project:

UNDRESSING A CRAB

Less of a recipe, more of a demolition job, undressing a crab is great fun. Cookbooks usually call this process "dressing a crab," but we think that "undressing" describes it a bit more accurately. Buy a cooked crab from the fishmonger and eat it on the same day.

Before you start, take a minute to have a really good look at your crab. Admire its astonishingly hairy legs and marvel at the power of its pincers. Could those tiny eyes actually see anything, peering out from under that massive shell?

For 2 people to share:
Free-range egg, 1
A freshly cooked large crab
Parsley, a small handful
A little paprika
A lemon

Small saucepan, tablespoon, 2 bowls, large cutting board, paper towels, teaspoon, hammer, heavy knife, skewer

1. Put the egg in the small saucepan, pour in enough cold water to cover, then place on the stove. Bring the water to a boil and boil the egg for 5 minutes.

2. Take the egg out of the pan with the tablespoon and put it in a bowl of cold water in the sink under the tap. Run the cold water

gently for 2 to 3 minutes, so that the egg cools down as quickly as possible.

3. Now for the crab. First, like any predator hoping to eat a crab, you need to deal with its protective shell. Standing the crab on its side, press down on the tail end and you should be able to pry apart the shell from the body, as if you were opening up a book. Put the shell and its meat to one side for the moment.

4. With the body of the crab in front of you, pick off all the "dead men's fingers" – these were the lungs of the crab while it was alive and you mustn't eat them. They look like feathery, wispy claws. Also, remove the bony stomach sac that sits just behind the eyes and the mouth parts. (It's a good idea to have a bowl at the side of the cutting board where you can discard all these nonedible bits of the crab as you go.)

5. Using the handle of the teaspoon, scoop out all the meat from the shell. This is the brown meat, and it's all edible. Put it in a pile on the side of the cutting board.

6. Look carefully at the underneath of the shell and you'll see that there's a sort of "false" shell line. Gently use the hammer to tap away the inner raggedy parts inside this line so you can tidy up the shell and use it for serving your crab. Take the empty shell to the sink and scrub it under hot water really well. Dry it on some paper towels and put to one side.

freshly boiled crab

picking meat from the body

twisting off the claws

he stuffed shell ...

... with its garnish

7.   Holding each of the little legs in turn, twist them so that they come away from the main part of the body. Repeat with the bigger pincers. Put them to one side.

8.   The body of the crab needs to be cut in half. Using the heavy knife, carefully split the body down the middle, using your weight to press down on the knife (younger cooks will need a bit of help here). Pick out the white meat from the body with the end of the skewer. Put it in a little pile separate from the brown meat.

9.   Now for the really fun bit. Starting with the big claws, use the hammer to crack the fattest part of the claw near the pincer. Hold the other end of the claw (the bit that was near the body) while you do this. As soon as the claw cracks, put the hammer down, peel off the shell, and add the meat inside to the white meat pile. Repeat for the other big claw. With the smaller legs, hold the pincer bit and crack the other end, this time very gently. Stop as soon as you hear the shell "give" or you'll smash the shell into splinters, which will be hard to pick out. Pick out the flesh, using the skewer and your fingers to pry it out. Add it to the rest of the white meat. You can even pull out the meat from the pincers, if you like, or you can use them to decorate your crab when you serve it up.

10.   Take the egg out of the cold water, tap it on the cutting board to crack the shell, then peel off the shell. Separate the white from the yolk and chop each on a different part of the board. Chop the parsley finely.

11.   Now to serve your crab. Chop the white meat evenly and pile this into the middle of the shell. Put half the chopped yolk in a line to one side of the white meat and half to the other side. Divide the parsley and put this next to the egg yolks. The chopped white of the egg goes next to the parsley and the brown meat from the crab can be tucked right into each corner of the shell. You can sprinkle a little paprika over the white of the egg, if you like.

12.   Put the dressed crab on a plate. Cut the lemon into quarters. If you didn't pick out the meat from the pincers earlier on, you can arrange them around the crab now in a suitably crabby way. Take the hammer to the table and crack them there instead.

How to eat your crab

You could cut and butter a few slices of fresh bread to eat with your crab, or cook some Garlic, Rosemary, and Lemon Potatoes (see page 203) to go with it. Squeeze some lemon juice over the crab and eat, forking up a little of each type of meat and egg as you go.

A WHOLE FISH BAKED IN FOIL

This is one of the easiest and most delicious ways to cook many kinds of fish, and can be adapted for a fish of almost any size – as long as it's not too big to fit in your oven. Trout, sea trout, bass, and bream are perfect, as they're all round fish with firm flesh that bakes well. ("Round" fish are the kind of plump-bodied, fishy-looking fish – the type that cats always eat in cartoons – as opposed to flat ones such as flounder and Dover sole.) The lemony, buttery juices in the foil packet at the end of cooking are a ready-made sauce.

A fish of around 1 pound will generously feed one person, and a fish only a little bigger than that (say, $1\frac{1}{2}$ pounds) will do for two. If there are 3 or 4 of you eating, then you can either cook a whole small fish for each or cook one large one (2 pounds or more) and share it. If you have any fish left over, you could always make some fish cakes (see page 245).

You will need:
Soft butter
Salt and black pepper
A few bay leaves
A few sprigs of thyme
A few slices of onion

1 whole fish, cleaned and gutted by the
   fishmonger (or see page 226)
Lemon, $\frac{1}{4}$ per fish

Aluminum foil, baking sheet, small sharp knife

1. Preheat the oven to 400°F.

2. Tear off 2 sheets of foil a little bit longer than your fish and lay one on top of the other. Smear the dull side of the upper sheet generously with butter. Season the buttery foil with a good pinch of salt and a few twists of pepper and put a bay leaf, a sprig of thyme and a couple of onion slices on it.

3. Lay the fish on the prepared foil. Smear a bit of butter on the fish and lay a few more of the herbs on it. Push a bay leaf, a couple of slices of onion, and a tablespoon of butter into the belly cavity. Season again with salt and

pepper. Lift up and lightly scrunch the sides and ends of the foil, then squeeze the lemon quarter (or use half a lemon if the fish is a biggish one) into the packet without the juice leaking out.

4. Lay the foil packet on the baking sheet and seal the foil by scrunching the edges together. Oven gloves on. Place the pan in the hot oven and bake for about 20 minutes (for a 1-pound fish).

5. Oven gloves on. Remove the fish from the oven and open the foil. Check that the fish is cooked through by slipping the knife into

the thickest part. If the flesh is still a little translucent and sticking to the bone, wrap the foil back around the fish and let it rest for a few minutes to complete the transfer of heat. (Of course, if it looks alarmingly raw, then put it back in the oven for a few more minutes.)

How to eat your fish

The easiest way to eat your fish is simply to transfer it carefully straight from its foil wrapper onto a plate with a bowl of plain boiled new potatoes (in summer) or mashed potatoes (in winter) and some green peas or steamed spinach. You've already got a delicious sauce to eat with your fish: just carefully lift up the foil parcel and strain the buttery, fishy, lemony, herby juices through a sieve into a small saucepan. Taste them and add salt and pepper if you think it's needed. A splash of wine, a dash of cream, and some freshly chopped chervil or chives will make it a very smart sauce indeed. Bring it to a boil, give it a quick whisk, and take it to the table to serve with the fish.

GRILLED MACKEREL

If you can't get out on a boat to catch your own mackerel, the next best thing is to buy some really fresh fish from a fishmonger. Make sure they still look shiny, with a clear, bright eye. They should be firm, not soft, to the touch.

You can cook your mackerel on any kind of grill. Or, if you're a beach barbecue purist, you can gather some dry driftwood, make a fire, and grill the fish over the hot embers (see page 275). Younger cooks should always enlist the help of an adult when cooking over a fire.

You will need:
Mackerel, 1 per person
A little olive or sunflower oil
Salt and black pepper
Bay leaves and/or thyme sprigs (optional)

Good olive oil and chopped fresh parsley, to serve (optional)

Sharp knife, cutting board, paper towels, metal spatula

1. Light the grill or fire and wait until there are no flames left, just glowing coals or embers. Place a grill rack over the coals and allow it to heat up.

2. Prepare the fish while the fire is burning. Mackerel are easy to gut: just run the point of the sharp knife from the hole at the back of its belly up to its throat. Put your hand into the belly and, holding the fish over a bowl or sink, pull out the guts. Slosh the fish in some fresh water (this could be under a running tap, or in a bucket of sea water if you're on the beach), then wipe the fish dry with paper towels or a clean rag.

3. Now lightly rub the surface of each cleaned fish with a little oil, using your fingertips to massage it on. This will help prevent the fish

from sticking to the bars of the grill grids. Sprinkle a little salt and pepper over the fish and, if you like, tuck a bay leaf and/or a sprig of thyme inside the belly.

4. Oven gloves on. Carefully lay the fish on the grill. Leave for at least 4 minutes before turning. This will not only ensure that the fish is cooked through but also, by allowing the hot grill grids to burn neat lines across the skin of the fish, it should prevent it from sticking and make it easier to turn over. It might take 5 to 6 minutes if it's a big fish.

5. Use the metal spatula to help you turn the fish over and, if it has stuck a bit, run the spatula between the skin of the fish and the grill grids to loosen it. Cook the fish on the other side for 4 to 5 minutes. Then, with oven gloves

on again, use the spatula to lift the fish off the grill and onto a plate. Season with another sprinkling of salt and pepper and, if you like, trickle over a teaspoon of good olive oil and a sprinkling of chopped fresh parsley.

How to eat your mackerel

Freshly caught, freshly grilled mackerel is wonderful with a simple, summery green salad and a few boiled new potatoes. But if you're on the beach, a hunk of fresh brown bread, thickly buttered, is just as good. A wedge of lemon on the plate is always welcome, but there's no need to squeeze more than a few drops onto the fish. Mackerel have nice, fat, round fillets that are quite easy to lift away from the backbone. But watch out for the bones running just below the skin along the back of the fish, and the fine, hairlike bones on the inside of the belly cavity.

FRIED WHITEBAIT

Whitebait aren't a type of fish like cod or turbot, they're the small offspring of various members of the herring family. They're almost always sold frozen, but they defrost very quickly. They cook in no time at all, and you crunch them up heads, tails, and all. The fish are so small that you don't notice their bones – they just seem to be nicely crisp.

To serve 4 as a snack or starter:
Lemon, 1
Tiny whitebait, max 2 inches long,
  about 7 ounces
All-purpose flour, 2 to 3 tablespoons
Salt and black pepper
Sunflower or olive oil, 4 to 5 tablespoons

Sharp knife, cutting board, small plate, serving bowl, large mixing bowl, colander, clean cotton cloth, large flat plate, heavy frying pan, sieve, knife, metal spatula, paper towels, slotted spoon

1. Cut the lemon into quarters and put it on the table on the small plate, ready for serving with the fish. Turn on the oven to 250°F. Put the serving bowl in the oven to warm up (this is so you can keep the first batch of whitebait warm while you cook the second).

2. Fill the mixing bowl with cold water, add the whitebait, and slosh them about in it to clean off any sand or dirt. Admire their shiny, chromelike skin and the way it catches the light. Drain them in the colander, then shake them gently in a clean cotton cloth.

3. Measure the flour onto the large plate and grind in some salt and pepper.

4. Pour the sunflower or olive oil into the frying pan, put it on the stove, and turn the heat to medium. Leave it for a minute or so to get good and hot.

5. Empty half the whitebait onto the flour on the plate and toss them about with your fingers so each fish is well coated. Then put the floured fish in the sieve, hold it above the floury plate, and shake it gently so that any excess flour just drops back onto the plate.

6. When the oil is hot, use the sieve to add the fish carefully to the pan – just enough of them to cover the base in a single layer. Fry for a couple of minutes, until they've started to turn golden brown. Gently flip them over with the long-handled metal spatula and fry them for another minute or two, until they're golden brown and crisp all over.

7. Meanwhile, line the warm bowl with some paper towels (remember to put on oven gloves when you get the bowl out of the oven). Scoop the whitebait out of the oil with the slotted spoon and put them into the warm bowl. Put

the bowl back into the oven while you cook the second batch. Add a little more oil to the pan (the fish will have absorbed quite a lot of the first lot), turn the stove back on, and let the oil heat up. Flour and cook the second batch of fish as before, remembering to turn off the stove when you have finished.

How to eat your whitebait

Serve the whitebait straight away, sprinkle a little lemon juice on them, and eat them with your fingers. They make a nice way to start a meal or are good eaten with bread and butter and a tomato salad (page 216). It's slightly greedy, but delicious, to have some garlic mayonnaise to dip them into (see page 212).

. . . .

FISH FINGERS

A nice, clean boneless fillet of white fish, such as sea bass, halibut, or lingcod, is perfect for making your own fish fingers — which will be much tastier than anything you have bought frozen and ready-made. Use good unsliced white bread to make the crumbs.

To make about 16 fish fingers:
Slightly stale bread, 3 thick slices, with
   the crusts cut off
Fillets of firm fish, such as sea bass, halibut,
   or lingcod, about 1 pound, skinned if
   possible
All-purpose flour, about ¼ cup
Salt and black pepper
Free-range eggs, 1 to 2

Butter, 1 tablespoon
Sunflower oil, about 2 tablespoons

Grater or food processor, small flexible
sharp knife, cutting board, 3 shallow bowls,
fork, 2 large plates, frying pan, metal
spatula, paper towels

1. Switch on the oven to 250°F (this is so you can keep the first batch of fish fingers warm while you cook the second).

2. Make bread crumbs from the bread either using a grater or in a food processor. The crumbs should be nice and small — not great flakes of bread.

3. If the fish still has its skin on, you will need to skin it. Lay the fillet, skin-side down, on the board. Take the sharp knife and, starting at the thinner, pointier end of the fillet, slide the blade between the flesh and the skin. As soon as you have released a small flap of skin, hold onto it with one hand while you slide the blade between the skin and the flesh. Angle

the blade very slightly down toward the board, so that you don't slice any of the flesh away with the skin. This takes practice, but you'll soon get the hang of it (see the picture on page 228). Throw away the skin. Cut the fish into strips like long, fat fingers and feel each strip carefully for any little bones. You might like to make your fish fingers a bit chunkier than the ones you buy frozen.

4. Take 3 shallow bowls. The idea is to dust each fishy finger with flour to get it nice and dry, slosh it about in some beaten egg (which works as a sort of tasty glue), and then coat it in bread crumbs. So you set up a production line with bare fish fingers at one end and dressed ones at the other.

5. Shake the flour into the first bowl. Grind on some black pepper and mix in a large pinch of salt.

6. Break an egg into the second bowl. Whisk it with a fork until you have a nice eggy liquid.

7. Add the bread crumbs to the third bowl.

8. Dip a fish strip into the flour, shake it so it doesn't have too much flour sticking to it, then swim it in the egg. Let the excess egg drip off, then place it in the bread crumbs, turning it once or twice and pressing the crumbs gently onto the fish so they stick. Transfer the fish finger to a clean plate. Repeat with the rest of the strips.

9. Put the butter and sunflower oil in the frying pan and place it over medium heat. When the butter starts to foam, place some fish fingers gently in the pan, without over-crowding. Let them cook for 2 to 3 minutes, then turn them over with the spatula. You'll see that the fluffy coating has turned to a crisp, golden brown crust.

10. Let the other side cook for a couple of minutes, then scoop them out with the spatula onto a clean plate lined with paper towels – this will absorb any excess oil. Keep them warm in the oven while you cook the remaining fish fingers in the same way, adding more oil and butter as necessary.

How to eat your fish fingers

These fish fingers are delicious for lunch or supper, with a good dollop of ketchup. You can fry some potatoes to go with them – and serve some peas on the side, too.

For a change, make homemade "mushy" peas by sautéing some finely chopped garlic and mint in a little butter, then mashing it into some slightly overcooked peas with a potato masher.

SALMON CAKES

Smooth and crisp on the outside, fluffy on the inside — homemade fish cakes are absolutely delicious. You can either buy salmon especially for them or improvise a recipe using any leftover cooked fish. Smoked haddock is very good, too.

To make 8 fish cakes:
Baking potatoes, 1 pound
Salmon fillet, about 10 ounces
  (or a similar amount of leftover
  cooked fish)
Milk, enough to cover the fish
A bay leaf
A strip of lemon zest, cut off a lemon
  with a vegetable peeler
Black peppercorns, 3 or 4
Parsley, a small handful
Slightly stale bread, 2 thick slices,
  crusts cut off

All-purpose flour, 2 tablespoons
Free-range egg, 1
Butter, a good chunk
Olive oil, 1 tablespoon
Salt and black pepper

Sharp knife, cutting board, 2 medium saucepans, colander, potato masher or ricer, sieve, 3 plates, 4 small bowls, grater or food processor, fork, heavy frying pan, metal spatula

1. Peel the potatoes and cut each one into 2 or 3 chunks. Put them in a medium saucepan and add just enough water to cover them. Add a little salt, then bring to a boil over high heat. Reduce the heat a little and simmer the potatoes for 15 to 20 minutes, until you can pierce one through easily with a knife. Drain the potatoes in a colander standing in the sink (the colander, not you).

2. While the potatoes are cooking, put the fish in another saucepan and just cover it with milk. Add the bay leaf, lemon zest, and black peppercorns, which will give a little flavor to the fish and the milk. Add a sprig of the parsley, too. Set the pan over medium heat and let the milk come slowly to a boil. As soon as it starts to bubble, turn off the heat. Allow the milk to cool down. Notice how the fish changes color from orange to soft pink.

3. Return the potatoes to their pan and mash them until smooth, adding a couple of tablespoons of the warm, fishy milk. Season with some salt and pepper.

4. When the fish has cooled, place the sieve over a bowl and pour the contents of the fish saucepan into the sieve. Lift out the fish and put it on a plate. Feel the chunks of fish between your fingers so you can pick out any bones and bits of skin; throw these away. Put the chunks of boneless fish into the potato pan.

peel ...

mash ...

feel for any bones

make some bread crumb

set up the production line ...

5. Chop the parsley with the sharp knife (or snip it with scissors) and add it to the fish and potato. Mix the fish, potato, and parsley gently together. Have a clean plate ready. With floured hands, so the mixture doesn't stick, pick up a golf-ball-sized lump of potato mixture and shape it gently into a smooth cake. Put the cakes on the clean plate as you make them, then put the plate of fish cakes in the fridge.

6. Make bread crumbs by rubbing the bread against the large-holed side of the grater. Or, if you like, you can whiz the slices in a food processor until you get small crumbs.

7. Now take the 3 bowls and set them in a row on the work surface. Put the flour into the first, break the egg into the next, and add the bread crumbs into the third. Beat the egg with a fork. You now have a sort of fish-cake production line.

8. Get the plate of fish cakes out of the fridge. Take the first one and dip it into the flour, turning it over so that it's coated on both sides.

Then dip it into the beaten egg, turning it over as before, and finally into the bread crumbs. The idea is that the egg works as a kind of edible glue, so that the bread crumbs stick to the surface of the potato. Put the coated fish cakes on a clean plate.

9. Put the butter and olive oil in the frying pan over medium meat. When the butter starts to sizzle gently, put 4 fish cakes into the pan and let them fry gently for about 4 or 5 minutes, until they're crisp and golden brown underneath. Turn them over and cook for another 3 or 4 minutes, checking from time to time that they're not cooking too quickly and adjusting the heat as necessary. When they're cooked, use the spatula to put them on a warm plate while you fry the others.

How to eat your fish cakes

Eat these fish cakes hot from the pan. A pile of green salad leaves such as watercress would taste nice with them. Ketchup is practically essential.

CREAMY FISH PIE

This fish pie is filled with a mixture of smoked and unsmoked fish, plus a few shrimp for added interest. The parsley is important because it not only tastes good (especially if you've grown it yourself) but also adds a splash of color to an otherwise pale pie.

To serve 4 to 6:

2 fillets of any firm white fish, such as
   sea bass, halibut, or lingcod,
   about 1¼ pounds in total
Undyed smoked haddock, a small fillet
   (about 6 ounces)
Cooked and shelled shrimp, 2 handfuls
Milk, 3 cups
Onion, 1 medium
Carrot, 1 large
Celery, 1 stalk
A bay leaf
Parsley, a good bunch
A few peppercorns

Baking potatoes, about 2 pounds
Butter, ½ cup (1 stick), plus extra to grease
   the dish and dot on top of the pie
Salt and black pepper
All-purpose flour, ½ cup

Medium-sized saucepan with lid, large bowl, cutting board, sharp knife, vegetable peeler, large saucepan, teaspoon, colander, potato masher or ricer, dinner knife, sieve, large pitcher, wooden spoon, balloon whisk, plate, large deep pie dish about 8 x 12 inches, tablespoon

1. Put all the fillets of fish in the medium-sized saucepan (leave the shrimp to one side for now). Pour in the milk. Peel and coarsely chop the onion and carrot, and clean and chop the celery. Add the vegetables to the milk, along with the bay leaf, a couple of stalks of parsley, and the peppercorns.

2. Put the pan on the stove over low heat. Let the milk heat up gently; then as soon as it comes to a simmer, turn off the heat and cover the pan. The fish will carry on cooking in the hot milk.

3. Meanwhile, peel the potatoes, cut them into even-sized chunks, and put them in the large pan. Add just enough water to cover and put the pan on the stove over high heat. Add a teaspoon of salt and let the water come to a boil. Lower the heat to a simmer and cook the potatoes until they are just tender (when you stick a knife into a chunk, it should feel soft, but drain them well before they start to fall apart).

4. Carefully drain the potatoes in a colander set in the sink and let them steam off for a minute or two. Return them to the pan and mash them, adding 3 tablespoons of the butter, cut into cubes.

5. Stand the sieve over the large bowl and add the fish and its milk. Wash the pan in which the fish was cooked and dry it well. You can now

add 3 to 4 tablespoons of the fishy milk in the bowl to the mashed potatoes and stir it in well. Grind in some black pepper, taste the potatoes, and add some salt if needed. Put the potatoes to one side while you make a béchamel sauce. Preheat the oven to 400°F.

6. Put the remaining butter in the clean pan and melt it over medium-low heat. Add the flour and stir well with the wooden spoon to make a roux (see page 71). Let this cook over the heat for a couple of minutes, stirring it every few seconds. Then gently whisk in a third of the hot fishy milk. The paste will quickly turn into a very thick sauce. Add another third of the milk, whisking all the time, and then the final third so that you end up with a creamy sauce that will pour nicely but isn't too thin. Season the béchamel with salt and pepper, turn the heat down to very low, and let the sauce bubble gently for 5 minutes while you sort out the fish.

7. Remove the cut-up vegetables and the herbs and peppercorns – they've done their job of flavoring the milk for the béchamel. Now carefully pick up a chunk of fish. Peel off any skin and throw it away, then feel the flesh for bones. Do this gently or you'll end up over-shredding the fish. When you're happy it's bone-free, put it on a clean plate. Repeat with the rest of the fish.

8. Turn off the heat under the sauce and add the fish to the béchamel. Add the shrimp, then chop the remaining parsley and stir this in too. Taste the sauce once more and add any salt and pepper if you think it needs it.

9. Generously butter the pie dish and pour in the fishy béchamel. Spoon the mashed potatoes over in great dollops and spread them carefully across the surface of the sauce, roughing them up with the flat blade of a knife. Dot a little extra butter over the top of the pie.

10. Oven gloves on. Put the pie in the oven and bake for about 25 minutes or until the top is starting to brown and the sauce is bubbling up the sides. Serve at once, with buttered, minted peas and lots of crusty bread to mop up the sauce.

KEDGEREE

This is an Anglo-Indian classic. It's not always made with a hint of curry powder, but if you haven't tried it this way we think you should. Buy pale golden-brown undyed smoked haddock rather than bright yellow smoked haddock. The dyed fish contains unnecessary colorings and additives and has a less subtle taste as a result.

To serve 4 to 6:
Basmati rice, 1 cup
Undyed smoked haddock (or pollack, or
    cod) fillets, 1 pound
Whole milk, 1 cup
Onion, 1
Sunflower oil, 1 tablespoon
Butter, 3 tablespoons
Mild curry powder, 1 tablespoon

Free-range eggs, 4
Parsley, a large handful
Salt and black pepper

Mug, large bowl, sieve, medium saucepan with lid, slotted spoon, plate, cutting board, sharp knife, large saucepan, small saucepan, fork

1. Put the rice in the large bowl and add plenty of cold water. Swish the rice about to wash it, then pour off the water. Do this 4 or 5 times, until the water is relatively clear, then pour the rice into the sieve and leave to drain.

2. Now, cook the fish. Place the smoked haddock in the medium saucepan and pour over the milk, plus just enough water to cover the fish. Place the pan over medium heat. Bring to a boil and turn the heat down to low. Put the lid on the pan, simmer for just 2 minutes, then take the pan off the heat. Leave the pan with the lid on for 10 minutes; the fish will finish cooking in the heat that's left in the pan.

3. With the slotted spoon, lift the cooked fish fillets from the pan and lay them on a plate. When they are cool enough to handle, pick away the skin and flake the fish with your fingers, discarding any small bones.

4. Peel the onion and chop it finely. Now take the large saucepan and heat the oil and 1 tablespoon of butter over medium heat. Add the chopped onion, turn the heat down, then cover the pan and let the onion cook gently for about 5 minutes, until it begins to soften. Stir in the curry powder and cook the mixture for another 2 minutes.

5. Now add the drained rice to the pan and stir so that the grains mix with the softened onion and are lightly coated in the oil and butter. Measure 2½ mugs of the reserved cooking liquid from the fish and pour it over the rice. Bring very gently to a slow simmer, cover with the lid, then simmer over a very low heat for

about 15 minutes. Turn off the heat, but leave the pan on the stove, with the lid on, for another 10 minutes.

6. While the rice is cooking, put the eggs in the small saucepan, cover with cold water, and bring to a boil. Boil hard for 5 minutes exactly, then transfer the eggs to a bowl of cold water in the sink. Run cold water over them gently for at least 2 minutes so that the eggs cool down as quickly as possible. Let sit for a minute or so, then peel them under a gently running tap. Cut the eggs into quarters or eighths.

7. Chop the parsley finely, cutting away any tough stalks.

8. Now put the kedgeree together. Take the lid off the rice pan, add the prepared fish, remaining 2 tablespoons of butter, and the chopped parsley and mix everything gently with a fork. Taste for seasoning. You'll probably need a little extra salt and pepper despite the saltiness of the fish. Garnish with the pieces of hard-boiled egg and serve at once.

How to eat your kedgeree

Kedgeree doesn't need anything with it, but it's nice to have a crunchy green salad afterward.

Variations

This is such a great dish that it's always worth buying good smoked haddock to make it from scratch. But very respectable versions can be made using leftover cooked fish.

Almost any kind will do, although you'll need at least 6 ounces to make a worthwhile dish for 2 or more. You might have to cook the rice in plain water, rather than the liquid from cooking the fish, but you can compensate by doubling the onion. A couple of handfuls of cooked peas will also help to jazz it up a bit.

ROAST SQUID

Cephalopods like squid are such bizarre-looking sea creatures – like something from a science-fiction film – that it's a good idea to buy them from a fishmonger whole and uncleaned, just so that you can take a good look at their strange anatomy at home.

Preparing a squid for cooking seems a bit complicated, but once you've done it for the first time, it's actually very quick and easy. You can often buy cleaned, fresh squid bodies at the fishmonger's (which will take you straight to stage 7, below). Or you can buy frozen squid rings in the supermarket – but they won't be quite as good as fresh. Roasting squid rings in this way is an easy and safer alternative to deep-frying them – and it's just as delicious.

To serve 4 as a snack or starter:
All-purpose flour, 2 tablespoons
Salt and black pepper
Lemon, 1
Squid, about 1 pound
Sunflower oil, ¼ cup

Shallow bowl, cutting board, sharp knife, small plate, tablespoon, roasting pan, wooden spoon, kitchen tongs or metal spatula, large bowl, paper towels, slotted spoon, large serving plate

1. Preheat the oven to 500°F or as hot as it will go.

2. Measure the flour into the shallow bowl. Grind in some salt and pepper and mix well.

3. Cut the lemon into quarters and put it on the table on the small plate, ready for serving with the squid.

4. Rinse the squid under cold water and lay it out on the cutting board, flat white body sacs to the left, stringy tentacles to the right.

5. With your fingers, feel your way up the suckered tentacles until you get to a hard part. Squeeze just to the left of this, and a hard, round little ball will pop out. Throw this away.

Trim the flesh at the top of the tentacles so that you get a ring of squiddy flesh with lots of bobbly tentacles hanging down. This is edible, so set it to one side.

6. Holding the firm white body of the squid in one hand, pull out the head with your other hand. Lots of white innards will come out too (sometimes you find a tiny fish inside as well – the squid's last supper). Squid squirt their enemies with ink, and you may find that the ink sac will come out with the innards (or it may have punctured so that you just get a rather black, gunky mess). You don't need the ink for this recipe so this can all be thrown away. Put your hand inside the pouch and pull out the hard cartilage. This looks exactly like a quill-shaped piece of clear plastic. Pull out any other

wispy bits from inside the pouch and clean it well under the cold tap so that it's completely hollow. Pull away the kite-shaped flaps attached to the pouch as well as the speckled skin. Pull away as much of this skin as possible from the tentacles too. Throw away the flaps and the skin.

7. Lay the pouch on the cutting board and cut it from side to side in thin strips, so that you end up with lots of rings. Toss the rings and the crown of tentacles in the seasoned flour so that they're well coated.

8. Pour the sunflower oil into the roasting pan. Put the pan in the oven for 2 minutes or until the oil is smoking hot. Oven gloves on. Very carefully get out the pan and set it on the stove. Carefully add the floured squid pieces to the oil. Give them a quick stir with the wooden spoon to coat them in the hot oil, then return the pan to the oven.

9. Roast the squid for 6 to 7 minutes or until it is turning golden brown underneath. Oven gloves on. Carefully take the pan out of the

oven and use the kitchen tongs or metal spatula to turn the squid over. Return the pan to the oven for another 5 to 6 minutes, until the squid is nicely colored all over.

10. Line the large bowl with a double layer of paper towels. Using the slotted spoon, transfer the squid pieces to the paper towels for a few seconds. This will absorb any excess oil. Then pile them on a plate and serve.

How to eat your squid

Serve straight away, with the lemon quarters and the pepper grinder at hand. If you want to make more of a meal of it, you could add a salad and some bread. It's also very nice with a garlicky, lemony mayonnaise for dipping the squid rings into (see page 212 for the recipe).

MUSSELS À LA MARINIÈRE

Mussels are very easy to prepare and cook. They do, however, show you just how important timing can be. Overcook them by just a minute or two, and they will be small, shriveled, and rubbery instead of plump, juicy, and lovely.

This is the easiest way to cook them, and also one of the best known and most popular – with garlic, butter, and a splash of white wine. You could add a little cream to make them a bit richer, and more soupy.

To serve 4 as a starter:
Live mussels, 3 to 4 pounds
Garlic, 3 cloves
Parsley, a small bunch
Butter, 3 tablespoons
A dash of oil
White wine, ½ cup
Water, ½ cup

Heavy cream, ½ cup (optional)
Black pepper

Colander, large serving bowl, cutting board, sharp knife, large wide saucepan with a well-fitting lid, wooden spoon, slotted spoon, ladle

1. Just before you cook the mussels, you need to wash and "debeard" them. Put them in the colander and rinse them quickly by sloshing them under cold water. Then pick up each mussel and give it a quick inspection. Some will be quite clean, tightly closed, and can be put straight into a "good" pile. Others may have a bit of "beard" – a kind of hairy fringe, usually at the narrow end. Pull this off with your fingers, then put these mussels in the "good" pile, too. If a mussel is tightly shut, it means that the muscle it uses to close its shell against a predator (i.e., you) is working and therefore the mussel is still alive and good to eat. One or two mussels may be slightly open. Give them a tap or a flick – if they don't close, it means that they may be dead or dying. You should throw these away.

2. Once you've sorted and cleaned the mussels, you can cook them, but bear in mind that they only take a few minutes. Make sure everyone is standing by, ready to eat them.

3. Turn the oven on to 250°F and put the large bowl in it to get warm. Peel the garlic. Wash the parsley, shake it dry, then pick off the tougher stalks. Then chop the garlic and the parsley fairly finely (not together, but in 2 separate piles).

4. Put the saucepan over a fairly high heat. Add the butter with a dash of oil (which will help to stop the butter burning), then add the chopped garlic straight away. As the butter melts and the garlic sizzles, spread it around the pan with the wooden spoon.

5. You don't want the garlic or the butter to burn, so after just a minute or two, add the wine and the water. Wait for another minute or two, until the liquid in the pan is bubbling fiercely.

6. Now, you can add the mussels. Unless you have a very big pan, it's probably best to add them in 2 batches, so they are not more than 2 mussels deep in the bottom of the pan. Give the pan a shake to spread the mussels around, then put the lid on the pan straight away.

7. After no more than 1 minute, take the lid off, check the mussels, and give them a quick shake and a stir. Some, at least, should have started to open. Replace the lid and cook for just 1 more minute. If most are now open, you can remove them with the slotted spoon, piling them into the large warm bowl you have standing by. If only a few, or no more than half, are open, replace the lid for another 30 seconds or so, then check again. Throw away any mussels that refuse to open.

8. Once you've taken out the first batch, you can add the second batch to the same bubbling liquid in the pan. Repeat the procedure.

9. When you've removed the last mussel, the juice left in the pan makes a lovely sauce. Stir in the parsley and the cream if you are using it. Grind in some black pepper, and let the sauce bubble for just a minute. Serve the mussels in the big bowl, with the sauce poured over, or divide them between individual bowls and ladle a little sauce over each bowlful.

How to eat your mussels

You eat mussels by picking them up with your fingers and pulling them out from the shells. You can choose a big half mussel shell and use it like a spoon to slurp the soupy juices from. Serve with plenty of buttered bread for dunking (warm baguettes are perfect for this).

MEAT

You probably know whether you prefer a bacon sandwich, a plate of herby roast chicken, or a skewer of garlic-scented lamb grilled over charcoal. But there's a little more you should know about meat. There's how best to cook it, of course. But also what kind of animal it came from, how that animal lived — and why that matters. The more you know about your meat, the more you'll enjoy it.

roast chicken, page 295

beef burgers, page 284

lamb kebabs, page 292

steak, page 268

spicy lamb pie, page 289

campfire cooking, page 275

ausages, page 272

spaghetti bolognese, page 287

MEAT

If you're out walking in the countryside, you're sure to see farm animals grazing in the fields. Do you think about them at all? In particular, do you ever think about the fact that many of these animals will eventually end up on our plates – as meat? Maybe you'd prefer not to think about it. It's much easier to see a sausage as just a sausage, rather than as a form of meat from an animal that once snuffled and grunted – before it was killed, cut up, and ground, ready for cooking.

Do try to think about it, though. If you're going to eat meat, shouldn't you eat it with your eyes wide open as to how that burger, how that chicken breast, how that pork chop, might have gotten to your plate? Then it's up to you to make the decision about the kind of meat you choose to eat. Far too many animals, both in the U.K. and abroad, are raised in miserable conditions. Largely, they are the animals that you won't see when you go out for a walk.

Of the four main animals that we raise for meat in the U.K. – cattle, sheep, pigs, and chickens – it's the last two that tend to get the worst treatment. This is because they are mostly farmed intensively – bred, raised, and fattened indoors in crowded conditions in very large sheds. Out of every 100 chickens eaten in this country, 98 will have been produced in this way.

Cattle and sheep, on the other hand, tend to be farmed extensively here, which means that most of them will spend most of their lives outdoors in fields where the food – the grass under their feet – is free.

Why are some animals farmed intensively?

The plain truth is that producers (often large companies rather than what we think of as farmers) can make money out of rearing pigs and chickens on intensive farms, but it's much more difficult to do this with cattle and sheep. Pigs and chickens are capable of putting on weight very quickly – and the faster an animal grows, the faster it can be sold for slaughter. What's more, the faster that animal can be grown, the cheaper it is to produce – so a chicken that's taken only six weeks to get to slaughter weight will be much cheaper to produce than one that's taken ten weeks.

In contrast, cattle are kept for at least 15 months, and very often $2^1/_2$ years, before they go to slaughter. If they are kept inside, they'll eat a lot of very expensive food in that time. Sheep may be quick to grow and fatten, but it's still too expensive for most farmers to raise them intensively. Indoor sheep are expensive to feed and need lots of care and attention to stay fit and free from disease, so most farmers choose to raise them cheaply out of doors.

So it all comes down to money. Most pigs and chickens are raised in vast numbers in huge sheds, simply because it's cheaper that way. They live in crowded conditions, never get to see daylight, and are often fed things they would never choose for themselves (feed containing antibiotics to keep them healthy in such unnatural conditions, for instance). They simply don't get a chance to behave in a natural way, doing the things that pigs and chickens like to do. Pigs enjoy rooting around, but it's impossible to do this on a concrete floor. A pregnant sow likes to make a nest before she gives birth, but she can't do this if she is confined in a space so narrow it prevents her from even turning around. Chickens reared out of doors like to peck and scratch at grubs and grit and grain. But chickens reared in huge numbers have nothing to peck and scratch at except each other.

Free-range and organic meat

In the case of pigs and poultry, finding an alternative to intensive farming means looking for meat that is certified as free range or organic. *Free range* means that the animals are free to roam and behave more naturally, while an organic label goes even further. It means the animals have been reared according to a strict code of high-welfare practice and have been given feeds produced without the use of agrichemicals and artificial fertilizers. In fact, it's not just their feed but the very land on which they live that has been organically farmed.

Organic and free-range, or naturally raised, meat is more expensive than intensively farmed meat. This is hardly surprising, given that the whole point of intensive farming is to make meat as cheap as possible. Those who

support organic and free-range farming take the view that meat should be more expensive. And they believe we should be prepared to pay more to ensure that the animals we raise for meat, whose lives are our responsibility from the moment of their birth to the moment of their death, live well. Only by caring for them properly when they're alive can we feel okay about eating them when they're dead.

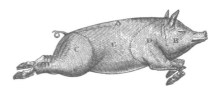

Shopping for meat

If we are going to buy only the more expensive, welfare-friendly meats, it may be that we can't afford to eat meat as often as we are used to. But perhaps that's not such a bad thing. If everyone were ready to spend a little more money on a little less meat, we would soon see a vast improvement in the welfare of millions of farm animals.

But why does so much intensive farming go on? Surely nobody really thinks it's right to buy chicken from a bird that can't stand on its own two legs? And that's the problem: it seems that hardly anyone does stop to think about it. At least, not at the vital moment when they pick up a pack of meat and put it in their shopping cart.

The trouble is, it has been made all too easy for us to buy intensively produced pork and chicken. If it's a lot cheaper for a farmer to raise it, then it's a lot cheaper for a shopper to buy it. It's hard to pay twice as much for something that looks very similar to the cheaper version. And there's really not enough information on the label for anyone to make a proper decision about which meat to buy. The label will say nothing about the lifestyle of the intensively raised pig or chicken, just that it's a "fresh pork chop" or a "fresh British chicken." If the label said "never sees daylight," or "denied the chance to scratch at the ground" or even "reared in severely crowded conditions," the alternative might not look so expensive after all.

How you can make a difference

We often forget who really controls the way animals are treated and meat is produced. We do. The reason factory-farmed meat is produced in such vast quantities is because we are buying it in vast quantities.

The fact is, farmers rear the kind of meat that people want to buy. If people buy cheap, intensively farmed meat, then farmers will continue to produce it. But if people change to buying free-range meat, then farmers will produce that instead. If free-range sausages sell out quickly every day, then shops will demand more and more free-range sausages. It's simply a matter of supply and demand. You demand it from the shops. They demand it from the farms. The farms supply it.

Which means that, if lots of us were to decide that we were no longer going to buy intensively farmed meat, we could make a big difference in a short time.

Where to buy meat

While farmers are responsible for the care of an animal while it's alive, butchers are responsible for what happens to it when it's dead. For a steak to taste good, a butcher must pay as much attention to the care of the dead carcass as the farmer paid to the living animal. Having said that, good butchers should know all about the meat they sell long before it gets into their fridges.

Really good butchers will be able to tell you about the meat in their shops – where it came from and how the animals were raised. Local farmers' markets and farm shops should also be able to tell you about the meat that they sell, and in some cases they will have raised the animals themselves. You'll be supporting local businesses in your area if you shop from them, too. If you buy your meat at a supermarket, you'll have to rely on the information given on the label. Try not to be influenced by meaningless terms such as *farm fresh*. Remember that a packet of pork chops or chicken thighs will be from intensively farmed animals unless it says otherwise.

If you want to be a really good meat cook, then undoubtedly the first challenge is to find yourself some really good meat. Once you've done that, the next bit isn't so hard.

Cooking meat

A crisp-skinned roast chicken straight from the oven. A lamb kebab sizzling on the grill. A pot of herby beef stew bubbling away. Few things make you as hungry as the sight and smell of meat cooking.

Heat does incredible things to meat. Take a leg of lamb, cold from the fridge. Hardly tempting, is it? But salt and pepper it, stick strips of garlic and sprigs of rosemary into it, put it in the oven for an hour or two, and you have a miraculous transformation. The warm, tender slices of meat will melt in your mouth; the fat, turned crisp and golden brown, is now utterly delicious. The heat has not only tenderized the meat, making it easier to chew, swallow, and digest, it has also created a whole new set of flavors that weren't there before.

We also cook meat to make it safer. Cooking kills the tiny bugs that may be present in meat – bacteria and parasites that might cause anything from minor tummy upsets to fatal poisoning. To be absolutely safe, some meats have to be cooked more thoroughly than others.

Poultry (chickens, turkeys, etc.) must always be completely cooked through before you eat it, as these birds can harbor nasty parasites and bacteria, which are killed only by cooking. Pork, too, should always be well cooked. Follow the cooking times given in recipes, but also check for yourself that the meat is done. Stick a sharp knife or skewer into the thickest part of the meat (the thigh of a chicken, for example). If the juices come out clear, then the meat is cooked. If they're still pink or bloody, it needs to cook longer.

It's slightly different with beef and lamb. Many people like to eat a leg of roast lamb when it's still a little bit pink in the middle. Some people like to eat a steak "rare" or even "blue" – where the steak only says a quick hello to a hot frying pan before it's whisked onto a serving dish. You can even eat certain cuts of beef completely raw in dishes such as steak tartare and carpaccio. However, beef that you've bought already chopped or ground should always be well cooked because more of the surface area has been exposed to possible contamination.

Whatever meat you're going to cook, you should always be careful how you handle and prepare it. Raw meat must never come into contact with other foods. So if, for example, you use a knife and a cutting board to cut up some raw meat, then you shouldn't use the same knife and board to make a salad afterward, or to slice some cooked meat to go in a sandwich. Wash your hands before handling meat, and again afterward before you handle any other foods.

Different kinds of meat

While it's possible to make a few important points that apply to all meats, the meat of different animals looks different, tastes different, and is often cooked in very different ways. Over the following pages are a few thoughts about the animals we rear for meat, and the way to cook and eat them . . .

CATTLE AND BEEF

Show someone a picture of a large animal with four legs, horns, and a stringy tail and they'll probably call it a cow. But cows, strictly speaking, are just the females.

For centuries, the same type of cattle would have provided us with both milk and meat. Modern farming separates the two jobs, and we have bred different sorts of cattle to do them. A pure dairy cow wouldn't give a beef farmer many good steaks (her coat-hanger-shaped hips support a huge udder rather than a meaty back end), and a beef cow wouldn't keep a dairy farmer in business for long.

Beef "suckler" cows are female cattle that give birth to calves that will be raised for beef. It's not the cow herself that will be eaten, it's the calves that she raises, year after year. These cows are called suckler cows because, unlike dairy cows, the milk they produce goes straight to the calf, which sucks it from her udder for around six months. Suckler cows will stay on a farm for several years, usually producing a calf each spring or summer.

Both the male calves (bulls) and female calves (heifers) of suckler cows can be reared for beef. The males usually have their testicles removed (castration) to make them less aggressive and less interested in the cows, so they can be reared more easily for meat. They are then called steers or bullocks.

When female beef cattle (heifers) are around 18 months old, they are either sold at a cattle auction or taken to a slaughterhouse.

The male steers take slightly longer to mature and are usually killed at two years of age or a little older (up to 30 months).

Not all beef cattle are raised with their mothers in this way. Almost half of all calves destined for meat are born on dairy farms, the offspring of a dairy cow mother and a beef bull father. These calves are taken from their mothers a couple of days after birth. (See also "The Problem of Dairy Calves," page 58.)

Cooking beef

Cattle are big animals, and just one carcass can produce hundreds of pounds of meat; typically they weigh 600 to 800 pounds. Some of this beef tastes best cooked quickly over high heat, while some of it needs to be cooked gently for a long time to make it tender.

Markets sell different cuts of beef, most of which are called "steak": filet steak, braising steak, chuck steak, sirloin steak . . . a steak is just a chunk of meat (at least, until we start talking about steak and chips – more about this in a moment). What makes these steaks look, cook, and taste different from each other is that they come from different parts of the beef carcass. Different muscles doing different jobs while the animal was alive result in different cuts of meat, as they are called. Each has its own character and its own uses in the kitchen.

The quick-cooking meat comes mostly from the animal's back and back end – the part that does the least work. This is where rump, tenderloin, and sirloin all come from – the sort of steak that arrives sizzling on your plate in a restaurant. The meat from the neck, which obviously does a lot of work stretching up and down all day to eat grass, takes long, slow cooking to make it tender, and gives you rich beef stews that melt in your mouth.

Some beef recipes

Beef Burgers, page 284
Spaghetti Bolognese, page 287

Veal

Beef is not the only meat that comes from cattle. Veal is the name given to the meat taken from the calves of dairy cows. It is pale in color and is valued for its delicate, "milky" flavor. It has been controversial for many years because of the practice of rearing veal calves in crates in which they can barely turn around. This is supposed to keep the veal tender, and although it is not practiced in Britain, it still happens on the Continent.

There is a humane alternative. Some British dairy calves are raised in open barns, where they are fed a milk- and cereal-based diet and may even be allowed to suckle their mothers. The resulting meat, often called "rosé, or pink, veal," is darker and more tasty. Veal calves are usually slaughtered when they are 5 to 6 months old, which seems young, but is about the same age as most lambs. Given the problem of unwanted dairy calves (see page 58), this pink veal is worth supporting.

OFFAL FROM NOSE TO TAIL Most of the meat that we eat is the muscle tissue of the animals we take it from — what we call flesh. But that accounts for only about 60 percent of any carcass. The rest of the animal, however, is not inedible. Far from it. Almost all the internal organs – the liver, kidneys, intestines – can be eaten, as can specialized muscles, such as hearts, tongues, and tails. These edible body parts are what we call "offal" (derived from the phrase "off fall" – because, when the stomach of a slaughtered carcass is cut open, most of the internal organs tumble out onto the abattoir floor).

Many people are squeamish about eating offal – some seem to assume that they won't like it before they have even tried it. This is partly because it seems so different from the meat they are used to. And partly perhaps because, unlike ordinary red meat, when you look at a piece of offal it is hard to forget where it comes from – a once living animal.

But the offal cuts are often some of the most interesting and delicious parts of an animal – sweeter, more tender, and usually more interestingly flavored than the muscle meat. Try it; you might like it. And if you do, you can also feel good about the fact that you are showing maximum respect to an animal that has died to feed you – by helping to put every last part of its carcass to good use.

Project:

EXPERIMENTING WITH A STEAK

Good butchers will hang the carcasses of their animals on a hook to age in their cold store for somewhere between two and four weeks. You might think that this would make the meat spoil, but it actually helps it to develop flavor and become more tender. Red meat that hasn't been hung is tough and chewy. Properly hung, well-produced beef is generally quite dark in color and should have a network of creamy fat lines running through it, a bit like a road map. These fat lines, called "marbling," stop meat drying out as it cooks and make it less tough to eat. Fat also means flavor.

The most sought-after cuts of beef are the steaks cut especially for quick grilling and frying. They come generally from the tenderloin (the most expensive cut, because it is the most tender), the sirloin (which often has the best marbling), and the rump (which is tougher, but very tasty). These are the kinds of steaks that many beef enthusiasts like to eat rare and bloody, and with chips (French fries).

You've probably already decided about the chips, but it may take a while to decide whether you like your steak rare, medium, or well done. You certainly won't know how you like it until you've tried it each way.

Buy a good steak and experiment a bit. You're not only learning how you like your steak, you're learning the art of cooking it well.

You will need:

A good sirloin steak, about ¾ inch thick (8 to 10 ounces)
A little oil
Salt and black pepper

To accompany (to make a meal of it!):

Chips (French fries) or fried potatoes and a tasty green salad

2 plates, cutting board, sharp knife, a heavy frying pan (the heavy bottom means that the pan heats up and cooks the meat evenly), metal spatula or tongs

1. It's best not to cook a steak straight from the fridge, so unwrap it, put it on a plate, and leave it somewhere safe (from the dog) for about an hour before you cook it. Then cut the steak into 3 equal pieces with the sharp knife.

2. Put the frying pan over high heat for a couple of minutes, then turn the heat down to medium. Add a little oil to the pan.

3. The idea of the experiment is to cook the 3 pieces of steak for 3 different lengths of time, so that you can taste the difference between well done, medium, and rare. So, put the first piece of steak in the pan and let it cook, without turning, for 2 minutes.

4. Turn the steak over with the spatula or tongs and, as soon as you have done so, put the second piece in the pan. Wait another 2 minutes, turn over both steaks, then put the third piece in the pan.

5. Now wait just 1 minute, then turn over all 3 pieces of meat. Season all of them lightly with a sprinkling of salt and pepper. After 1 more minute, turn them again and season them again. Leave for 1 minute, turn, and then leave for 1 last minute. Remove them from the pan and put them straight away onto a warm, but not hot, plate. Let them rest for a couple of minutes.

It may pickle your brain to do the math, but take it from us that the 3 steaks have had 8 minutes, 6 minutes, and 4 minutes each. They have also been nicely seasoned, and turned several times to get a well-browned, tasty crust. Provided you started with a nice thick steak, they will be well done, medium, and rare (but not very rare – that would be just 1 minute on each side).

Taste each of the pieces, starting with the well-done one. You should find it has a well-browned crust but isn't even a little bit pink in the middle. It shouldn't be completely dried out, though (that would be very well done, 10 to 12 minutes).

Next, try the medium one. It should still be a bit pink in the middle. Now try the rare. It will be really quite pink, a bit bloody and, if the meat is good, more tender than the first two. Do you like it like that? If you think the rare one is best, you might try giving it 3 minutes' overall cooking next time. Of course, your decision now doesn't have to become the habit of a lifetime – in fact, the better the steak, the more likely you are to enjoy it rare.

Rare

Medium

Well done

PIGS AND PORK

If you stand a pig on its back legs, it's eerily similar to a human being. And oddly enough, we call the front legs of pork not legs but "hands" and the cuts of bacon around its front shoulder "collar bacon" — almost as if pigs should be wearing shirts and ties.

It's true that pigs and humans have had a very close relationship since people first started to domesticate wild animals. It's said that dogs look up to you, cats look down on you, but pigs look you straight in the eye. But how could we look a pig in the eye when we think about the shameful conditions that so many of them endure on intensive farms?

Pigs are smart, friendly animals that, like dogs, are able to form bonds with us humans. Even more reason to treat them with respect. We suggest you don't even consider buying pork unless it is clearly labeled "naturally raised," "free range," or "organic."

Beyond roast pork

Roast pork, with its armor of crackling, is an irresistible classic. But one of the reasons pigs have always been prized is because pork can be transformed into so many different foods. For thousands of years, our ancestors salted nearly all their meat — pork, beef, even lamb — to stop it from going bad. Now, although we have fridges and freezers, we still go to the trouble of salting some meat, particularly pork, simply because it tastes so good. Think of hot, crisp bacon or slices of honey-roasted

ham. It's not unusual in French towns to come across an entire shop — called a *charcuterie* — devoted to dishes made by salting, smoking, and processing pigs: pâtés, terrines, hams, and salami.

Most sausages are made from pork, though of course they can be made with any meat. Salami-style sausages, which you'd find in a delicatessen rather than on a fresh meat counter, are made from meat that has been carefully salted and spiced, stuffed into casings, and then hung up to dry for several weeks (it's safe to eat raw pork in this instance, because of the salt and the lengthy drying-out process). They are thinly sliced and eaten on their own or with bread.

The best fresh sausages, or "bangers," are made by stuffing good meat, bread crumbs, and seasonings such as salt, pepper, and herbs into natural casings — usually sheep intestines. Far too many sausages on sale today are made from poor-quality meat (all the nasty bits salvaged from a pig carcass) bulked out with too much bread, salt, and many artificial additives, even colorings, designed to make them keep longer and look better in your fridge. They are stuffed into artificial casings, which can turn hard as you fry them.

Some pork recipes
Macaroni and Cheese with Bacon, page 71
Homemade Bacon for a Bacon Sandwich,
  page 326
Spicy Bean Stew with Sausages, page 330

Project:

MAKING YOUR OWN SAUSAGES

The best way to set a standard for the very finest sausages is to make some yourself. It's also one of the best possible ways to have fun in the kitchen. Clear yourself a large work surface – sausage making takes up lots of room – and recruit a partner/assistant (it's much easier and far more fun when there are two or even three of you).

Most butchers who make their own sausages will be prepared to sell you a couple of yards of sausage casing, particularly if you buy the meat from them at the same time. Or you can get them by mail order (see page 407). If you can't get the skins, though, you can shape the sausage meat into little patties instead and fry them gently like mini burgers. They'll still be completely delicious.

You will need:
Sausage casing, 2 to 3 yards
Free-range, organic, or naturally raised
    pork shoulder, 1 pound ground
Free-range, organic, or naturally raised pork
    belly, 8 ounces, ground
Fine dried bread crumbs, ¼ cup (optional)
Salt (start with 1 level teaspoon)
Sage leaves, 16 small ones
Black pepper
White pepper, if you have some
Nutmeg or mace, a good grinding or
    ¼ teaspoon
A little oil for frying

2 large bowls, wooden spoon, sharp knife, cutting board, teaspoon, frying pan, wide-necked funnel (hardware stores sell cheap ones), something to act as a plunger to push the meat down the neck of the funnel (the handle of a rolling pin, perhaps), butcher's string, scissors, an assistant

1. Put one of the large bowls in the sink and fill it with cold water. Drop the length of casing into it. Find one of the ends and hold it close under the faucet. Turn the cold water on a little. You'll see the water run in and the skin will gradually swell as the water travels down, so it looks like a long, curly snake – an amazing sight! Keep running the water through the casing for a minute or two, and then let the casing soak in the bowl of water while you make the sausage meat.

2. Put all the ground pork in the other large bowl. Add the bread crumbs if you are using them (a small amount is good for the texture of the sausage), then add the salt and stir well with the wooden spoon.

3. Chop the sage leaves and add them to the mixture with some pepper and a good pinch of nutmeg or mace.

4. Before you start going into sausage production, make a little cake of a couple of teaspoons of the sausage meat and fry it for a couple of minutes on each side until cooked through. Taste it for seasoning – do you need more herbs, more salt, more pepper?

5. Now to fill the sausages. Take the casing out of the water and slide your fingers down it to push out any water trapped inside. Find one end of the casing and draw it over the spout of the funnel. Gather up all the casing over the spout (rather like putting a leg warmer on over your foot), leaving a little bit of the casing overlapping the tip of the funnel so it catches the stuffing.

6. Take a spoonful of the sausage meat and push it down through the neck of the funnel. When the meat appears in the tip of the casing, tie a piece of string around the bottom to pinch it closed (if you tie the casing closed before you put the meat in, you'll get a big bubble of trapped air).

7. Take turns with your assistant to keep pushing the sausage meat through the funnel and into the casing, which will slide off the spout of the funnel as it fills up with meat. Try not to make the sausages too thick and fat, or they'll burst when you twist them into lengths. It's difficult to make them really even at first, and you'll probably find that the end of your string of sausages is a bit more professional looking than the start.

8. When you've used up all the sausage meat, you'll need to twist the filled casing into individual sausages. Starting at the tied-up end, gently pinch the casing and twirl the sausage clockwise every so often, so that you get a classic string of sausages, like something out of a cartoon. Then find the middle of the string (roughly) and start twisting "opposite" sausages into pairs. There is a clever butcher's way of twisting them into bunches of 3, but it's too hard to explain!

9. When you get to the end, tie it up with string and snip off any remaining casing. Hang up the sausages somewhere cool and airy for a few hours, and then either cook them straight away or, better still, though you'll need unbelievable patience, put them on the bottom shelf of the fridge overnight to let the flavors mingle and settle.

10. When you want to cook your sausages, heat a little oil in a frying pan over low heat. Fry the sausages fairly gently, turning them every few minutes so that they brown all over without burning. They should cook gently for at least 15 minutes, depending on their thickness; cut one open to make sure they are cooked all the way through.

How to eat your sausages

A hot dog bun, or just a simple, crusty white-bread sandwich, filled with your own home-made sausages and a bit of ketchup or mustard, is very hard to beat for breakfast, lunch, or supper. In fact, the only thing that probably comes close is good old bangers and mashed potatoes (see Best-Ever Mashed Potatoes, page 199).

Project:

BUILDING A CAMPFIRE FOR OUTDOOR COOKING

Grilling is a way of cooking food (especially meat) directly on a metal grid suspended over red-hot charcoal or the hot embers of a wood fire. Some people build permanent brick barbecues at home, while others have portable barbecues that can be moved around. You can also buy disposable kits. These are handy when you're picnicking away from home or down on the beach.

Sometimes, though, it's even more fun to build a proper campfire from scratch, using paper, leaves, twigs, and dry branches and logs. You can grill the food on a rack propped over the fire, as for a barbecue, or, much easier, you can use the rack as a stovetop, taking a frying pan or saucepan, cutting board, and knife with you along with all your raw ingredients, and actually cook properly outside.

Younger cooks should always enlist the help of an adult when cooking over a fire.

You will need:
Bricks or stones to encircle the fire
* and support the grill*
Dry fire-lighting material, such as
* newspaper or dead leaves*
Dry sticks and twigs
Matches
Thicker sticks and logs
A grill rack or oven rack for grilling

Whether you're on the beach, out on a picnic, or just in your own back garden, think carefully about the best place to put your fire. It should be well away from overhanging trees and branches or anything that might catch fire, like dry, dead grass. Always ask permission from whoever owns the land. If you're camping, keep the fire well away from any tents. See which way the wind's blowing and how strongly – you don't want to be driven away from where you're sitting by thick clouds of smoke (and neither does anyone else). Once you've decided on the right spot, brush away any dead leaves or twigs – anything that might catch fire.

Place a few bricks or stones in a circle just far enough apart to support the rack that will act as your grill or stovetop. Keep your fire quite compact, otherwise it will take a long time to get cooking. It will also become too hot to sit near.

Scrunch up some sheets of newspaper into balls and place them on the ground in the middle of the stones, or make a pile of dead leaves. Starting with twigs and small dry sticks, arrange them in a rough sort of pyramid on top of the paper or leaves so that they criss-cross each other. Light the newspaper in several places with a match. The fire will flare up as it burns the newspaper, but it's only when the sticks start to crackle that you know they've really caught fire. Add some slightly bigger sticks just a few at a time. You don't want to choke the fire with too much fuel too quickly.

As the fire strengthens, add four or five small logs. If it's a very calm day, you may need to blow on the base of the fire or fan it to give it some extra oomph to get going.

It's very tempting to start cooking straight away, but wait until the flames have died down and the logs have started to turn white and ashy before you cook (if it's already dark, you'll see them glowing red). Carefully place the rack on the bricks or stones, and you're ready to start cooking.

Things to cook on your campfire
All sorts of recipes can be adapted for cooking over a campfire. Here are a few ideas:

Sausages Whether you grill them on the barbecue or fry them gently in a pan, they'll taste delicious, especially if you've made them yourself (see page 272). Go whole hog and you could even fry some of your own home-cured bacon alongside (page 326).

Spicy bean stew with sausages What's the point of a campfire if you don't cook a campfire stew? Ladle it into bowls and hand them round with hunks of bread and butter to mop up the sauce (see page 330).

Lamb kebabs Marinate the meat in the kitchen and thread it onto the prepared skewers next to your fire (see page 292). You could make mixed vegetable kebabs to eat with the meat ones by marinating chunks of onion and green and red peppers in olive oil, lemon, and bay

leaves. Thread the vegetable chunks alternately onto skewers and grill the kebabs alongside the lamb ones; watch them carefully as they may not take as long to cook.

A juicy steak Get a frying pan good and hot and let your steak sizzle in the pan until it's cooked just as you like it (see page 268).

Homemade burgers A burger cooked over an open fire or barbecue, delicious with the flavor of wood smoke, is in a different league from one cooked at home in a pan on the stove (see page 284). Remember to take the buns, ketchup, and mustard too.

A freshly caught mackerel Clean it and gut it (see page 226) and pop it in a pan with lots of butter. Or, maybe even better, you could grill it over charcoal (page 240).

Flat breads Use the recipe on page 38, taking a bowl, board, and rolling pin, plus all the ingredients, with you. Make them outside and cook them in a heavy frying pan. Once cooked, smear them with a little butter and eat them with your fingers. Best of all, you can use them to wrap up your campfire meats, such as sausages, burgers, or steaks.

Marshmallows Find each person a long stick. Spear a marshmallow on the point of each stick and toast it gently over the fire until it just starts to melt (see page 368).

SHEEP AND LAMB

Walk past a field of sheep with their young lambs in the early evening in spring and you'll see some pretty crazy behavior. Lambs running races, playing king of the castle on old bales of hay, or standing on the backs of their long-suffering mothers. Could you really eat one of those gallivanting cuties?

It's confusing that we use the word *lamb* to describe both the very young animal and the meat that we eat. But by the time they're ready to go to market, to end up on your Sunday lunch table, lambs have changed out of all recognition. Sheep grow up very quickly – one minute they're impossibly charming and gangly legged, the next they're hard to distinguish from their placid mothers, head down, sober citizens, their whole world seemingly one long mealtime.

Lambs are raised either for meat or to join a flock as breeding stock. Few sheep in the U.K. are kept for their wool. Shearing the thick fleece from a ewe in June will make her more comfortable in the hot summer months, and the fleeces will certainly be bundled up and sold, but a farmer will get only around two pounds for each fleece.

You're more likely to see sheep in a field than any other farm animal. Although beef cattle are fairly common, outdoor pig farms are usually few and far between, and you're lucky indeed to spot a flock of chickens (either egg-laying or roast-dinner ones) pecking the ground. But sheep seem to be everywhere, scattered across the countryside like cordless lawnmowers.

This is because they thrive on even quite poor grazing. They love the outdoor life. Whereas if you take a flock of sheep into

MOVING SHEEP Generally speaking, most lambs are still extensively rather than intensively farmed, which means that they're sent out to graze rather than brought in to consume. In this respect, they get a much better deal than the poor pig. But the one big welfare issue for lambs is the way, or  rather the distance, they are sent for slaughter. Farmers sometimes pack their lambs up in huge trucks and send them halfway across the country, or even abroad, for slaughter if they think they can get a better price that way. Supermarkets often have one central slaughterhouse that may be a long way from where the animals they are buying have been raised.

If you want to avoid supporting the long-distance transport of live sheep when you buy lamb, then always try to choose local lamb. You'll see it labeled by most good butchers, and of course if you buy it direct from the farmer, at a farm shop or a farmers' market, you'll know it's local.

a barn for a few weeks, pamper them with the best dry food and the sweetest hay – then some of them will start to get sick. Sheep tend to struggle without grass or vegetation and plenty of space to roam around.

Lamb for Easter

It's traditional to eat lamb at Easter, which seems strange if you think that Easter is actually the time that most lambs are being born rather than growing big enough to eat. Lambs are generally slaughtered from about four months after birth, so in fact the best time of year to buy young, "new-season" lamb is from June onward.

However, some breeds of sheep can produce lambs at any time of year rather than just in the spring. For other breeds, it's necessary to introduce hormones into the mother ewes so they give birth out of season. These November- and December-born lambs are kept indoors with their mothers for the harshest months of winter. The mothers are fed plenty of hay and "cake" (sadly, only cereal-based concentrated feed pellets), and the lambs feed on their mother's milk and eat a bit of cake themselves. They may be turned out briefly on the early spring grass, but the idea is generally to have the lambs ready for the Easter market. This milk-fed lamb is pale pink in color and a bit porky in taste, lacking the deep flavor of older, grass-fed lambs.

The tradition of eating lamb at Easter may well go back to the time when we ate mostly "hogget" lamb – lamb that's a year or so old and therefore has eaten a whole year's worth of milk and grass. Some people like the deep flavor of sheep that are kept, like beef cows, for two or more years. These are not called lamb at all but referred to as mutton. Mutton has been unfashionable for many years now, but it is making a bit of a comeback. If you like well-flavored meat, you should give it a try. You'll need to ask for mutton and hogget from a butcher, farm shop, or farmers' market, as supermarkets don't currently stock it.

Eating lamb

For an animal that eats its greens and takes so much exercise, a sheep is surprisingly fatty. In terms of its eating, this is no bad thing. It's the fat in lamb that makes its meat so sweet and juicy and gives it so much flavor. The fat that drips from a roast can always be poured off, and you don't have to eat the fat on the edge of your lamb chop. But without it the meat wouldn't be so succulent and tasty.

Because of its strong flavor, lamb is particularly good cooked with spices or herbs such as rosemary and garlic, which contrast well with the fattiness of the meat. A lot of lamb is eaten in Middle Eastern countries, marinated and grilled as kebabs, or ground and made into *koftas* – little meat patties flavored with onion and parsley.

Some lamb recipes

Spicy Lamb Pie, page 289
Lamb Kebabs, page 292
Liver and Bacon, page 294

POULTRY

Birds are one of the few creatures we ever buy whole to cook and eat. Pork, beef, and lamb mostly come already cut up — into steaks, chops, chunks, and ground meat. Often it's difficult even to tell what kind of animal they once came from.

Even so, it's still hard to link a plucked chicken in a plastic-wrapped polystyrene tray with the feathered bird that once walked around pecking the grass (if it was lucky). Without its head, feathers, and feet, neatly trussed up for the oven, it lies on its back, breast up, horizontal not vertical. Next time you get a bird ready for the oven, prop it up on its legs and take a few seconds to imagine what it looked like when it was alive. Imagine the wings covered in feathers, all ready to flap; the feet scratching at the soil; the breast of the bird covered in soft, downy feathers. Pull up the flappy bit of neck and imagine a feathered head on it.

Why? Because it's always good to understand what you're cooking and eating — link the meat to the bird and you can't help but think about the life that your chicken's had.

If it's a free-range chicken, it must have had some freedom to roam outside during the day, to peck and scratch the ground and stretch its wings. If it's an organic bird, then it will have had the freedom of a free-range chicken, possibly more, plus a diet of organic food. But chickens that are farmed intensively in broiler houses are bred to put on vast amounts of weight very quickly. So quickly, in fact, that sometimes their legs cannot bear their own weight and their hearts give out under the stress of too large a body. These birds will have had hardly any more room to move around in than the size of this page.

Roasting a chicken

A roast chicken is a great treat that everyone looks forward to. But however you cook chicken, it will always taste more interesting from a bird that was used to running over a grassy field. It will have had the chance to peck at the grass and search for insects, so its diet will have been more varied and it will have a better flavor. Free to run around, its legs become strong and muscular. It may not be as big as the bird that was raised in the broiler house, and it will certainly cost you more. But every mouthful will be ten times tastier, and you will have the tremendous satisfaction of knowing that the bird you are eating has had a far better life.

IS IT COOKED? It's very important that chicken meat, and the meat of other reared poultry such as turkeys, is cooked thoroughly before you eat it. Whether you're cooking the whole bird or just a joint or breast, pierce the thickest part of the meat with a sharp knife or skewer at the end of the recommended cooking time and look at the juices that ooze out — they should be clear. Any hint of pink and the chicken needs to cook longer.

Turkey

While chicken dominates our poultry eating throughout the year, turkey makes up for it

 in grand style on one or two big feast days. Turkeys were brought back from the New World in the sixteenth century

and quickly took over the role of "occasion" food from birds such as swans, peacocks, and even herons. The outlandish appearance of the turkey-cock probably appealed to Elizabethan cooks used to dressing, say, a roast peacock carcass with its own spectacular tail feathers. Today's roast turkey hardly looks different from a very large chicken.

Turkey can be tasty when it's been raised slowly and given good food to eat. But an ordinary turkey, kept in an overcrowded barn, stuffed with food until it's so big that you can barely wedge it in the oven, is no happier, and no tastier, than a factory-farmed chicken.

Roasting is such a simple cooking technique that it's vital to start with a really good turkey – there's no fancy sauce to disguise the fact if you've cooked a second-rate bird. No wonder so many people prefer the leftovers, when lots of other flavors can be added: a creamy, herby turkey pie, perhaps, or slices of cold turkey with a curried mayonnaise.

So, if you want to make sure your Thanksgiving or Christmas roast turkey really is special and not just sandwich fodder, search out a free-range or organic bird.

Ducks and geese

After chickens and turkeys, ducks and geese are the most popular farmed poultry in the U.K. While ducks are quite common, geese make up just a tiny fraction of the poultry market, and they are mostly sold at Christmas.

The meat of ducks and geese is similar, and quite different from chicken and turkey. You could say that geese are "big ducks," just as you might describe turkeys as "giant chickens." Although ducks and geese are waterfowl – they like to spend some time swimming on, or at least splashing in, water – they both eat grass and grain, such as wheat and corn. The best-tasting and happiest birds are those that have been reared outdoors on grass (with a bit of water to splash in, even if it's an artificial pond or just a bathtub) and fed on grain.

In the case of ducks, look for a free-range or organic label for reassurance. Goose farming is still on such a small scale that almost any bird you buy from a butcher is likely to be free range. Organic geese will be expensive, but should be top quality.

At their best, the meat of both birds is rich, dark, and far more deeply flavored than the white meat of chickens and turkeys. It's also helped by the generous layer of fat that the birds put down between the meat and the skin. Roasting either bird is not that difficult, but is likely to take over two hours in the case of a large duck, and nearer three for a goose. You can make fabulous roast potatoes using the fat that runs out of the birds.

GAME

Not all meat is from farmed animals. Some of it is wild. Rabbits, hares, and deer have all been eaten for centuries – by anyone crafty enough to catch or shoot one. Birds that are shot for sport and enjoyed for their meat include partridge, woodcock, pigeon, and mallard (the most common kind of wild duck).

The meat of all these creatures, whether they are birds or mammals, is usually referred to as "game." But the most common game meat we eat in the U.K. is pheasant.

Pheasant

Pheasants are not truly wild. The vast majority have been reared to be shot. Most of them are hatched from eggs in incubators and raised in very large numbers, spending the first few weeks of their lives in similar conditions to intensively farmed chickens. After that, they are a bit more fortunate, being transferred to large pens in the woods, where it is probably best to think of them as free range.

A few weeks before the shooting season begins, they are released from their pens to roam and fly wherever they please. They have a chance, at least, to become wild. But they generally don't wander too far away, as the gamekeeper who is looking after them will continue to feed them at various places in the woods where he wants them to stay.

More than half the pheasants reared on any shoot are shot in the first winter after their release. Those that survive the shooting season learn to live in the hedges and woods and, if they are not eaten by foxes, hawks, or other predators, will face the guns a second time. But very few will nest and breed successfully, and in that sense there is hardly a wild pheasant population at all in Britain.

However you feel about shooting, there is no doubt that the meat of pheasants makes good eating. If you want to roast one, follow the recipe for roast chicken on page 295, but spread a couple of slices of bacon over the breast of the bird. After the first 15 minutes on high heat, remove the bacon, then continue to roast at the lower temperature for just 30 to 45 minutes. This will be enough to cook the bird through.

Some poultry and game recipes
Roast Chicken, page 295
Chicken Curry, page 298
Pheasant Casserole, page 300

Venison
Venison, the meat of various species of deer, is butchered in a similar way to lamb – except that its leg, which, as with lamb, is one of the most popular roasting joints, is referred to as a *haunch*. The meat is leaner than lamb, and a strip of pork fat is often tied over a joint of venison to keep it moist while it roasts.

If it's well butchered and carefully cooked, venison is not a particularly gamy meat, though it is full flavored, like the best lamb. If you are curious to try it, then venison sausages or burgers are a good way to get started.

BEEF BURGERS

Making your own beef burgers gives you the chance to have a burger that's seasoned, cooked, and dressed exactly the way you like it.

The beef is the most important ingredient. It's best not to buy it already ground, as you don't know which cut of meat has been used. It's often the worst quality and ground so finely it turns out like pâté. Ask for "top round" or "rump." A little bit of beef fat on the outside of the meat (although not too much) will improve the flavor and texture of your burger. Ask the butcher to grind it on a coarser setting than usual, or, even better, take it home and grind it yourself if you can. Some food processors and mixers have grinding attachments that you can use, but a simple, old-fashioned meat grinder that clamps to the table and has a handle that you crank is much more fun. You can sometimes find old ones for sale very cheaply in secondhand stores and garage sales.

If you are confident of the quality of the beef and you've ground it yourself at home the same day as you are making the burgers, then you can eat your burgers, like your steak, medium or medium-rare – a little bit pink in the middle. If the beef is really good, your burgers won't really need any seasoning until the cooking stage. If you want to give them a bit of a tweak, a little finely chopped onion and a few herbs can be good, as below. But don't overdo it.

To make 4 burgers:

Coarsely ground top round or rump of beef, about 1 pound
Onion, 1/2 small
Chopped parsley, a small bunch
Thyme leaves, stripped from their stalks, about 1 teaspoon (or a pinch of dried mixed herbs)
Salt and black pepper
A little oil for frying

To serve:
Hamburger buns, 4

Plus some or all of the following:
Tomato ketchup
Mustard
Pickles
Mayonnaise
Sliced tomatoes
Sliced onions
Lettuce leaves
Slices of Cheddar cheese

Mixing bowl, sharp knife, cutting board, large, heavy frying pan

1. Put the ground beef into the bowl. Chop the onion very finely – or grate it coarsely, if you like – and add it to the meat. Chop the parsley and add that too, along with the thyme, a pinch of salt, and a twist of pepper.

2. Mix the meat and seasonings thoroughly with your hands. Divide into 4 roughly equal portions and form each into a ball with your hands. Then start flattening out the ball with your palms.

3. Keep pressing and molding to get the burger well compacted. You should be aiming for a burger that is (a) nice and wide (so it goes to the edges of the bun); (b) fairly flat (so it cooks evenly); and (c) not too raggedy at the edges (so it doesn't break apart when you cook it and turn it over). Around ¾ inch thick is about right – or a little thicker if you know you want to eat it medium-rare.

4. Heat a little oil in the frying pan over medium heat. Place the burgers in the pan. They should sizzle, but not too fiercely. Cook them for a couple of minutes, then turn them over and cook for a couple more. Keep turning every minute or so, seasoning lightly with salt and pepper each time.

5. The burgers should be completely cooked through (i.e., well done) in 7 to 10 minutes, depending on their thickness. If you want your burger a bit pink (medium or medium-rare), cook it for just 5 or 6 minutes overall. Of course, you don't have to fry the burgers in a pan. You can broil them or cook them on a grill. If you cook them over too high a heat, though, they'll be burnt on the outside before they're cooked in the middle.

How to eat your burgers

Toast the cut side of the buns lightly if you like them like that. Place a burger on each one. Have all the sauces and toppings laid out in bowls so that everyone can choose how to dress their burger.

SPAGHETTI BOLOGNESE

Once you've learned how to make a spag bol, you've begun to master a range of skills that will introduce you to a whole family of different recipes. The ingredients may vary quite a lot from recipe to recipe, but the techniques remain the same: the proper browning of the meat, the slow sautéing of the chopped vegetables in oil or butter, the gentle stewing of the meat in a highly flavored sauce. Changes in ingredients, spices, herbs, and quantities make for completely different end results. Add potato, chile, and cumin to a very similar sort of stew and you get a Latin American *picadillo* to eat with tortillas and rice. Make the stew meatier and less tomatoey, ladle it into a dish, cover it with buttery mashed potatoes, then bake it in the oven, and you have a cottage pie. A similar stew, well seasoned with cumin and chile and simmered with beans, gives you chili con carne.

To serve 4 to 6:
Spaghetti or dried tagliatelle, about 1 pound
Parmesan cheese, to serve

For the bolognese sauce:
Onion, 1 medium
Carrot, 1 large
Celery, 2 stalks
Olive oil, 3 tablespoons
Ground beef, 1 pound
Butter, 2 tablespoons
Salt
Garlic, 2 cloves

Tomato purée, 2 cups
Bay leaves, 2
Black pepper
White wine, 1 large glass (about $3/4$ cup)
Organic vegetable or chicken stock, $3/4$ cup
Milk, 1 cup

Sharp knife, cutting board, tablespoon, heavy frying pan with lid, wooden spoon, slotted spoon, bowl or plate, large saucepan, colander, grater

1. Peel the onion and carrot. Trim the celery and give it a wash if it looks muddy. Chop the vegetables fairly finely. You need roughly equal quantities of each. Set the prepared vegetables to one side while you get ready to fry the meat.

2. Spoon the olive oil into the pan, tilt the pan around to cover the surface evenly, then put the pan on the stove and turn the heat to high. Let the oil get really good and hot, almost but not quite smoking.

3. Add the meat and spread it in a layer across the pan with the wooden spoon. Let it sit, without stirring, and cook for 3 to 4 minutes, until it starts to turn brown underneath – not just change color from pink to beige. If it sticks in a couple of places, it doesn't matter at all. In fact, it's a good thing because those little burnt bits are actually where the juices in the meat have caramelized on the hot pan and are going to give your sauce plenty of flavor.

4. Turn the meat over with the wooden spoon to let the other side brown in the same way, breaking up the lumps with the back of the spoon if necessary. When you think it's cooked enough, use the slotted spoon to transfer the meat from the pan to a bowl or plate at the side of the stove. Turn the heat down.

5. Add the butter to the pan. Add the onion, carrot, celery, and a good sprinkling of salt and stir them into the butter, scraping up all the meaty bits that have stuck to the bottom of the pan. Put the lid on and let the vegetables "sweat" over a very low heat for about 10 minutes, stirring from time to time, until they soften and seem to shrink.

6. Peel the garlic and chop it very finely. Add it to the pan and fry the mixture a minute or two longer.

7. Add the tomato purée and bay leaves, then grind in some pepper and give everything a good stir. Return the meat to the pan and pour in the wine and stock. Stir in the milk. Bring the mixture to a simmer, cover the pan with the lid, and keep the heat very low so that the ragù cooks very gently. Stir from time to time. It should bubble away for at least an hour,

preferably 2 hours. At the end of the cooking time, taste a teaspoonful of the sauce – does it need more salt and pepper? Remember, though, that you are going to be cooking the spaghetti in quite salty water as well as perhaps adding salty grated Parmesan.

8. Fill the large saucepan three-quarters full with water and bring it to a boil. Just as it comes to a boil, add a tablespoonful of salt (there's no real scientific reason for adding the salt now; it's just that it's a good habit to get into because if you add it earlier you won't remember if you've added it or not!). Add the pasta to the pan and stir the water gently until all the pasta is submerged. Set the timer for a minute or two less than the cooking time on the pasta package, but remember to stir every now and again. Stand the colander in the sink.

9. Taste the pasta and, when you're happy that it's cooked as you like it (see page 29), carefully drain it into the colander. Then pour the pasta back into the pan and add the sauce. Stir well and serve, handing around the Parmesan cheese and the grater.

SPICY LAMB PIE

This pie is a tasty mixture of herby, spiced meat and crumbly pastry. If you prefer, you can make lots of little pies instead. However, one big pie (especially one that you've decorated with bits of leftover pastry) always gets people wowing, and it's even quicker and easier to make.

To make 1 big pie:

For the pastry:
Unsalted butter (or a mixture of butter
    and lard), 3/4 cup (1 1/2 sticks)
All-purpose flour, 2 1/4 cups, plus extra for
    dusting the work surface
A pinch of salt
Water, 3 to 4 tablespoons

For the filling:
Onion, 1 small to medium
Garlic, 2 cloves
Olive oil, 2 tablespoons
Ground lamb, 12 ounces
Ground cinnamon, 1/2 teaspoon

Ground cumin, 1/2 teaspoon
Ground cloves, a good pinch
Salt and black pepper
Chopped tomatoes, 14 1/2-ounce can
Flat-leaf parsley and/or cilantro leaves,
    a big handful
Free-range egg, 1

Small knife, sieve, mixing bowl, tablespoon, plastic wrap, sharp knife, cutting board, frying pan, wooden spoon, teaspoon, large baking sheet, rolling pin, 10-inch metal pie plate, pie funnel or egg cup (optional), small bowl, fork, pastry brush

1. First, make the pastry. Cut the butter up into little cubes. Sift the flour into the mixing bowl and add the salt and butter. Now rub the butter into the flour with your fingertips, breaking down the butter lumps until the mixture looks rather like tiny bread crumbs (see also page 34 if you want a little more help with making pastry).

2. Add enough cold water (start with 3 table-spoons) to make a firm, unsticky dough with a little gentle kneading. Divide the dough in half, wrap each piece in plastic wrap, and put them in the fridge while you make the filling for the pie.

3. Peel the onion and garlic and chop them finely. Heat the olive oil in the frying pan, add the onion, and fry over low heat for 10 minutes or so, stirring occasionally with the wooden spoon, until the onion is lightly golden and starting to soften. Add the chopped garlic and fry for a couple of minutes longer.

4. Add the ground lamb, turn up the heat, and brown the meat so that it loses its raw look, breaking it up with the back of the wooden spoon. Stir in the cinnamon, cumin, and cloves. Season with 1/2 teaspoon of salt and plenty of pepper and add the chopped tomatoes. Give everything a good stir.

prepare the filling

roll out the pastry

roll on the lid

fill the pie

pinch the edges together

brush with beaten egg

5. Let the mixture simmer over low heat for about half an hour, stirring occasionally. Most of the liquid should evaporate in this time, so that you're left with a thick, meaty sauce. Turn off the heat. Break off any tough stalks from the parsley and/or cilantro and chop up the leaves. Stir them into the meat mixture and let it cool while you roll out the pastry.

6. Preheat the oven to 425°F. Place the baking sheet in the oven to get hot. Sprinkle a little flour on the work surface and the rolling pin. Take one half of the pastry from the fridge, unwrap it, and start to roll it out gently but firmly, giving it a quarter turn after every couple of rolls so that you know it hasn't stuck and so that you get a fairly even circle. Always roll away from you rather than battering the pastry by rolling the pin back and forth.

7. When the circle of pastry is just a little bigger than the pie plate, roll it up on the pin and line the plate. Roll out the other piece of pastry in the same way.

8. Place a pie funnel or upturned egg cup in the middle of the pie dish, then spoon in the filling.

9. Break the egg into the small bowl and beat it lightly with the fork. Brush a little of the egg around the edge of the pastry. Roll up the second circle of pastry onto the pin and cover the pie. Trim the sides, then pinch them together to make a wavy edge. If you haven't used a pie funnel or egg cup, cut a quarter-sized hole in the center of the top crust.

10. Brush the pie with more of the egg and use any pastry trimmings to decorate the top. Oven gloves on. Place the pie on the preheated baking sheet and bake for about 35 minutes, until the pastry is golden brown.

How to eat your pie

You could eat it piping hot at home, but eaten warm it makes particularly good picnic food. If you serve it with a sauce made by stirring some chopped tomatoes into thick Greek yogurt along with salt, pepper, and some chopped mint, it will taste even better.

Variation: lots of little pies

Instead of one big pie, you could make lots of little ones. Make more pastry (3 cups flour and 1 cup fat) and bind it with 6 tablespoons of water. Roll out the pastry as before, but this time cut out as many circles as you can with a 3-inch pastry cutter. Repeat this with the other half of the dough, then clump the pastry trimmings back into a ball and roll it out again to cut out some more. Get about sixteen 2-inch tart pans and line each with a circle of pastry. Put a heaping teaspoon of filling into each pastry shell. Brush the edge of the remaining circles with egg and cover the pies with them, pressing the edges together. Finally, brush the tops with beaten egg and bake in the oven as before, but for just 15 to 20 minutes or until golden brown.

LAMB KEBABS

Lamb grilled over a barbecue is perhaps one of the most delicious meats you can imagine. The easiest way to do it, and the most fun way to eat it, is by skewering juicy cubes of lamb on a stick and placing these on the grill.

Lots of recipes for lamb kebabs have all kinds of things, such as mushrooms, bits of onion, and squares of red or green pepper, threaded on the sticks between the chunks of lamb. We reckon these never quite work — the vegetables always end up too raw or too burnt, and the amount of meat always seems too small. So in this recipe, our kebabs are all lamb. You might want to serve them with a good green salad on the side (see page 218).

Leg meat is by far the best for kebabs, and you can either buy half a leg from the butcher, off the bone, or ask for thick leg slices.

To serve 4 to 6:
Boned leg of lamb, about 2 pounds
Lemon, $1/2$
Fresh rosemary, a few sprigs
Fresh thyme, a few sprigs (optional)
Fresh oregano, a small bunch (optional)
Garlic, 2 cloves

Olive oil, 2 tablespoons
Salt and black pepper

Cutting board, 2 sharp knives, large mixing bowl, citrus juicer, wooden spoon, about 6 wooden skewers, a grill with charcoal

1. You will need to cut up and marinate the meat at least an hour before you want to eat it. This allows the herbs, oil, and lemon to flavor it. Cut the meat into large, rough cubes (they don't have to be tidy, and in fact it's good to vary the shape and size a bit). Cut off any gristly bits or large lumps of fat, as too much fat can flare up in the heat of the grill. Put the meat in the bowl.

2. Squeeze the juice from the lemon half. Coarsely chop the herbs and peel and finely chop the garlic. Add them to the meat in the bowl, along with the olive oil, lemon juice, and a few twists of black pepper, then mix well with the wooden spoon. Let the meat marinate in a cool place for at least an hour, giving it a stir once or twice. At the same time, place the skewers to soak in a sink of water (this sounds odd — but it helps to stop them catching fire on the grill).

3. Prepare the grill, or a campfire, as described on page 275. Wait until you have nice hot coals to cook over, with no leaping flames.

4. Remove the meat from the marinade and wipe it lightly (you don't want the cubes of

lamb dripping with oil), but leave bits of garlic and herbs sticking to the meat. Push about 5 or 6 pieces of meat onto each skewer. Spread them out a little so they are just touching. This will help them cook more quickly and evenly, and they'll pick up more of that lovely barbecue flavor, too.

5. Oven gloves on. Place the kebabs on the grill. Turn them after a couple of minutes, and again 2 minutes later. They'll take 6 to 10 minutes overall (any more, and they'll get too dried out; any less, and they might still be a bit bloody). In the end, you have to work out how you like them.

How to eat your kebabs

You can nibble your kebabs off the skewer, while enjoying a salad and some crusty bread on the side. Or you can slide them off the skewers and make them into a sandwich by filling a pocket of lightly grilled pita bread or a split bread roll with them. If you go down this sandwich route, then some hummus (see page 333), loosened with extra olive oil and lemon juice and maybe with some chopped parsley stirred in, makes a lovely sauce. Some sliced raw onion, some shredded lettuce, and a dash of chile sauce for the brave, and you have a homemade version of the kebab-shop classic.

LIVER AND BACON

This traditional meaty combination is usually served up with lots of creamy mashed potatoes and gravy. But if you're a liver novice, then this is a quick and appealing way to give it a try. Maybe you'll want the full-blown version next time.

For 4 people as a starter or snack:
Flat-leaf parsley, a small handful
Free-range or organic bacon,
  smoked or unsmoked, 4 to 5 slices
Garlic, 1 clove
Lamb's liver, about 8 ounces
All-purpose flour, 2 tablespoons
Sea salt and black pepper

A little olive oil
Bay leaves, 2

Serving plate, cutting board, sharp knife,
2 shallow bowls, scissors, tablespoon,
heavy frying pan, wooden spoon,
slotted spoon

1. Turn the oven to low and put the serving plate in it to get warm.

2. Chop the parsley quite finely and put it in a bowl to one side.

3. Cut each bacon slice in half crosswise and then in half again lengthwise to make 4 slim strips of each one. Peel the garlic and chop it very finely.

4. Cut the liver into strips ¾ inch wide. Spoon the flour into a shallow bowl and add some sea salt and plenty of black pepper. Toss the liver strips in the seasoned flour until they are well coated.

5. Pour a little oil into the frying pan, turn the heat to medium, and add the bacon, garlic, and bay leaves. Fry them gently until the bacon is brown and slightly crisp, stirring with the wooden spoon. With the slotted spoon, transfer the bacon and garlic to the warm serving plate.

6. Turn the heat up slightly and add a little extra oil if the pan looks dry. Shake the excess flour off the strips of liver and gently lower them into the pan. Let them sizzle nicely for about a minute, turning them gently so that they brown on all sides.

7. Scoop out the liver with the slotted spoon and add it to the bacon on the plate. Sprinkle the chopped parsley over the meat and serve.

How to eat your liver and bacon

You could eat this dish Spanish *tapa* style, with cocktail sticks (tapas are little portions of food eaten in bars across Spain), serving it with a potato tortilla (page 106), a tomato salad (page 216), and plenty of crusty bread.

ROAST CHICKEN

It's always useful to have a simple roast chicken recipe up your sleeve, as it were. This chicken is cooked with a little white wine and plenty of herbs – ingredients that not only flavor the bird as it roasts but also form the basis of a delicious gravy once it has finished cooking.

You will need:

A free-range or organic chicken
Softened butter, 5 tablespoons
Lemon, 1
A few bay leaves, sprigs of thyme
 or oregano
Salt and black pepper
Onions, 2
Carrots, 2
White wine, $1/2$ cup

Heavy cream, 2 tablespoons (optional)

Scissors, roasting pan, butter knife, sharp knife, cutting board, large glass measuring cup, large spoon, sharp knife or skewer, 2 large forks, large serving plate, tablespoon, mug, wooden spoon, sieve, small saucepan, teaspoon, small pitcher or gravy boat

1. Preheat the oven to 450°F, or its hottest setting if it doesn't go that high.

2. Unwrap the chicken from its packaging and snip away any pieces of elastic or string that hold the legs together. Check inside to see whether a bag of giblets (the chicken's heart, liver, and gizzard) is included. If it is, take it out (you could use it to make stock – see page 192).

3. Put the chicken in the roasting pan, breast side up. With a knife or your fingers, smear the breast and legs of the bird with the butter. Cut the lemon in half and squeeze the juice over the buttered bird. Put the squeezed halves inside the chicken. Tuck some bay leaves and herb sprigs around the chicken and some in the cavity. Grind some pepper and sprinkle a little salt over the bird.

4. Peel the papery skin from the onions and cut each one into quarters. Cut off the top and tail of the carrots, peel them, then slice them into big chunks. Put the onion and carrot pieces in the roasting pan around the chicken. Pour the wine into the pan.

5. Oven gloves on. Carefully put the roasting pan in the oven and cook the chicken for about 15 minutes, until the skin of the chicken has started to brown. Turn the oven down to 325°F and cook for 1 to $1\frac{1}{2}$ hours; the exact cooking time will depend on the size of your chicken. Every 20 minutes or so, baste the chicken by scooping up the cooking juices in the bottom of the pan with the large spoon and pouring them over the bird. If you can manage this 3 times during the roasting, you've done well.

(continued)

6. Test the chicken to find out if it really is cooked (see page 281) by piercing the thigh with a sharp knife or skewer to see whether the juices run clear. If they look pink or bloody, then the bird isn't cooked. Put the pan back in the oven and test again in 15 minutes.

7. With a couple of big forks, lift the chicken carefully onto a warmed plate and let it sit for 10 minutes or so. This gives the meat time to relax and let the juices settle back into it.

8. While the chicken is "resting," you can make a very simple gravy. (Although, of course, you don't have to make a gravy. You can just leave the chicken in the roasting pan and spoon out the delicious juices from the pan as you carve.) Let the roasting pan sit propped up slightly at one end so that its juices collect at the other end. You'll see that the oily fat rises to the surface, as it's lighter than the liquid underneath. Skim off as much of this fat as possible with the tablespoon and put it in a mug at the side of the stove to throw away.

9. Unprop the pan and put it on the stove (wear your oven gloves), then turn the heat under the pan to low. Stir with the wooden spoon to loosen any chickeny bits that may be stuck to the bottom of the pan. If there aren't many juices, you can add another tablespoon or two of white wine.

10. Stir again. Place the sieve over the small saucepan and carefully pour the juices into it. Then set the saucepan on the stove over low heat and let it come to a very gentle simmer. Use a teaspoon to scoop up a little of the gravy, blow on it to cool it down, then taste it. Do you think it needs salt and pepper? You may want to add a couple of tablespoons of cream just to soften the flavor. Let it simmer for a minute longer, then pour the gravy into a warm pitcher or gravy boat ready to serve.

How to eat your chicken

It's your roast, so you get to carve. Make sure that everyone gets the bit of the bird they like best and pass the gravy around. The pieces of onion and carrot may look a bit wizened, but they're actually quite tasty.

You could serve the chicken with some mashed potatoes (see page 199) or, in the summer, with Garlic, Rosemary, and Lemon Potatoes (page 203) and a green salad (page 218).

CHICKEN CURRY

The general idea of this dish is that you make a sauce (a *kari*) from vegetables and spices first, then add the meat and stew it until it is cooked through. The sauce is then thickened with yogurt, and the sweetness of the curry is balanced with a little sour lime juice.

If you want your curry to be hot as well as spicy, include some or all of the chile seeds.

To serve 4:

Tomatoes, 4 to 6 medium
Onion, 1 medium
Vegetable oil, $1/4$ cup
Fresh ginger, a $1 1/4$-inch piece
Garlic, 2 cloves
Mild green chiles, 1 or 2
Ground coriander, 1 teaspoon
Ground cumin, 1 teaspoon
Ground turmeric, $1/4$ teaspoon
Salt and black pepper

Water, scant $1/2$ cup
Free-range chicken, a whole bird cut
  into 8 pieces, or 8 thighs and/or drumsticks
Plain yogurt, 2 tablespoons
Lime (or lemon), 1
Cilantro leaves, a small bunch

Sharp knife, 2 cutting boards, bowl, plate, tablespoon, large, heavy saucepan with lid, wooden spoon, fork, teacup

1. If you're cooking rice to eat with your curry, wash and soak it now (see page 324).

2. First, you need to peel the tomatoes. Nick the skin of each tomato with the point of the sharp knife, then put the tomatoes in a bowl next to the sink and pour over some very hot water from the kettle to cover. Count to 20, then carefully pour away the water. When the tomatoes are cool enough to handle, pull away the skin, halve the tomatoes, and squeeze most of the seeds and juice into the empty bowl, ready to throw away. Chop the flesh coarsely and put it on a plate to one side.

3. Peel and finely chop the onion. Add the oil to the saucepan, turn on the stove, and add the onion. Fry it over medium-low heat for about 10 minutes, stirring from time to time so that it turns an even golden brown, and watch carefully to make sure it doesn't burn.

4. Meanwhile, peel the thick, knobbly skin off the ginger and the papery skin from the garlic, then chop them very finely. Slit the chile using a sharp knife while holding it down with the fork, and slice the flesh away from the cluster of seeds in the middle. (Avoid touching any part of the chile with your fingers if you can — it's very easy to get chile in your eyes, which will sting terribly. Or wear rubber gloves when handling chiles.) Chop the chile finely. Use the seeds only if everyone eating the curry likes quite spicy food.

5. Measure the ground spices into the teacup. Add the ginger, garlic, and chile to the pan, stir them around, and fry for another minute or so. Then add the spices in the cup. Fry the spices for a minute or two, stirring all the time so that they do not stick. Wonderful smells will start to rise up from the pan as the spices heat up. Grind in some salt and pepper.

6. Pour in the water and the tomatoes, bring to a boil, turn down the heat a little, and let the sauce simmer for 5 to 10 minutes.

7. Add the chicken pieces to the pan and stir them around so they are covered with the sauce. Put the lid on the pan, turn the heat down, and

let the chicken cook for 30 to 40 minutes, stirring occasionally; chicken thighs will take longer to cook than breast pieces. (If you're cooking rice, drain it and start to cook it while the chicken is gently simmering.)

8. Now, add the yogurt to the chicken and stir it in. When the sauce is gently bubbling again, scoop up a little in a teaspoon, blow it cool, and taste it. The sauce will probably taste quite sweet because of the tomatoes. Cut the lime in half and squeeze its juice into the sauce. Stir and taste again, as before. Do you think it needs the juice from the other half?

9. Finally, chop the cilantro leaves on a separate board with a clean knife and sprinkle them onto the curry just before serving.

How to eat your curry

You could eat your curry very simply with some rice and a little extra yogurt spooned on the side.

Alternatively, why not make your own banquet, where everybody gets to prepare a special part of the meal? You could cook the curry along with flat breads (page 38), Fragrant Rice (page 324), a raita (page 83), and Potatoes with Spinach (page 200). Pile each onto a dish, and arrange down the length of the table. Little bowls of mango chutney and lime pickle can complete the feast. And if you can lay your hands on a fresh coconut, thin slivers of it make a lovely extra garnish.

PHEASANT CASSEROLE

The outdoor life of a pheasant means that it's generally a lot tastier than your average chicken. Once they have been shot, game birds such as pheasants are "hung" before being plucked and gutted. Hanging makes the meat more tender. But pheasants needn't be strong tasting, or "gamy" if they're not hung for too long. All good butchers, and some supermarkets, sell oven-ready pheasants, plucked, gutted, and ready to go, throughout the shooting season (November to January). For this recipe, you'll have to ask your butcher to cut the bird into four pieces.

This is a simple pheasant casserole, which ends up with a lovely creamy, tangy sauce. You can easily adapt it for a chicken or a rabbit. In fact, you can buy chicken thighs, wings, and drumsticks especially to make this dish, but do, please, choose free-range or organic poultry.

To serve 4:
All-purpose flour, 2 tablespoons
A plump pheasant, cut into 4 pieces
Salt and black pepper
Free-range or organic bacon, 4 slices
Onion, 1
Carrots, 2
Celery, 2 stalks
A little sunflower oil
Cider, 1 cup
Red currant jelly, 1 teaspoon
English mustard, 1 heaping teaspoon

Heavy cream, 2 tablespoons
A sprig each of rosemary and thyme
Vegetable stock, organic chicken stock, or water, $1\frac{1}{3}$ to $1\frac{2}{3}$ cups

Sharp knife, cutting board, 2 large plates, heavy frying pan, wooden spoon, slotted spoon, casserole dish (or good heavy saucepan) with a lid, large glass measuring cup, wooden spatula

1. Put the flour on one of the plates and grind some salt and pepper over it. Dust the pheasant pieces lightly with the seasoned flour, shaking off any excess (the flour will help thicken the sauce as the casserole cooks). Keep the floured pheasant portions ready on the other plate.

2. Cut the bacon slices into 5 or 6 pieces each. Peel the onion and carrots and chop them into fairly chunky pieces. Wash and chop each celery stalk into 3 or 4 pieces.

3. Preheat the oven to 250°F.

4. Heat some oil in the frying pan over medium heat. Add the bacon and fry gently for a few minutes until it's lightly browned. Then use the slotted spoon to transfer the bacon pieces to your casserole dish.

5. Now gently fry the vegetables in the same oil in the frying pan. After about 5 minutes, when they are just lightly colored (golden, not

brown) and softened a little bit, add them to the bacon in the casserole dish. By gently browning the bacon and vegetables, you'll be creating some delicious flavors that will all contribute to the sauce.

6. Now put the pheasant pieces in the pan (you might want to add another tablespoon of oil to the pan first if it's looking a bit dry). Fry at a good sizzle for 6 or 7 minutes, turning them several times, until the pieces are nicely browned on the outside.

7. Transfer the pheasant pieces to the casserole, but keep the frying pan on the heat. There are some tasty morsels sticking to the bottom of the pan, and it would be a crime not to get them into your casserole! The best way to do this is to pour about half the cider into the pan. As the cider begins to bubble, gently scrape the wooden spatula over the bottom of the pan to loosen all the tasty bits. This is called "deglazing," and it's a clever trick to get all the delicious burnt bits to dissolve into a liquid, which will then become a gravy or sauce.

8. Add the rest of the cider to the pan, along with the red currant jelly, mustard, cream, and the sprigs of rosemary and thyme. Season with salt and plenty of black pepper. Pour this mixture into the casserole and top with enough stock or water just to cover the pheasant.

9. Put the casserole on the stove and bring the liquid to a very gentle simmer – so that a few bubbles are just popping on the top rather than bubbling furiously. Oven gloves on. Put the lid on the casserole, transfer it to the preheated oven, and leave for about 1¼ hours to complete the cooking. Then check that the pheasant meat is nice and tender; it might need another 15 minutes in the oven.

How to eat your casserole

Serve with plain boiled or mashed potatoes (see page 199), and some nice, lightly cooked greens, such as kale or cabbage.

THE CUPBOARD

Take a closer look at the dried and canned ingredients on your pantry shelves: packets of lentils and rice, cans of tomatoes and beans, jars of spices. Gathered from all over the world, there are comforting staples for everyday eating alongside rare exotics to be used by the pinch for bursts of extraordinary flavor. Think about their journey as you use them, and you'll enjoy them all the more.

pear and almond pudding cake, page 334

homemade bacon, page 326

flapjacks, page 320

salt, page 318

THE CUPBOARD

Somewhere in your kitchen there's probably a cupboard or shelf where the "dry goods" are kept. Often this means dusty jars of spices; half-opened packets of rice, pasta, and lentils; cans of tomatoes, beans, chickpeas — all that sort of stuff. At first glance, it's not a very exciting collection. But take a second look. These are some of the kitchen's most useful ingredients and appealing flavors.

Few of these foods were grown in the U.K. or the U.S.; nearly all were shipped in from overseas. Rice from India or Indonesia, spices from Sri Lanka, Jamaica, and Zanzibar, beans from Latin America — the very names are

exciting and exotic. Many were grown in tropical countries, where the temperature is sweltering all the time. Hot, aromatic curries and sweet, spicy stews may originate from countries where the sun always shines, but in our cold British climate, when the wind is howling and the skies are slate gray, they can do a brilliant job of cheering us up.

A couple of hundred years ago, before imported ingredients like these became so widely and cheaply available, most cupboards were filled with "preserved" foods. These were made from homegrown ingredients that were plentiful in summer and needed to be laid down for the lean days of winter. In the early summer, when fresh food was abundant, the cupboard would be more or less bare, except for staples such as flour, oats, and sugar, which were useful for baking all year round.

The cupboard filled up as the months went by. Jams and jellies were made in the summer, to be eaten later in the year when the trees and bushes were bare of fruit. Other jars or pots might be filled with dried peas and beans, if the harvest had been good enough to save some. Jars of pickled eggs were packed up in autumn when the days began to shorten, as the hens would soon stop laying. A couple of hams and a side of bacon would soon be hanging from the ceiling, made from a pig born in the spring, fattened through the summer and autumn, and killed a few weeks before Christmas.

Modern cupboard ingredients are very different. Nowadays, our cupboards are stocked with foods that don't change from season to season. Some of these are "emergency standbys" – foods that can be rustled into easy meals at short notice, when the fridge and the vegetable basket suddenly turn out to be bare. But mostly they are there so we can create interesting and varied meals – lamb curry and rice one day, couscous and roasted vegetables the next, and a big pot of spaghetti carbonara the day after that.

Not that we are always very good at exploring these possibilities. Sometimes that packet of pretty dried beans or the jewel box of saffron that seemed so exciting when we picked it off the shelf in the store can still be sitting at the back of the cupboard, gathering dust, a year, two, or even three later.

However, for every item bought on the spur of the moment that gets neglected, there are many others we turn to regularly. It might be oats for daily porridge and occasional biscuits. Long-grain rice to serve with stir-fries and curries. Half a dozen types of pasta – a favorite for each member of the family. Dried fruits, such as currants and raisins, that might sit there for months, until suddenly it's time to make hot cross buns or the Christmas pudding. Plus various cooking oils, vinegars, dried herbs, and spices that get used day after day.

We take these cupboard foods for granted, but the time you *really* notice them is when they aren't there. Imagine spending an hour or two lovingly putting together a big pot of bolognese sauce for family and friends. You go to the cupboard, open the door, poke around for a minute, and find there's no spaghetti. Not so much as a strand. It's a minor catastrophe. Bolognese with macaroni just isn't the same.

So what is the secret of the long shelf life of all these different ingredients? What do they have in common? There are two main techniques for preserving them, and it's pretty easy to spot them by looking at the containers the foods come in.

Preserving in jars and cans

If the food comes in a can or jar and includes some kind of liquid, then it was preserved by heating it, to kill all the bugs and bacteria that might spoil it, and sealing it inside the container so that no other bugs can get to it.

This applies to all foods in cans and jars, from sardines to peaches, from a canned meat pie filling to a pot of strawberry jam or a jar of olives. In most cases, the food is cooked, sealed in its container, then cooked again – the sealed can or jar is superheated one last time to ensure the contents are completely sterile. Foods preserved in this way can last not just for months but for years.

Food in jars doesn't keep quite as well as food in cans. The acidity in jams and bottled fruits can very slowly corrode the lids, which means that bacteria can get in and spoil the food. But cans of sardines in oil, for example, have been opened after 50 years or more and found to be not only safe but actually quite pleasant to eat (assuming you like canned sardines, that is).

Having said that, you shouldn't eat the contents of any cans or jars that have been hanging around in your cupboard for years. You can't be sure they are safe without doing proper laboratory analysis. And even if they look completely fine, it simply isn't worth the risk, so always check the sell-by date.

Preserving in bags and boxes

What else is in the cupboard? If it doesn't come in a jar or tin, the chances are it's in a bag or a box. Shake it and it probably rattles. Many of these foods – rice, lentils, beans, popcorn – are actually seeds. And if they are not whole seeds, they are probably ground-up or processed seeds. Rolled oats, for example, are made from whole oat grains, while couscous and all that pasta are made from flour that has been ground from wheat.

What these foods have in common is that they have been dried. If you take all the water out of a food, you remove – or at least greatly reduce – the risk of it spoiling or decaying. This is because all the molds and bacteria that spoil food require some moisture to do their work. To produce their spores and multiply, they need to feed off the food. And without moisture, they just can't do it.

This is why a packet of bullet-hard dried beans or split peas can sit on a shelf for months. Left fresh in their pods in the vegetable basket, peas or beans would become a perfect breeding ground for some interesting molds in days. Even in the fridge, the same would happen after a week or two. But the dried-out versions are stable and safe as long as they remain completely dry.

Rehydrating grains and legumes

It isn't just the tiny food-spoiling bacteria that need food to be moist before they can feed off it. So do we. Swallow these grains and pulses dry and they may do us serious harm. It's very important that they are prepared carefully. Water needs to be added, and plenty of it, so that they can swell back up again and become tender. Some dried foods rehydrate very quickly. Rice, most lentils, and dried pasta will simply swell and become tender enough to eat when they are boiled in plenty of water. This might take anywhere from ten minutes for small and thin types of pasta to over half an hour for some kinds of rice.

But other larger dried seeds, particularly those known as legumes, such as dried beans and peas, need special treatment. They must be soaked in cold water for several hours or overnight before you cook them. Even after that, they sometimes need boiling for an hour or two to make them safe and tender enough to eat. When cooking with dried grains and legumes, always read the back of the package to see what you should do.

RICE

Measure out ¼ cup Arborio rice – the kind known in the U.K. as pudding rice – and spread it out, one grain deep, on a dinner plate. It will barely cover the surface of the plate. But these chalky grains have one extraordinary talent. They swell. Combine this small amount of rice with a bottle of milk, a scrap of butter, a pinch of salt, and some sugar, bake it gently in the oven for a couple of hours, and you have one of the most delicious puddings you can imagine, enough for four people. Rice is little short of a miracle food. It's no wonder that these grains fill the stomachs of half the people on the planet.

Grass plants such as wheat and barley can only be grown on well-drained land, but rice can be grown on land that floods, too, such as paddy fields. This means that it can be grown alongside rivers that flood during rainy seasons, and explains why it is a vital food for people all over the world.

Rice comes in many shapes and sizes, colors and flavors. Long and thin, short and fat, white, red, and even black. All of which look, taste, and cook quite differently.

Fat little short-grain rices, such as Italian Arborio, cook into a sticky mass. These are the ones to use if you're making a risotto or a rice pudding, where you want a creamy, oozy kind of rice. If you want a rice to eat with Indian food, then the long grains of a rice like basmati will stay fluffy and separate. If you're eating with chopsticks, you might like to choose a slightly stickier Thai long-grain rice that clumps together – or you'll be chasing grains of rice around a bowl for hours.

Some rice comes precooked, which means that it has already been partly cooked before being dried again for packaging. It may make perfect-looking rice, but it usually isn't as tasty as start-from-scratch rice. You can tell as soon as you open the packet: precooked rice smells of not very much, whereas raw rice has a pleasant, fragrant smell – almost as if the rice grain has been packed with a hint of spice.

Cooking rice

Some people cook rice by simply boiling it in lots of salted water for 12 to 15 minutes, then draining it through a sieve. Others measure out rice and water very precisely, bring it to a gentle simmer, and let it cook very slowly until the rice absorbs all the water and finishes cooking in its own steam.

Whichever way you cook it, it's a good idea to rinse and soak the rice in water first. The rinsing washes away the chalky starch that clings to the rice, while the soaking helps the grains get ready to swell. Let the rice drain in a sieve for a few minutes after it's finished soaking, and you're ready to go.

Some rice recipes

Kedgeree, page 250
Rice Pudding, page 322
Fragrant Rice, page 324

LEGUMES

Legumes – beans, peas, and lentils – are plants also known as pulses. They are all plants that bear their seeds in pods.

Beans and peas (but not lentils – they need a hotter climate) are often grown in the U.K. as part of a five-year crop rotation plan, where different crops are grown in a field year after year. One of the reasons farmers and gardeners like growing leguminous plants is that they put back a valuable nutrient, nitrogen, into the soil as they grow. This means that the following year the soil will be sufficiently enriched to cope with "greedy" crops, such as wheat and potatoes, which need so much of this nutrient to grow well.

Cooks, on the other hand, like legumes simply because they're so tasty. All three seeds can form the backbone of the kind of delicious soups and stews that are just what you want to eat when it's blowing a gale outside. So it's odd to think that they play the same comforting role in extremely hot countries such as India, where dried peas, beans, and lentils form a major part of the daily diet. Here are a few notes about the main legumes . . .

Beans
You've probably eaten young green beans, long and thin with their ends topped and tailed. And you're sure to have eaten cans of baked beans, whitish ovals in their pinky-orange sauce. The two beans may look completely different, but they are much more closely related than you might think. "Baked bean" beans are simply varieties of young green beans that have been left to swell and mature in the pod until the pod has turned brown and withered and the beans are as fat as they can get. The beans are then shelled from the pod and dried out. So, if they weren't made into baked beans, they could be used as the seeds for another crop of green beans.

The small, dried white beans used for baked beans are sometimes called navy beans, because the navy used to take them to sea as part of the sailors' rations. But there are dozens of other varieties of beans, in all sorts of colors and shapes, with names like pinto, kidney, cannellini, flageolet, or borlotti. Each one tastes a little different from the rest, and the textures vary too. But they are similar enough to swap one kind for another in a recipe without worrying too much, though the bigger ones may take longer to cook.

Remember, all these dried beans need to be soaked in plenty of cold water for several hours or overnight before cooking. This is fine if you're planning today what you're going to cook tomorrow, but as a standby for more last-minute cooking decisions it's always useful to have a few cans of beans in stock. These are presoaked and precooked, and usually canned in lightly salted water. They can be rinsed, then added straight to soups, stews, and curries and heated through for immediate eating.

Lentils

If you have a bag of lentils in your pantry, the chances are that you'll have half a dozen of these little seeds lying at the bottom of the cupboard, in the cupboard next door, and probably underneath the cupboard as well. Like sand on the beach at picnic time, lentils just get everywhere.

The little flying-saucer-shaped seeds come in all sorts of colors and sizes. You can buy biggish pale green ones, brown ones, and – most commonly – tiny split ones that are called "red" but are actually orangey-pink, like cooked salmon. Because they are split, they cook very quickly. Others, such as French lentils, are a beautiful mottled green and blue-black, rather like a toad's skin.

Different lentils cook differently, too. Some, like the red ones, cook to a mush, which is perfect when you want them to have a soft, sloppy texture. Other types hold their shape better, so they're good to use when you're eating lentils in a "vegetable" rather than in a "soupy" sort of way.

Lentils have a fairly bland taste, so they're at their best when they're cooked with things that have plenty of flavor. In India, where lentils are an important part of most people's daily diet, they are simmered with spices such as turmeric and ginger, which helps to make them easier to digest.

Peas

Dried peas are exactly what they say they are. The same peas that we eat sweet and fresh from the pod or buy frozen at the supermarket can also be dried and kept for months, or even years. Once they're soaked and cooked like dried beans, they make delicious soups – some especially good ones are made with bits of chopped ham or bacon. In fact, a traditional pea soup is made from the leftover liquid used to cook a big ham, plus presoaked dried peas, simmered in this stock until completely tender. Look out also for yellow split peas – they are more like giant lentils. Cooked in a well-flavored stock, they will slowly dissolve into a creamy, thick purée, almost like mashed potatoes. In the U.K., this is called pease pudding and is delicious served with baked ham or boiled bacon.

Chickpeas are a distant relation of green peas but grow in much hotter countries. If you've tucked into a bowl of smooth, creamy hummus, scooping it up with pieces of pita bread or sticks of carrot, then you've already eaten them. Before being mashed into hummus, chickpeas (also called garbanzo beans) are large, nutty-looking legumes like outsized beige peas. You might also have tried falafel – fried patties made of herbed and spiced ground chickpeas and crushed wheat. They are delicious stuffed into warm pita bread with some chopped salad and plain yogurt.

Some recipes with legumes

Lentil and Bacon Soup for Lots of People, page 328
Spicy Bean Stew with Sausages, page 330
Hummus, page 333

NUTS

Nuts present challenges. Can you throw a stick high enough to get that chestnut down from the tree? Can you break a hazelnut open  with those big metal nutcrackers without mashing the nut inside to a pulp? Can you crack a walnut and get its knobbly kernel out whole?

Nuts are the edible kernels of the seeds of certain fruits. A sweet chestnut tree, for instance, produces prickly, spiny pods (fruits). Stamp on it and you'll see the shiny chestnut inside. And inside that dark brown shell is the sweet, edible kernel (make sure you don't confuse sweet chestnuts with the similar, but inedible, horse chestnuts, with slightly less prickly casings).

Some nuts are native to Britain – you might well find hazelnuts or chestnuts while you're out walking in the autumn. Shake the trees and you'll be doing what your early hunter-gatherer ancestors did thousands of years ago to supplement their diet. Check very carefully, though, that these nuts really are edible before you put them anywhere near your mouth. If in doubt, leave them for the squirrels to decide.

Most of the nuts we eat and cook with in the U.K. are imported – including pecans for desserts and pies, cashews for stir-fries, pistachios for ice cream, and peanuts for a spicy sauce. (Technically, though, peanuts are only an "honorary" sort of nut, being more closely related to peas and beans than nuts.)

When it comes to cooking, probably the most versatile of all nuts is the almond. You can buy it whole, flaked, chopped, as oil, or as extract. Ground almonds mixed with egg white and sugar make marzipan for coating fruitcakes or for molding into sweets. They sometimes replace some or all of the flour in a cake recipe, which doesn't make the cake taste nutty – just moister in texture and richer in flavor. Incidentally, the best, freshest-tasting ground almonds are the ones you grind yourself. Put whole blanched almonds in a food processor and whiz them up until they are the consistency of granulated sugar.

It's always important to check whether the people you're cooking for have any sort of nut (or seed, in the case of peanut) allergy. Some schools have a ban on any form of nut cooking, so bear this in mind if you're cooking for, say, a school bake sale.

Some nutty recipes

Roast Chestnuts, page 331
Pear and Almond Pudding Cake, page 334
Double-Chocolate Brownies, page 403

SPICES

Take down a jar of spice from your kitchen shelf. Open the lid, take a cautious sniff, and breathe in its extraordinary scent. Is it the sweet smell of cinnamon, the nose-tickling intensity of ginger, or perhaps the heavy perfume of cardamom pods?

The jars themselves tell you little – often just the name of the spice and what foods it's usually cooked with. They rarely tell you where the spices come from or what they actually are. They certainly don't tell you about the sailors who set sail for the East Indies in the sixteenth and seventeenth centuries, risking death for a share of the spice trade.

Imagine sailing from Britain bound for islands that you have heard stories about but that are not even marked on your map. You know nothing of Australia, little of America. You've heard rumors that the earth is probably round like an orange but, on the other hand, it may be flat. Perhaps you'll sail off the edge. "Here be dragons," it says on the map – and that seems like a real possibility. These early traders sailed across the world in their wooden ships, at the mercy of winds and tropical storms. Diseases like dysentery wiped out half the crew, and scurvy caused their teeth to drop out (see page 134 to find out about the cure). Even when they finally reached the Spice Islands, after months or even years of traveling, they might face hostile islanders and rival traders from Holland or Portugal. Murder, cannibalism, mutinies, riots – just a few of the hazards they might encounter. Why would anyone risk all this?

It was because spices that cost just a few pennies in the East Indies were worth bags of gold back in Europe. We may take these spices for granted, tossing them into the shopping cart without a second thought, but since medieval times English cooks were gripped by a passion for any spice they could get their hands on. Not only did spices liven up the endless winter diet of salted meat, but, just as importantly, using spices in your food meant that you were wealthy enough to afford them. Spices were a status symbol and were kept locked away. People even thought they protected you against the plague.

Cooking with spices

Spices look intriguing, smell wonderful, and taste extraordinary. To cook with them is to become a wizard in the kitchen. You're in charge of your own cauldron, adding a little bit of this and a little bit of that to arrive at a magical blend of flavors.

Many dishes require a complex blend of spices to get the desired overall taste. A traditional recipe for an Indian chicken dish, for instance, might include cumin seeds, cardamom pods, peppercorns, ginger, cayenne pepper, turmeric, and a stick of cinnamon – all to be measured, lightly toasted in a pan, ground to a powder, and sprinkled in. It's enormous fun. Spoon them all out into little piles on a white plate and take a few seconds to enjoy the look of them. Orange, black, red, beige – seeds, pods, sticks, and powders.

Understanding how much to use of different spices is simply a matter of getting to know them. If you're not accustomed to eating chiles, for example, then you'll want to go easy when it comes to using chile in its dried forms – cayenne pepper or red pepper flakes. Not all spices are hot, though. The point of spicing food isn't to burn the roof of your mouth off and deaden your taste buds, it's to tickle your tongue with flavor. Grate a little nutmeg into milky foods such as rice puddings and white sauces for lasagne and creamed cauliflower. Use cloves when you want spiciness without heat, but add them sparingly – the reliable rule with most spices is that a little goes a long way.

Spices are sold either whole (like sticks of cinnamon or peppercorns) or ground up into a powder. Whole spices tend to keep their

A PINCH OF HERBS
Just as a dried bean is completely different from a fresh green bean that you eat as a vegetable, so a dried herb bears no resemblance to a fresh green herb that you'd add to a salad. You might chop a small bunch of parsley, chives, or basil to toss with some cooked pasta. But that's not something that would work with dried herbs.

Dried herbs work best when they're used like spices – in pinches to flavor and add depth to something that you're cooking. A bouquet garni, for instance, is sometimes a little bag of mixed dried herbs that you drop into a stew to give it a subtle flavor while it simmers away in the pot. You fish the bag out again before you eat the stew. Dried oregano and thyme are good staples for adding to stews, sauces, and pizzas. But many herbs simply don't taste that interesting after they've been dried. A pinch of dried basil has none of that distinctive, knock-you-out scent that you get if you rub a fresh basil leaf between your fingers. Dried parsley can't compare to fresh. Spend the money instead on little herb plants from the garden center to put in the garden or in a pot on the windowsill.

flavor longer than ground ones. They're also more fun, because they have shape and texture and you can grate them and grind them, breathing in the fantastic smells as you do so. Vanilla extract is always useful for flavoring cakes and desserts, but slim, black vanilla pods are even more interesting.

Keep them buried in a jar of sugar to make the sugar fragrant.

Whole spices reveal more about themselves, too. Look at a whole clove and you'll see it's really the dried base of a flower, while a stick of cinnamon is a piece of bark from a tree, which has been dried and rolled into a tight quill. Nutmegs are giant seeds that have come out of a fleshy covering, just like the pit in a plum or a peach. The yellow, pollen-bearing stigmas of a special crocus flower give us threads of precious saffron.

It can be a good idea to toast your spices before you grind them, as this will make their flavor stronger. If your recipe tells you that you need a teaspoon of ground cumin, put a teaspoon of cumin seeds into a dry frying pan and toast them for just a minute or two over medium heat, giving them the occasional stir with a wooden spoon. You can then grind them up (either in a mortar, if you have one, or in a stout paper bag with the end of a rolling pin if you haven't). Preparing and cooking food like this is almost as much fun as eating the finished dish.

. . . .

SALT

There's an old Russian folktale about a czar who happily hands over three bags containing gold, silver, and precious stones in exchange for a bag of salt. It's only when you leave salt out of your cooking that you realize he was probably getting a bargain. Bake a loaf of bread and forget the salt and you might as well throw it to the ducks. Leave it out of the water when you boil rice or pasta and you'll know straight away that there's something missing. Salt basically makes a food taste of what it ought to taste of.

But too much salt isn't good for us at all. Many convenience foods, like some cans of baked beans for instance, contain large amounts of salt to make you think you're eating something very tasty when actually you're only eating something very salty. Manufacturers of processed foods sometimes add lots of salt to their recipes because it helps disguise the poor quality of some of the other ingredients. So one of the skills in cooking is knowing when you need to use salt and when you can leave it out.

Salt isn't just something that we use to flavor food – it has other uses, too. For example, it draws water out of things. Sprinkle a thinly sliced cucumber with a little salt and watch the water drip out of it – a good trick if you want to make unsoggy cucumber sandwiches or a yogurty rather than watery cucumber raita (see page 83). Recipes sometimes tell you to sprinkle salt over watery vegetables such as eggplant and zucchini to draw some of the water out of them before they're fried. This is because wet foods don't fry well – they steam rather than brown. (If a recipe asks you to do this, remember to rinse the vegetables after salting and pat them dry on paper towels.)

Long before we had freezers to preserve our food, meat and vegetables were kept in salt or salty water (brine) to prevent them from going bad. Although we eat much less salted meat than our ancestors did, we still eat plenty of ham and bacon. A ham is a leg of pork that has been salted and is then simmered in water or baked in the oven to cook. Bacon is a joint of pork that has been salted before being sliced, ready for cooking.

Fish, too, are often salted to preserve them a little longer. Smoked salmon hasn't just been smoked, it's been salted first. You may have seen salt cod for sale in markets, particularly in France, Spain, and Portugal. It's generally available as long, dusty gray fillets, almost as stiff as a plank of wood. Cod salted like this needs to be soaked in fresh water for several days before it can be cooked.

Where salt comes from

Much of the salt we eat comes from dried inland salt lakes, often some way under the ground, and is called rock salt (towns in England ending in *wich* – like Norwich – are the sites of old salt works). The salt is extracted from these salt mines by pumping in fresh water, which dissolves the salt to make brine. The brine is then pumped back out of the mine and evaporated in huge tanks to leave behind white salt crystals.

You can also buy salt that comes from the sea. In hot countries, the heat of the sun causes the water to evaporate, or dry up, leaving the salt behind. In colder climates, including the U.K., the sun isn't strong enough to rely on for most of the year, so the water has to be evaporated artificially by boilers.

A salty recipe

Homemade Bacon for a Bacon Sandwich, page 326

Project:

MAKING YOUR OWN SALT

Next time you visit the beach, take a large watertight container and fill it with seawater (but only if you're sure it's an area with a good record of clean water). If you're abroad in a hot climate, transfer the water to a wide, shallow container, so that it's no more than a couple inches deep, and stand it where it will catch the full hot sun all day long. The heat from the sun gradually causes the water to evaporate, leaving the salt behind. You can scrape it up into a jar and cook with it.

If it's cold and gray out, though, you'll need a bit of artificial heat to help things along. Line a sieve with a clean handkerchief or a piece of cheesecloth and place it over a large, wide pan (the larger the surface area of the water, the quicker it will evaporate away into steam). Carefully pour the seawater through the sieve so that you filter out any bits of sand. Most of the sand will be left behind in the bottom of the container, and any grains that aren't should be caught by the handkerchief.

Place the pan on the stove, turn on the heat, and bring the water to a steady, bubbling boil. The steam should rise up and away and, after a few minutes, you'll notice the water level start to drop. How long it takes for the water to boil away will depend on how much water you started with. Keep a close eye on the pan, and when you've come down to the last inch or so of water, watch it like a hawk.

This is when the whole process speeds up and things get quite exciting. Now you'll believe that there really is salt in the pan – you'll see that a film of salt is starting to appear on the surface of the water.

The water becomes cloudier and cloudier. Clumps of salt form in the base of the pan. Stir the salt and water with a wooden spoon, pushing the salty bits around the bottom of the pan. Turn the heat down a little as the water disappears. Keep stirring, and you're left with a soggy, damp mass of snowy white salt. Switch off the heat, scrape the salt into a shallow bowl, and let it dry out slowly in a warm place. You can break up the salt with your fingers as it dries out.

Unless you've taken your seawater from an unusually salty piece of coastline (near a salt marsh, for instance), you'll probably get around a tablespoon of salt from a quart of seawater. You can use your homemade salt in any of your cooking – for boiling with pasta, for flavoring stews, or for sprinkling on, say, a chicken before you roast it. Or you can even add it to your own homemade butter (see page 64), then melt this over your freshly boiled homegrown potatoes (see page 181). Keep this up, and soon you'll never have to go to the shops again!

collect some seawater

boil it down ...

salt!

NICOLA'S ZESTY FLAPJACKS

Hugh's friend Nicola Greenway makes the best flapjacks! (In the U.K., flapjacks are a kind of oatmeal bar cookie.) The secret's in the orange and lemon — the sharp flavor of the citrus cuts through all that buttery sweetness. You can adapt the recipe according to what you have in the cupboard. Instead of raisins, try chopped dried apricots or prunes. And instead of pine nuts, try pistachios, cashews, pecan nuts, sunflower seeds, or pumpkin seeds.

You will need:

Orange, 1
Lemon, 1/2
Raisins, 1/2 cup
Golden syrup or light corn syrup, 1/4 cup
Unsalted butter, 3/4 cup (1 1/2 sticks),
    plus a little for greasing the pan
Brown sugar, 1/2 cup
Rolled oats, 2 3/4 cups

All-purpose or white pastry flour, 2/3 cup
Pine nuts, 3/4 cup

Baking pan about 9 inches square, parchment paper, grater, large saucepan, citrus juicer, small saucepan, wooden spoon, mixing bowl

1. Preheat the oven to 325°F. Grease the inside of the pan with a little butter and line the bottom with parchment paper.

2. Grate the zest (but not the white pith) from the orange and lemon into the large saucepan. Then squeeze the juice from both and put this in the small saucepan, with the raisins. Turn the heat on low and bring the juice to a gentle simmer. Remove the pan from the heat, but leave it in a warm place for the raisins to plump up in the juice.

3. Meanwhile, measure the syrup into the large saucepan containing the zest; you can help it off the spoon with a (clean!) finger. Add the butter and brown sugar. Heat very gently, stirring occasionally with the wooden spoon,

until the butter has melted and the sugar has dissolved. Turn off the heat.

4. Mix together the oats, flour, and pine nuts in the mixing bowl. Pour the oat mixture into the saucepan containing the melted butter mixture and add the raisins, along with any juice left in the pan. Mix everything very thoroughly.

5. Spread the mixture out in the lined pan. Oven gloves on. Place the pan in the oven and bake for 25 to 30 minutes or until golden brown.

6. Oven gloves on. Remove the pan from the oven and let sit for a few minutes, then mark the flapjack cookie into squares with a knife. Let cool slightly and eat the first few warm — they are irresistible.

RICE PUDDING

Rice pudding isn't a quick pudding, but it's a very easy one to make and well worth the wait. You can cook it with the lid on – in which case you'll simply have a bowl of delicious creamy rice – or with the lid off, when it will form a golden-brown skin on top. This will make enough for 2 people, or 4 if you're eating it with something else.

You will need:
Arborio rice, ¼ cup
Unsalted butter, 2 tablespoons, plus
   a little extra for greasing the dish
Whole milk, 2 cups
Superfine sugar, ¼ cup

A pinch of salt
Vanilla bean or whole nutmeg (optional)

*Sieve, medium ovenproof dish or pan
(with a lid if you don't want a skin to form),
measuring cup, wooden spoon, grater*

1. Preheat the oven to 300°F.

2. Measure the rice and look through it carefully just to make sure there's no grit lurking in it. Wash it in a sieve under cold water to remove any dust, give it a shake, then let it drain for a few minutes.

3. Rub the inside of the ovenproof dish with a little butter. Add the washed rice, the 2 tablespoons of butter, the milk, sugar, and salt. If you like, you can add a whole vanilla bean (split lengthwise with a sharp knife) or grate in a little nutmeg.

4. Oven gloves on. Put the dish in the pre-heated oven and bake for 45 minutes. Oven gloves on again. Take the dish out of the oven and stir the milk and rice gently with the wooden spoon. Put the dish back in the oven. Take it out again half an hour later and you'll notice that a light skin has started to form on the surface of the pudding. Stir this in and scrape up any rice that may have started to stick on the base of the dish.

5. Return the dish to the oven (with the lid on if you don't want a skin to form on the pudding) for 1 to 1½ hours, until the rice is tender and creamy. Keep an eye on it to check that it doesn't dry out at all – you can gently stir in a little more milk if it does.

How to eat your rice pudding

There are all sorts of delicious ways to eat rice pudding. You could stew some fruit to go with it. The following are all very good:

Washed and chopped rhubarb, stewed with a little orange juice and sugar in the oven.

Topped and tailed gooseberries, stewed gently on the stove with a little sugar until they burst.

Peeled, cored, and chopped Granny Smith or Golden Delicious apples, cooked gently with a little sugar and water.

A tangy jam, such as raspberry, simply dolloped on top of the rice.

If you want a complete cupboard experience, hot rice pudding and cold canned pears makes a very good, easy standby, particularly with a little cream poured on top.

As well as eating it hot, you can let the rice pudding get cold and then chill it until firm. It can then be eaten with hot or cold versions of any of the above.

If you've used a vanilla bean, this can be rinsed afterward and used again. Put it in a jar of superfine sugar and after a week or two it will have given the sugar a delicious vanilla scent. Use this sugar when you make custards or puddings to give them just a hint of the spice.

Variation

Give your rice pudding a slightly Spanish feel by baking it (lid on) with a wide piece of zest that you've peeled from a lemon (scrape off any white pith). When you serve the pudding, shake a little ground cinnamon over the top.

. . . .

FRAGRANT RICE

In this recipe, the rice is fried for a minute or so in a little butter, which helps the grains stay fluffy rather than clumping together.

Serves 4 to 6 as a side dish:
Basmati rice, 1½ cups
Cumin seeds, 1 teaspoon
Cloves, 4 or 5
Cardamom pods, 4 or 5
A bay leaf
Butter, 3 tablespoons

Water, 2 cups
Salt, 1 teaspoon

Large glass measuring cup, large mixing bowl, sieve, teaspoon, teacup, medium saucepan with a tight-fitting lid, wooden spoon, aluminum foil, fork

1. First, wash and soak the rice. Put the mixing bowl under cold water in the sink and pour the rice into the bowl. Turn the tap on, fill the bowl with water, and gently swirl the rice in the water. Let the rice sink to the bottom again and carefully pour the cloudy water off. Repeat this 4 or 5 times, until the water is reasonably clear. Pour more water into the bowl and let the rice soak for half an hour.

2. Drain the rice into the sieve and rinse one last time. Let the water drip away while you put the spices and bay leaf in a teacup.

3. Put the saucepan on the stove. Add the butter and turn the heat to low. When the butter has melted and is just starting to sizzle, add the spices and stir them around in the pan with the wooden spoon for a few seconds to heat up and start releasing their wonderful smell. Add the drained rice into the pan and very gently (rice is fragile stuff) stir-fry it for a minute so that all the grains are lightly coated in the spicy butter.

4. Pour the water onto the rice, using the wooden spoon to rescue any grains of rice stuck to the side of the pan. Add the salt, stir the rice, and turn the heat up to bring the water to a boil.

5. As soon as the water starts to bubble, turn the heat down as low as it will go without turning off the burner. Put a sheet of foil on top of the pan and put the lid on top of the foil. This will help stop any steam escaping from the pan if the lid doesn't fit absolutely tightly. Cook like this for 25 minutes, then turn off the heat. Let the rice sit undisturbed for about 5 minutes.

6. Oven gloves on. Raise the lid and lift up the foil. The rice should have swelled and the liquid completely disappeared. Very gently use a fork to stir and lift the grains – called "fluffing the rice" in many cookbooks – but take care not to crush them. Serve the rice right away.

How to eat your rice

Rice as fragrant as this is wonderful simply eaten on its own, perhaps with a little extra butter on top. You could serve it with an Indian curry (see page 298) or eat it with dal, a spiced lentil soup. You can vary the spices – add a cinnamon stick, which will give the rice a sweet flavor, or add a chopped fresh chile for a little heat. Leave the spices out and you have plain fluffy rice, which will go with almost any stew.

HOMEMADE BACON FOR A BACON SANDWICH

Everyone loves bacon, but not everyone knows how easy it is to make your own — or how much more delicious homemade bacon is than most of what you buy in the store.

Any salted pork can technically be called bacon, but the best cuts to use for this recipe (and your sandwich) are loin (Canadian bacon), belly (regular bacon), or spareribs (for collar bacon, as in the picture opposite). Ask your butcher to leave the rind on (unscored), but take any bones out.

You will need:
Free-range piece of pork (loin, spare ribs, or thick end of belly), about 1½ pounds

For the dry-cure mix:
Bay leaves, 2
Juniper berries, 10
Coarse salt, a little over 1 pound
Brown sugar, ½ cup
Coarsely ground black pepper, 1 tablespoon

To serve:
A little oil for frying
Bread and butter
Ketchup

Large cutting board, sharp knife, large mixing bowl (not metal), large plastic container with lid, plastic wrap, paper towels, butcher's string, waxed paper or cotton cloth, carving knife, heavy frying pan

1. First, make up the cure for your bacon. Finely chop the bay leaves, lightly crush the juniper berries, and add both to the (nonmetal) bowl along with the salt, sugar, and black pepper. Mix thoroughly together.

2. Put the piece of pork on the board. Grab a handful of the dry-cure mix and start rubbing it with your fingers into all the surfaces of the meat. When you have thoroughly salted it all over, put it in the plastic container. Put the lid on and place it in the fridge. Cover the bowl of cure mix with plastic wrap — you'll need it later.

3. After about 24 hours, take the container out of the fridge and take off the lid. The salt will have drawn the moisture out of the pork, which will now be sitting in salty liquid. Take the pork out and put it on a board, then carefully pour the liquid in the container down the sink. Rub the meat with a couple more handfuls of cure mix before returning it to the container and placing in the fridge, as before.

4. Repeat this process every day. The bacon will be lightly cured (ready to make your bacon sandwich) after 4 days, though you could cure it for longer (up to a week). The longer it's cured, the longer it will keep and the saltier it will become — less suitable for bacon slices but very good for adding to stews and pasta sauces (which won't need any extra salt).

5. When you've finished curing your bacon, take it out of the fridge, rinse the excess salt under cold water, and pat the meat dry with paper towels. Ideally, you should then hang it to dry in a cool, airy place for 24 hours – but if you're getting impatient, it's not essential.

6. Wrap your finished bacon in waxed paper or a cotton cloth (this will let it "breathe," whereas plastic wrap or aluminum foil would make it "sweat").

7. Now for the sandwich . . . Put the bacon on a large cutting board and find a long, sharp carving knife. Do your best to slice some nice, thin slices from your bacon (it might be a good idea to get some adult help with this!). If it's tricky, just cut off little slivers of bacon instead – you'll need a few more to make your sandwich.

8. Heat a very little oil in the frying pan over medium heat. Add the bacon slices (cook just 3 or 4 at a time) and fry well, turning them over as necessary until they're just as you like them. Keep these on a warm plate if you have to fry any more bacon. Meanwhile, put a plate of bread and butter on the table and find the ketchup.

9. Store leftover bacon well wrapped in waxed paper in the fridge. It should keep for a couple of weeks (much longer if you have cured it for longer), or you can freeze it.

How to eat your homemade bacon

Bring the plate with the bacon to the table and let everyone assemble their own sandwich.

If this seems rather a long process for making a bacon sandwich, then rest assured your bacon has plenty of other uses. You could use it to serve with macaroni and cheese (see page 71), fry it with liver (see page 294), or use it in savory, custardy tarts like quiche Lorraine. Chunky cubes of homemade bacon are a very good way to add flavor and richness to all kinds of stews (e.g., Pheasant Casserole, page 300). Cut into smaller pieces (matchsticks) and fried, they can be tossed with pasta (and peas), sprinkled on pizza or over salads, or added to a tomato sauce for pasta.

LENTIL AND BACON SOUP FOR LOTS OF PEOPLE

It's traditional in Fizz's household that her friend Richard Johnson make this lovely lentil soup for lunch whenever he and his family come to stay. A mixture of red and green lentils is used because the two sorts have a different texture when they're cooked – the green have a bit of bite to them, while the red soften into a kind of mush.

This recipe makes quite a lot of soup, but it tastes even better the next day (and freezes well, too).

To serve about 12:

Onions, 3
Carrots, 3 to 4
Celery stalks, 4 to 5
Bacon slices, about 10
Olive oil
A mixture of red and green lentils, 3⅔ cups
Water, 3 quarts (or use homemade chicken or vegetable stock, or bouillon, and leave out the stock cubes)
Organic chicken stock cubes, 3 to 4
Salt and black pepper

Oregano or thyme, 1 tablespoon dried (or use 2 tablespoons of chopped fresh oregano and a handful of thyme sprigs, if you have them)
Tomato purée, 1 tablespoon
Worcestershire sauce, a few good shakes
Shredded Cheddar or grated Parmesan, to serve

Sharp knife, cutting board, scissors, a really big pan with a lid, wooden spoon, large bowl, large saucepan

1. Peel the onions and chop them finely. Peel the carrots and trim the celery stalks (rinse them if they look muddy). Finely chop the carrots and celery. You're aiming for equal quantities to match the amount of onion that you've chopped. Cut any thick rind off the bacon slices with the scissors and snip the bacon into little pieces.

2. Pour plenty of olive oil into the pan – enough to cover the base completely. Turn the heat to low. Add the onions, carrots, celery, and bacon. Put the lid on the pan and let the vegetables cook very gently, for 10 to 15 minutes.

They mustn't burn or brown too quickly, but should just become tender and slightly shrunken down in the pan. From time to time, remove the lid and stir the vegetables. Fill the kettle and put it on to boil.

3. Add the lentils to the pan.

4. Heat the 3 quarts water in a large saucepan. Put the stock cubes in the bowl and add 1 quart of the hot water. Stir gently to let the stock cubes dissolve, then add this stock to the lentils in the pan. Add the remaining water to the pan. Turn the heat to medium.

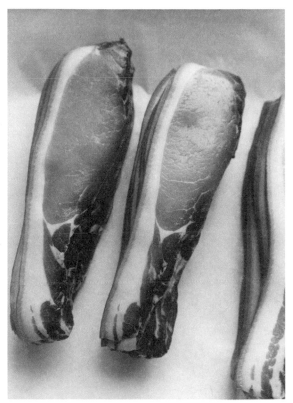

5. Now stir in lots of freshly ground black pepper, a little salt (the stock will be quite salty), and the oregano and/or thyme. Add the tomato purée and Worcestershire sauce.

6. Bring to a boil, turn the heat down again, and simmer the soup gently, with the lid not quite covering it, for at least half an hour, until the red lentils are soft and the green ones are cooked but still with a bit of bite to them. It really doesn't matter if it cooks a bit longer. Check for salt and pepper and bring your soup bubbling to the table.

How to eat your soup

Serve the soup with bread to dunk and a big bowl of shredded or grated cheese (aged Cheddar or Parmesan) to hand around for sprinkling over the top. If you have soup left over, you can let it cool, cover it, and keep it in the fridge for a day or two. Reheat it over low heat until it's piping hot.

SPICY BEAN STEW WITH SAUSAGES

This is a lovely, easy stew that will sit good-naturedly on the stove for an hour or two, filling the kitchen with wonderfully spicy smells.

To serve 4:

Olive or canola oil, 3 tablespoons
Pork sausages, 8 good free-range ones
Onion, 1 medium
Garlic cloves, 2
Cannellini beans, 14½-ounce can
Kidney beans, 10-ounce can
Brown sugar, 1 teaspoon
Nutmeg, a good grinding from a whole
  nutmeg, or ¼ teaspoon ground nutmeg

Cayenne pepper, ¼ teaspoon
Ground cloves, ¼ teaspoon
Thyme, ½ teaspoon dried, or 2 sprigs fresh
Plum tomatoes, two 14½-ounce cans
Salt and black pepper

Large heavy saucepan with lid, tablespoon, plate, cutting board, sharp knife, colander, wooden spoon, grater

1. Place the saucepan on the stove and spoon in the oil. Turn on the heat to medium, add the sausages, and fry them, turning them over until they are browned on the outside. Fish them out of the pan, setting them aside on a plate.

2. While the sausages are browning, peel the onion and garlic and chop them as small as you can. Drain the cans of beans into a colander and rinse them with cold water.

3. Add the onion to the pan, turn the heat down to low, cover the pan, and cook the onion gently in the pan for about 10 minutes, stirring from time to time so that it doesn't stick on the bottom of the pan. It will pick up all the lovely sausagey goo in the bottom of the pan.

4. Add the garlic and fry for another couple of minutes. Add the brown sugar and grate in some nutmeg. Stir in the cayenne, cloves, and dried or fresh thyme.

5. Pour in the tomatoes and break them up with a wooden spoon or a potato masher. Add the sausages to the pan, along with the beans.

6. Season with salt and lots of black pepper. Give everything a good stir and turn up the heat to medium. When the stew starts to simmer, put the lid on, turn the heat down, and let it bubble away gently. Stir occasionally to make sure it isn't burning on the bottom of the pan. You can leave it for at least an hour or up to 2 hours.

How to eat your stew

This stew makes a great dish when it's cold and miserable outside. It's also nice and easy for a bit of campfire cookery (see page 275). Serve it with baked or mashed potatoes.

ROAST CHESTNUTS

If toasting yourself in front of an open log fire is part of your cold-weather ritual, why not get some plump chestnuts to roast in the coals? If you don't have a fireplace, a roasting pan in a hot oven will do the job just as well. You can buy fresh chestnuts from produce markets in the autumn.

You will need:
A handful of chestnuts for each person

A small sharp knife, an old pan (like a cake pan), an old roasting rack (the kind that goes in a roasting pan – not essential if you don't have one), a bowl, an old tea towel

1. Let the fire die down, so that you'll be roasting the chestnuts in hot ash and embers.

2. With the sharp knife, carefully make a slit in the rounded end of each chestnut (be certain that you've slit every single one, as you don't want an exploding chestnut covering you with hot ash). Put them in the pan, allowing plenty of space for the chestnuts to move around when you shake them.

3. Carefully stand the rack in the embers of the fire and put the pan on top (alternatively, just place the pan at the edge of the embers). Line the bowl with the tea towel and place by the fire.

4. Oven gloves on. Shake the pan every few minutes so that the chestnuts cook evenly. Keep a close eye for burning spots, and test a chestnut for doneness when the slits on the shell start to peel back. Empty the cooked chestnuts into the bowl lined with the tea towel, then wrap them and let cool for a few minutes.

Variation

If you want to roast your chestnuts in the oven rather than over the fire, preheat the oven to 400°F. Slit the chestnuts as before and place them in a roasting pan. Roast the nuts, opening the oven door every 3 or 4 minutes to shake the pan (oven gloves on) until they're cooked as described above.

How to eat your chestnuts

Peel back the shell and you'll get to the nugget of sweet, tender chestnut meat inside. Whether you've cooked them in the oven or on the fire, chestnuts are food to be eaten at dusk or later. Somehow, broad daylight just doesn't feel right. In the U.K., we wrap hot cooked chestnuts in foil and munch on them while watching the bonfire and fireworks on Guy Fawkes Night.

HUMMUS

The benefit of making this hummus from scratch with dried chickpeas is that you get a lovely dip that you can scoop up with pita bread while it's still slightly warm.

You will need:
Dried chickpeas, ½ cup
A bay leaf
Salt
Lemon, 1
Garlic cloves, 2
Tahini, 2 to 3 tablespoons

Black pepper

Large bowl, sieve, heavy medium saucepan with lid, spoon, citrus juicer, sharp knife, cutting board, tablespoon, blender or food processor, serving bowl

1. Rinse the chickpeas thoroughly, then place in the large bowl with plenty of fresh water — enough to cover them very generously. Soak for at least 12 hours, or overnight.

2. Drain the chickpeas in a sieve and put them in the saucepan. Add enough clean water to cover them by a few inches, then add the bay leaf. Put the pan on the stove, turn the heat to high, and bring the water to a boil.

3. Turn the heat right down, put the lid on the pan, and simmer the chickpeas gently for 2 to 3 hours, until they mash easily if you press one of them against the side of the pan with the back of a spoon. Check that they don't run dry at any point — add a little boiling water from the kettle if this looks possible. Add ½ teaspoon of salt near the end of the cooking time.

4. Stand a sieve over a bowl and drain the chickpeas through it. Keep the liquid but throw away the bay leaf.

5. Squeeze the juice from the lemon and peel and finely chop the garlic cloves.

6. Put 5 to 6 tablespoons of the chickpea cooking liquid into the food processor, then add half the chickpeas, 2 tablespoons of the lemon juice, and all the garlic. Put the lid on and whiz the chickpeas for a few seconds. Take the lid off; add the remaining chickpeas and 2 tablespoons of tahini paste. Whiz again.

7. Once the chickpeas have blended properly, scrape the hummus into a bowl. Taste it. Season it with some salt and plenty of black pepper. If you think it needs more lemon juice or tahini, add some a little at a time until it tastes just the way you like it.

How to eat your hummus

Warm plenty of pita bread, either in the oven for 2 to 3 minutes or in the toaster, and use it to scoop up the hummus. You could eat it with some lamb kebabs (see page 292).

PEAR AND ALMOND PUDDING CAKE

This recipe uses two sorts of almonds, yet it's not aggressively nutty at all, showing that almonds are used as much for texture as for flavor. If you have a food processor, use it to whiz up whole blanched almonds (the ones without their papery brown skin). If you don't have one, just use ready-ground almonds.

It's called a pudding cake because you can eat it warm with lots of cream at lunchtime and if there's any left over, you can eat it cold for tea.

To serve 6:

Unsalted butter, ⅔ cup, soft but not melted
Superfine sugar, ½ cup
Eggs, 2
Almond extract, 1 teaspoon
Whole blanched almonds or ground
    almonds, ½ cup
Self-rising flour (see page 18), ½ cup

For the pears:
Pears, 3, firm but ripe
Unsalted butter, 2 tablespoons
Granulated sugar, 1 tablespoon

Cake pan about 8 inches in diameter and 2 inches deep (a springform pan is best), parchment paper, vegetable peeler, sharp knife, cutting board, medium saucepan, tablespoon, large mixing bowl, wooden spoon, food processor, sieve, palette knife or rubber spatula, wire rack

1. Preheat the oven to 325°F. Grease the cake pan with a little butter and line the bottom with parchment paper (see page 407).

2. Peel the pears and slice the flesh off each one in 4 pieces, lengthwise around the core (if you nibble off the extra flesh around the cores, you'll know just how sweet and ripe your pears are and how much extra sugar they need).

3. Put the saucepan on the stove and turn the heat to medium. Add the 2 tablespoons butter and let it start to sizzle. Add the tablespoon of granulated sugar (a small one if your pears are

ripe and sweet, a heaping one if they're rather hard and unsweet) and stir the butter and sugar together to make a bubbly sauce.

4. Add the pear slices and fry them in the mixture for a couple of minutes until they start to pick up a few brown flecks. If at any time the pears start to fall apart or look as if they're about to burn, turn off the heat. Set the pan aside to cool down a little.

5. Make the cakey bit. Put the butter and sugar in the mixing bowl and cream together with the wooden spoon until well blended.

Break in the first egg and beat this in well. Beat in the other egg, along with the almond extract. The mix will look quite bitty and eggy, which is fine for the time being.

6. Whiz the whole blanched almonds in the food processor for about a minute to grind them up. Add them to the cake mixture (or add the already-ground almonds). Sift in the self-rising flour. Fold in the dry ingredients gently but completely until all the flour has disappeared (see page 91 for more about folding in). By now the cake mix should have a thick, moussey sort of texture.

7. Scrape the mixture into the prepared pan and spread it out with the palette knife or spatula – do this very gently so you don't knock any air out of it. Pick up the pieces of pear with the wooden spoon, leaving the juices behind in the pan, and arrange them evenly on top of the cake in whatever pattern you like.

8. Oven gloves on. Put the pan in the preheated oven and bake for about 45 minutes. The cake is ready if, when you slide a knife into the middle, the blade comes out clean. Place the hot pan on a wire rack to cool. If you've used a springform pan, you can unclip the sides to serve. Otherwise it's easier to serve the cake from the pan.

How to eat your pudding cake

You can eat the cake warm and serve it with cream, custard, crème fraîche, or Greek yogurt, or you can let it cool completely and have it for tea.

If you have a lot of juice left in the saucepan after cooking the pears, while the cake is in the oven you can simmer the juice for a few minutes to reduce and thicken it slightly. Pour the syrupy juice over the finished cake to make a nice, shiny glaze.

SUGAR & HONEY
(and ice cream)

Once our ancestors had to search for sweetness high up in the trees, risking painful stings and fatal falls. Now it's all so easy — sugar at the flick of a spoon, in our tea, on our cereal, wherever we want it. All the more reason to experiment and discover what amazing things happen to sugar when it's baked, boiled, whisked, and even frozen. Then share your sweet discoveries with family and friends.

marshmallows, page 368

honey-ginger cake, page 364

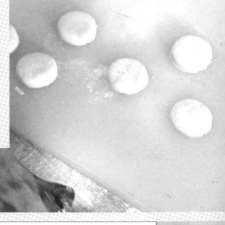
peppermint creams, page 363

peach parfait, page 373

custard ice cream, page 374

an ice cream maker, page 356

honey fudge, page 379

ice lollies, page 358

Turkish delight, page 376

SUGAR & HONEY

Imagine that you are a Neolithic hunter-gatherer, roaming the forests and following the herds. Think about the kind of food you'll be eating – wild boar, an elk or two, fruits and berries when you can get them, roots and leaves when you can't, perhaps oysters and the occasional fish if you are close to the sea.

You're working incredibly hard, hunting and gathering to get the food just to keep yourself fit and strong enough to hunt and gather some more. It's a pretty tough life. Imagine, then, the sheer luxury and indulgence of finding a food that is so packed with luscious, energy-giving sweetness that a few mouthfuls is all you can manage. After that you feel filled up by its richness and intoxicated by its sheer deliciousness. You might have had to shin up a tree and brave a few stings, but it's easily the best day's hunting you've had in weeks. Because what you have found is honey.

Our sweet tooth evolved over thousands of years to help us seek out sugary foods high in energy to sustain our very active hunting, gathering, wandering lives. But whereas once we had to use all our wits to find any sort of sweet treat, nowadays it's all too easy. That sweet tooth is highly developed, yet the closest we get to hunting and gathering for its gratification is picking up a chocolate bar in the corner store.

A sweet tooth that can be satisfied so easily can lead us into all kinds of trouble.

High-sugar foods are indeed packed with energy. But if we don't use up that energy – if there is no tree for us to climb – then it can quickly turn to fat.

It would be hard for anyone to argue that sugar is a health food, and it is thought to contribute to obesity. But, as with most foods, a little bit of sugar now and then is unlikely to do us much harm, provided that we think of sugary foods as treats rather than natural, everyday parts of our diet. Making your own sweet treats is better than grabbing something off a store shelf, because not only do you have all the fun of preparing them but you can't help but be aware of exactly what you're eating. You can see just how much sugar went into that sweet or cake when you measure it out and add it to a bowl. All the food labeling in the world is no substitute for simply seeing a pile of ingredients in front of you.

What is sugar?

Think of sugar and you probably think of a canister of fine white crystals sitting on a shelf in your kitchen ready to sweeten your tea or make a cake. But if you look at a shelf of sugar in a store, you'll see different-colored crystals, granules, and cubes, even jars and cans of liquids. We use the word *sugar* to describe a whole mass of different foods. They may even come from completely different plants that are not related at all.

In the same way that a flour is just the ground-up powder of any grain or food, whether it be wheat, barley, or even rice, a sugar is the boiled-down, concentrated juice of any sweet plant. In Canada, the sap of maple trees is drained and boiled to make maple syrup and maple sugar. In India, a sugar called *gur* is made from the sap of palm trees. In the U.K., though, nearly all the sugar we eat comes from two main plants: sugarcane, which is grown in hot regions such as the West Indies and Mauritius; and the sugar beet, which is grown in cooler climates, including Britain.

How sugar came to Britain

Although sugar from plants had been eaten in India and China for thousands of years, sugar came late to Britain and the rest of Europe. It wasn't until the seventeenth century, when British adventurers established sugarcane plantations in their colonies in the New World and the West Indies, that it became truly widespread. Sugar production soon became a massive and highly profitable part of our colonial trade operation.

For over a century, the demand for sugar across European countries seemed never-ending. Whatever could be produced would be consumed. But a huge amount of labor was required to plant, harvest, and process the sugarcane crop. The solution to this problem was a terrible and brutal one. Hundreds of thousands of Africans were captured and transported in dreadful conditions to the West Indies and other colonies to work as slaves on sugar plantations.

Homegrown sugar

In 1748, a German scientist, Andreas Marggraf, succeeded in making sugar from the root of the sugar beet plant — a close relation to the beets and rutabagas that had previously been used as a fodder crop for animals. Over the next 150 years, most European countries started to grow sugar beets. This meant they were no longer entirely dependent on their faraway territories for sugar — although both plants and both methods of production competed to provide the world's sugar, as they still do to this day.

How sugar is made

If you were to dip a finger into a bowl of white cane sugar and then into a bowl of white beet sugar, you wouldn't be able to taste the difference between the two. This is odd when you think about how different the two plants look. Cane is tall and leggy, a thick, bamboo like stem harvested under a sweltering tropical sun. Sugar beets are short and stumpy, looking just like turnips or rutabagas, and are dug from the sticky, muddy ground under often gloomy skies.

To make cane sugar, the stems are cut down when their sugar content is highest. The sweet juice is pressed out of the stems by steel rollers on a giant industrial mangle. This juice is purified and then boiled down slowly to a syrup, so that most of the water evaporates away as steam. Small sugar crystals are added, and the tiny sugar particles in the syrup cling to these crystals, which grow into bigger crystals. They are then spun dry (rather like in a washing machine) to get raw cane sugar. Further washing, cleaning, and filtering at sugar refineries turns this raw sugar from a damp, brown mass into the fine, white crystals of sugar that we mostly use today in cooking and sweetening.

Sugar beet processing is a little different. The bulbous roots are sliced and left to stand in hot water so that most of the particles of sugar in the plant cross into the water. The slices are then crushed to a pulp, which is pressed to make sure that as much of the sugar as possible goes into the syrupy juice. The juice is then filtered and further processed in roughly the same way as sugarcane.

Different sorts of sugar

Sugar comes in many shapes, forms, and colors and each kind is suited to particular tasks in the kitchen. You don't always have to use exactly the kind of sugar specified in a recipe, but if you don't you might end up with some subtle differences in the end result.

Superfine sugar is made up of small, white crystals that blend quite easily into other ingredients, making it a good sugar to use for cakes and biscuits. It dissolves very quickly in a liquid, particularly a warm liquid – for example, when you make a sugar syrup or an icing. You can make your own superfine sugar by whirling granulated suger in a blender.

Some recipes with superfine sugar

Shortbread, page 80

Meringues, page 108

Victoria Sponge Cake, page 111

Lemon Curd, page 143

Banana Bread, page 153

Lemonade, page 159

Pear and Almond Pudding Cake, page 334

Granulated sugar has larger crystals than superfine sugar. As it is coarser, it's usually a little cheaper. It can make cakes and biscuits rather gritty in texture. But then if you're sprinkling sugar on something creamy, such as porridge, a little grittiness may be just what you're after. Generally speaking, granulated sugar is best used in recipes where the sugar is going to be dissolved in a hot liquid – for example, when you're making jam.

Some recipes with granulated sugar

Bramble Jelly, page 156

Sweet Chile and Red Currant Jam, page 163

Confectioners' sugar has been ground very finely and had a little cornstarch added. It behaves quite differently from other sugars. It dissolves instantly if a little is stirred into a large amount of liquid. And when you add a little liquid to a large amount of confectioners' sugar, something quite dramatic occurs – its powdery bulk immediately shrinks into a glossy, smooth paste. This is how the simplest of icings is made, known as confectioners' icing.

Add a lightly beaten egg white to confectioners' sugar instead of water and you end up with a thick sugar paste, which can be molded or rolled out into a sheet. This is sometimes called royal icing. Laid over a cake, it sets pure white and rock hard, forming a complete seal over a rich fruitcake, for example, which will help it keep for months. The same paste can be flavored with very concentrated essences to make fondants. The simplest of these is peppermint creams (see page 363).

Just like other powders, confectioners' sugar tends to lump together in the packet, so it needs to be shaken through a sieve before you use it. Because it dissolves instantly, it's good for sweetening desserts that aren't going to be cooked, such as fruit fools.

Some recipes with confectioners' sugar

Strawberry Fool, page 141
Orange and Strawberry Jellies, page 154
Peppermint Creams, page 363

Brown sugar is simply white sugar that has had molasses added. You can buy both light and dark brown sugar. Both have a soft moistness to them, and a more distinctive flavor than refined white sugar. This is the flavor of molasses, which is a form of unrefined sugar in its liquid state. You can buy a bottle of dark, sticky molasses and use it for the best kind of spicy ginger cake – but you wouldn't want it on your strawberries.

The darker the sugar, the more intense the flavor. Light brown sugar has a soft, creamy texture and a mild taste and always seems good in recipes with other tropical ingredients in them, such as bananas, cinnamon, and ginger. Bananas sprinkled with light brown sugar and lemon juice, wrapped in buttered foil, and roasted in the oven make a fine dessert (particularly if you cook it in the hot embers of a campfire).

Some recipes with brown sugar

Baked Apples, page 144
Nicola's Zesty Flapjacks, page 320

Demerara sugar is a distinctive kind of golden brown sugar with large, even crystals, a little bigger than most granulated sugar. It's called Demerara after the area of Guyana, South America, where it used to be produced. The taste is similar to light brown sugar, but it is a bit more "cooked," or toffeeish. In fact, this is an excellent sugar for making toffee and fudge. If you like the flavor of brown sugar and the gritty texture of granulated, you might well enjoy Demerara sugar sprinkled on your cereal or a bowl of porridge.

HONEY

Sugary liquid is taken from a naturally sweet plant, the liquid is filtered and purified, and the water is evaporated from that liquid to make it thicker, sweeter, and more concentrated. This sounds pretty much like a summary of the manufacture of sugar from cane or beet. But this time we're talking about making honey, and with honey it's bees, not people, who do all the work.

How honey is made

A colony of honeybees is made up of one queen, a few hundred male drones, and between 10,000 and 40,000 female workers who run the hive as a nectar-processing factory. Bees collect nectar – a sugary water produced by flowers – turn it into honey, and store it in hexagon-shaped wax cells so that they have plenty of food to see them through the winter months when flowers are scarce.

Each bee in the hive has a particular job – whether it be harvester, processor, or packager. The harvester bees use their tongues to suck up nectar from each flower they visit, storing the nectar in one of their two stomachs. When this nectar stomach is full, they return to the hive.

The second lot of bees sucks the nectar out of the bees' stomachs and gives it a good chew. Substances in the bees' saliva change the sugars in the nectar to different sugars that they can digest more easily. They then spit the chewed nectar into the waxy cells.

As the nectar is still very runny at this stage, the bees fan the liquid nectar with their wings to dry it out. When it's just sticky enough, the youngest bees in the hive seal up each hexagonal cell in the honeycomb with a layer of the beeswax that they produce from their bodies.

In other words, the teaspoon of honey that you trickle lovingly onto your buttered toast is simply a mass of slurped-up, regurgitated, chewed-up, spat-out, wing-dried sugar water that has been collected from thousands of flowers by several thousand bees and enclosed in a cell made of their hardened bodily fluids. And very delicious it is, too.

The history of honey harvesting

For thousands of years, honey was a wild food for hunter-gatherers. Good honey-seekers were honored members of the tribe. They knew about following certain birds, and the bees themselves, and looking up into trees to spot the nest where the treasure of honey would be. And they knew about using a handful of smoking leaves to waft at the bees so that they became sleepy and less likely to sting. Having found the honey, they probably plundered the lot, more or less destroying the nest.

But when the first farmers started growing crops in settlements rather than following grazing herds of wild beasts, people began farming bees rather than searching for their nests. They worked out how to build artificial hives, from wood, mud, clay, and straw. They learned how to catch a swarming colony of

wild bees and introduce them to a hive, where a little honey would be waiting as a welcome gift. The bees did so well, and

reproduced so successfully, that soon the colony could be divided into two, with a new queen, and another hive could be started. Several times a year, the beekeeper could take off a good helping of honey, leaving just enough for the bees to stay healthy and set busily about making some more.

The success of honey farming meant that, for years before sugar came to Europe, we already had an excellent product with which we could sweeten our food. There were beehives in and around every town and village. Cakes, drinks, milk, cheeses, and sour or unripe fruits were all sweetened with a trickle of local honey.

The uses of honey today

Nowadays, natural honey has given way to processed, refined sugar as the chief way of sweetening most of the food we cook and eat. Sugar's main advantage is that it doesn't interfere with the flavors of delicate food. Whenever honey is used as a sweetener, especially the darker honeys, you don't just taste sweetness. You get a strong hit of the heavy, almost perfumed flavor that is unique to honey. Sometimes this is just what you want. And sometimes it isn't!

If you're making a sponge cake layered with jam, you want to taste the jam and the airy, delicate sponge rather than the musky scent of honey. Similarly, a strong-flavored honey in a cup of tea can overpower the taste of the tea — and most people would agree that honey in a cup of coffee tastes disgusting. It's an unfortunate clash of strong flavors.

These days we mainly appreciate honey in its pure state, as something to spread on our bread and toast or trickle on pancakes and scones. But honey can still come into its own as a sweetener in recipes, if that unique flavor is exactly what you want. It's perfect in sticky ginger cakes, light, crisp cookies, or as a highly distinctive way to flavor an ice cream or a batch of fudge.

Different types of honey

What honey looks like, how thick it is, and how it tastes depends on the kind of flowers the bees that made it were feeding on. Some of the nicest, most distinctive honeys are made from a single type of flower, such as heather, orange blossom, or lavender. You can quite clearly taste the scent of the flower in the honey. This is achieved by deliberately placing the hives in an area where one kind of flower dominates the landscape — for example, right in the middle of fields of cultivated lavender, or on Scottish hills almost entirely covered in wild heather. Honeys like this are sometimes called "mono-floral" (which means "single flower" in Latin), and they are often quite expensive.

Pale, cloudy, thick-set honey, which can be almost rock solid when cold, comes mainly from crop flowers such as rapeseed – those fields of bright yellow that you see in late April and May. It is not the most subtle of honeys, but it still tastes pretty good.

Some honeys are labeled "wildflower" honey. They usually come from hives that are placed away from any particular cultivated flowering crops, such as rapeseed. It will never be possible to be sure exactly what flower the bees have taken their nectar from, but it's likely to be a happy mixture, and this honey is often richly scented and delicious.

If the label on the jar doesn't say what sort of flower honey it is, then it will probably be a blended honey – taken from different crops or maybe even different countries.

Some recipes with honey

Honey-Ginger Cake, page 364
Honey Fudge, page 379

HEATING SUGAR

Sugar reacts to heat very quickly indeed. If you place a thin layer of sugar in a pan and put the pan on high heat, the sugar will quickly melt and turn brown. Then, if you're not careful, it will turn black and start smoking. You'll be left with a black, sticky mess – and probably a ruined pan.

However, if you can catch the melting sugar before it burns, at the golden brown stage, you have caramel. The sugar, which is only a little bit burnt, has a delicious, toffeeish taste. Chefs make caramel in this way to flavor various kinds of sweets and puddings. They may add toasted almonds or hazelnuts to the caramel to make praline.

Deliberately burning sugar in this way is a tricky and dangerous business, best left to trained experts. It's certainly not something you should attempt unless you are supervised by an adult – and ideally one who knows about making caramel!

A simple sugar syrup

A less risky way of heating sugar is to dissolve it in a little water first. This is how you make a sugar syrup. You can easily make a sugar syrup by putting 1 cup superfine or granulated sugar in a small, heavy-based saucepan with $^1/_2$ cup cold water. Put the pan over low heat. The sugar and water need to be heated very gently to begin with and stirred continuously until all the crystals have completely dissolved. The heat is then turned up so that the syrup comes to boil. At this point, you stop stirring the syrup, otherwise you encourage sugar crystals to form once more. The longer the syrup boils, the thicker and more concentrated it becomes, as the water evaporates into steam.

Boil it hard for a few minutes, and you'll get a light sugar syrup that's useful in all kinds of recipes.

Paint a little on a fruit loaf as you take it from the oven, and it makes a lovely sticky glaze that shines in the light. A syrup can be a sweet salad dressing, turning an ordinary mass of sliced-up fruit into a shiny bowl of glistening fruit salad, glowing with color. Sherbets and sorbets are fruit syrups that have been churned and frozen. And some of the best ice creams are made by whisking hot syrup into egg yolks and then adding cream. See pages 351 to 361 for more on homemade ices.

Sometimes, syrups are poured onto cakes when they come out of the oven to make them extra moist. Baklava, for example, a Middle Eastern cake, is made from wafer-thin sheets of buttered pastry layered with chopped nuts and then smothered in syrup flavored with rosewater. A lemon syrup poured over a sponge cake that you've just taken out of the oven makes the cake damp inside and crunchy on top. This is the trick that gives us the mouthwatering lemon drizzle cake.

Some recipes with sugar syrup
Raisin Bread, page 43
Fruit Salad, page 366

Hard-boiled sugar
If you keep boiling a simple syrup, it slowly begins to change. Whereas water boils at 212°F and starts to evaporate into steam, sugar in a syrup keeps getting hotter and hotter as the water evaporates. As the syrup gets hotter, the consistency begins to change.

This means that, depending on the precise temperature you heat it to, you can do all sorts of different things with it. Boil a syrup to 241°F and you'll find that when it cools it becomes a thick, almost moldable goo called fondant (like the cream filling you find in some boxes of chocolates). Boil further, taking the temperature to 252°F, and you'll reach the hardball stage, suitable for whisking with egg whites to make marshmallows. Boil more water away, and raise the temperature to around 266°F, and you get a syrup that will harden as it cools. Colored and flavored, this is more or less how hard candies are made.

Keep boiling, and you'll eventually get to a point, at about 320°F, where the syrup begins to change to a golden color. Once again, you're beginning to burn the sugar, and you will get that delicious caramel flavor. Let it cool and it will set as hard as glass – and shatter like glass too. At this point color and temperature can change fast. Be careful!

Cooking with a candy thermometer
A syrup doesn't have to be pure sugar. The most interesting boiled-sugar recipes are made from syrups flavored with other ingredients. Jam is made by boiling chopped or crushed fresh fruit with sugar. Hard candies are made from a syrup flavored with real or artificial flavorings and color. Fudge and toffee are made by dissolving sugar not in water but in

milk, with a bit of butter added too, to give them a rich creaminess.

The trouble is that when you're cooking these boiled-sugar recipes you can't easily see the important changes happening – for most of the time the mixture just looks like a furiously bubbling liquid. The only noticeable change is that the syrup gets quieter and quieter as more and more water evaporates away into steam and the syrup gets hotter. It's only when the syrup cools down that you can see it thicken or harden.

There are various traditional tests that can tell you whether a boiling sugar syrup has reached the required temperature for your recipe. Most of them involve dropping a little of the syrup into a glass of cold water and seeing what it's like. If it can be stretched, it's called "the thread," which sounds rather odd but means that it's the right temperature for setting jam. If it can be rolled into a ball, it's called "softball," and the temperature is right for fudge. A higher temperature will take it to the "hardball" stage, which is used for making toffee, marshmallows, and nougat. If it instantly becomes hard, it's called "hard crack," and it means your syrup will set into a brittle, pale caramel. When a caramel like this is mixed with nuts, and left to set, you have made a praline.

Some experienced cooks can work with these tests, but by far the safest and most accurate way of getting a syrup to exactly the right temperature is to use a candy thermometer, which you stand in the saucepan and watch

very carefully. If you are interested in making jams, toffee, fudges, and other boiled-sugar treats, you should definitely buy such a thermometer. You'll soon discover that once the temperature gets past 230°F, the mercury gallops up the thermometer faster than you might think – so be prepared to act quickly.

A word of warning. Boiling sugar is *very* hot – much hotter than boiling water. Always have an adult standing close by when you cook with hot sugar. Resist the temptation to dip your finger in a boiling sugar mixture to taste it – you will be severely burned. If you do get burned, completely immerse the affected area in cold water for ten minutes or until it no longer feels hot to the touch. In the case of serious burns, dial 911 – a cool bath may be the best option until medical help arrives.

Some recipes with boiling sugar

Bramble Jelly, page 156
Sweet Chile and Red Currant Jam, page 163
Marshmallows, page 368
Turkish Delight, page 376
Honey Fudge, page 379

ICES

It's a long, hot summer's day. You're scrabbling over the pebbles on the beach or feeling the heat rise as you walk along the pavement. Fancy an ice cream? Of course you do. Something sweet is always a treat. But something that's both sweet and ice cold has come to be one of the biggest treats we know. *Everybody* loves ice cream.

A scoop of vanilla ice cream melting over a hot blackberry and apple crisp is delicious even on the coldest day. But it's summer that really draws us to ice cream. The heat, the dust, the salty sweat on our lips — it makes us long for something cold. It's such a craving that hundreds, even thousands, of years before fridges and freezers were invented we found a way to cool our throats during the hot, dusty months of July and August. Ice.

A thousand years ago, the Moorish kings of North Africa used to send servants into the High Atlas Mountains to cut a block of ice, then run home with it on their backs. If they were fast enough, the king could enjoy a cold drink in the heat of the day. If they were too slow, the ice would melt and the king would stay hot and bothered. The consequences for the servants could be dire.

Centuries later, ice was shipped from Norway and taken by railway to country houses across Britain to make frozen desserts for the wealthy. You, though, can walk to the freezer, take out a plastic tub, and scoop up a ball of ice cream. No long-distance running necessary, no risky sea journey. What will it be today? Raspberry, peach, gooseberry, chocolate . . . ?

Real ice cream

Traditional ice cream is just cream, sugar, and perhaps some flavoring. Eggs might be added to give a smooth, silky texture. Yet the ice creams sold in most shops today quite often don't contain any cream at all. They are mixtures of vegetable fat, skimmed milk powder, and artificial flavorings — strange ingredients that have no place at all in proper ice cream. Many of these ingredients are simply there to make the ice cream last longer and spoon more easily, besides making it much cheaper to produce. Learn to make your own real ice cream, and you'll notice a world of difference.

Quite magical things happen when you freeze cream and fruit together. Most of the time we use our freezers to preserve things, keeping them full of bags of green peas, perhaps, or loaves of bread ready for eating in a month or two's time. But ice cream is different. It's a food that uses the freezer as a sort of "cooking" appliance. You put a cake mixture into an oven to cook it with heat; you put an ice cream mixture into a freezer to "cook" it with cold.

When you make ice cream, you transform one food into another. Freezing completely alters the eating qualities of the food. Most obviously, it turns a liquid into a frozen solid — a very different feeling when we put it in our

mouths. However, freezing changes not just the texture but the way we experience the taste. When we eat foods that are very cold, our taste buds don't work quite as well as they usually do. Sweet things become less sweet and sharp things become less sharp. Flavors are less intense. As ice cream melts in your mouth, changing from a solid into a liquid once more, the sweetness, the sharpness, and the complex flavors all become more intense again. When you eat the best strawberry ice cream, it's as if real strawberries are actually ripening in your mouth. And what could be more exciting than that?

Different ways to make ice cream

In its purest form, ice cream is simply cream that has been flavored – perhaps with some drops of vanilla extract or mashed-up fruit – sweetened with sugar, and frozen until it's more or less solid. It's quick and delicious and pretty simple to make. But ever since the late seventeenth century, when Europeans learned the basic art of freezing a liquid food to make it solid, we've dreamed up all kinds of variations on the ice cream theme. By the end of the eighteenth century, people realized that frozen custards of milk, eggs, and cream made an even better ice cream – richer, smoother, and creamier. Another method was to whisk a very hot sugar syrup gradually into a mass of egg yolks to make a kind of soft mousse. This was then blended with whipped cream and frozen solid to give a very smooth ice cream, known as a parfait.

Flavoring ice cream

While you could, of course, just freeze cream and sugar together and it would still taste pretty good, we really expect our ice cream to come flavored. Vanilla, chocolate, strawberry – all irresistible, particularly when they're eaten together as a Neapolitan ice cream.

But you needn't stop there. Think of your favorite fruits and flavors and you can find a way of turning them into creamy ices. Soft fruits such as strawberries and raspberries can simply be crushed, sieved, or blended into a purée, then sweetened with superfine sugar. Fruits, such as gooseberries and plums, can be cooked gently until they soften. Picked a glut of sun-ripened blackberries? Simmer them gently with a tablespoon or so of water until they're soft, push them through a sieve with the back of a spoon to leave the seeds behind, and fold them into your ice cream base. And in the depths of winter? A couple of tablespoons of your favorite fruit jam added to a cream or custard ice cream base makes a pretty good alternative to a basket of underripe, overpriced berries.

Freezing ices

If you're lucky enough to have an electric ice cream maker, then making ice cream and sorbet can be amazingly quick. You pour the liquid mixture into the chilled bucket part of the machine, switch it on, and a set of motorized paddles stirs the mixture as it freezes. Some ice cream makers have their own little refrigeration units. You simply turn them on, wait a couple of minutes, and get churning. Others have a bucket that you have to put in the freezer the day before you want to make ice cream. Ice cream makers produce very smooth, whipped-up ice cream, because the turning paddle stirs lots of air into the mixture as it freezes.

But you can still make very good ice cream – better than anything you can buy in most stores – if you have nothing more than a shallow plastic container or a loaf pan, plus a fork or whisk. It just takes a little longer and needs a bit more attention.

If you put a container of ice cream or sorbet mixture into a freezer and let it sit there for several hours it will certainly freeze, but usually into a solid block full of hard ice crystals rather than a mass of smooth ice cream. During the freezing process, you need to break down the ice crystals that start to form by stirring the mixture with a fork every so often before letting it start to freeze once

FROM ICE TO ICE CREAM

Before fridges and freezers came into every home during the twentieth century, getting something really cold in the heat of summer was a long, time-consuming, and very expensive process. In fact, the only people who could get food really cold were those who had access to ice. And where on earth do you find ice in the middle of July?

Just as wheat and barley are harvested in August and kept in grain stores over the winter, so ice can be harvested in the depths of winter and stored for summer. Icehouses and ice pits, insulated from summer warmth with thick layers of straw, were built especially for this purpose. As long as 4,000 years ago, the wealthy people of what is now Iraq sipped drinks chilled by stored ice in the height of summer. Incredibly, it was another 3,500 years before the first ice pit was built in England. But when Charles II served up a dish of ice cream at a dinner in the seventeenth century, he caused a sensation. Suddenly, every wealthy family wanted ice.

Many built special icehouses on the grounds of their large country houses. Ice was cut from the surface of lakes, ponds, or flooded fields in winter, chopped up finely, and stored in special and sometimes extraordinarily ornate houses. Ornate or not, these icehouses were basically deep pits lined with bricks. There was usually a drain at the bottom so that water from any melted ice could flow away. The ice wasn't put into drinks or added to food – it must have been completely filthy. Instead, foods that needed to be chilled were placed in containers of ice.

354   SUGAR & HONEY

more. You have to become a sort of ice cream paddle yourself.

So when you've made the mixture, pour it into the plastic container or loaf pan and place it in the freezer. After about an hour or so, go back and you'll find that the sides have started to freeze (the shallower the mixture in the freezer, the quicker it will freeze). With a fork, mash it all up, turning the frozen sides into the still-liquid center until it's smooth once more. Repeat this a couple of times over the next two or three hours — remembering that it's absolutely essential to sample it each time — and then freeze it to proper ice cream firmness. If you leave ice cream in the freezer overnight and it gets too solid to scoop, take it out about half an hour before you plan to eat it to soften it up a little.

Some ice cream recipes

Strawberry Parfait, page 371
Custard Ice Cream, page 374

So why did it take so long for ice cream to be invented? The trouble is that ice can chill a drink or a pudding, but on its own it isn't enough to freeze cream to a solid lump. The ice melts long before the cream has begun to freeze.

The trick is to mix ice with salt. Water freezes at 32°F, but saltwater freezes at much lower temperatures. You can see this for yourself if you have a cooking thermometer: just pour a couple of tablespoons of salt over a few ice cubes, stick the thermometer in, and watch the temperature plummet to around 1°F. At temperatures as low as this, cream quickly freezes.

The building of the railways in the mid-nineteenth century meant that for the first time ice could be transported easily across the country. But it wasn't until commercial refrigerators were invented and became widely available toward the end of the nineteenth century that ice cream became anything other than a treat for the wealthy few. For hundreds of years ice had signified luxury and frivolity — the ability to produce a frozen pudding at a posh dinner party or a carved ice sculpture to impress your neighbors was a sign that you had "arrived."

Oddly enough, although ice is no longer necessary for keeping foods cold, and although it's so cheaply made, it still feels luxurious. Food presented in a snowy bed of ice looks smart — think of oysters on a tray of crushed ice in a fancy restaurant, or a bottle of Champagne in its silvery bucket of ice. Chunks of pink watermelon served on a bed of ice look far more exciting than piled on a white plate. Maybe it's because chipped ice looks like diamonds. Or could it be that diamonds are so highly prized because they look like chips of ice that never melt?

Project:

CREATING YOUR OWN ICE CREAM MAKER

Can it really be possible, your own scoop of ice cream in 30 minutes without an ice cream maker or a freezer? Read on.

You will need:
Well-chilled heavy cream,
   2 or 3 tablespoons
Flavoring, e.g., vanilla extract,
   2 or 3 strawberries, 2 teaspoons of your
   favorite jam, a little melted chocolate
Confectioners' sugar, 2 teaspoons

Clean half-pint Mason jar or jam jar with lid, 5 cups of ice cubes straight from the freezer, 1 cup of salt, plastic/metal container with lid (large enough to contain all the ice and the jar – a cookie or cake pan, for example)

1. Spoon the cream into the clean jar. Add your flavoring: for vanilla ice cream, add a few drops of the vanilla extract; for strawberry, crush the strawberries until they're runny and stir them in, or mix in 2 teaspoons of good jam; for chocolate, stir in melted chocolate. Add the sugar.

2. Screw the lid tightly closed. Place the jar in the fridge while you sort out the ice and salt.

3. Get the ice from the freezer. The ice should be as cold as possible. If that sounds a bit silly, remember that the temperature of ice can vary a lot. Straight from the freezer, it could be as low as 14°F. Ice that's been sitting around in a bowl and is just beginning to melt will be only 30° or 28°F. Put the ice and salt into the container and mix them together well. The temperature of the ice will fall rapidly.

4. Make a well in the ice mixture. Take the jam jar out of the fridge and stand it in the well. Put the lid on the container and let it stand somewhere cool.

5. After 10 minutes, take off both lids and carefully stir the cream mixture, making sure you don't get any of the salt in it. It will have turned very cold but it won't have started to freeze yet. Replace both the lids. Repeat this stirring process at 10-minute intervals until the cream turns to ice cream. It will do this quite suddenly, so be ready.

6. This makes a small amount of ice cream, just right for a single cone or to sandwich between a couple of wafers. You could use a bigger pan and add more jam jars (you can see in the picture that we used 3). Just keep the proportions of ice to salt the same.

Variations
Once you've got the hang of it, you can use this technique to make all sorts of homemade sorbets and ice creams. See pages 371 and 374 for some more ideas.

Ice lollies and other creamless ices

You don't have to use cream to make flavored ices. If you're a fan of ice lollies, also called frozen pops (and who isn't?), you'll know this already. What you might not know is that pops you make yourself with fresh fruit taste much better than anything you can buy in a store, because the flavors will be natural and true.

Ice lollies are the easiest ices to make. They are simply sweetened fruit purées or syrups (or, in the case of most store-bought lollies, artificially flavored sugar syrup) frozen solid, with a stick in the bottom to hold them by.

A sorbet is made from a similar base of sweetened purée or highly flavored syrup, but instead of being frozen solid in one go it is whisked at intervals during the freezing process (or whisked continuously if you make it in an ice cream machine). As with ice creams, this "freeze-churning" procedure gives a silkier consistency. Sometimes, a lightly whisked egg white may be added to the mix to create a softer, more luxurious texture.

A granita, which is an Italian ice, is a kind of halfway house between a lolly and a sorbet. The sweetened mixture, usually a fruit purée but sometimes a syrup flavored with wine and spices, is frozen solid in a lump, without churning. But instead of being served on a stick, the mixture is scratched with a fork into frozen shards, then piled into a glass. You can turn any granita into a "snow-capped" peak by trickling over a little cream, which should instantly freeze onto the fruity ice pile.

Project:

MAKING ICE LOLLIES

Ice lollies are very straightforward to make. The only remotely tricky part is knowing when to insert the stick – it has to be put in when the mixture is frozen enough to hold it upright but not so frozen that it won't go in.

In many good cookware stores, you can now buy reusable lolly-making kits, usually consisting of plastic molds with a "stick" built into the lid. After you've made the lollies, you dip the molds in warm water to release them, then pull the "stick-lid" out with the lolly attached. Some more traditional kits provide wooden lolly sticks that you stick in the molds when the mixture inside is half frozen.

You can easily buy a few lolly sticks (or save them from frozen lollies you have bought – but do wash them thoroughly) and then improvise your own molds. The kind of paper cups you use for parties (the narrower the better) can be used, and even old yogurt containers will do. Taller, thinner ones are more suitable than short, fat ones – but then homemade pops don't have to be quite as streamlined as bought ones.

You will need:
1 cup superfine sugar, medium saucepan, 1 cup water, wooden spoon, fruit flavorings (see suggestions below), lolly-making kit (or improvised lolly molds and wooden sticks, plus baking tray or large plastic lid), small pitcher, bowl or cloth

With most lolly flavors, you need to make a simple syrup first. Put the superfine sugar into the saucepan and pour in the water. Place the pan on the stove over low heat and stir with the wooden spoon until the sugar has completely dissolved. Turn up the heat and bring the syrup to a steady boil for 5 minutes. Turn off the heat and allow the syrup to cool completely.

Now you can flavor the syrup to create your favorite frozen pops. Below are a few suggestions, but you could always improvise. (Any of the mixtures below can be "freeze-churned" by hand into a sorbet instead of ice lollies by pouring it into a plastic container or metal loaf pan, putting it in the freezer, and whisking it every half hour or so with a fork until the mixture freezes firmly.)

Citrus flavors

For citrus-flavored ice lollies, add enough freshly squeezed lemon, lime, orange, or tangerine juice (or combinations of these) to the syrup to give a tangy, sharp, but sweet flavor. Try about ⅓ cup fresh lemon juice for the quantity of syrup above. Or try ¼ cup lemon juice and 1¼ cups freshly squeezed orange juice. Remember the flavor will be slightly muted when the mixture is frozen, so at room temperature it should taste a little too sharp and a little too sweet.

Berry flavors

Fresh berries such as strawberries, raspberries, and blackberries can just be crushed with a fork (or clean hands) in a bowl and rubbed through a nylon sieve to make a purée. Use about 4 cups fresh berries, plus about ¼ cup fresh lemon juice, for the quantity of syrup above. Mix the purée with the cold syrup and taste the mixture. If you think it needs to be a little sweeter, whisk in some sifted confectioners' sugar. If sharper, then add an extra squeeze of lemon.

Cooked fruit flavors

Fruits that are normally cooked, such as gooseberries, plums, black currants, and rhubarb, can also be used to flavor lollies (or to make sorbets). There's no need to make a syrup first, as the fruit can be cooked with enough sugar and water to get the right consistency. Cook 2 pounds of fruit with about 1 cup sugar (you may well need more sugar but it can be added later, to taste.)

Prepare the fruit first: top and tail gooseberries or black currants; trim rhubarb and cut it into chunks; halve and pit plums. Put the fruit in a saucepan, barely cover it with water, and add the sugar. Stir carefully over low heat until the sugar has dissolved, then simmer for about 5 minutes, until the fruit is completely tender.

Let cool for a few minutes, then pour the fruit and its juices into a large sieve (ideally nylon, rather than metal) set over a bowl. Rub the fruit through the sieve with the back of a spoon to make a purée. Taste the purée and, if it needs it, whisk in some sifted confectioners' sugar, a tablespoonful at a time, to adjust the sweetness.

To make the lollies

If you are using a lolly-making kit, simply follow the instructions. If not, sort out your improvised molds and arrange them fairly snugly together on a tray or a plastic container lid. Check that this will fit in a suitable space in your freezer and that it can be placed level.

Have your fruity mix(es) in a small pitcher ready for pouring. Fill each mold about three-quarters full (the mixture will expand as it freezes). Place the tray of molds in the freezer. If you haven't got enough molds for the amount of mixture, or enough space in the freezer for the molds, you can always freeze them in batches.

After about an hour, check the molds. If the mix has begun to freeze, try putting a stick in. If the mix is not firm enough to hold the stick upright, try again in another hour. You are sure to end up with some sticks at wonky angles. But that hardly matters!

When the lollies are all sticked and frozen solid, you can, if you like, unmold them, wrap them in plastic wrap, and refreeze in a more space-saving manner in the freezer.

To unmold a pop, you can either dip the mold into a bowl of warm water for just a few seconds or you can make a "nest" of a warm, damp cloth and wrap that around the mold. If the lolly is a bit reluctant, don't pull the stick too hard or it might come out. Just redip, or rewrap, and try again.

Remember that some freezers are *very* cold, and a lolly that's just come out of one could even freeze to your tongue. Best give

it a few minutes to warm up a bit before you go for your first lick.

How to eat your lollies

I don't think we really need to tell you how to eat an ice lolly, do we? On the other hand, there's one rather indulgent bonus you might enjoy. Try pouring a couple of tablespoons of heavy cream into a saucer, then rolling your just-unmolded lollies in it. The cream freezes instantly on the lolly, forming a luscious coating. If you wanted a really swanky coated lolly, you could do the same trick with homemade English custard (see page 113).

keep adding sugar ...

... till you can handle the dough

rolling out the first batch (white)

coloring the second batch (green)

stamping out

PEPPERMINT CREAMS

This is probably the easiest bit of cooking you'll ever do. Not that anything actually gets cooked. You're really just making edible, mint-flavored Play-Doh.

You will need:

Confectioners' sugar, 2 cups, and then some more
Free-range egg white, 1 (see page 88 for details of how to separate eggs)
Peppermint essence
A few drops of cooking oil (sunflower or peanut)

Green food coloring (optional)

Sieve, mixing bowl, wooden spoon, cup, fork, large square of waxed paper, rolling pin, plastic container

1. Sift about two-thirds of the sugar into the mixing bowl, tapping the sides of the sieve to shake the sugar through, then rubbing through any hard lumps at the end with the back of a wooden spoon.

2. Lightly whisk the egg white in a cup with a fork. It should be well mixed and lightly frothy, but not really moussey.

3. Pour the beaten egg white and a few drops of peppermint essence onto the sugar in the bowl, then use the same fork to start mixing the liquid with the sugar.

4. As the mixture begins to stiffen, scrape it off the fork and start using your hands to work it into a paste. It will probably be very sticky, and you'll have to keep adding a shake or two of sugar. You can taste it at any time and add another drop or two of peppermint essence if you'd like it to taste mintier.

5. Keep kneading the mixture and adding sifted sugar until you have a smooth paste you can mold like Play-Doh. Keep your hands dusted with sugar all the time.

6. Now prepare the sheet of waxed paper by rubbing it lightly all over with a few drops of oil.

7. You can shape your peppermint creams in various ways. First roll out the dough to about 3/8 inch thick with a rolling pin – but dust the work surface with confectioners' sugar first or it will stick horribly. You can then cut the dough into squares, triangles, or diamonds. Or you can use small cutters to stamp out any shape you like. Then squish up the leftover mixture, reroll it with a fresh dusting of confectioners' sugar on the work surface, and make more shapes. (If you like, you can add a few drops of green food coloring to some or all of the mixture. Knead it well and the dough will turn a very pale green.)

8. Or, if you don't have a rolling pin, you can simply roll little balls of the mixture between the palms of your hands (also dusted with confectioners' sugar), then flatten each ball a bit with your finger or thumb.

9. Place the finished peppermint creams on the lightly oiled sheet of paper. Leave them uncovered in the kitchen to dry out for a few hours. Keep them in a plastic container.

How to eat your peppermint creams

You can nibble one a little at a time or gobble it up all in one go. But remember, they are almost pure sugar, and overdoing it will make you feel sick.

If you want to find out how to coat your homemade peppermint creams (and other homemade sweets) in melted chocolate so you can put together your own little box of chocolates, then go to page 394.

. . . .

HONEY-GINGER CAKE

This is a very easy cake to make – all the sugary ingredients and the butter are melted together in a saucepan and then poured over the flour and spices in the bowl. The cake rises gently with the help of a little baking soda dissolved in some warm milk and water, which is added at the end of the recipe after the eggs have been beaten in. You end up with a lovely dark batter that you pour, rather than spoon, into the pan.

You will need:
All-purpose or white pastry flour, 1½ cups
Ground almonds, 6 tablespoons
A pinch of salt
Ground ginger, 1 heaping teaspoon
Ground cloves, a pinch
Lemon, 1
Brown sugar, ½ cup plus 2 tablespoons
Butter, 7 tablespoons
Honey, ¼ cup
Syrup taken from a jar of stem ginger,
   3 tablespoons

Molasses, 1 tablespoon
Stem ginger in syrup, 3 to 4 lumps
Eggs, 2
Baking soda, 1 teaspoon
Milk, 2 tablespoons

8½-inch square shallow cake pan, aluminum foil, mixing bowl, teaspoon, grater, medium saucepan, tablespoon, cutting board, sharp knife, citrus juicer, wooden spoon, cup, skewer or knife, wire rack

1. Preheat the oven to 350°F. Cut a piece of foil a little bigger than the cake pan and use it to line the pan (see page 407 for more on how to do this).

2. Put the flour, ground almonds, salt, ground ginger, and cloves into the mixing bowl. Grate the zest of the lemon carefully (leaving behind the white pith) and put that into the bowl, too.

6. Spoon the baking soda into a cup and add the cold milk and a tablespoon of hot water from the kettle. Stir well to dissolve the soda and add this mixture to the bowl, beating it in gently at first and then really well to get everything blended together.

7. Pour the mixture into the foil-lined pan. Oven gloves on. Put the pan into the hot oven and leave for 30 to 40 minutes. Test to see if the cake is ready by sticking a skewer or knife into the center — it should come out just clean, not gummy. Remove the pan from the oven and leave for a few minutes, then lift out the cake in its foil wrapper and allow to cool completely on a wire rack.

How to eat your cake

While this cake tastes nice just warm from the oven, its flavor really starts to develop if, when it's cold, you wrap it in more foil and keep it in an airtight container for a couple of days. If you can't wait that long, then it also tastes good eaten warm with a generous slosh of English custard (see page 113) or even ice cream (see page 374).

3. Now put the brown sugar (it doesn't matter if it's gone hard) and butter into the saucepan. Add the honey, the ginger syrup from the jar, and the molasses. Finely chop the pieces of stem ginger and add them to the pan. Squeeze the juice from the lemon and add it too.

4. Place the saucepan on the stove and switch the heat to low. Stir from time to time with the wooden spoon until the butter and sugar have melted. Switch off the heat.

5. Pour the honey mixture into the bowl of flour and spices. Stir well until you get a thick mixture. Break in the eggs, one at a time, beating them in well with the wooden spoon.

FRUIT SALAD

The fruit doesn't have to be exotic, although you can certainly experiment with all sorts of different fruits if you like. Steeping everyday fruits in a lemony sugar syrup transforms them out of all recognition. Cut the fruit in reasonably large pieces, not little dice like canned fruit cocktail. If you can bear to wait, leave the fruit salad in the fridge for at least a couple of hours, preferably more. All the fruit flavors will flood into the syrup, making every spoonful absolutely delicious and very useful (see "How to Use Up Leftover Syrup," opposite).

The lemon juice in the syrup helps to stop the cut apple and bananas from turning brown, because the acid in the juice slows down the chemical reaction that takes place when the fruit is cut. It also seems to bring out the best flavor in all the other fruits. So, even though it might feel like you're only adding a bit of juice, don't be tempted to leave it out!

To serve 4 to 6:
Juicy oranges, 2 smallish ones
Ripe peach, 1
Strawberries, 1 basket
Golden Delicious apple, 1
Bananas, 2 small
Grapes (the more fragrant, seeded ones
   are best), a handful (optional)

For the sugar syrup:
Granulated sugar, ½ cup
Water, ½ cup
Lemon, 1

Medium saucepan, large glass measuring cup, wooden spoon, cutting board, knife, citrus juicer, serving bowl, small pitcher or bowl, vegetable peeler, plastic wrap

1. Make the syrup first. Put the sugar and water into the saucepan and put it on the stove over low heat. Heat gently, stirring with the wooden spoon until all the sugar has dissolved. Turn the heat up to medium, bring the syrup to a boil, and let it boil for 2 minutes. Turn off the heat. Move the hot pan of syrup safely to the back of the stove to cool down.

2. When the syrup is nearly cold, cut the lemon in half and squeeze out the juice. Stir it into the syrup. Pour the syrup into the bowl you plan to serve the fruit salad in.

3. Peel the thick skin off the oranges. Cut away the white pithy stuff, then break each orange into segments and pull away any strings. Slice the segments lengthwise in two so you expose a long, gleaming side of flesh. Drop them into the serving bowl. Let any juices drip into the bowl, too.

4. Put the kettle on. Make a little cross in the skin of the peach with a sharp knife and put it in a small pitcher or bowl. When the kettle starts to boil, pour enough of the water over the peach just to cover it. Count to 20, then pour

the hot water carefully down the sink. Prepare the strawberries while the peach cools down.

5. Give each strawberry a wipe with a clean damp cloth, and cut out the stems. Cut each strawberry into halves (or quarters, if they're large ones) and add them to the bowl. Stir the fruit every now and then to coat it in the syrup.

6. When the peach is cool enough to touch, you should find that the skin peels away easily. Cut the peach in half, pull out the pit, and cut the flesh into thin slices. Add to the bowl.

7. Peel the apple, if you like. Stand it upright on the board and cut off 4 slices, so you're left with a rectangular core. Chop the apple into pieces, drop them into the bowl, and stir straight away to stop them from turning brown.

8. Peel the bananas, pulling away those annoying strings that always cling to your fingers, and slice the bananas thickly, straight into the bowl. Stir well.

9. If using grapes, cut them in half and take out the seeds, then add the grapes to the bowl.

10. Cover the bowl with plastic wrap and leave in the fridge for several hours for the flavor to develop.

How to eat your fruit salad

Spoon the salad into bowls and eat with softly whipped cream, ice cream, or even some of your own cream cheese (see page 72). Leftover fruit can be whizzed into milkshakes and smoothies (see pages 85 and 139).

How to use up leftover syrup

Once you've eaten your fruit salad, you may well end up with a puddle of colored fruit syrup in the bottom of the serving bowl (in fact, it's worth not being too generous with the syrup as you ladle out the fruit salad). Keep it!

As you'll no doubt have found out, the syrup is now incredibly tasty, having soaked up all the fruity flavors. It can transform a container of cream into the most delicious and unbelievably easy ice cream. Whip $1\frac{1}{4}$ cups or so of cream, and, just as it starts to thicken, pour in as much of the syrup as you have left over – hopefully 7 to 10 tablespoons – in a steady stream. Keep whipping until the cream starts to hold its shape, and then turn the mixture into a shallow plastic container. Freeze until just firm, gently mixing the semifrozen sides into the center after about an hour.

MARSHMALLOWS warning – boiling sugar!

When you're cooking with hot sugar, it's important that you have everything at hand. If you'll be using a food mixer to do all the whisking, plug it in as close to the stove as you can. It's never a good idea to walk about with saucepans of hot syrup.

As this recipe involves boiling sugar, it's important that an adult always be present at the stove. Be well prepared, and take care.

You will need:

Confectioners' sugar, 1 tablespoon
Plain cornstarch, 1 tablespoon
Canola oil for oiling the pan and knife
Gelatin powder, 1 packet (1 tablespoon)
Red food coloring, 2 to 3 drops (optional)
Free-range egg whites, 2 (see page 88
   for details of how to separate eggs)
Granulated sugar, 2 cups
Water, 1 cup

Sieve, 2 small bowls, shallow cake pan about 8 inches square, large glass measuring pitcher, wooden spoon, stand mixer, medium heavy saucepan, candy thermometer, pitcher, cutting board, dinner knife

1. Sift the sugar and cornstarch together into a small bowl. Rub the pan lightly with just a few drops of oil and shake a little of the sugar mixture around the pan to coat the bottom and sides. Set the pan to one side.

2. Bring the kettle almost to a boil, then measure out ½ cup water. Pour it into the second small bowl and sprinkle the gelatin on top. Stir with the wooden spoon until the gelatin has all dissolved. If you want the marshmallows to be tinted pale pink, add the red food coloring to the gelatin and stir again. (It's all too easy to get carried away with the coloring, so it's a good idea to measure the drops into the cap of the bottle first.) Leave the dissolved gelatin to stand near the stove.

3. Put the stand mixer on the work surface near the stove and plug it in. Put the egg whites into the bowl of the mixer.

4. Put the granulated sugar into the medium saucepan and add the water. Turn the stove on low and stir with a wooden spoon until the sugar has completely dissolved and you can't see any grains left if you carefully tilt the pan. Now, stop stirring. Rinse the candy thermometer under hot water for a few seconds so it doesn't get too much of a shock, then clip it to the inside of the pan. Raise the heat so the syrup comes to a boil. Meanwhile, turn on the mixer and beat the egg whites until stiff peaks form. Stand a pitcher with a little hot water in it near the stove.

on the way to hardball

it pours into moussey ribbons

5. The sugar needs to boil fiercely until it gets to 252°F – the hardball stage. Watch the thermometer carefully, especially in the later stages of the sugar boiling. As the sugar gets hotter and more of the water is boiled away, the temperature rises more quickly. When it gets to 252°F, immediately turn off the stove. Using oven gloves or a thick cloth to protect your fingers, take out the candy thermometer and put it in the pitcher of water to cool down.

6. Pour the dissolved gelatin into the pan of syrup, stirring all the time with the wooden spoon. The syrup will bubble up a little, although not dangerously so. Stir until the mixture is well blended.

7. Turn the mixer to low so that the egg whites keep on whisking. Very carefully pour the syrup into the beating egg whites in a steady, gentle trickle – avoid pouring it onto the beaters or it will splash. You'll see the mixture turn creamy. After you've poured in all the syrup, let the machine keep on beating until the mixture turns really thick and bulky but is still pourable. If you lift up the beaters, a ribbon of marshmallow should remain on the surface for a few seconds before sinking back down into the mix.

8. Pour the marshmallow into the prepared pan. Let set in a cool place, though not the fridge – this will probably take an hour or two. You won't want to wait that long, obviously, but try to be patient.

9. Dust the cutting board with the rest of the cornstarch mixture. Coat the butter knife in a little oil. Carefully ease the marshmallow out of the pan onto the board, helping it out where necessary with the butter knife. Make sure the surfaces of the marshmallow are entirely dusted with the cornstarch mixture – sift over extra confectioners' sugar and cornstarch, if necessary. Cut the marshmallow into squares, oiling and dusting the knife as it needs it (probably between every cut).

How to eat your marshmallows

You can eat a marshmallow just as it is, but it's great fun to toast them over a campfire (see page 275) until they're just starting to singe and melt a little. If you have any marshmallows left over, store them in an airtight tin lined with parchment paper, or they'll dry out.

Variation

Some people like marshmallows completely plain, as in this recipe, but you can always flavor them if you like. Prepare two smaller pans as above. Pour half of the thick, well-whisked mixture into a bowl and whisk in a teaspoon or two of vanilla extract. Add a teaspoon of rosewater, orange flower water, or even peppermint essence to the other half.

STRAWBERRY PARFAIT warning – boiling sugar!

French for *perfect*, and once you've tasted it you'll probably agree. This recipe is based on making a hot syrup of sugar and water, which you then whisk into egg yolks and cream. In some ways, it's a very easy ice cream to make because once you've put it in the freezer you don't have to worry about stirring it regularly to break up the ice crystals.

Finally, of course, remember that when you boil sugar it gets very, very hot. Always be careful when you're carrying hot pans.

To serve 4 to 6:

Free-range egg yolks, 3 (see page 88 for details of how to separate eggs)
Superfine sugar, ½ cup
Water, ½ cup
Strawberries, 3 cups
Lemon, ½
Heavy cream, 1 cup
Vanilla extract, 1 teaspoon

Good strawberry jam, 1 tablespoon (not necessary if your strawberries are really tasty ones)

Free-standing food mixer or handheld electric beater and bowl, pitcher, small heavy saucepan, wooden spoon, candy thermometer, potato masher or fork, bowl, citrus juicer, shallow plastic container or loaf pan

1. Place the stand mixer on the work surface near the stove and plug it in. Place the egg yolks in the bowl of the mixer (or put them in a large bowl and use a handheld electric mixer).

2. Put the sugar and water into the small saucepan, place on the stove, and turn on the heat to medium. Stir with the wooden spoon until the sugar dissolves completely and the syrup comes to a boil. Stop stirring. Stand a pitcher with a little hot water in it near the stove.

3. Rinse the thermometer under hot water for a few seconds so it doesn't get too much of a shock, then clip it to the inside of the saucepan and carefully watch the temperature rise. As it starts to approach 226°F, turn on the mixer to start whisking the egg yolks. (You'll notice that as the syrup reaches the right temperature, the bubbles will get a lot smaller, the noise of the boiling mixture will start to quiet down, and much less steam will pour up.) When it reaches 226°F, turn off the heat and very carefully take the very hot saucepan over to the mixer. Remove the thermometer and put it in the pitcher of water. Gradually pour the hot syrup in a thin stream over the egg yolks, whisking all the time. Avoid pouring it directly onto the whirring beaters, which might make it splash.

4. As the machine continues to whisk, you'll see the mixture thicken and become paler until

it's creamy colored. After 3 or 4 minutes, stop the machine and raise the beaters so that the mixture runs down from them into the bowl. It should leave a brief ribbon trail that rests for a few seconds on the top of the mixture before sinking in. If it sinks straight away, whisk a little longer.

5. Hull the strawberries and mash them with the potato masher or a fork in the bowl. Squeeze the juice from the lemon.

6. Whisk the cream and the vanilla extract into the egg and sugar mixture. Add the strawberries and the lemon juice, along with the tablespoon of strawberry jam, if using.

7. Pour the mixture into the container and place it in the freezer. Let freeze for 3 to 4 hours.

How to eat your parfait

Ice cream made like this has a wonderfully smooth texture, so it's delicious eaten just as it is, in a bowl or a cone. Let the ice cream soften at room temperature for 30 minutes or so before serving.

Variation: peach parfait

Instead of strawberries and strawberry jam, flavor the mixture with the puréed flesh of 5 to 6 ripe, juicy peaches.

Skin the peaches first by nicking the skin with a sharp knife, then putting them in a deep bowl in the sink. Pour enough boiling water over the peaches to cover them, count to 20, then turn on the cold tap to cool the water down. Drain the peaches. The skins should now peel off easily.

Halve the peaches and take out the stones, then either mash them thoroughly with a fork or whiz them in a food processor until you get a smooth purée.

Add the peach purée (and the lemon juice) to the egg, sugar, and cream mixture and freeze as above.

CUSTARD ICE CREAM

This is the classic method for making ice cream — whisking egg yolks and sugar with hot cream so that they thicken it into a custard sauce. Heavy cream is then stirred in to enrich the mixture. This custard ice cream is flavored with vanilla, but you could stir in some mashed soft fruit (raspberries or bananas, for instance), or some sweetened cooked fruit (such as black currants or gooseberries) that you've puréed by passing them through a sieve.

To serve 6:
Half-and-half, 1¼ cups
Vanilla bean, 1
Free-range egg yolks, 4 (see page 88
   for details of how to separate eggs)
Superfine sugar, ½ cup
Heavy cream, 1¼ cups

Medium saucepan, sharp knife, cutting board, medium bowl, balloon whisk, wooden spoon, sieve, ice cream machine or plastic container and fork

1. Pour the half-and-half into the saucepan. Slit the vanilla bean open lengthwise with the sharp knife and drop it into the pan. Turn the heat to medium and heat the half-and-half until it just starts to steam a little, then turn off the heat. Let the saucepan just sit there, and the heat will draw the vanilla flavor into the half-and-half.

2. Meanwhile, put the egg yolks into the bowl and add the sugar. Whisk them well together for a minute with the balloon whisk, until they turn thick and a little paler.

3. Pour the saucepan of hot half-and-half into the sugary egg mixture and whisk again until smooth. Pour it all back into the saucepan. Rinse out the bowl for later.

4. With the heat set very low, stir the creamy mixture all the time with the wooden spoon so that it doesn't stick to the bottom of the pan but heats slowly and evenly. To see if the custard has heated enough, check from time to time with this classic test: take the spoon out of the custard and look at the back of it — the film of custard over it should look noticeably creamier. Draw your finger across the back of the spoon and, if the line stays clear and distinct, your custard has thickened enough (see the picture on page 95). Turn off the heat and carry the saucepan over to the work surface. Keep on stirring for a few more seconds so that the cooking process is halted and the custard starts to cool down. Strain the custard through a sieve into the rinsed-out bowl you used earlier.

5. Fish the vanilla bean out of the sieve, rinse it under cold water, and let it dry (you could put it in a jar of superfine sugar to give the sugar a vanilla flavor).

6. As soon as the custard has cooled to room temperature, put the bowl in the fridge for half an hour, then stir in the heavy cream.

7. Either pour the mixture into an ice cream machine and churn it until it freezes or pour it into a plastic container. Freeze it for about an hour or until the sides start to get solid. When this happens, mash up the mixture with a fork, mixing the frozen sides into the liquid center. Put it back in the freezer straight away for another hour. Repeat this twice more at hourly intervals and then let the ice cream set solid. Notice just how much tastier it is the colder it gets.

How to eat your ice cream

You could make some hot chocolate sauce (see page 392) to pour over your ice cream, or eat it with fruit salad (see page 366).

Variation: black currant ice cream

For black currant ice cream, gently simmer 3 cups of black currants with 2 tablespoons of water for about 10 minutes, or until the fruit is soft and pulpy. Wait 10 minutes, then pour the black currants and their juice into a sieve set over a bowl. Press as much of the pulp as possible through with the back of a metal tablespoon. Let the pulp cool down, then stir it into the custard and cream mix. Taste for sweetness — you may think that it needs a tablespoon of sieved confectioners' sugar . . . on the other hand, you may not. Pour the mixture into a container and freeze as before.

TURKISH DELIGHT   warning – boiling sugar!

Turkish delight is a jellylike sweet flavored with orange, lemon, and rosewater. This version has a soft, rather than a rubbery, texture. As it sets, it looks rather uninteresting, but when you turn it out onto a board dusted with confectioners' sugar it becomes completely spectacular. Make it the day before you want to eat it, as it needs to set well in the fridge before you turn it out – particularly if you want to keep it for more than a day or two.

As this recipe involves boiling sugar, it's important that an adult always be present.

You will need:
Granulated sugar, 2 cups
Lemon, ½
Orange, ½
Cream of tartar, ¼ teaspoon
Cornstarch, ½ cup plus 1 tablespoon
Canola oil, a few drops for greasing the pan
Runny honey, 2 tablespoons
Rosewater, a few drops

Red food coloring, a few drops
Confectioners' sugar, 3 to 4 tablespoons

Medium heavy saucepan, 1 small and 1 large glass measuring cup, citrus juicer, wooden spoon, candy thermometer, 2 teaspoons, large heavy saucepan, shallow cake pan about 8 inches square, paper towels, mug, wooden cutting board, butter knife

1. Put the granulated sugar into the medium saucepan. Measure ½ cup water and pour it into the pan. Squeeze the juice from the half lemon and half orange and add this to the pan, too. Put the pan on the stove, turn the heat to medium, and stir the mixture with the wooden spoon until the sugar has completely dissolved and you can't see any grains remaining.

2. Rinse the candy thermometer under hot water for a few seconds so it doesn't get too much of a shock, then stand it in the pan. Turn the heat up so that the syrup starts to boil. Boil the syrup steadily without stirring, watching the thermometer the whole time. As soon as the temperature reaches the softball stage (241°F),

turn off the heat. Carefully stir in the cream of tartar (this will help stop the sugar from recrystallizing when you have to stir the syrup later on). Set the pan aside to cool a little.

3. Put the kettle on. Pour a scant ½ cup cold water into the small measuring cup and mix in the cornstarch so that you have a thin, white liquid. Pour hot water from the kettle (it doesn't have to be boiling) into the large measuring cup up to the 2-cup mark. Then add the cornstarch mixture and stir to combine.

4. Pour the cornstarch mixture into the large saucepan, set the pan on the stove, and bring the mixture slowly to a boil over low heat,

stirring all the time until it is really thick and smooth. Turn off the heat.

5. Carefully pour a little of the hot sugar syrup into the thick cornstarch mixture. Stir it in gently with the wooden spoon. Add the rest of the syrup a little at a time, stirring well. Then move the pan to the back of the stove, turn the heat to very low, and bring to a simmer. Let the syrup cook very gently for 25 minutes, stirring occasionally to prevent it from sticking. Bubbles should blip gently on the surface, but it shouldn't be any fiercer than that.

6. Meanwhile, prepare the pan: pour a few drops of canola oil into it and rub it all over the inside with some paper towels.

7. When the 25 minutes are up, your syrup won't look very different, although it may have started to turn slightly darker. Turn off the heat. Carefully stir in the honey with the wooden spoon. Stir in a few drops of rosewater (this can be strong stuff, so it's best to measure it out into a teaspoon over a mug just in case your hand slips) and just a drop or two of red food coloring (ditto!). A dark rose pink looks stunning. Let the mixture cool just a little and then pour it into the prepared pan. Rinse the empty saucepan right away in warm water or it will be a nightmare to get it clean.

8. When the Turkish delight is cold, put it in the fridge to set firmly.

9. Next day, or at least several hours later, sift the surface of the wooden cutting board with 2 tablespoons of confectioners' sugar. Run a knife around the edge of the pan of Turkish delight, then quickly turn the pan upside down onto the board. The Turkish delight should just fall out. Sift the remaining confectioners' sugar all over the surface and cut it into little squares. Store in an airtight tin in a cool place.

How to eat your Turkish delight

Being pretty well pure sugar, Turkish delight is something to have in small quantities, so it's a good thing to make for parties when there are lots of you to eat it up – a very nice Christmassy treat, in fact.

HONEY FUDGE warning – boiling sugar!

This is a lovely recipe because it shows that the choice between honey and sugar isn't always an "either, or." In this case it's a "both, and."

You will need:
Granulated sugar, 4 cups
Evaporated milk, 13-ounce can
Water, scant ½ cup
A pinch of salt
Honey, heaping ¼ cup
Canola oil, a few drops to grease pan
Butter, 7 tablespoons

Large glass measuring cup, large heavy saucepan, long-handled wooden spoon, tablespoon, candy thermometer, jelly roll pan, sharp knife

1. Put the sugar, evaporated milk, and water in the saucepan. The pan should be no more than about a third full at this stage, as the hot mixture will bubble up dramatically later. Place over low heat and stir until the sugar has dissolved. Then stir in the salt and honey. Clip the candy thermometer to the inside of the pan.

2. Raise the heat and bring the syrup to a fierce, bubbling boil, stirring every half a minute or so to ensure it isn't sticking to the bottom of the pan. When the temperature on the thermometer reads 241°F, turn off the heat and allow the mixture to cool for a few minutes. Oil your pan lightly.

3. Cut the butter into 5 or 6 pieces and drop it into the mixture. As you do so, stir vigorously with the wooden spoon. The butter will melt into the thickening syrup. Keep stirring. As the mixture cools and thickens, it will start to become grainy. Now it's time to pour it into the pan. Don't hang around, or it may start to set while you are pouring it!

4. Use a sharp knife to mark the fudge into squares before it has completely set. This means pressing the knife partly but not completely through the fudge. It will then be very easy to break up the fudge into squares when it has cooled.

How to eat your honey fudge

A square of homemade fudge is a real treat. Have one whenever you feel you deserve it. Chopped-up fudge sprinkled over vanilla ice cream is delicious.

Variation: honey fudge sauce

Put 6 ounces of fudge in a small pan with a couple of tablespoons of milk and one of honey. Stir over low heat until the fudge is smooth and melted (don't let it boil). Pour over ice cream.

CHOCOLATE

There are times when only something chocolatey will do: a cake for a birthday, a tray of brownies on the weekend, a mug of steaming hot chocolate when the rain is lashing against the windows. Five hundred years ago, chocolate was served to emperors in gold cups. Now it comes in gold wrappers. And still no other food has the same feeling of luxury and indulgence.

chocolate chip cookies, page 400

brownies, page 403

real hot chocolate, page 388

éclairs, page 397

chocolate mousse, page 391

chocolate sauce, page 392

a box of chocolates, page 394

CHOCOLATE

How do you like your chocolate? As a spongy cake, covered in smooth icing, or as a gooey mousse? Whizzed into a frothy hot drink, or churned into chilly ice cream? Or simply as it comes – undressed from its shiny gold wrapper and munched one square at a time?

Of all the cakes in the shop window, it's the chocolatey ones that tempt most of us to stop and stare. Think of almost any special occasion where food is part of the celebration, and chocolate is almost always there. A birthday, wedding, Christmas, Easter – you'd be quite surprised if chocolate didn't feature somewhere in the day. Few chefs would dare to leave it off the dessert menu. There's no doubt that, for most of us, it's the ultimate treat food.

While no one could say that eating a lot of chocolate is good for you, a little bit every now and again is no bad thing for most people. Compared to other sweet treats, good-quality chocolate does at least contain small amounts of minerals like iron, magnesium, and potassium. Neither is it quite as bad for your teeth.

And chocolate gives you something that most other sweets just can't – that rich, velvety feeling in your mouth as it starts to melt on your tongue. But the reasons we love chocolate may be to do with more than just a taste sensation. Scientists have discovered that chocolate contains substances that send messages of contentment to the brain (once you've eaten it, that is). No wonder, then, that a chocolate cookie is so often eaten with a mug of tea – the great comfort food meets the great comfort drink.

How is chocolate made?

Chocolate comes from a bean produced by the cacao tree, which can only grow in tropical countries. The tree grows large pods, a bit like long, thin melons, which turn yellow and red when they ripen. After the ripe pods are harvested, they are split open and the beans (about 40 in each pod) are scooped out. Heaped in piles, they are covered and left for a few days until the whitish pulp that surrounds each bean has turned to liquid and drained away. The beans are then dried and roasted to bring out their flavor, then cracked open. Inside the shell of each bean is a little nutlike kernel, and it's this that is made into chocolate.

These roasted kernels now need to be blended. There are many different kinds of beans. Some are very strong, others mild, so they are mixed together to get the exact flavor that a chocolate manufacturer is aiming for. After blending, the kernels are ground up into a thick paste. What happens next depends on the quality of chocolate being made. The cacao bean kernel consists of cocoa solids and cocoa butter. In really good chocolate, extra cocoa butter is added to the chocolate paste. But in cheaper chocolate, some or all of the cocoa butter is taken out of the paste and vegetable fat is added instead.

THE FIRST CHOCOLATE LOVERS

However much you like chocolate, the chances are you don't feel quite as passionate about it as many of the ancient peoples who lived in Mexico and Central America a thousand years ago did. The Mayan tribes used cacao beans as money (the first chocolate money, perhaps?) and drank chocolate as part of their religious rituals. The Italian explorer Christopher Columbus came upon a large Mayan canoe loaded with cacao beans off the coast of Honduras in 1502. Columbus's son noted that the Mayans were incredibly careful with these strange, almond-like beans: ". . . for when they were brought on board ship together with their goods, I observed that when any of these almonds fell, they all stopped to pick it up, as if an eye had fallen."

The Spanish explorer Hernán Cortés, who arrived in Mexico in 1519, was the first to realize just how important the cacao bean was. He couldn't help but notice how the Aztecs cherished this drink, chocolate. Montezuma, emperor of the Aztecs, had chocolate brought to him in pure gold cups, and 2,000 foaming jugs of the drink were served up at the great banquets he held. If the Mexicans, who seemed to drip with gold and riches, rated the cacao bean so highly, Cortés reasoned, then these beans were certainly worth taking back to Spain.

Within only a few years, the Aztec Empire had been ruthlessly overthrown and the Spanish were cultivating their cacao plantations. They made great efforts to keep their extraordinary drink a secret. British pirates who captured Spanish trading ships were said to have thrown sacks of cacao beans overboard in disgust – the captured Spanish crew had told them they were sacks of sheep droppings, saved as fuel.

However, something as exciting as chocolate could hardly be kept quiet for long. Soon, the fashion for chocolate was sweeping across Europe. It was popular in the morning as a breakfast drink and as a sort of pick-me-up, like coffee today. Samuel Pepys, who wrote a diary about life in seventeenth-century London, went out the morning after King Charles II's coronation in 1661 for a cup of chocolate "to settle my stomach."

It wasn't until the nineteenth century that scientists discovered that chocolate could be turned into a food as well as a drink. Even then, it was only because people were searching for a better way of making drinking chocolate that they came to make chocolate bars (read on). Once the chocolate-making process had been fully understood and its manufacture had been industrialized, it was made on such a huge scale that nearly everyone could enjoy it, at least once in a while.

All chocolate made for eating (as opposed to cooking) has to be sweetened – it would be unbearably bitter otherwise – so sugar is added. Flavorings such as vanilla are added too, as well as milk powder if it is to become milk chocolate. Finally, the chocolate has to be mixed and beaten (this is called "conching"), then warmed and cooled (which is known as "tempering") to precise temperatures, so that when it is finally molded and cold, it has just the right texture.

Cocoa

In 1828, a Dutchman called Coenraad Van Houten developed a machine that could press most of the cocoa butter out of the basic chocolate paste. This left a fine, crumbly cake of cocoa mass that could be ground up to make cocoa powder. It was then found that if the pressed-out cocoa butter was added to another batch of basic chocolate paste and the combination was sweetened with fine sugar, chocolate could for the first time be made into solid bars.

The dry powder, cocoa, immediately took off as the new, cheaper way to enjoy chocolate, a drink that all but the poorest could now afford. Chocolate manufacturing was turned into big business in Britain by the Cadbury and Fry families. The new product was considered "good for the people." More and more people were leaving the countryside to look for work in the new factories of the big towns, only to find dull work and dreadful living conditions. Beer and gin were cheap,

and people drank heavily to escape their lives of drudgery. The chocolate companies were keen to promote cocoa as a healthy alternative to alcohol.

In stores today, you'll find unsweetened cocoa powder and instant cocoa mixes. Cocoa mixes can be very sweet and often not that chocolatey – sugar and milk powder with added cocoa, rather than the other way around. Nor is it good for cooking with. Cocoa powder makes good, basic hot chocolate when it's mixed with hot milk and a little sugar. Like bars of chocolate, there are good cocoas and there are better ones, but even the cheaper ones taste of chocolate. Cocoa is useful for giving foods such as cakes and biscuits a chocolate flavor but you wouldn't use it to make chocolate mousse or truffles. For these, you need the creamy texture of actual chocolate, as well as its flavor.

Some recipes with cocoa

Chocolate Sauce for Ice Cream, page 392
Double-Chocolate Brownies, page 403

Choosing chocolate for cooking

Chocolate comes in so many forms: Unsweetened (baker's chocolate), semisweet, milk, white, spiced, orange, mint, nutty, and fruity. And of course there are hundreds of different chocolate bars, too. You probably already know what your favorites are.

You wouldn't want to cook with your favorite chocolate bar because you'll be adding ingredients such as sugar, butter,

cream, and milk to the recipe anyway. If you're making a mousse or a cake, you want to get as much real chocolate flavor in it as possible. So whenever you're choosing chocolate for cooking, look carefully at the list of ingredients on the back of the package. The main ingredient of a food is always listed first. So if sugar is first, you'll know that it contains more sugar than chocolate. Instead, choose a bar that puts "cocoa mass" first. A chocolate suitable for cooking will contain at least 45 percent cocoa mass. But the best ones are more like 60 to 70 percent.

Melting chocolate

Chocolate burns easily, so if you want to melt chocolate for an icing, say, or for a dessert like chocolate mousse, then you need to do it gently. The traditional way of melting it is in a stainless-steel bowl placed over a pan of hot water – the hot air rising from the water is enough to soften the chocolate. Or you can put it in a bowl in a low oven (not more than 250°F) for ten minutes or so. This works best if you're melting the chocolate with a bit of butter. Or you can add squares of chocolate to already hot ingredients such as melted butter or cream. Just keep it away from direct heat.

Baking with chocolate

One of the tastiest ways to enjoy chocolate is to use it as a flavoring for cakes and cookies. The simplest chocolate sponge cake is made by adding cocoa powder to the usual mix of butter, sugar, flour, and eggs (see page 111, and replace 3 tablespoons of the flour with 2 tablespoons of cocoa powder). To make it extra chocolatey, you can then make a simple chocolate butter icing by creaming 7 tablespoons softened butter with 1 cup sifted confectioners' sugar and a tablespoon of sifted cocoa powder. This makes a delicious filling to sandwich together two chocolate sponges, and can be spread on top too.

A richer icing is just as easy to make. Simply melt some good dark chocolate with a little unsalted butter – just as in steps 1 and 2 of the chocolate mousse recipe on page 391. Spread this mixture evenly over the top of the chocolate cake, letting it trickle down the sides, and you have a rich, velvety, smooth icing for the best of chocolate cakes. Alternatively, if you want a slightly sweeter, fudgier icing, see page 397.

Cookies can also be made using cocoa powder, but perhaps the best kind you can make at home are the ones with lots of bits of real chocolate in them – chocolate chip cookies (see page 400).

REAL HOT CHOCOLATE

If you want to experience the excitement felt by the very first chocolate drinkers, you'll have to do a bit better than a heaped teaspoon of cocoa mix in a mug of hot milk. So here's a recipe for the creamiest hot chocolate you'll ever drink. Think of it as hot chocolate mousse in a mug.

For each cup, you need:

Good dark chocolate (at least 70 percent cocoa solids), 4 or 5 squares

Free-range egg yolk, 1 (see page 88 for details of how to separate eggs)

Whole milk, ¾ cup

Superfine sugar, 1 teaspoon

A small saucepan, a stainless-steel bowl that will fit on the pan without touching the water, wooden spoon, balloon whisk, teaspoon, ladle

1. Put 2 inches of water in the saucepan, place it on the stove over medium heat, and bring it to a simmer.

2. Break the chocolate up and put it in the stainless-steel bowl. Put the bowl over the pan of gently simmering water and turn the heat off. Stir occasionally with the wooden spoon until the chocolate has melted completely. Oven gloves on. Take the bowl off the saucepan.

3. Drop the egg yolk into the melted chocolate and whisk until thick and smooth. (Yes, this "drink" is almost like a kind of chocolate custard.)

4. Pour the hot water carefully down the sink. Now add the milk to the empty saucepan along with the teaspoon of sugar. Place the saucepan back on the stove over medium heat.

5. Watch the milk carefully (it boils over very quickly), giving it a stir every few seconds. Wait till it is hot and steaming but not quite boiling, then pour a little of it onto the melted chocolate and egg yolk. Stir it in, then add the rest of the milk. Now whisk vigorously until very frothy. (The Mayans and Aztecs made their chocolate frothy by pouring it from one container into another. You could try this, but maybe outdoors.)

6. Ladle the hot chocolate into a cup or small mug for each person.

How to drink your hot chocolate

Slurp the froth, and glug the chocolatey drink underneath. You might need a spoon to get the last trickle out of the mug.

CHOCOLATE MOUSSE

This is a lovely, rich mousse that sets nice and firm. The two chocolates are sweetened with just a little sugar. There's no cream in the mousse, so you can add the cream when you eat it!

This recipe contains raw eggs (see page 88).

To serve 6:
Good dark chocolate, 3 ounces
Milk chocolate, 3 ounces
Unsalted butter, 5 tablespoons
Vanilla extract, 2 teaspoons
Free-range eggs, 4
Superfine sugar, 2 tablespoons

A small saucepan, 2 mixing bowls, one stainless-steel bowl to set over the saucepan without touching the water, butter knife, wooden spoon, balloon whisk, rotary whisk, balloon whisk, or handheld electric mixer, tablespoon, ramekins or sundae glasses (or a large serving bowl)

1. Pour 2 inches of water into the saucepan. Set it on the stovetop and turn the heat to medium. Bring the water just to the simmering point and switch off the heat.

2. Meanwhile, break the chocolate into small chunks and cut the butter into small cubes. Put both chocolate and butter into the stainless-steel bowl and carefully place the bowl on top of the saucepan of hot water. Stir it from time to time with the wooden spoon. When the chocolate and butter have just about melted, take the bowl off the pan (oven gloves on; it will be hot) and put it on the counter to cool.

3. Stir the vanilla extract into the cooled melted chocolate and butter.

4. Separate the eggs (see page 88), putting the yolks in one of the remaining bowls and the whites in the other. Add the sugar to the yolks and whisk together with the balloon whisk until the mixture becomes thick and a little paler. Stir the whisked yolks gently into the bowl of butter and chocolate until they are thoroughly mixed.

5. Now using the (clean) balloon whisk, a rotary whisk, or an electric mixer, whisk the egg whites until they are thick and just stiff enough to make mountains when you raise the whisk; there should be no liquid egg white left at the bottom of the bowl.

6. Take a tablespoon of the fluffy egg white and whisk this into the chocolate mixture. Now, put down the whisk and take up the tablespoon — the rest of the egg white needs to be folded in gently all at once until you can't see any trace of it in the mixture. This may take a little while but keep folding, turning the spoon over and over like a paddle.

7. Spoon the mousse into individual ramekins or sundae glasses or into one big bowl. Put it in the fridge to chill and set.

How to eat your mousse

The mousses are ready to eat when set firm, which will take just a few hours. You can pour a little cream (or a lot) over them as you eat them. Or you could whip up some cream and serve each mousse with a blob of whipped cream on top. Or you may find that they're just right on their own, without any cream at all. Fresh raspberries taste really good with this mousse, too.

Variations

If you like orange chocolate, then finely grate the zest of an orange into the mixture at the same time as you add the vanilla extract. Or dissolve a teaspoon of instant coffee powder in a teaspoon of very hot water and add this instead for just a hint of coffee flavor.

CHOCOLATE SAUCE FOR ICE CREAM

This is a perfect sauce for ice cream – thick, fudgy, and not too sweet. It's incredibly quick to make.

To serve 4 to 5:
Unsalted butter, 3 tablespoons
Brown sugar, ¼ cup
Cocoa powder, heaping ¼ cup
Milk, 3 tablespoons

Small saucepan, wooden spoon, whisk

1. Put all the ingredients into the pan and put it on the stove. Turn the heat on low.

2. Heat very gently, stirring all the time with the wooden spoon, until the butter melts and the sauce thickens. Change to a whisk if the sauce looks in any way lumpy or grainy. Simmer gently for just a minute and then take off the stove.

How to eat your sauce

Serve warm, poured over vanilla ice cream. Or you could create a delicious chocolate dessert by making a small chocolate Victoria sponge cake, following the recipe on page 111 but using 2 eggs and replacing 1½ tablespoons of the flour with cocoa powder. Bake it in just one pan rather than two and eat it warm with the hot chocolate sauce and a pitcher of cream.

Variation: chocolate icing

If you sift 4 to 5 tablespoons of confectioners' sugar into this sauce and add a tablespoon of cream, it makes a fantastic icing for the top of a chocolate sponge cake (see above and page 387).

CHOCOLATE TRUFFLES

A real truffle is an underground fungus that grows in woodland areas and is usually sniffed out by pigs or dogs. Truffles are one of the most highly prized ingredients, and one of the most expensive foods you can buy. The word *truffle* was probably first used to describe these chocolates because they are dark and knobbly, rich and delicious like black truffles.

You'll need to sniff out a bar of really good dark chocolate for this recipe. Look on the label for one that contains at least 70 percent cocoa solids.

You will need:

Good dark chocolate, 5 ounces
Heavy cream, 1 cup plus 2 tablespoons
Cocoa powder

Cutting board, sharp knife, medium bowl, small saucepan, wooden spoon, baking sheet, parchment paper, sieve, small shallow bowl, 2 teaspoons

1. Break the chocolate into chunks and then chop it into fairly small chips. Place these chips in the bowl.

2. Pour the cream into the saucepan and place on the stove over low heat. Heat gently, stirring with the wooden spoon, until the cream is just about to boil. Turn off the heat and remove the saucepan from the stove.

3. Pour the hot cream onto the chocolate. Stir it from time to time as the chocolate melts until you get a thick, shiny mixture.

4. Place the bowl in the fridge until the truffle mixture sets firm enough to handle – 2 hours, perhaps a little longer.

5. Line the baking sheet with parchment paper and sift some cocoa powder into the small bowl, ready for dusting the truffles.

6. Take teaspoonfuls of the truffle mixture and drop them into the cocoa powder, pushing them off the spoon with another teaspoon. Turn them over and over with the spoons until they're well covered in cocoa. They'll look rough and craggy rather than perfectly round – more like those real truffles the pigs are after. Drop each truffle onto the baking parchment. Let them set in a cool place.

How to eat your truffles

Because they have fresh cream in them, these truffles are best stored in the fridge and eaten within a week – not that you're likely to hang onto them for that long. If you're going to make a box of homemade chocolates (see page 394), then a batch of chocolate truffles is a very good start!

A BOX OF CHOCOLATES

If you can make truffles as good as any professional *chocolatier* (see page 393), what's to stop you from going a stage further? Making your very own box of chocolates may sound a bit daunting, but there's really nothing to be afraid of. Dipping homemade sweets in a coating of milk or dark chocolate is really easy. It might be a little bit messy the first few times — but it will be a very delicious mess. And once you've taken the nicely coated chocolates away from the mess and put them neatly in a box, they are sure to look as lovely as they taste.

You can try dipping just about any homemade sweets in chocolate, but two recipes from this book will work particularly well: Peppermint Creams (page 363) and Honey Fudge (page 379). Add to these the chocolate truffles on page 393, and you have a choice of three kinds of chocolates in the box. If you like nuts, then whole Brazil nuts (shelled, obviously) are easy to dip.

Most good kitchenware stores sell tiny paper cups that you can use for presenting your chocolates. If you don't want to make your own candy boxes, you can buy them, along with molds and other decorating equipment, on the Internet (see page 407).

Besides your ready-made sweets, you'll need:
Good dark chocolate, 6½ ounces

Small saucepan, a stainless-steel bowl that will fit over the saucepan without touching the water, wooden spoon, baking sheet, parchment paper, 1 or 2 forks, small spoon, boxes, ribbons, and decorating materials

1. Put 2 inches of water in the saucepan, place it on the stove over medium heat, and bring it to a simmer.

2. Break the chocolate up and put it in the metal bowl. Put the bowl over the pan of gently simmering water and turn the heat off. Stir occasionally with the wooden spoon, until the chocolate has melted completely. Oven gloves on. Take the bowl off the saucepan.

3. Line the baking sheet with baking parchment. Have your "centers," e.g., small squares of fudge or whole peppermint creams, standing by, nicely cool from the fridge. Scoop one of them up with a fork and place it gently in the chocolate. Turn it over carefully so that it is entirely encased in chocolate. Lift it up with the fork, scrape the bottom of the fork against the side of the bowl, and transfer the sweet to the lined baking sheet. Some fillings, like peppermint creams, look particularly good half-dipped.

4. Repeat the process with the next center. You may find that 2 forks come in handy — especially when you drop one of the centers and it sinks to the bottom of the chocolate. Incidentally, if the dipping chocolate starts to set while you've still got centers left to dip, place

can buy pretty boxes from stationer's or paper goods shops.

7. As you are arranging the chocolates, touch them as little as possible with your bare hands – the heat from your fingers will be enough to make them start to melt. Use a fork and a small spoon to handle them instead. It's a good idea to put pieces of card stock between the layers of chocolates to stop them melting together. And, once the chocolates are packed up, keep them in the fridge until it's time to give them away. A beautifully wrapped box of chocolates has to be one of the loveliest presents you can give. In fact, if it doesn't persuade someone to be your Valentine, then realistically nothing else will.

the bowl back on the pan of hot water, place the pan over low heat, and stir, until the chocolate flows again.

5. When all the centers have been coated, put the chocolates in the fridge straight away to set.

6. Now, for the presentation. You can be as creative as you like in how you present and wrap your chocolates. You could save the little frilly paper cups from other boxes of chocolates, you could buy some from kitchenware stores, or from companies that sell chocolate supplies on the Internet (see page 407), or you could cut out little squares or circles of waxed paper to make your own. You can make little boxes, too, from colored or foil-coated card stock, or again you

CHOCOLATE ÉCLAIRS

Chocolate éclairs are long, puffy pastries stuffed with whipped cream (although in France it's usually a thick pastry cream) and topped with rich chocolate icing. The pastries are made with choux pastry, which is made by bringing butter and water to a boil, adding the flour, and then beating in the eggs.

Éclair is French for "a flash of lightning." They take a little longer to make than that, but they disappear about as fast.

To make about 12 éclairs:
Butter, 5 tablespoons
Water, ⅞ cup
A pinch of salt
All-purpose flour, scant ⅔ cup
Free-range eggs, 3
Heavy cream, 1 cup

For the chocolate icing:
Superfine sugar, ½ cup
Water, 6 tablespoons

Dark chocolate, 2 ounces
Unsalted butter, 2 tablespoons

Butter knife, medium saucepan, medium bowl, wooden spoon, sieve, 2 small bowls, fork, small plastic freezer bag (or piping bag), plastic spatula, scissors, 2 baking sheets, parchment paper, small sharp knife, wire rack, whisk, small saucepan, 2 teaspoons

1. Preheat the oven to 400°F. Dice the butter, put it into the medium saucepan with the water and salt, and turn the heat to low. Stir from time to time with the wooden spoon as the butter melts. Meanwhile, sift the flour into a small bowl.

2. When the butter has melted, turn up the heat and bring the mixture to a boil. Turn off the heat and quickly add the flour to the saucepan. Immediately beat the flour into the liquid with the wooden spoon to mix all the ingredients together. After a few seconds or so, you'll find that the mixture swells into a smooth dough that comes away from the sides of the saucepan. Stop beating.

3. Remove the pan from the heat. Let the mixture cool for 3 or 4 minutes. Crack the eggs into the medium bowl and whisk them with the fork. Pour a little of the egg into the flour mixture and beat it in well. Keep adding and beating in the egg, a little at a time, until the dough looks thick, smooth, and shiny and still holds its shape well. You may not need the last 2 or 3 table-spoonfuls of egg if your eggs are large ones.

4. Spoon the mixture into the freezer bag (you'll need to scrape it out of the pan with the plastic spatula). Fold down the top of the bag to squeeze the dough to the bottom. Snip off one of the bottom corners of the bag to give you a hole about ⅜ inch long.

5. Line the baking sheets with parchment paper. Squeeze the mixture into sausage shapes about 4 inches long onto the parchment, allowing about 1½ inches of space between each one (they should at least double in size in the oven). You should be able to make about 12.

6. Oven gloves on. Place the baking sheets in the hot oven and leave for about 30 minutes. When the éclairs are ready, they should be puffed up, a good golden brown all over, and feel hard when you poke one with a knife. Oven gloves on again. Take out the baking sheet and turn off the oven.

7. Immediately take each éclair off the sheets (they will be very hot, so wear oven gloves) and, with the point of a knife, gently slit the side to let out the steam. (Otherwise, the steam sits trapped in the éclair and turns back to water, leaving you with a soggy pastry.) Let them cool and dry out on the wire rack.

8. Whip the cream in the small bowl with the whisk until it's just thick enough to hold its shape. Put it in the fridge while you make the chocolate icing.

9. For the icing, put the sugar and water in the small saucepan, place it on the stove, and turn the heat to low. Heat gently, stirring all the time with a wooden spoon to dissolve the sugar. Bring to a boil and boil fast for 3 minutes. Remove the pan from the heat and wait for a few minutes for the syrup to cool down (you can speed this up by dipping the bottom of the pan in a bowl of cold water, if you like). Meanwhile, break up the chocolate and cut the butter into chunks.

10. When the syrup is very warm, rather than very hot, add the chocolate and butter. Stir until both have melted and blended to a smooth, glossy sauce. Let cool, stirring occasionally. When the sauce starts to thicken, it's ready to ice your éclairs.

11. When the pastries are cool, use a teaspoon to fill the inside of each éclair with whipped cream (you may need to enlarge the slit that you made before). Then take a different teaspoon and smear the chocolate icing generously over each éclair. Leave the éclairs on the wire rack until the icing has set. In the unlikely event that you're not going to eat them straight away, you can put them in the fridge for a few hours.

Variation: profiteroles

The great thing about the icing for the éclairs is that while it is still warm it is a fantastic chocolate sauce. This means you can easily adapt your éclairs to become the irresistible dessert known as profiteroles. Just make the éclairs round instead of long (pipe them into blobs on the baking sheet, like little meringues, rather than long sausages). Bake, let cool, and fill with cream just as before. Put 2 or 3 in each dessert bowl and pour over the warm chocolate sauce as you hand them out. You may need to lighten the sauce a little with just a tablespoon of milk.

CHOCOLATE CHIP COOKIES

A delectable treat that can be rustled up quickly and eaten almost straight from the oven.

To make about 12 large cookies:
Good dark chocolate, 3½ ounces
Unsalted butter, ½ cup (1 stick)
Granulated sugar, scant ½ cup
Brown sugar, ⅓ cup
Free-range egg, 1
Vanilla extract, 2 teaspoons
All-purpose or white pastry flour, 1 cup

Baking powder, ½ teaspoon
A pinch of salt

2 large baking sheets, parchment paper, sharp knife, cutting board, small saucepan, mixing bowl, wooden spoon, teaspoon, sieve, tablespoon, wire rack

1. Preheat the oven to 375°F. Line each baking sheet with a piece of parchment paper. Chop the chocolate into little chunks and set aside.

2. Heat the butter in the small saucepan very gently until it has just melted. Meanwhile, put the two sorts of sugar into the mixing bowl. Pour the melted butter on top of the sugar and beat well with the wooden spoon.

3. Break the egg into the bowl and add the vanilla. Beat until the mixture is well blended.

4. Sift the flour, baking powder, and salt into the mixing bowl and stir them in, then add the chopped chocolate. You should have a pretty sloppy sort of mixture.

5. Dot heaping tablespoonfuls of the mixture on the the lined baking sheets, leaving plenty of space in between them — these cookies really spread out.

6. Oven gloves on. Put the baking sheets in the oven and bake for 8 to 10 minutes, until the cookies are just turning golden brown. (If you have a glass door in your oven, watch the extraordinary transformation as these cookies bake — one moment you've got lumpy brown dough, the next, you have pale golden cookies, their shiny surface a network of cracks.)

7. Let the cookies set on the baking sheets to harden for a couple of minutes, then carefully lift up the parchment paper and transfer them to a wire rack.

How to eat your cookies

Sample a cookie as soon as it's set a little and isn't too bendy but is still warm, and while the chocolate is still a little messy. They're also very good cold, and they store well in an airtight tin. If you're feeling *really* greedy, you could try sandwiching a couple of them together with some ice cream — chocolate or vanilla would work best.

pour in the chocolate mixture

sift the flour and cocoa

mix it all in

very nearly done ...

DOUBLE-CHOCOLATE BROWNIES

These have both cocoa powder and real chocolate in them – hence the "double chocolate." They are much easier to make than a cake, as they are meant to be dense and fudgy, not light and airy.

To make about 18 brownies:

Good dark chocolate, 8 ounces
Unsalted butter, ¾ cup plus 1 tablespoon
Superfine sugar, ⅞ cup
Free-range eggs, 3
All-purpose or white pastry flour, ¾ cup
Cocoa powder, ½ cup
Broken walnuts, 1 cup (optional)

Small saucepan, butter knife, 1 mixing bowl, 1 stainless-steel bowl to set over the saucepan without touching the water, wooden spoon, balloon whisk, rubber spatula, sieve, baking pan about 8 x 12 inches and at least ¾ inch deep, aluminum foil, wire rack

1. Preheat the oven to 325°F. Put 2 inches water in the saucepan and bring it to a simmer over medium heat.

2. Break the chocolate up, cut up the butter, and place both in the stainless-steel bowl. Put it over the pan of gently simmering water and turn the heat off. Stir occasionally until melted together and smooth.

3. Meanwhile, in the other bowl, whisk the sugar with the eggs, using the balloon whisk, until the mixture is smooth and creamy.

4. Add the chocolate mixture to the eggy mix, using the rubber spatula to get all the chocolate out of the bowl. Mix thoroughly together with the wooden spoon.

5. Sift in the flour and cocoa powder and mix thoroughly. Stir in the walnuts if you've decided to use them.

6. Line the baking pan with a piece of foil (see page 407) and pour in the mixture, again using the spatula to get everything out of the bowl. Smooth the top of the mixture with the spatula.

7. Oven gloves on. Place the pan on a shelf in the middle of the oven and bake for 20 to 25 minutes. A knife pushed into the middle should come out just a bit smeared. Don't cook them for too long – better a bit gooey than too solid.

8. Oven gloves on. Take the pan out of the oven and place it on the wire rack. Let sit until cool enough to cut into squares.

How to eat your brownies

You can eat your brownies as soon as they are cool enough to touch. If you're eating them hot, they are delicious with ice cream. Once they've cooled, keep them in a plastic container. They're less cakey, more fudgy the next day.

GLOSSARY

Want to know what brine is, or what to do with a palette knife or a potato ricer? Here's a short roundup of culinary terms that you will often come across when cooking – not just in this book, but in any recipe book that you use.

Al dente. Italian for "to the tooth" – a term commonly used to describe the texture of cooked pasta, which means it's just tender but with a little bit of chewiness to it.

Apple corer. A tool shaped like a hollow cylinder, used for taking the core out of a whole apple.

Baking blind. Cooking a pastry shell without any filling.

Batter. A runny uncooked flour-and-liquid mixture.

Beat. To stir vigorously, usually with a wooden spoon.

Boil. To heat a liquid until it bubbles furiously.

Brine. Salt dissolved in water. Used for soaking joints of pork to turn them into ham or bacon.

Candy thermometer. A cooking thermometer that is suitable for standing in boiling liquids.

Caramelize. If you heat a pan of sugar until it melts, it will quickly turn from a colorless liquid to a brown, bittersweet one. This is called caramelization. Rather confusingly, caramelization is also used to describe the browning of meat and even vegetables such as onions.

Carcass. The dead body of an animal before it's cut up into pieces.

Cereals. Crops such as wheat, barley, and rice that produce edible seeds.

Colander. A large plastic or metal bowl with holes in it for draining pasta or vegetables from their cooking water.

Cream. To blend ingredients together by beating them with a wooden spoon. You cream butter and sugar together, for instance, when you make a Victoria sponge cake.

Dough. A thick uncooked flour-and-liquid mixture.

Durum wheat. A wheat grown in hot climates that's particularly suitable for making dried pasta.

Evaporation. When water boils away as it turns to steam.

Fillet/filet. In fish, fillets are long, slim pieces of flesh cut away from the backbone. In meat, a beef filet is simply a piece of boneless flesh cut from the tenderloin. It's expensive because it is particularly tender.

Fold. A gentle way of combining ingredients by scooping up tablespoonfuls of the mixture gently but firmly in an up-and-over motion.

Herbicide. A spray that farmers use to kill weeds on their crops.

Knead. To stretch and fold a dough until it becomes smooth and elastic.

Live yogurt. Yogurt that contains active bacteria. Add warm milk and it will breed to make more yogurt.

Organic. Organic farming does not use artificial fertilizers and pesticides. Instead, organic farmers rely on natural methods to enrich the soil (for example, by using manure) and natural predators (such as ladybugs) to control pests. Animals raised on organic farms are guaranteed a high standard of welfare and must be fed an organically produced diet.

Palette knife. A broad, flat, round-bladed knife that's useful for pancake making or flipping things over in a pan.

Parchment paper. Also known as baking parchment, this nonstick paper is used for lining baking sheets and pans for foods such as meringues and cakes, which might otherwise stick to the pan.

Pâtisserie. A French word for a pastry shop. The person who makes the pastries is a *pâtissier*.

Pectin. A natural substance found in many fruits. Jams made from fruit high in pectin (like apples) set more easily than fruits that don't contain so much (such as blackberries) – a reason blackberry and apple jelly is such a good combination.

Pesticide. A spray that farmers use to kill the bugs on their crops.

Pie. A food that's covered with a pastry or potato top. A double-crust pie has pastry beneath and above the filling.

Poach. Cooking food in hot or gently simmering water. Eggs and fish are sometimes cooked this way.

Potato ricer. A tool for making mashed potatoes. Hot boiled potatoes are put into the ricer, the bottom of which is a mass of tiny holes. The lever part of the machine then presses down on the spuds so that they're forced through the holes, emerging as a mass of tiny white worms into a bowl or pan beneath. Very satisfying.

Ripeness. A combination of sweetness and tenderness that means you have a really tasty piece of fruit.

Roux. A paste made by beating flour into melted butter or other fat. Whisk in hot milk and you have a simple béchamel sauce.

Rub in. A technique for making pastry in which you rub little cubes of butter into flour between the pads of your fingertips to break them up. Eventually, you end up with a sandy, crumb-like mixture. Stir in a little liquid, clump the mixture into a round disk, and you have a pastry dough.

Salad spinner. A simple little machine for drying washed lettuce so that a salad dressing will cling to its leaves. The spinning of the lettuce in its slotted bowl forces the water out of the leaves into an outer solid bowl.

Serrated knife. A sharp knife with a jagged cutting edge, like teeth. Good for cutting slippery or crumbly foods.

Sift. To stand a sieve over a bowl, add a dry ingredient – often flour or confectioners' sugar – and either shake it through the sieve or push it through with the back of a spoon. This gets rid of any lumps and allows more air between the particles.

Simmer. To heat a liquid until tiny bubbles rise and break on the surface. Turn the heat down to maintain this temperature or it will rise to a rolling boil.

Slotted spoon. A large, usually metal, spoon with slits in it – useful for scooping food out of a liquid, e.g., taking the browned meat out of a frying pan and leaving the oil behind.

Spatula. A flexible plastic spatula is a good (maybe too good) way of scraping every scrap of cake mix out of bowls. A metal spatula is used to remove foods like fish or meat from a frying pan.

Steak. A piece of meat or fish.

Sterilize. Some recipes call for jars and utensils to be sterilized or scalded before you start to cook, otherwise bacteria can spoil the food. To sterilize utensils such as bowls and spoons – for example, when you're making yogurt or cheese – it's usually enough to scald them by standing them in a clean bowl in the sink and pouring boiling water over them. When you make jam or jelly, however, you will need to put the jars and their lids in a pan, cover them with cold water and boil them for 10 minutes, then dry them in a low oven. Alternatively, you can put the clean jars through a hot dishwasher cycle. Use the jars immediately afterward.

Stock. Water that has been simmered with vegetables and sometimes meat or fish bones to make a well-flavored liquid that you can use in soups, sauces, risottos, etc.

Tablespoon. A standard 15-ml measurement – the kind of spoon you'd use for serving food rather than eating it.

Tart. A pastry shell containing a sweet or savory filling.

Teaspoon. A standard 5-ml measurement – the kind of spoon you'd use for adding sugar to tea.

Tender. Food that has been cooked until you can easily insert a knife into it.

Whip. Another word for "beat" or "whisk," as in whipped cream, which is cream that has been beaten until it holds its shape.

Whisk. A rotary whisk has two interlocking metal beaters and a handle that you turn. It's good for whisking cream and egg whites. A balloon whisk is a mass of wire loops set into a simple handle. It's good for small whisking jobs – making béchamel sauce, say, or a smooth pancake batter. It will also whisk cream and egg whites . . . eventually.

Zest. The thin, brightly colored layer of skin covering a citrus fruit.

A few basic techniques

Chopping garlic. Pull as many cloves, or little segments, of garlic as you need away from the bulbous head of the plant. Cut away either end of each clove, then put the clove on a cutting board and squash it with the flat side of a knife blade (or use the back of a tablespoon instead, if you like). It's then easy to peel off the papery covering. With a sharp knife, cut the clove into slices and then chop these slices into tiny pieces.

Chopping an onion. Cut off either end of the onion with a sharp knife and strip away the layers of papery skin. Cut the onion in half from top to bottom, then put the cut sides down flat on the cutting board. Taking the first half, carefully cut the onion into thin slices from top to bottom, then turn it and cut across these slices to make little dice. Do the same with the other half. There's no hurry and you can always chop separately any odd slices that fall away. Try not to bend over the onion too much as you chop, or the chemicals that are released when the onion is cut may sting your eyes. If a recipe asks you to chop an onion finely, then make the little dice as small as possible. If it says to chop it roughly, then keep the pieces large. If it doesn't say either way, then simply chop the onion into average small pieces.

Washing and trimming leeks. Leeks can be muddy not just on the outside but inside their many layers, too, so they need to be carefully washed. Trim off the very bottom of the leek with its frondy ends and also cut away the darker, coarse green leaves at the top. Lie the leek flat on the board and cut down its length with a sharp knife but only to the white part. Strip away the tough outer layers and then rinse away any mud and grit that might be caught between the layers of green leaves. Many recipes call for just the more tender white and very light green parts of the leek to be used – the green parts can be used to make stock (see page 192).

Lining a cake pan. To keep a cake from sticking to the pan, it's always a good idea to line the bottom of the pan with parchment paper. Stand the pan on the parchment paper, draw around it with a pencil, and cut out the shape. Lightly grease the bottom of the pan with a little canola oil or butter so the paper will stick, then put the paper in it. Alternatively, you can line a pan with aluminum foil. Turn the pan upside down, gently wrap the foil around it so that it molds to the shape of the pan, then take it off, turn the pan the right side up, and use the foil mold to line the pan. Gently grease the foil with a little softened butter.

Useful websites

Chocolate supplies. You can buy chocolate-making equipment such as molds and wrappers from www.candylandcrafts.com.

Farmers' markets, farm shops, and u-pick farms. For details of your nearest farmers' market, contact www.localharvest.org.

Fish. For advice on fish to buy and fish to avoid, contact www.mbayag.org/cr/seafoodwatch.asp.

Paper chef's hats. You can buy these online from www.growingcooks.com.

Sausage casings. If you can't get these from your local butcher, try www.sausagemaker.com/making_sausage.

INDEX

Page numbers in *italic* refer to the illustrations

A

agriculture, 123
all-purpose flour, 17
almonds, 313
   pear and almond pudding cake, *302*, 334–5, *335*
animals, farming, 261–3
apples, 122, 125, 127–8, 129, 131
   baked apples, *118*, 144, *145*
   French-style apple tart, *119*, 150–1, *150*
apricots, 123
asparagus, 176
avocados, 123
   guacamole, *214*, 215
Aztecs, 384

B

bacon, 270, 317
   homemade bacon for a bacon sandwich, *302*, 326–7
   lentil and bacon soup for lots of people, 328–9
   liver and bacon, 294
   macaroni and cheese with bacon, 71–2
   spaghetti carbonara, 51
bacteria
   cheese-making, 67
   in meat, 265
   preserving food, 305, 306
   yogurt, 70, *70*
baked beans, 310, 317
baking blind, pastry, 36, *37*
baking powder, 47

baking soda
   soda bread, 27, 46
   Sultana scones, 47
bananas, 125, 128
   banana bread, *152*, 153
barbecues, 275–7, *276*
barn eggs, 93
basil, 190, 315
   pasta with four herbs, 207
bass, 225
batter cakes, 97
bay, 190
beans, 304, 306, 310–12, *311*
   spicy bean stew with sausages, 277, 330
béchamel sauce, 59–61
beef, 58, 265, 266–9
   beef burgers, *258*, 277, 284–5, *285*
   spaghetti bolognese, *259*, *286*, 287–8
   steak, *258*, 268–9, *269*, 277
bees, honey, 344–6, *345*
biscuits
   cheese straws, 79
   chocolate biscuits, 387
   chocolate chip cookies, *380*, 400, *401*
   shortbread, 80, *81*
blackberries, 127, 138
   bramble jelly, *119*, 156–7, *157*
   ice lollies, 360
   summer fruit tart, *118*, 148, *149*
black currants, 127
   black currant ice cream, 375
blue cheeses, 68
boiled egg, *86*, *100*, 101
bolognese sauce, 287–8
bouquet garni, 315
bramble jelly, *119*, 156–7, *157*
bran, 23

bread, 19–27
   banana bread, *152*, 153
   cheese and onion bread, 22
   easy flat breads, *14*, 38–9, *39*, 277
   eggy bread, *87*, 103, *103*
   flour, 21–2, 23
   fresh white bread, *15*, 40, 41–2
   kneading, 21
   raisin bread, *15*, 43–5, *44*
   salt, 22
   seed bread, 22
   shapes, 22
   soda bread, 27, 46
   sourdough bread, *14*, 24–6, *25*
   tomato bread, 23
   yeast, 19–21, 24
bream, 225, *227*
broccoli, 176, 177
brown sugar, *342*, 343
brownies, double-chocolate, *380*, *402*, 403
Brussels sprouts gratin, 75
bullaces, 138
burgers, beef, *258*, 277, 284–5, *285*
butchers, 263
butter, 63–5
   cooking with, 63
   making butter, *55*, 64–5, *64–5*
   shortbread, 80, *81*
buttermilk
   homemade cream cheese, *54*, 72–4, *73*

C

cabbages, 170
   quick-fried onion and cabbage with black pepper, 206
cacao trees, *382*, 383, 384
cake pans, lining, 407

cakes
  banana bread, *152*, 153
  chocolate cake, 387
  double-chocolate brownies, *380*, *402*, 403
  honey-ginger cake, *336*, 364–5
  pear and almond pudding cake, *302*, 334 5, *335*
  Victoria sponge cake, *87*, *110*, 111–12
calves, dairy farming, 58, 266, 267
campfires, 275–7, *276*
candies, *see sweets*
candy thermometers, 348–50, *349*
canned foods, 305–6
cannellini beans
  spicy bean stew with sausages, 277, 330
caramel, 347, 348, 350
carrots, 169, 170, 177
casseroles and stews
  pheasant casserole, 300–1
  spicy bean stew with sausages, 277, 330
cattle, 261, 266
cauliflower, 177
cheese, *66*, 67–8
  cheese and onion bread, 22
  cheese straws, 79
  cooking with, 68
  homemade cream cheese, *54*, 72–4, *73*
  macaroni and cheese with bacon, 71–2
  spaghetti carbonara, 51
  types of, 68
cheesecake, *54*, *76*, 77–8
cherries, 127
chestnuts, 313
  roast chestnuts, 331
chicken, 92–3, 261–2, 265, 281
  chicken curry, 298–9, *299*

chicken stock, 192
  roast chicken, *258*, 295–7, *296*
chickpeas, 312
  hummus, 333
chiles, 123, *164*, 177, 315
  sweet chile and red currant jam, 163–5
chocolate, 380–403
  baking with, 387
  a box of chocolates, *381*, 394–5, *395*
  chocolate chip cookies, *380*, 400, *401*
  chocolate éclairs, *380*, *396*, 397–8
  chocolate mousse, *381*, *390*, 391–2
  chocolate sauce for ice cream, *381*, 392
  chocolate truffles, 393
  choosing, 385–7
  double-chocolate brownies, *380*, *402*, 403
  history, 384
  icing, 387, 392
  making chocolate, 383–5
  melting, *386*, 387
  profiteroles, 398
  real hot chocolate, *380*, 388, *389*
chorizo, green peas with roasted red peppers and, 208–9
choux pastry
  chocolate éclairs, *380*, *396*, 397–8, *399*
  profiteroles, 398
cilantro, 190
cinnamon, 316
citrus fruits, 131–4
  ice lollies, 360
clementines, 131
clotted cream, 62
cloves, 315, 316

cocoa, 385
cod, *220*, 224, 229, 317
Columbus, Christopher, 384
confectioners' sugar, 340–3
cookies, chocolate chip, *380*, 400, *401*
corn, 170, 171
  vegetable fritters, *166*, 209–11, *210*
Cortés, Hernán, 384
cowpox, 69
cows' milk, 56–89, *57*
crab, *220*, 233
  undressing, 234–7, *235*, *236*
crab apples, 138
cream, 59, 61–2
  chocolate truffles, 393
  cooking with, 62
  creamy Brussels sprouts gratin, 75
  custard ice cream, *336*, 374–5, *375*
  homemade cream cheese, *54*, 72–4, *73*
  ice cream, 351, 352, 356
  making butter, 64–5, *64–5*
  rhubarb fool, 142
  strawberry fool, *140*, 141
  strawberry parfait, 371–3, *372*
  types of, 61–2
creamy fish pie, 248–9, *249*
crème fraîche, 62
crème pâtissière, 148
crudités with garlic mayonnaise, 212–13
crumble, gooseberry, *146*, 147
cucumbers, 123, 317
  cucumber raita, 83, *83*
cumin, 316
cupboard, 302–35
curds, cheese, 67, 68
curry, chicken, 298–9, *299*

custard, *87*, 94–6, 113
custard ice cream, *336*, 374–5, *375*

D

dairy farming, 58, 266, 267
dairy maids, 69
damsons, 127, 138
Demerara sugar, 343
dips
    guacamole, *214*, 215
    hummus, 333
double-chocolate brownies, *380*, *402*, 403
dough
    bread, 21
    pasta, 30, *31*
    pastry, 34
    pizza, 33
dried food, 306
drinking chocolate, 385
drinks
    frozen strawberry milkshake, *55*, *84*, 85
    lemonade, *118*, *158*, 159
    mango and orange smoothie, 160, *160*
    peach, pear, and raspberry smoothie, 161
    real hot chocolate, *380*, 388, *389*
    rhubarb and ginger smoothie, 162
    smoothies, 139
drop scones, 97, *116*, 117
duck, 282
duck eggs, 94

E

Easter, eating lamb, 279
éclairs, chocolate, *380*, *396*, 397–8, *399*
egg pasta, 28

eggplant, 169, 317
eggs, 86–117
    boiled egg, *86*, *100*, 101
    chocolate mousse, *381*, *390*, 391–2
    cracking, 88
    custard, *87*, 94–6, 113
    custard ice cream, *336*, 374–5, *375*
    drop scones, *116*, 117
    eggy bread, *87*, 103, *103*
    folding, 91
    French omelette, *86*, 104, *105*
    freshness, 92
    garlic mayonnaise, 212–13
    kedgeree, 250–1
    meringues, *86*, 108, *109*
    pancakes, *87*, 96–7, 114–15, *115*
    poached egg, 102, *102*
    scrambled eggs on toast, *87*, 101
    separating, 88–90, *89*
    spaghetti carbonara, 51
    Spanish omelette (tortilla), 106–7, *106*
    types of, 93–4
    Victoria sponge cake, *87*, *110*, 111–12
    whisking, 90, 91
    whites, 90
    yolks, 91–2
Eton Mess, 141
evaporated milk
    honey fudge, *378*, 379

F

factory farming, chicken, 93
Fair Trade products, 128
farfalle, *31*, 32
farming, 261–3
fava beans, 169, 171
fires, 275–7, *276*

fish, 220–57
    bones, 229
    catching, 224–5, 231
    creamy fish pie, 248–9, *249*
    fillets, 226–9, *228*
    fish farming, 225
    fish fingers, 243–4
    freshness, 225–6
    history, 230
    preparation, 226, *227*
    salted and smoked fish, 229–31
    whole fish baked in foil, *221*, 238–9, *239*
    see also individual types of fish
fish cakes, salmon, *221*, 245–7, *246*
flapjacks, Nicola's zesty, *303*, 320, *321*
flat breads, *14*, 38–9, *39*, 277
flour, 14–53
    bread, 21–2, 23
    and civilization, 18
    pasta, 28
    pastry, 34
    types of, 17–18
    uses, 16–17
foil, whole fish baked in, *221*, 238–9, *239*
folding mixtures, *90*, 91
food miles, fruit, 128
fools
    rhubarb fool, 142
    strawberry fool, *140*, 141
fragrant rice, 324–5
free-range eggs, 93–4
free-range meat, 262, 263
freezing
    ice cream, 351–5
    vegetables, 170–1
French omelette, *86*, 104, *105*

French-style apple tart, *119*, 150–1, *150*

fritters, 97
vegetable fritters, *166*, 209–11, *210*

frozen pops, *337*, 358–61, *359*, *361*

frozen strawberry milkshake, *55*, *84*, 85

fruit, 118–65
buying, 128–9
citrus fruits, 131–4
cooking, 131
fruit salad, 366–7
jam-type jellies, 137–8
jellies, 135–7, *136*
lollies, *337*, 358–61, *359*, *361*
organic fruit, 127
ripeness, 125–7
seasonal fruit, 127–8
smoothies, 139
see also individual types of fruit

fudge, honey, *337*, *378*, 379

G

game, 283
garlic, 185
chopping, 406
crudités with garlic mayonnaise, 212–13
garlic, rosemary, and lemon potatoes, *166*, *202*, 203
roast onion family, *167*, 204–5, *205*

geese, 282

gelatin, 135
marshmallows, 277, *336*, 368–70, *371*
orange and strawberry jellies, *119*, 154–5, *155*

gilthead bream, *227*

ginger
honey-ginger cake, *336*, 364–5

rhubarb and ginger smoothie, 162

goose, 282

goose eggs, 94

gooseberries, 122, *126*, 127, 129, 131
gooseberry crumble, *146*, 147

grains, 306

granitas, 358

granulated sugar, 340

grapefruit, 131–2, 134

grapes, 123, 125

gratin, creamy Brussels sprouts, 75

green beans, 169–170, 176, 177, 310

greengages, 127

growing vegetables, 171–6
potatoes, *180*, 181–2, *182*
salad vegetables, 187–9, *188*
tomatoes, 172–5, *172*, *174*

guacamole, *214*, 215

H

half-and-half, 61–2

ham, 317

heart, 267

heavy cream, 62

herbs, 190–1, 315
pasta with four herbs, 207

honey, 338, 344–7, *345*
honey fudge, *337*, *378*, 379
honey-ginger cake, *336*, 364–5

hummus, 333

I

ice cream, 351–6, *352*
black currant ice cream, 375
chocolate sauce for ice cream, *381*, 392
custard ice cream, *336*, 374–5, *375*
flavoring, 353

history, 354–5
peach parfait, *336*, 373
strawberry parfait, 371–3, *372*

ice lollies, *337*, 358–61, *359*, *361*

icehouses, 354

ices, 351–61

icing, chocolate, 387, 392

J

jams
jam-type jellies, 137–8
sweet chile and red currant jam, 163–5

jars, food in, 305

jellies
bramble jelly, *119*, 156–7, *157*
fruit jellies, 135–7, *136*
jam-type jellies, 137–8
orange and strawberry jellies, *119*, 154–5, *155*

Jenner, Edward, 69

K

kebabs, lamb, *258*, 277, 292–3, *293*

kedgeree, 250–1

kidney beans
spicy bean stew with sausages, 277, 330

kidneys, 267

kippers, 231

kiwifruit, 128

kneading bread, 21

L

lamb, 265, 278–9
at Easter, 279
lamb kebabs, *258*, 277, 292–3, *293*
spicy lamb pie, *190*, 259, 289–91

lamb's liver
    liver and bacon, 294
lasagne, 32
leeks, 185
    roast onion family, *167*,
        204–5, *205*
    washing and trimming, 407
legumes, 306, 310–12, *311*
lemons, 131, 132, *133*, 134
    garlic, rosemary, and lemon
        potatoes, *166*, *202*, 203
    ice lollies, 360
    lemon curd, 143
    lemon tart, 52–3, *53*
    lemonade, *118*, *158*, 159
lentils, 310, 312
    lentil and bacon soup for lots
        of people, 328–9
lettuces, 170
limes, 134
    guacamole, *214*, 215
Lind, James, 134
liquids, thickening, 16
liver, 267
    liver and bacon, 294
lobsters, *232*, 233
loganberries, 127
lollies, *337*, 358–61, *359*, *361*

M

macaroni and cheese with bacon,
    71–2
mackerel, *220*, 231, 277
    grilled mackerel, 240–1, *241*
mangoes, 128
    mango and orange smoothie,
        160, *160*
maple syrup, 339
Marggraf, Andreas, 339
marjoram, 190
marshmallows, 277, *336*,
    368–70, *371*

mashed potatoes, 199–200
Mayan tribes, 384
mayonnaise, 186
    crudités with garlic
        mayonnaise, 212–13
meat, 258–301
    buying, 262–3
    cooking, 265
    free-range and organic, 262,
        263
    see also individual types of meat
melons, 124, 125
melting chocolate, *386*, 387
meringues, *86*, 91, 108, *109*
    Eton Mess, 141
milk, 54–85
    cheese, 67
    cream, 59, 61–2
    frozen strawberry milkshake,
        55, *84*, 85
    homemade yogurt, 82
    real hot chocolate, *380*, 388,
        389
    rice pudding, 322–4
    types of, 59
    yogurt, 70, *70*
minestrone, pick-your-own,
    196–8, *197*
mint, 190
    peppermint creams, *336*, *362*,
        363–4
Montezuma, Emperor of the
    Aztecs, 384
mousse, chocolate, *381*, *390*,
    391–2
mushrooms
    mushroom noodle soup, 193
    vegetable fritters, *166*, 209–11,
        210
mussels, 233
    mussels à la marinière, 255–7,
        256

N

navy beans, 310
Nicola's zesty flapjacks, *303*,
    320, *321*
noodle soup, mushroom, 193
nutmeg, 315, 316, *316*
nuts, 313

O

oats
    Nicola's zesty flapjacks, *303*,
        320, *321*
offal, 267
olive oil, 186
    garlic mayonnaise, 212–13
omelettes
    French omelette, *86*, 104, *105*
    Spanish omelette (tortilla),
        106–7, *106*
onions, 169, 185
    cheese and onion bread, 22
    chopping, 406
    quick-fried onion and cabbage
        with black pepper, 206
    roast onion family, *167*,
        204–5, *205*
oranges, 128, 131–2, 134
    ice lollies, 360
    mango and orange smoothie,
        160, *160*
    Nicola's zesty flapjacks, *303*,
        320, *321*
    orange and strawberry jellies,
        119, 154–5, *155*
    rhubarb and ginger smoothie,
        162
    sweet chile and red currant
        jam, 163–5
organic produce
    eggs, 94
    fruit, 127
    meat, 262

ostrich eggs, 94
oysters, 230, 233

P
pancakes, *87*, 96–7, 114–15, *115*
    pancake races, *98*, 99
    sourdough pancakes, 26
parfaits
    peach parfait, *336*, 373
    strawberry parfait, 371–3, *372*
parsley, 190, 191, 315
    pasta with four herbs, 207
pasta, *14*, 28–32
    cooking, 29, 32
    dough, 30, *31*
    drying, 32
    macaroni and cheese with
        bacon, 71–2
    pasta with four herbs, 207
    shapes, 28, 32
    spaghetti bolognese, *259*, *286*,
        287–8
    spaghetti carbonara, 51
    types of, 28–9
pasteurized milk, 67
pastry, 34–6, *35*
    baking blind, 36, *37*
    cheese straws, 79
    choux pastry, *396*, 397–8, *399*
    flour, 17
    rubbing in, 34–6, *35*
    sweet pastry, 52–3
pastry cream, 148
peaches, 122, 123, 125
    peach parfait, *336*, 373
    peach, pear, and raspberry
        smoothie, 161
peanuts, 313
pears, 122, 128
    peach, pear, and raspberry
        smoothie, 161

pear and almond pudding
    cake, *302*, 334–5, *335*
peas, *168*, 169, 171
    green peas with roasted red
        peppers and chorizo, 208–9
peas, dried, 310, 312
peppermint creams, *336*, *362*,
    363–4
peppers, 123, 124, 171, 177
    green peas with roasted red
        peppers and chorizo, 208–9
Pepys, Samuel, 384
pheasant, 283
    pheasant casserole, 300–1
pick-your-own minestrone,
    196–8, *197*
pie, spicy lamb, *190*, *259*,
    289–91
pigs, 261–2, 270, *271*
pizza, *15*, 33, 48–50, *49*
plaice, *220*, 224
plain flour, 17
plums, 122, 127, 131
poached egg, 102, *102*
pollution, 128
pomegranates, *121*, 122
pork, 265, 270
    homemade bacon for a bacon
        sandwich, *302*, 326–7
    sausages, 270, 272–4, *273*
potatoes, 169, 176, 177, 178–84,
    179
    best-ever mashed potatoes,
        199–200
    creamy fish pie, 248–9, *249*
    garlic, rosemary, and lemon
        potatoes, *166*, *202*, 203
    growing, *180*, 181–2, *182*
    history, 183–4
    potatoes with spinach, 200–1
    salmon fish cakes, *221*, 245–7,
        246

Spanish omelette (tortilla),
    106–7, *106*
pound cake, *87*, *110*, 111–12
poultry, 281–2
preserving food, 305–6
profiteroles, 398
pudding cake, pear and almond,
    302, 334–5, *335*
pulses, *see legumes*
pumpkins, 123, 124, 176, 177

R
raisins
    Nicola's zesty flapjacks, *303*,
        320, *321*
    raisin bread, *15*, 43–5, *44*
    Sultana scones, 47
raita, cucumber, 83, *83*
raspberries, 127
    ice lollies, 360
    peach, pear, and raspberry
        smoothie, 161
    summer fruit tart, *118*, 148,
        149
real custard, *87*, 113
red currants, 127, 129
    sweet chile and red currant
        jam, 163–5
rennet, 67
rhubarb, 128, 131
    rhubarb and ginger smoothie,
        162
    rhubarb fool, 142
rice, 304, *308*, 309, *323*
    fragrant rice, 324–5
    kedgeree, 250–1
    rice pudding, 322–4
root vegetables, 169
rosemary, 190
    garlic, rosemary, and lemon
        potatoes, *166*, *202*, 203
    pasta with four herbs, 207

rowan berries, 138
rubbing in pastry, 34–6, *35*
runner beans, 169–70, 171, 177

S

safety, 13
    cooking chicken, 281
    cooking meat, 265
    eggs, 88
saffron, 316
sage, 190
salad dressings, 186
salads, 170, 186–9
    growing salad vegetables,
        187–9, *188*
    quick tomato salad, 216, *217*
    a simple green salad, 218
salmon, 225, 230
    salmon fish cakes, *221*, 245–7,
        246
salmonella, 88, 265
salt, 316–18, *319*
    bread making, 22
salt cod, 229, 317
salted fish, 229–31
satsumas, 131
sauces
    béchamel sauce, 59–61
    chocolate sauce for ice cream,
        381, 392
    honey fudge, 379
sausages, *259*, 270, 272–4, *273*,
    277
    green peas with roasted red
        peppers and chorizo, 208–9
    spicy bean stew with sausages,
        277, 330
scones, Sultana, 47
Scotch pancakes, 97
scrambled eggs on toast, *87*, 101
scurvy, 134, 314
seasonal fruit, 127–8

seasonal vegetables, 176
seed bread, 22
seeds 122, 306
self-rising flour, 18
shallots, 185
    roast onion family, *167*,
        204–5, *205*
sheep, 261, 278–9
shellfish, 233–7
    see also individual types of
        shellfish
shortbread, 80, *81*
shrimp, 222, 233
    creamy fish pie, 248–9, *249*
Shrove Tuesday, 97, 99
single cream, 61–2
sloes, 138
smallpox, 69
smoked fish, 229–31
smoked haddock, 231
    creamy fish pie, 248–9, *249*
    kedgeree, 250–1
smoked salmon, 231, 317
smoothies, 139
    mango and orange smoothie,
        160, *160*
    peach, pear, and raspberry
        smoothie, 161
    rhubarb and ginger smoothie,
        162
soda bread, 27, 46
sorbets, 358
soups
    lentil and bacon soup for lots
        of people, 328–9
    mushroom noodle soup, 193
    pick-your-own minestrone,
        196–8, *197*
    white winter soup, *194*, 195
sourdough bread, *14*, 24–6, *25*
sourdough pancakes, 26
soured cream, 62

spaghetti
    pasta with four herbs, 207
    spaghetti bolognese, *259*, *286*,
        287–8
    spaghetti carbonara, 51
Spanish omelette (tortilla),
    106–7, *106*
spices, 304, 314–16
spicy bean stew with sausages,
    277, 330
spicy lamb pie, *190*, *259*, 289–91
spinach, 169, 170, 171
    potatoes with spinach, 200–1
    vegetable fritters, *166*, 209–11,
        210
sponge cake, Victoria, *87*, *110*,
    111–12
spring onions, 185
squashes, 124
squid, *221*, 233
    roast squid, 252–4, *253*
steak, *258*, 266, 268–9, *269*, 277
stews and casseroles
    pheasant casserole, 300–1
    spicy bean stew with sausages,
        277, 330
Stilton, 68
stocks
    chicken stock, 192
    vegetable stock, 192
strawberries, 122, 125, 127, 129
    Eton Mess, 141
    frozen strawberry milkshake,
        55, *84*, 85
    ice lollies, 360
    orange and strawberry jellies,
        119, 154–5, *155*
    strawberry fool, *140*, 141
    strawberry parfait, 371–3, *372*
strong flour, 18, 21
sugar, 336–79
    hard-boiled sugar, 348

heating, 347–50, *349*

history, 339

honey fudge, *337*, *378*, 379

making sugar, 339–40

marshmallows, 277, *336*, 368–70, *371*

peppermint creams, *336*, *362*, 363–4

Turkish delight, *337*, 376–7, *377*

types of, 340

sugar beets, 339, 340

sugarcane, 339–40

sugar syrup, 347–8

fruit salad, 366–7

Sultana scones, 47

summer fruit tart, *118*, 148, *149*

superfine sugar, 340

supermarkets, 129, 170, 177

sweet chile and red currant jam, 163–5

sweet pastry, 52–3

sweets

a box of chocolates, *381*, 394–5, *395*

chocolate truffles, 393

honey fudge, *337*, *378*, 379

marshmallows, 277, *336*, 368–70, *371*

peppermint creams, *336*, *362*, 363–4

Turkish delight, *337*, 376–7, *377*

syrup, sugar, 347–8

fruit salad, 366–7

T

tagliatelle, *31*, 32

tahini

hummus, 333

tangerines, 131, 134

tarts

French-style apple tart, *119*, 150–1, *150*

lemon tart, 52–3, *53*

summer fruit tart, *118*, 148, *149*

tayberries, 127

thermometers, candy, 348–50, *349*

thickening liquids, 16

thyme, 190

pasta with four herbs, 207

toad-in-the-hole, 97

toast, scrambled eggs on, *87*, 101

tomatoes, 123, 124, 169, 176, 177

growing, 172–5, *172*, *174*

guacamole, *214*, 215

pizza, 48–50, *49*

quick tomato salad, 216, *217*

spaghetti bolognese, *259*, *286*, 287–8

spicy bean stew with sausages, 277, 330

tomato bread, 23

tongue, 267

tortilla (Spanish omelette), 106–7, *106*

tortillas, 38–9, *39*

trout, 225

truffles, chocolate, 393

turbot, 225

turkey, 282

Turkish delight, *337*, 376–7, *377*

V

vanilla, 316, 385

veal, 58, 267

vegans, 58

vegetables, 124, 125, 166–219

buying, 169–70

crudités with garlic mayonnaise, 212–13

freshness, 169–70

frozen vegetables, 170–1

growing, 171–6, *172*, *174*

pick-your-own minestrone, 196–8, *197*

seasonal vegetables, 176

vegetable fritters, *166*, 209–11, *210*

vegetable stock, 192

white winter soup, *194*, 195

see also individual types of vegetables

vegetarians, 58

venison, 283

Victoria sponge cake, *87*, *110*, 111–12

vinegar, 186

vitamin C, 134

W

walnuts

double-chocolate brownies, *380*, *402*, 403

whipping cream, 62

whisking eggs, 90, 91

white winter soup, *194*, 195

whitebait, fried, 242–3

whole-wheat flour, 16, 18, 23

Y

yeast, 19–21, 24

yogurt, 70, *70*

cucumber raita, 83, *83*

homemade yogurt, 82

Yorkshire pudding, 97

Z

zucchini, 123, 169, 176, 317

FIZZ AND HUGH'S ACKNOWLEDGMENTS

We are hugely grateful to the brilliant team that has made the writing and production of this book such a satisfying and enjoyable experience. Our editor Richard Atkinson has been unbelievably (heroically, in fact) skillful, thorough, calm, and patient in bringing the book together. Simon Wheeler's wonderful photographs and Georgia Vaux's gorgeous design have been a pleasure and an inspiration: together they have captured the whole spirit of the book, joyously and succinctly. Jane Middleton's deft and sensitive copyediting and recipe testing has given us great confidence in the text. Our agent Antony Topping, and his ever-helpful colleagues at Greene and Heaton, have provided rock-solid support whenever it was needed.

Thanks to Bryan Johnson, for sure and valuable support in the kitchen, to the whole River Cottage team, especially Leigh Goodman, for her kindness and patience, and Jess Upton, for vital logistical support. And thanks to the entire team at Hodder, especially Jo Seaton, Simon Shelmerdine, Karen Geary, Alasdair Oliver, and Briar Silich.

We'd like to thank all the friends, family, local shops, and food producers who have helped us with the food and in the kitchen, particularly Jackie and Peter Appleton, ID Bickerstaff, Geoff Brain, Bill of Bill's Produce Store, Miranda Bowen, Jo Carr, Jenny Compton, Angus Davison, Jaimie D'Cruz and Heidi Agbowo, Belinda Giles, Stephen Goldman, Bob Hill, Richard and Tiffany Johnson, John and Julia Rapson de Pauley, Pots and Ivan Samarine, Simon and Jenny at Washingpool Farm Shop, Ray Smith, Reg Smith, Fiona Wheeler, and Webbie.

And, of course, a massive thank-you to all our young cooks. They are:

Isabella Alfonzo-Plowright	Daisy, Jake, and Polly Johnson
Taylor Baugh-Pyke	Chloe Koy
Archie Burrows	Alexandra Legg
Charlotte, Georgie, Joey, and Mattie Carr	Adeeb Makda
Jack and Rafi D'Cruz	Mack and Nell Nixon
Fred Dimbleby	Dudley Odubela
Oscar and Freddie Fearnley-Derome	Lucie Parker
James Hibberd	Georgia and Josephine Rapson de Pauley
Chloë Jackson	Lily and Gabriel Samarine
Caroline and Hugh Jeffery	Alice, Molly, and Roisin Wheeler